AUTOMOBILE ENGINEERING SERIES OF LUBAN WORKSHOP

Structure and Maintenance of Automobile Electronic Control System

SHI JIANFEI

天津大学出版社
TIANJIN UNIVERSITY PRESS

Preface

The electronization, intelligentization and networking of automobile is an important symbol of the development of modern automobile. With the increasing requirements of consumers for the functions and performance of automobile, automobile has been converted from mechanical system to electronic system. In the process of compiling this book, we have carefully summarized the professional teaching experience of national transportation vocational colleges for many years, and adopted advanced concepts and methods of vocational education. We should actively promote curriculum reform and textbook construction, provide more rich, diverse and practical textbooks for vocational education teaching and training, and better meet the needs of vocational education reform and development. Closely combined with the actual needs of the current automobile maintenance industry, and referring to the relevant industry job skills appraisal norms, this book is compiled for the teaching of automobile maintenance specialty in vocational colleges.

This book is written for the Luban Workshop Project in Madagascar, with moderate difficulty, excellent pictures and texts, simple and easy to understand. Each project is a complete and independent teaching module, which can arrange the teaching content and process reasonably and flexibly according to the actual situation of the school and the needs of employers. This book has four chapters, including: overview of automobile electronic control systems, automobile engine electronic control systems, automobile chassis electronic control system, vehicle network technology. Its characteristics can be summarized as follows.

(1) The basic guiding ideology of the design of professional training objectives is to determine the training objectives of professional knowledge based on the post competence requirements of key technical operation posts and technical management posts in the industry, and to lay a good foundation for the smooth entry of graduates into the ranks of automotive application engineers in their career.

(2) In the selection of content, we pay attention to the knowledge and ability requirements of talents for professional posts in the automobile aftermarket, strive to

connect with the corresponding professional qualification standards, and reflect the contents of new knowledge, new technology, new technique, new methods and new materials.

According to the requirements of the talent training program, each chapter of this book takes the actual maintenance project as the expansion learning of the course, so as to improve the knowledge application ability of students and trainers in actual production. This book is suitable for automobile application technology, automobile electronic technology, automobile detection and maintenance and other related majors of all kinds of vocational schools, as well as automobile repairmen, drivers, automobile industry engineering and technical personnel.

This book is edited by Shi Jianfei, Tianjin Institute of Mechanical and Electrical Technology Technicians, and Liu Yanchao and Li Qi, Tianjin Institute of Mechanical and Electrical Technology Technicians, participated in the compilation.

In the process of compiling this book, we have consulted many publicly published documents home and abroad, and hereby express our gratitude.

Limited to the editor's experience and level, the content is difficult to cover the actual situation in all parts of the country, and improperness and errors are unavoidable, so readers are urged to put forward valuable opinions and suggestions for correction in the second edition and revision.

Editor

Contents

Contents

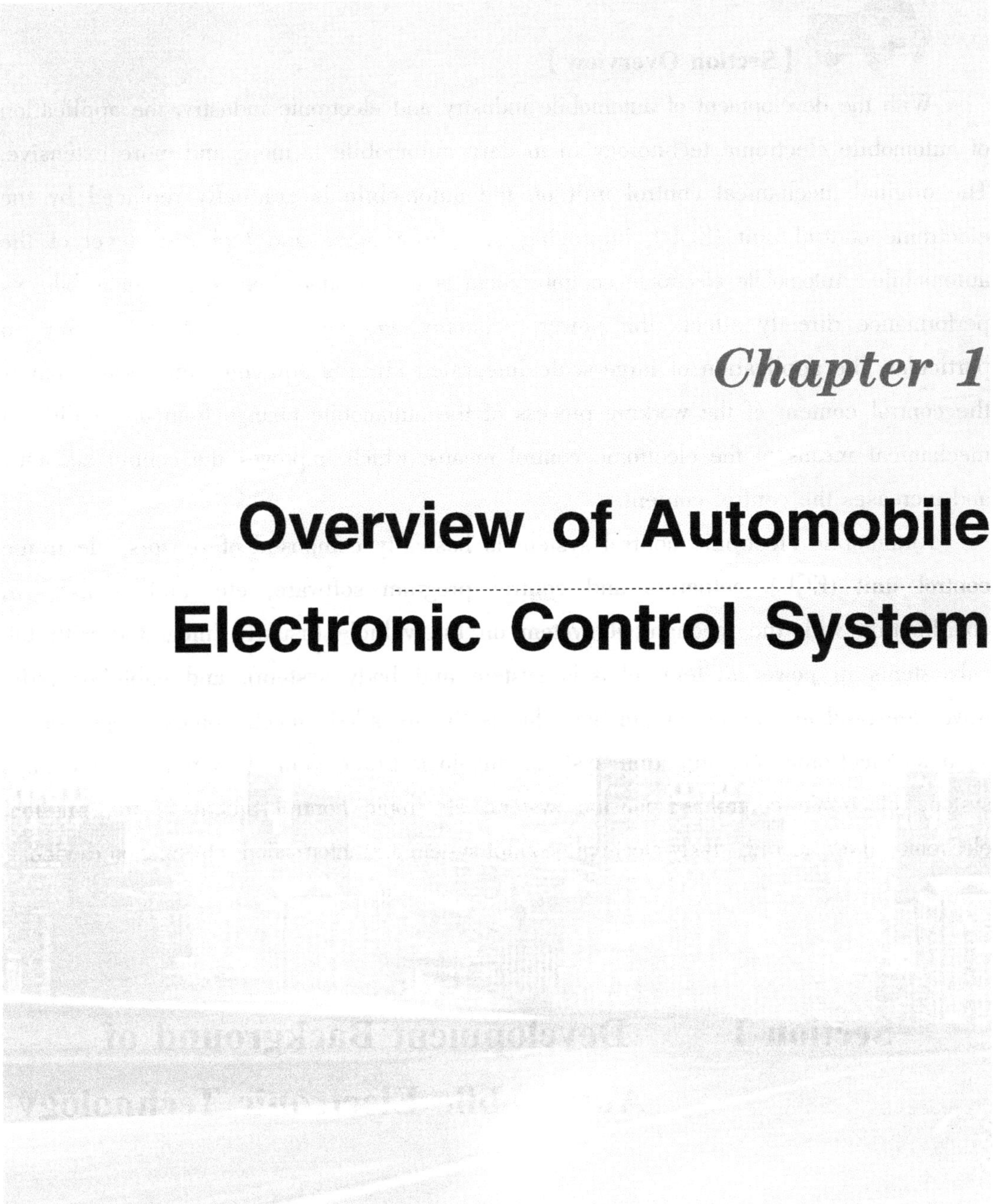

Chapter 1

Overview of Automobile Electronic Control System

【Section Overview】

With the development of automobile industry and electronic industry, the application of automobile electronic technology in modern automobile is more and more extensive. The original mechanical control unit on the automobile is gradually replaced by the electronic control unit (ECU), improving the performance and technical level of the automobile. Automobile electronic control system is an important part of the automobile, its performance directly affects the power, economy, emissions, comfort and so on. In particular, the application of large-scale integrated circuits and microprocessors makes the control content of the working process of the automobile change from the traditional mechanical means to the electronic control means, which improves the control accuracy and increases the control content.

Automobile electronic control system is basically composed of sensors, electronic control unit (ECU), actuators and control program software, etc. and is used in coordination with the mechanical system on the vehicle (usually integrated with the subsystems in power system, chassis system and body system), and cable or radio waves are used to transmit information, that is the so-called "mechatronics integration", such as electronic fuel injection system, anti-lock brake control system, skid control system, electronic control suspension system, electronic control automatic transmission, electronic power steering, body electronic control system and information transmission device.

Section 1 Development Background of Automobile Electronic Technology

Ⅰ. The development process of automobile electronic technology

As its name implies, automobile electronic technology is the combination of modern automobile technology and electronic technology, involving two technical fields.

The emergence of automobile electronic technology is an important revolutionary event in the development process of automobiles, and it has become an important technical symbol to measure the development level of modern automobiles. Throughout the history of automobile technology development, there are four main stages in the development of automobile electronic technology.

In the first stage, from the early 1950s to the early 1970s, automobile electronic products composed of discrete components and integrated circuits were mainly developed to replace traditional mechanical components, such as integrated circuit regulators, electronic igniters, etc. Valve radios and transistor radios were installed in automobiles one after another, which was the beginning of the application of electronic technology in automobiles.

In the second stage, from the mid-1970s to the mid-1980s, special independent systems were mainly developed, and electronic devices were used for complex control functions that could not be solved by mechanical devices, such as electronic control gasoline injection system, cruise control system, anti-lock braking system (ABS), etc.

The third stage, from the mid-1980s to the mid-1990s, the integrated system with various functions and the microcomputer control of various vehicles were developed. The electronic devices on the vehicles can not only automatically undertake the basic control tasks, but also process various external and internal information, such as the power transmission control which integrates the engine control and the automatic transmission control, anti-lock brake and anti-skid control, etc.

In the fourth stage, since the mid-1990s, we have mainly studied the intelligent control technology of vehicles, simulated the thinking and behavior of human beings to control, such as automobile automatic driving system, automobile automatic navigation system, etc. Intelligent integrated sensors and intelligent actuators have also been put into practice, and digital signal processing methods have been used for voice recognition, safety collision, timely diagnosis, navigation system, etc.

Ⅱ. The application status of automobile electronic technology

After a long time of accumulation, automobile electronic technology has entered a stage of comprehensive and rapid development, with the characteristics of functional diversification and technology integration. At present, the application of electronic technology has almost penetrated into all systems of automobiles. According to the impact on the driving performance of automobiles, automobile electronic products can be classified into two categories: one is automobile electronic control device, the other is vehicle electronics. At present, the mature automobile electronic control systems mainly include: engine electronic control, chassis electronic control, body electronic control, information transmission, etc.

(Ⅰ) Electronic control of engine

1. Electronic fuel injection (EFI)

On the modern automobile, the mechanical or electromechanical fuel injection system tends to be eliminated, and the electronic fuel injection device is getting more and more popular because of its superior performance. The electronic fuel injection system was developed in the end of 1960s. Compared with the traditional carburetor fuel supply system, its outstanding advantage is that the control of air-fuel ratio is more accurate, and it can achieve the optimal air-fuel ratio. Engine power and torque are significantly increased. This allows the engine to always operate at optimum operating conditions and improves overall engine performance.

2. Electronic spark device (ESA)

As early as the beginning of the 20th century, ignition systems have been used in automotive engines. Today, ignition systems have developed from the contact type, the ordinary non-contact type and the integrated circuit type to the microcomputer controlled electronic ignition system. The microcomputer control electronic ignition system can control and maintain the engine electronic spark advance (ESA) angle within the optimal range, the ignition time of the gasoline engine will be closer to the ideal state, so as to further tap the potential of the engine. In the computer-controlled electric ignition system, a distributorless ignition system (DLI) has emerged. It cancels the distributor in the common microcomputer control ignition system, and the power distribution of each cylinder is controlled by the ECU. In this way, the high voltage generated by the ignition coil can be directly sent to the spark plug for ignition without being distributed by the distributor. The distributorless ignition system can eliminate the spark discharge phenomenon between the distributor head and the cap electrode of the distributor, and reduce the electromagnetic interference.

3. Idle Speed Control (ISC) System

Idle performance is an important index to evaluate whether the engine performance is superior or not. Poor idle performance will lead to increased fuel consumption and serious pollution, so necessary control is needed. Modern cars generally have idle control system, which is controlled by ECU and maintains the engine idle speed within a stable range. Idle control usually refers to idle speed control. In essence, it is to adjust the air intake under idle condition (with the control of fuel injection quantity and ignition advance angle).

At present, in addition to the stability control of idle speed, the idle speed control can also realize the functions of starting control, warm-up control and load change control, which not only simplifies the mechanism, but also improves the accuracy of idle speed control.

4. Other control systems

In addition, the engine uses electronic technologies such as exhaust gas recirculation (EGR), electric fuel pump, generator output, cooling fan, engine displacement, throttle timing, secondary air injection, engine boost, fuel evaporation, and system self-diagnosis function etc. , which are used in different models to a greater or lesser extent.

(Ⅱ) Chassis electronic control

1. Electronically controlled automatic transmission (ECAT)

According to the engine load, speed, vehicle speed, brake working state and the parameters controlled by the driver, ECAT can automatically realize shift after the calculation and judgment of the computer, so as to realize the optimal control of transmission shift, the optimal gear and the optimal shift time. It has the advantages of good acceleration performance, high sensitivity, and can accurately reflect of the driving load and road conditions. It can not only simplify the operation of the car obviously, but also achieve the best driving dynamics and safety.

2. Anti-lock braking system (ABS)

Anti-lock braking system is an important safety component with the longest development time and the fastest popularization and application. It can ensure the best slip rate (15%-20%) between the wheel and the ground by controlling and preventing the locking of the wheel when the automobile is braked. When the automobile is braked on various road surfaces, the wheels and the road surface can reach longitudinal peak adhesion coefficient and larger lateral adhesion coefficient so as to ensure that unsafe working conditions such as locking, dragging, slipping, losing steering ability do not occur when the automobile is braked, to improve the operation stability and safety of the automobile, and reduce the braking distance. Acceleration slip regulation (ASR) is also called traction control system (TCS or TRC), which is a complement and supplement to ABS. It can prevent drive wheel slippage during starting and acceleration, and help improve traction and handling stability during acceleration.

3. Electronic steering power system

Electronic steering power system uses a direct current (DC) motor to replace the traditional hydraulic cylinder and uses the battery and motor to provide power. Compared with the traditional hydraulic system, this computer controlled steering system has the characteristics of fewer parts, smaller volume and lighter weight, as well as the optimal steering force and steering return characteristics, which greatly improves the steering ability and steering response characteristics of the car. It increases the maneuverability of the car at low speed and the stability at high speed.

4. Adaptive suspension system

According to the instantaneous load of the suspension device, adaptive suspension system can automatically adjust the stiffness of the suspension spring and the damping characteristics of the shock absorber in time to adapt to the load at that time and maintain the established height of suspension. In this way, it can greatly improve the stability of vehicle driving, operability and ride comfort.

5. Adaptive cruise control system (ACC)

Adaptive cruise control system is an intelligent automatic control system, which is developed on the basis of the already existing cruise control technology. It can continuously scan the road in front of the vehicle, while the wheel speed sensor collects the vehicle speed signal. When the distance from the front vehicle is too short, the ACC control unit can coordinate with the anti-lock braking system and engine control system to brake the wheels properly and reduce the output power of the engine, so that the vehicle can always keep a safe distance from the front vehicle.

(Ⅲ) Body electronic control

1. Automobile air conditioning control

According to the output signals of various temperature sensors set up inside and outside the vehicle, the microcomputer in ECU calculates the outlet air temperature that should be reached after passing through the air conditioning heat exchanger. The opening of the mixture regulator, the speed of the fan drive motor, cooler damper (or heater damper), compressor, etc. are controlled automatically to keep the temperature in the car within the set temperature range, so that the temperature and humidity in the car are always at the best value, providing a comfortable environment for the driver and passengers.

2. Information display system

Information display system is in the stage of development and perfection, and consists of three parts: vehicle condition monitoring components, on-board computer and electronic instrument. Vehicle condition monitoring is the improvement and development of the traditional mechanical instrument panel alarm function. Through the liquid level, pressure, temperature, light and other sensors, the fault of engine, brake system, power system and lamp can be monitored. The information provided by the on-board computer can improve driving safety, fuel economy and ride comfort. The electronic instrument provides the driver with the most basic operation information while driving, which is continuously displayed on the dashboard.

3. Airbag control system

Airbag control system is a passive safety protection device, which consists of a trigger device, a gas generator and an airbag. The trigger device includes a sensor, an electronic control device, a reserve power supply and a monitoring device. The electronic control system receives the signal sent by the acceleration sensor and analyzes it to determine whether there is a collision accident. If there is a collision, the gas generator will be instructed. The airbag is inflated rapidly, and the whole process takes about 0.03 s. The monitoring device in the triggering device continuously monitor automatically to ensure that the entire airbag system is ready for operation at all times.

4. Automobile Electronic Light Control System

Automobile Electronic Light Control System can automatically switch on or off the rear light and headlight according to the signal of the weather light outside the vehicle detected by the light sensor, so as to improve the convenience and driving safety of the vehicle.

(Ⅳ) Information transmission device

1. Information display and alarm

Information display and alarm system can process the working condition and other information parameters of the engine, and output useful information for the driver after the information was processed by the microcomputer, and display the information with numbers, lines or sound and light alarm. Besides the common parameters such as water temperature, oil pressure, vehicle speed and engine speed, the system can display the engine working conditions and other information parameters. There are also instantaneous fuel consumption, average fuel consumption, average speed, mileage, driving range, outside temperature, etc. The monitoring and alarm information mainly includes: fuel temperature, water temperature, oil pressure, charging, taillight, headlamp, exhaust temperature, brake fluid volume, hand brake, door not closed tightly, etc. In case of abnormal phenomenon or fault detected by self diagnosis system, sound and light alarm will be given immediately

2. Voice information

Voice information system includes voice warning and voice control. When the car is in abnormal conditions (in water temperature, water level, or oil level is not normal, brake fluid is insufficient, battery charging value is low, etc.), the electronic control unit outputs information to the loudspeaker after logical judgment, and sends a simulated voice to the driver to alarm. Most of them can also use lights to alarm at the same time. Voice control is to use the driver's voice to command and control a certain part and equipment of the car to move.

3. Vehicle navigation

Vehicle navigation system can select the best driving route in the city or highway network, and can display the map on the screen to show the position, direction and distance of the vehicle in the process of driving.

Ⅲ. The development trend of modern automobile electronic technology application

In the 1990s, the automobile electronic technology entered the stage of optimizing the overall relationship of human-automobile-environment, which developed toward the microminiaturization of ultra-miniature magnets, ultra-efficient motors and integrated circuits, and provided the basis for the centralized control of automobiles (such as the centralized control of braking, steering and suspension, as well as engine and transmission). Automobile electronic technology contributes to the future of the automobile industry, and the future automobile electronic technology will have the following development trends.

(I) Sensor technology

With the diversification and increase in the number of sensors used in vehicles, sensors are developing towards multi-function, integration, intelligence and miniaturization. Future intelligent integrated sensors can not only provide signals for simulation and processing, but also amplify the signals and so on. ECU can automatically carry out time drift, temperature drift and nonlinear self-correction, and has strong ability to resist external electromagnetic interference, so as to ensure that the quality of sensor signal is not affected, and that the sensor can still maintain high accuracy even under particularly harsh service conditions; It also has the advantages of compact structure and convenient installation, so as to avoid the influence of mechanical characteristics. Now, automobile manufacturers are stepping up the development of various sensors to develop autonomous vehicles, including vehicle position sensor, rear obstacle sensor, side obstacle sensor, front obstacle sensor, inter-vehicle distance sensor, road surface sensor, collision detection sensor, vehicle speed sensor, acceleration sensor, fire detection sensor, steering wheel angle sensor and driver state sensor.

(II) Microprocessor (ECU) technology

After ECU is applied to the control system of the automobile engine, the automobile electronic control system enters the new high speed development stage. In the near future, ECU will be applied to power transmission, vehicle body, safety and other control systems. In view of the special requirements of automotive ECU on reliability, information processing ability, real-time control ability and cost, it is difficult for ECU developed based on the universal chip to meet the requirements of automobile electronic control system. It is of great practical significance to develop multi-channel synchronous real-time control system with analog to digital (A/D) and digtal to analog (D/A), converter self-diagnosis, high input/output and other functions. With the control becoming more centralized, the amount of information that ECU needs to process is increasing. Therefore, 16-bit and 32-bit ECU will be the first choice for future automotive ECU. It is expected that the demand will increase by more than 50% in the next few years, and it will become the main stream of automotive ECU gradually.

In recent years, more than 2.5 billion ECU products have been sold home and abroad in Japan, and in 2005, more than 3 billion products will be sold, with a value of more than 1.5 trillion yen. At present, few Chinese users use 32-bit ECU, mainly focusing on some scientific research projects, such as the research and development projects of electric vehicles.

(Ⅲ) Actuator

At present, the actuators used in automobiles mainly include: electromagnetic type, electric type and pneumatic/hydraulic type. Electromagnetic type and electric type actuators are operating mechanisms powered by electricity, and have the characteristics of small volume, light weight, fast response and low energy consumption, but the output driving capacity is insufficient, especially after the replacement of 42 V new power supply system in the future, the output drive capacity will be greatly improved, which can completely replace the traditional pneumatic/hydraulic system.

(Ⅳ) Control strategy

At present, Proportion integral differential (PID) control theory is widely used in automobile electronic control system. It is the classical control theory for single input/single output linear constant system. Because the control object in automobile often has strong time-varying and nonlinear characteristics, there are more and more input and output parameters of control. Modern control theory based on state space and used for multi-input/multi-output, nonlinear time-varying systems has become inevitable, such as optimal control, adaptive control, fuzzy control and so on.

(V) Bus technology

Bus technology is used to connect various electronic control units (ECUs), intelligent sensors, intelligent instruments and so on in automobiles, thus forming an automobile internal LAN to realize the sharing of information resources among various systems. Its main advantages are as follows.

(1) Greatly reduce the number of harnesses, connection points and volume, and improve the reliability and maintainability of the system.

(2) Common sensors are used to achieve the purpose of data and information sharing.

(3) The flexibility of the system is improved, that is, the realization of the change of system function through the software of the system.

According to different functions, Society of automotive engineers (SAE) divides the bus into three types: A, B, and C. Type A is a low-speed network for sensors and actuators, mainly used for the control of rearview mirror adjustment, lighting control, and power windows, etc. Currently, the mainstream of type A is LIN. Type B is a medium speed network for data sharing between independent modules, mainly used for automobile comfort network, fault diagnosis, instrument display, four door central control, etc. At present, the mainstream of Type B is low-speed CAN; Type C is a multi-channel transmission network for high-speed and real-time closed-loop control, mainly used for the control of engine, ABS, automatic transmission, air bag restraint system, etc. Currently, the mainstream of Type C is high-speed CAN. However, with the development of the next generation of high-speed, fault-tolerant and time-triggered "X-by-Wire" control technology, it will gradually replace the high-speed CAN in Type C. In the next 5-10 years, the traditional automobile mechanical system will be changed into 100% electronic control system connected with high-performance CPU through high-speed fault-tolerant communication bus without the support of backup mechanical system, which is mainly represented by TTP/C and FlexRayo. In multimedia and communication system, MOST, IDB-1394, Bluetooth technology will become the mainstream of future development. Optical fiber is increasingly used as a high-speed signal transmission medium due to its high transmission rate and anti-interference capability.

(Ⅵ) Safety technology

The important development direction of future automobile electronic control is the field of automotive safety, the main directions are as follows.

(1) Radar technology and vehicle camera technology will be used to develop various automatic collision avoidance systems.

(2) Near-infrared technology is used to develop various safety systems that can monitor driver's behavior.

(3) High-performance tire comprehensive monitoring system.

(4) Adaptive automatic driving system.

(5) Driver Identification System.

(6) Airbag, ABS/ASR and body dynamic control system.

(Ⅶ) Multimedia entertainment and intelligent communication system

With the development of the third generation mobile communication technology and computer network technology, the future automobile is developing in the direction of mobile office and home cinema, providing drivers and passengers with real-time communication and entertainment information in motion, and combining the automobile with the road and other remote service systems to build a future intelligent transportation system (ITS). The specific functions are as follows.

(1) It can provide rich multimedia facilities and environment, and use global positioning system (GPS) and global system for mobile communications (GSM) network to realize navigation, driving guide, wireless internet, and interaction between automobile and external environment such as home.

(2) It has the function of remote automobile diagnosis, and can guide rescue service agencies to the fault or accident site in emergency.

【Thinking and Practice】

1. What are the stages of automobile electronic control technology?

2. What is the development trend of automobile electronic control technology in the future?

3. What are the electronic control technologies currently available in automobiles (name at least five)?

Section 2 Fundamentals of Automobile Electronic Control Technology

Ⅰ. The composition of the engine electronic control system and the functions of each part

(Ⅰ) Introduction to the electronic control system of the engine

Engine electronic control system, also called engine management system (EMS), engine centralized control system, is to centralize the control of multiple items in a power control module (PCM) or engine control unit (ECU), common use sensor, which is mainly composed of sensors, ECU and actuators.

(Ⅱ) Composition of engine electronic control system

1. Sensors

The sensor is a kind of signal acquisition device, which is installed in various parts of the car. It is used to detect engine operating parameters and convert them into electrical signals to be transmitted to the control unit. The greater the number of sensors, the more accurate the detection. The more actuators, the stronger the function. The composition of the engine electronic control system is shown in Figure 1-2-1.

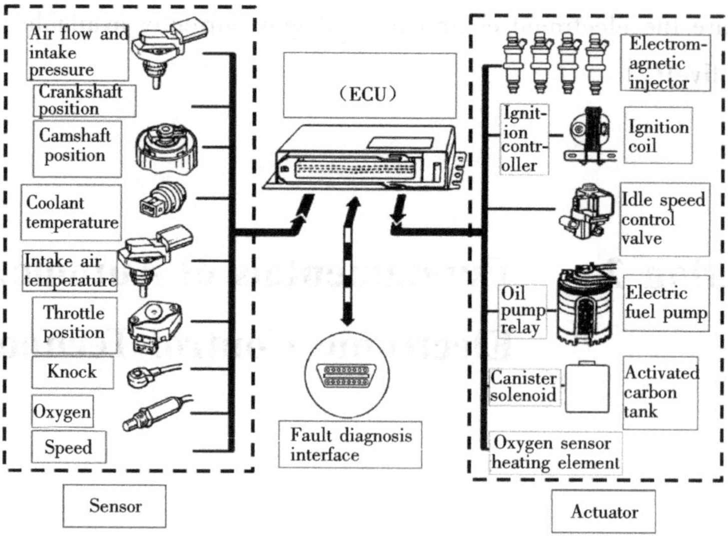

Figure 1-2-1 Main Sensors and Actuators of Electronic Control System of Automobile Engine

2. Electronic control unit (ECU)

Electronic control unit, also known as driving computer, car computer and so on. In terms of use, it is a special microcomputer controller for automobiles, also known as the special single-chip computer for automobiles. It is the same as the ordinary single-chip microcomputer, consisting of microprocessor (CPU), memory (ROM, RAM), input/output (I/O) interface, analog to digital (A/D) converter, shaping, driving and other large-scale integrated circuits. The physical diagram of ECU is shown in Figure 1-2-2.

The voltage range of ECU is generally 6.5-16 V (voltage stabilizer is available at key points inside), and the working current is 0.015-0.1 A, the working temperature is minus 40-80 ℃. It can bear the vibration below 1 000 Hz, so the probability of ECU damage is very small. CPU is the core part of ECU, which has the function of operation and control. When the engine is running, it collects the signals of each sensor, operates, and converts the operation results into control signals. It controls the work of the controlled object. It also controls the memory (ROM, RAM), input/output (I/O) interface and other external circuit. The program stored in ROM is based on the data obtained through accurate calculation and a large number of experiments. When the engine is working, this inherent program constantly compares and calculates the signals of various sensors collected. The comparison and calculation results are used to control the ignition, air-fuel ratio, idle speed, exhaust gas recirculation and other parameters of the engine. It can also automatically record fault codes in RAM and use protective measures to read alternative programs from the above inherent programs to maintain the operation of the engine, so that the car can drive to the maintenance site at the basic speed.

Figure 1-2-2 Harvard H6 Engine ECU

Main functions of the electronic control unit ECU are as follows.

(1) Acceptance of control information, mainly refers to accepting various control instructions from the operator, such as throttle instructions.

(2) Acquisition and processing function of system parameters, using rich interface resources of MCU to collect working conditions and state parameters of the engine, and then convert them.

(3) Completing various control functions, judging the working condition according to the collected system parameters, and realizing the control of fuel injection quantity and fuel injection timing, under the management of control software.

(4) Output drive function, according to the control information obtained after the system processing, the output signal is amplified to drive the oil quantity control mechanism and timing control mechanism.

(5) Self-diagnosis function system, if a fault is detected, the backup function will be enabled.

(6) Real-time communication with the monitoring system.

Installation of ECU: pay attention to against water, vibration, heat, overvoltage and magnetism. It is usually installed under or behind the seat filter in the instrument panel, glove box or other parts of the console, as shown in Figure 1-2-3.

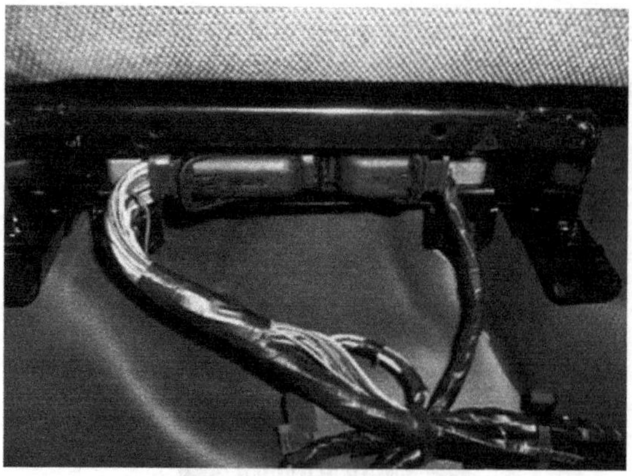

Figure 1-2-3 Installation Location of ECU

3. Actuator

Actuator is controlled by the ECU, it receives the output signal of the control unit, and generates execution actions to realize various controls. It is a device that performs a specific control function. Generally, the ECU controls the ground circuit of the solenoid coil of the actuator. Some electronic control circuits are controlled by the ECU, such as electronic ignition controller and so on. See Figure 1-2-1 for the main actuators of the engine. The composition of the engine electronic control system is shown in Figure 1-2-4. Figure 1-2-5 shows the fuel injector of Great Wall Haval H6.

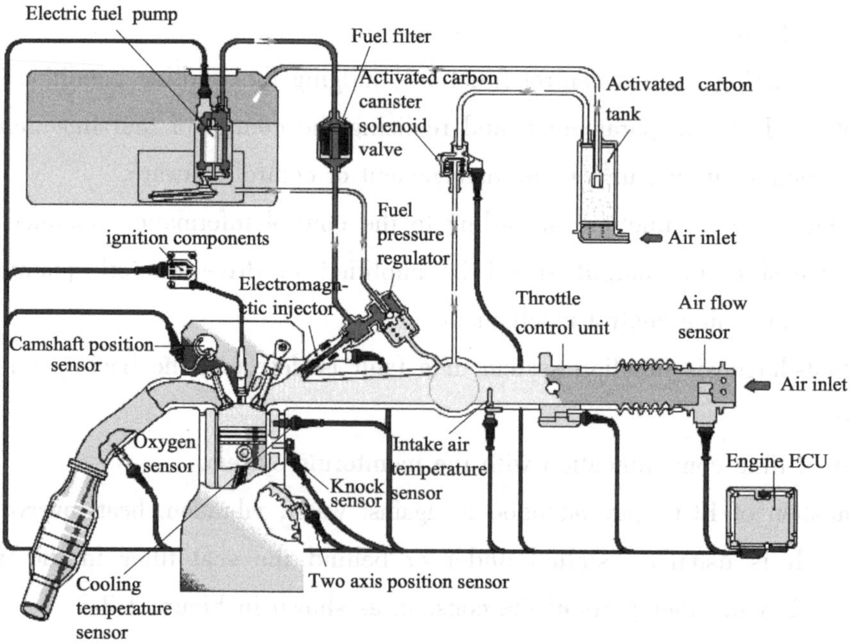

Figure 1-2-4 Great Wall Haval H6 Injector

Figure 1-2-5 Composition of Engine Electronic Control System

Summary: the electronic control engine is composed of air supply system, fuel supply system and electronic control system, of which the electronic control system is composed of sensors, ECU, actuators, etc. The sensors are the "intelligence officers" , the ECU is the "headquarters" , and the actuators are the "working organizations" or "combat forces" . Only when the three aspects cooperate with each other can the engine work normally.

ECU controls the normal operation of the engine, and the "intelligence" required includes crankshaft position and speed, camshaft position, air flow, throttle position, water temperature and other aspects, so the engine is equipped with sensors in many aspects. In addition, the "working mechanism" needed to maintain the normal operation of the engine includes fuel injection, ignition, fuel supply, idle control system, etc., so the engine will be equipped with various actuators.

(Ⅲ) Functions of each part of the engine electronic control system

1. Electronic fuel injection system (EFI)

The electronic fuel injection system (EFI) was developed at the end of 1960s. Compared with the carburetor fuel supply system which was widely used in the early time, its outstanding advantage is that the control of air-fuel ratio is more accurate, and it can achieve the best air-fuel ratio. In addition, EFI technology improves the atomization and evaporation performance of gasoline, has better acceleration performance, and significantly increases engine power and torque. At present, the EFI system mainly adopts the combination of open-loop and closed-loop control (feedback control). According to the different installation positions of injectors, the EFI system can be divided into three types: single point injection (SPI), multi-point injection (MPI) and cylinder direct injection.

Function of the electronic fuel injection system: the basic fuel injection quantity is determined according to the intake air quantity, and then the fuel injection quantity is corrected according to the signals of other sensors (such as coolant temperature sensor, throttle position sensor, etc.), so that the engine can obtain the mixture with the best concentration under various operating conditions, thereby improving the power, economy and emission performance of the engine.

2. Electronic ignition control system (ESA)

At the beginning of the 20th century, the ignition system has been used in the automobile engine from the contact type, the ordinary non-contact type and the integrated circuit type to the present microcomputer control electronic ignition system. The microcomputer controlled electronic ignition system can control and maintain the engine electronic spark advance (ESA) within the optimal range. The best ignition time of ESA can be achieved, and the engine can be controlled in advance.

In the computer controlled ignition system, there is a distributorless ignition (DLI) system, which cancels the distributor in the general computer controlled ignition system, and instead, the ECU controls the power distribution of each cylinder. In this way, the high voltage generated by the ignition coil is directly sent to the spark plug for ignition without distribution by the distributor. The control form of combination of open loop and closed loop is also adopted.

The function of the electronic ignition control system: according to the signals of the relevant sensors, the operating conditions and conditions of the engine are judged, and the ideal ignition advance angle is selected to ignite the mixed gas, so as to improve the combustion process of the engine, achieving the purpose of improving the power and economy of the engine and reducing emission pollution.

3. Idle speed control system (ISC)

Idle performance is an important index to evaluate the engine performance. Poor idle performance will lead to increased fuel consumption and serious pollution. Therefore, it is necessary to carry out necessary control. Idle control usually refers to idle speed control. Its essence is to adjust the air intake under idle condition (with the control of fuel injection and ignition advance angle). The basic principle of idle speed control is that ECU calculates the target speed according to the cooling water temperature, air conditioner load and neutral signal, and compares it with the actual speed. At the same time, ECU detects the full throttle signal and vehicle speed signal to determine whether it is in idle speed. After confirmation, ECU drives the actuator to adjust and control the air intake according to the difference between the target speed and the actual speed.

Function of idle speed control system: under the condition of engine idle speed, according to the temperature of engine coolant, whether the air conditioning compressor is working, and whether the transmission is in gear, etc., the air intake of the engine is controlled by the idle speed control valve, so that the engine can run at the best idle speed at any time.

4. Exhaust gas recirculation electronic control system (EGR)

Early research abroad found that a small amount of exhaust (5%-20%) was recirculated into the cylinder and mixed with fresh combustible mixture for combustion, which could effectively inhibit the production of NO_x. In fact, in addition to the internal EGR mode of valve overlap to produce exhaust reflux, the more commonly used measure is to use a special pipeline to guide part of the exhaust to the intake pipe. The ECU controls the EGR valve to change the flow section to adjust the exhaust volume and realize the change of recirculation exhaust rate.

The function of the exhaust gas recirculation electronic control system: electronically control the operation of the engine emission control device.

The items of emission control mainly include exhaust gas recirculation (EGR) control, activated carbon canister solenoid valve control, oxygen sensor and air-fuel ratio closed-loop control, secondary air injection control and so on.

5. Air intake control system

Function of air intake control system: controls the air intake of the engine according to the change of engine speed and load, so as to improve the charging efficiency of the engine and improve the power of the engine.

6. Booster electric control system

The installation of turbocharging system in the engine is increasing day by day. The turbocharger is usually designed to match the low-speed and small-load working conditions of the engine to improve the intake efficiency. At present, the electronic control exhaust turbocharging system is commonly used.

Function of supercharging electronic control system: control the work of engine intake supercharging device. On the vehicle equipped with exhaust turbocharging device, ECU controls the supercharging device according to the detected pressure of intake pipe, so as to control the intensity of supercharged intake air.

7. Fault self-diagnosis system

At present, in the electronic control system of the car engine, the ECU is generally provided with a fault self-diagnosis system which can automatically monitor and diagnose the faults of each part of the engine control system; the fault self-diagnosis system can constantly monitor the working conditions of each control system, and when a fault occurs, the fault indicator lamp on the instrument panel of the car can flicker to alarm. At the same time, the fault information is stored in the memory of the microcomputer in the form of codes, which can not only be displayed by the intermittent flashing of the fault indicator lamp during maintenance. The fault code can also be displayed in digital form by special testing instruments, so as to further find out the cause of the fault through the manual. The self-diagnosis system solves the problem that it is difficult to judge the fault of complex electronic control system.

Function of fault self-diagnosis system: prompt the driver that there is engine fault. At the same time, the system stores the fault information in the memory in the form of set number (fault code), so as to help the maintenance personnel to determine the fault type and range.

8. Fail-safe system and fail-back control system

When the self-diagnosis system detects the sensor and its circuit failure, the fail-safe system in the ECU will automatically start to play its role. The fail-safe system will replace the abnormal signal input by the failure part with the programmed data for direct control. The fail-safety system is usually realized by software programming.

Function of fail-safe system and fail-backup control system: when the control system computer fails, the backup system (backup integrated circuit) will be started automatically, and the engine will be controlled to enter the forced running state according to the set signal, so as to prevent the vehicle from stopping on the road.

9. Cruise control system

Function of the cruise control system: after the cruise control mode is set, the ECU automatically controls the engine to work according to the vehicle operating conditions and operating environment information, so that the vehicle can automatically maintain a certain speed.

10. Other electric control systems

(1) Intake swirl electronic control system: the intake swirl can promote gasoline evaporation and uniform mixing with air, and improve combustion efficiency.

(2) Variable intake control system: improves the power performance of the engine by increasing the intake volume and improving the intake efficiency. Practice has proved that the variable intake control system can enhance the power performance and economy of the engine.

(3) Intake air temperature preheating control system: promotes gasoline evaporation and improves emission performance by adjusting the intake air temperature at low temperature start.

(4) Fuel evaporation power control system: used to reduce the pollution caused by the gasoline vapor in the fuel tank discharged to the atmosphere. At present, the activated carbon canister evaporation power control device has been widely used, which can effectively prevent the escape of gasoline vapor and reduce the HC emission pollution.

(5) Electric control system for forced crankcase ventilation: circulates the gas permeating into the crankcase through the piston ring gap in the cylinder into the intake pipe again, so as to reduce the pollution caused by the direct discharge of this part of gas to the atmosphere.

(6) Secondary air injection system: as one of the early measures to control pollutant emissions, secondary air injection is currently used in conjunction with catalytic converters.

Ⅱ. Automobile chassis electronic control system

The main parts of the automobile chassis electronic control are as follows.

1. Electronic control automatic transmission

Advantages of automatic transmission: saving driving effort, smooth starting acceleration, avoiding overload and engine stall, improving the life of engine and transmission system.

There are three main types of automatic transmissions.

1) Automatic mechanical transmission

Automatic mechanical transmission is electronically controlled by the traditional clutch and manual gear transmission for automatic transmission. It has a certain commonality with the parts of manual gear transmission, and retains the advantages of high transmission efficiency. At present, it is widely used in heavy trucks.

2) Electrically controlled hydraulic-mechanical automatic transmission

Electrically controlled hydraulic-mechanical automatic transmission consists of torque converter, automatic mechanical transmission and hydraulic-electronic control system. At present, the technology is mature and widely used. The loading rate of cars in developed countries has reached 80%-90%.

3) Electronically controlled mechanical continuously variable transmission (CVT)

Electronically controlled mechanical continuously variable transmission (CVT) is continuously variable by a V-shaped metal steel belt and a pulley with adjustable radius. There is also an automatic clutch between the V-shaped metal steel belt and the engine, as shown in Figure 1-2-6.

Figure 1-2-6 Electronically Controlled Continuously Variable Transmission (CVT)

2. Anti-lock braking system (ABS)

The function of ABS is to automatically control the braking force of the brake when the car is braking, so that the wheels are not locked, and are in a state of rolling and sliding, so as to ensure that the adhesion between the wheels and the ground is at the maximum value. The ABS operation schematic diagram is shown in Figure 1-2-7.

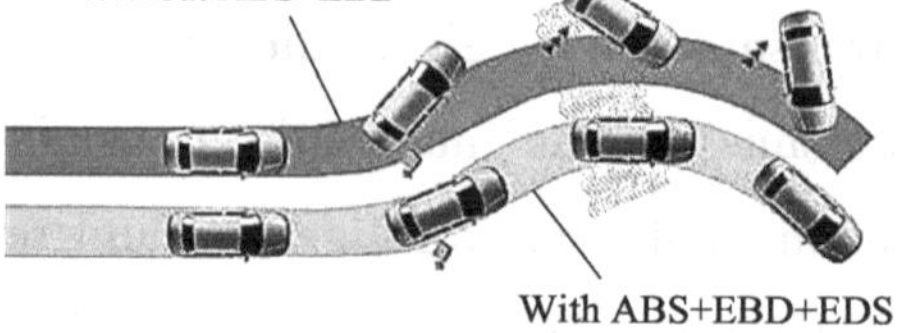

Figure 1-2-7 ABS Operation Schematic

EBD–Electronic Brake force Distribution; EDS–Electronic Differential System

The functions of the anti-lock braking system are as follows.

(1) Shorten the braking time and distance.

(2) Prevent the vehicle from sideslip and tail flick during emergency braking.

(3) The direction can be controlled in case of emergency braking.

(4) Reduce the wear of tires.

3. Drive anti-skid system

Drive anti-skid system is to apply braking force to the skid wheel or control the power output of the engine to inhibit the skid rotation of the wheel when the wheel skids. Its purpose is to avoid the decline of automobile traction and driving stability. The schematic diagram of the driving anti-skid system is shown in Figure 1-2-8. Because the driving wheel slip control is usually achieved by adjusting the driving wheel traction, it is also called traction control system (TCS).

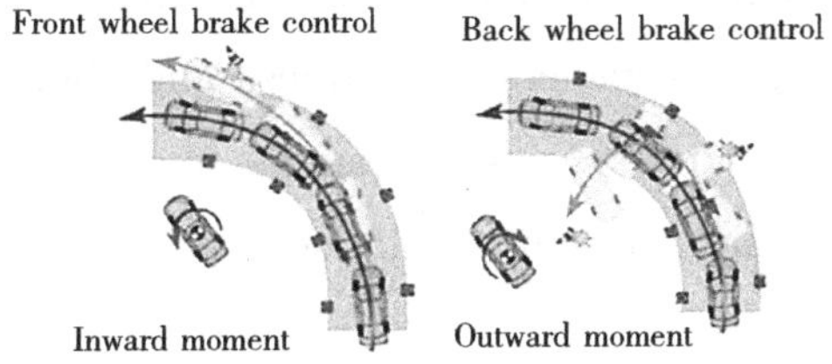

Figure 1-2-8 Drive Anti-Slip System Schematic

4. Electronic control suspension system

Electronic control suspension system is the general name of all the parts and components connecting the body and the wheel, which is mainly composed of springs (such as leaf springs, coil springs, torsion bars, etc.), shock absorbers and guide mechanisms, which is shown in Figure 1-2-9. It can effectively restrain and reduce the dynamic load and vibration of the vehicle body and wheels, thus ensuring the smoothness and handling stability of the vehicle. The ride comfort and handling stability of the automobile are the main indicators to measure the suspension performance. An ideal suspension would have different spring rates and shock absorber damping under different service conditions. It can not only meet the requirements of ride comfort, but also meet the requirements of handling stability.

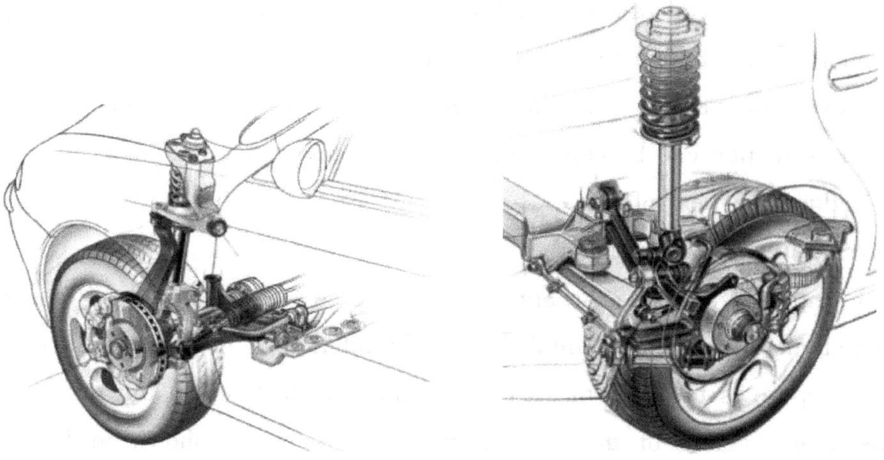

Figure 1-2-9 Electronic Control Suspension System

The functions of the automobile electronic control suspension: electronically controlled automotive suspension breaks through the limitation of passive suspension by controlling and adjusting the suspension stiffness and shock absorber damping; The automotive suspension characteristics shall adapt to the road conditions, and the mutually exclusive performance requirements of ride comfort and handling stability shall be met.

Active suspension: the state signal of the motion of the detection system is fed back to the electronic control unit, and the electronic control unit sends instructions to the main power generator to form a closed-loop control. The active control force generated by external energy acts on the system to control. Besides vibration control, active suspension can also control vehicle attitude and height.

5. Steering control system

The rear wheels of the four-wheel steering control system (4WS) participate in steering together with the front wheels, which is a key technology to improve the reactivity and stability of the vehicle. The schematic diagram of the four-wheel steering system is shown in Figure 1-2-10. Turning the rear wheels in phase with the front wheels can reduce the rotational movement (yaw) of the vehicle during steering and improve the stability of high-speed driving. It can improve the maneuverability of the vehicle at medium and low speed, and improve the fast steering.

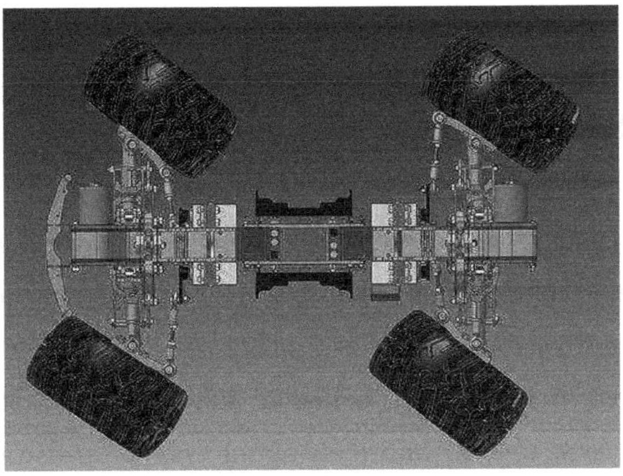

Figure 1-2-10 Four-Wheel Steering Control System Schematic

6. Automobile Electronic Stability Programme (ESP) System

ESP system can help the driver avoid vehicle instability. Electronic stability program belongs to the active safety of the vehicle, and the electronic stability system of the vehicle is shown in Figure 1-2-11. ESP system can identify the unstable state of the vehicle, and control the brake system, engine management system and transmission management system, so as to make up for vehicle sliding

Figure 1-2-11 Automobile Electronic Stability Programme System Schematic

ESP system is developed on the basis of ABS. ESP system can recognize emergency driving conditions such as driver's panic reaction and maintain vehicle stability by applying brakes to individual wheels and intervening in engine control system. This software can integrate signals such as ideal steering angle, yaw angle, lateral force and wheel speed difference. The moment when the car lost control was quickly identified. Then no matter how the driver operated, the vehicle was braked or accelerated, and the ESP system began to play a role in stabilizing the car.

Ⅲ. Automobile body electronic control system

Automobile body electronic control technology involves a lot, such as the car's visibility, convenience, comfort, entertainment, communication functions, etc. Automobile body electronic control mainly includes: safety control (electronic control airbag, electronic control seat belt, vehicle collision safety system, etc.), comfort control (central electric door lock system, anti-theft alarm system, cruise control system, etc.), instrument control(electronic instrument, multi-functional integrated screen display, etc.).

(Ⅰ) Safety control

1. Supplant Restraint System (SRS)

Airbag is a common passive safety device on the car. When the car crashes, the ECU provides current to detonate the nitrogen compound in the airbag placed in the center of the steering wheel and behind the dashboard (glove compartment), which is like "gunpowder" . A large amount of nitrogen gas is produced by the rapid combustion of air, and the air bag is filled in an instant. The whole process is completed in about 0.02 s. In this way, a cushioning cushion is formed between the driver and the steering wheel, the co-driver and the instrument panel (glove compartment) at once, so as to avoid serious injuries and deaths caused by hard impact. More and more vehicles now adopt it as the standard equipment.

2. Electric control seat belt

In order to ensure the safety of passengers, in addition to the effective absorption of impact energy in the body structure design to ensure the effective living space for passengers, the seat belt, as one of the restraint devices for passengers, is required to prevent passengers from large deceleration in the event of collision and rollover accidents, and at the same time restrain passengers from secondary collision to reduce the degree of injury to passengers. When the structural performance of the seat belt is improved and matched with the seat structure and the airbag, the ideal occupant protection effect can be achieved, and the injury index of the occupant can be further reduced.

3. Vehicle collision safety system

Vehicle collision safety system includes the collision prevention safety system, the rear-end collision prevention system, the reverse collision warning system and other safety systems. The collision prevention safety system can retract the slack of the front seat belt before collision, and make the brake control system enter the brake auxiliary state, so as to reduce the injury to the driver and passengers. Rear-end collision prevention system is also called automatic braking control rear-end collision prevention system. This is a new type of active safety technology. Reversing anti-collision alarm system, also known as reversing radar system or sonar ranging system, can prevent collision during reversing.

(Ⅱ) Comfort control

1. Electric control door lock system

For vehicles with central power door locking, when the driver locks the driver's door, several other doors (including the rear door or the trunk door, etc.) are automatically locked at the same time. When the driver's door is opened, other doors can be opened at the same time; Passengers can still open and close the doors with mechanical or spring lock of each door.

2. Anti-theft alarm system

In order to prevent the theft of vehicles, many car companies have already taken the car anti-theft device as a standard configuration of cars. Anti-theft alarm system usually works with the car door lock system. When the car is in the anti-theft alarm function state, if someone attempts to force into the car or open the hood, luggage door, anti-theft alarm system, on the one hand, alarms, such as light flashing, the horn sounds. On the other hand, to prevent the vehicle from running, such as cutting off the ignition circuit, starting circuit and fuel supply circuit, etc.

3. Cruise control system

According to its characteristics, the automobile cruise control system is also called constant speed control system, automatic speed control system and so on. The system can automatically control the automobile speed at the target speed set by the driver without the need for the driver to manipulate the accelerator pedal. The system will automatically increase or decrease the throttle opening according to the driving resistance, so as to keep the automobile speed at a certain level, thus eliminating the driver's frequent action of stepping on the accelerator pedal. During driving, as long as the driver grasps the steering wheel, he can drive easily. When the road condition changes, the driver can operate the car again, such as acceleration, deceleration, parking, etc., so that the whole driving process becomes simple, easy and comfortable.

4. Automobile air conditioner

Automobile air conditioner is used to adjust the temperature, humidity, flow rate and cleanliness of the air in the cab and carriage, and to prevent or remove the fog, frost and ice on the windshield, so as to ensure the health, vision and driving safety of the passengers. Automobile air conditioner is refrigerated by refrigerant circulation. The liquid refrigerant absorbs the heat of the object to be cooled at the low temperature in the evaporator and is vaporized to cool the object to be cooled. It also transfers heat to the surrounding medium at high temperature and condenses into liquid. In this way, it circulates continuously, and achieves the purpose of refrigeration by means of the state change of refrigerant.

(Ⅲ) Instrument Control

1. Electronic instrument

The traditional instrument monitors, transmits and displays the information of vehicle speed, engine speed and fuel consumption, etc. With the development of automobile industry, the demand for information of the working state of each system in the driving process of automobiles is significantly increased, that is, the requirements for the functions of automobile instruments are increasing. Therefore, the traditional automobile instruments are gradually replaced by electronic instruments. It uses microprocessor to collect and process different sensor signals, control and display various information such as vehicle speed, engine speed, fuel consumption and mileage.

2. Multifunctional integrated screen display

With the rapid development of automobile electronic technology, the electronic display system of automobile dashboard has developed from simply displaying sensor information to an integrated information system that can analyze, calculate and process all kinds of information. The integrated information system can select all kinds of information required by the driver from a large number of information, including electronic driving map, maintenance, rearview mirror and other information It can also display TV, radio, telephone and other information.

3. Auxiliary electrical system

The automobile auxiliary electrical system mainly includes electric windows, electric seats, windshield wiper system and so on.

The electric windows system is composed of a glass lifting drive motor and a reducer on the basis of the manual glass lifting system. The master switch on the side of the driver's seat can control the lifting of all door glasses, and each window lifting switch can control the lifting of its own door glass independently. Automobile electric seat system is also known as the seat position (seat) adjustment system. By operating the seat control switch, the front and back sliding, front vertical and rear vertical position of the seat, the tilt position of the back and headrest and the position of the waist cushion can be adjusted. The function of the windshield wiper system is to wipe off the rain, snow, dust and dirt on the windshield, to provide a good view for the driver and ensure the driving safety.

Ⅳ. Information and communication system

Automobile information communication system is a kind of device for communication between automobile and outside, mainly including on-board multimedia system, driver information system, language system, intelligent transportation system (ITS), global positioning system (GPS), computer network communication system, on-board short-distance wireless communication system, state monitoring and fault diagnosis system etc.

The components of the automobile information communication system mainly include a roaming device, a mobile phone, an electronic mail and internet terminal, a video or electronic game center console, etc. A relatively complete information communication system has the electronic control functions of assisting the driver, connecting the automobile with the outside world and coordinating all parts of the automobile, so that the driver can obtain a large amount of information, so as to improve the comfort of driver operation and the safety of vehicle driving.

(Ⅰ) Navigation system

With the development of science and technology, the automobile navigation system has developed rapidly. At present, it has developed into a relatively advanced integrated system with the functions of automobile navigation, anti-theft, dispatching and monitoring and alarming of the main working conditions of the automobile. From the equipment point of view, it has developed into a global satellite positioning system using "3C technology", that is, the combination of computer, communication and control technology. A comprehensive system with navigation, control and other functions has been established, and the accuracy of civil use has reached the meter level.

(Ⅱ) Vehicular network system

Since the 1990s, more and more electronic control devices have been used in automobiles, such as electronic fuel injection device, anti-lock braking device (ABS), airbag device, active suspension and so on, so the electronic control area network (CAN) came into being. It uses different coded signals to indicate different switching actions. After decoding the signals, the corresponding electrical equipment (headlamp, wiper, electric seat, etc.) is switched on or off according to the instructions. In this way, the special line system of one line for one use in the past is changed to one line multi-purpose system, which reduces the number of wires on the car and reduces the diameter of wire harness.

【Knowledge Development】

Ⅰ. Equipment preparation

Great Wall Harvard H6, one lift, one set of general tools, one set of engine compartment protective cover, one set of "three-pieces set" (seat cover, steering wheel cover, foot pad).

Ⅱ. Practical training steps

(1) Open the door, lay the "three-piece set" and pull the handle of the engine compartment cover.

(2) Open the engine compartment cover, lay the engine compartment shield, and

remove the engine guard.

(3) Find out the air filter and air inlet pipeline, and observe their structure and arrangement.

(4) Find out the air flow meter (or intake pressure sensor), inlet air temperature sensor, throttle and throttle position sensor, camshaft position sensor, knock sensor, oxygen sensor are shown in Figure 1-2-12 to Figure 1-2-17, and observe their respective positions.

Figure 1-2-12 Air Flow Meter

Figure 1-2-13 Inlet Air temperature Sensor

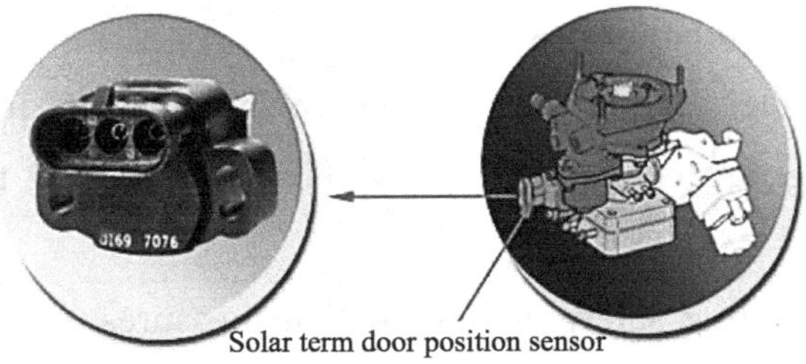

Figure 1-2-14 Throttle Position Sensor

Figure 1-2-15 Crankshaft Position Sensor

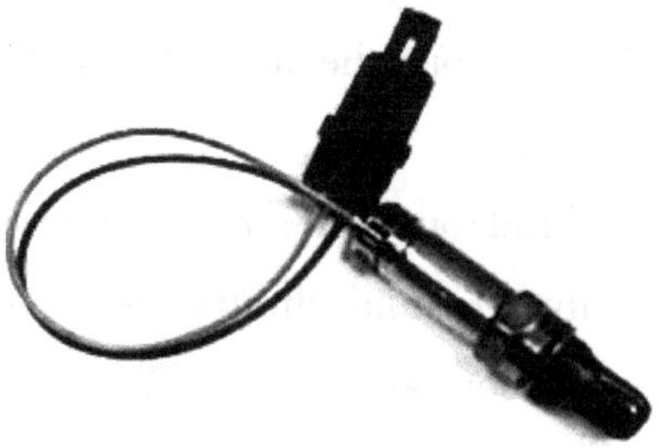

Figure 1-2-16 Knock Sensor **Figure 1-2-17 Oxygen Sensor**

(5) Find out the idle valve and ignition module of each injector, and observe their respective positions.

(6) Find out the power distribution box (or relay box) in the engine compartment (or under the dashboard in the cab), open the cover, and observe the position of each relay and fuse (commonly known as fuse).

(7) Find out the ECU in the engine compartment (or under the dashboard in the cab), and observe its installation position.

(8) Open the luggage compartment of the car, remove the fuel tank cover plate at the bottom of the luggage compartment, and observe the fuel tank and electric fuel pump.

(9) Take corresponding safety and protection measures according to the operation requirements of the lift, and lift the car with the lift.

(10) Reset the vehicle and the lift in the reverse order, and check whether the reset condition is good.

Ⅲ. Training requirements

(1) Be able to skillfully find out each sensor, actuator, ECU, electric fuel pump and relay box.

(2) Habitually use "three-piece set", engine compartment shield and other automobile protective articles, and develop good professional habits.

(3) Develop the habit of "taking safety protection measures".

(4) Cultivate the professional habit of "three not falling to the ground" for tools, parts and oil. Tools and dismantled parts and components should be placed in the tool car and parts tray neatly.

【Thinking and Practice】

1. What is the English abbreviation of anti-lock braking system?
2. What are the three major components of the automobile electronic control system?
3. What are the auxiliary systems of electronic control system of automobile engine?
4. What are the sensors that detect engine working conditions?
5. Name at least three actuators and their roles.

[Thinking and Practice]

1. What is the English [illegible] building [illegible]?
2. What are the three [illegible] system?
3. What are the [illegible]
4. What [illegible]
5. [illegible]

Chapter 2

Electronic Control System of Automobile Engine

【Section Overview】

The automobile engine electronic control system mainly includes three major parts, the electronic fuel injection system, the electronic ignition system as well as the auxiliary control system. The core part is the electronic fuel injection system and electronic ignition system. With the rapid development of electronic technology, more and more advanced technologies are applied in the engine electronic control system, a large part of which is reflected in the auxiliary control system control projects, control accuracy and complexity. This chapter focuses on the electronic fuel injection system and electronic ignition system, with the general introduction and understanding of the auxiliary control system.

Section 1 Electronic Fuel Injection System

Ⅰ. The role of the electronic fuel injection system

The function of the fuel supply system is to use the electric fuel pump to supply fuel with enough pressure to the fuel injector, and the fuel injector injects a certain amount of fuel to the upper part of the intake valve in the intake manifold according to the control signal from the ECU, that is, to control the fuel injection timing, fuel injection quantity, fuel cut-off and fuel pump.

Ⅱ. The advantages of the electronic fuel injection system

The electronic fuel injection system uses various sensors to detect engine working conditions and vehicle driving conditions. The engine ECU controls the fuel injection timing and fuel injection quantity according to the engine working condition information detected by the sensors. The basic composition of the electronic fuel injection system is shown in Figure 2-1-1. Compared with the traditional carburetor engine, the electronic control fuel injection system has many advantages as follows.

(1) Distribute different concentrations of mixed gas according to the working conditions.

(2) Three-way catalytic device is installed to carry out closed-loop control of air-fuel ratio and reduce HC, CO and NO_x emissions.

(3) It has high injection pressure and good atomization.

(4) Compensate and control the fuel injection according to the atmospheric pressure and temperature change.

(5) It has the function of deceleration and fuel cut-off to reduce fuel consumption.

(6) Without the throttling effect of carburetor, the inertia air intake is used, and the power is strong.

(7) It has warming up idle speed control, which can warm up fast.

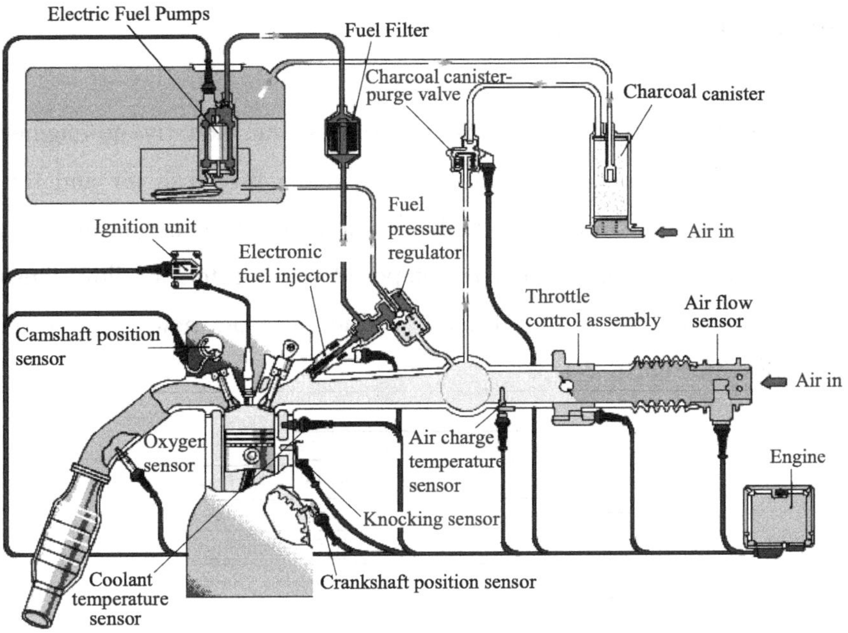

Figure 2-1-1 Composition of Electronic Fuel Injection System

Ⅲ. Composition and function of electronic fuel injection system

A complete electronic fuel injection system usually consists of three subsystems: air supply system, fuel supply system and electronic control system. Figure 2-1-2 shows the Great Wall Haval H6 engine compartment.

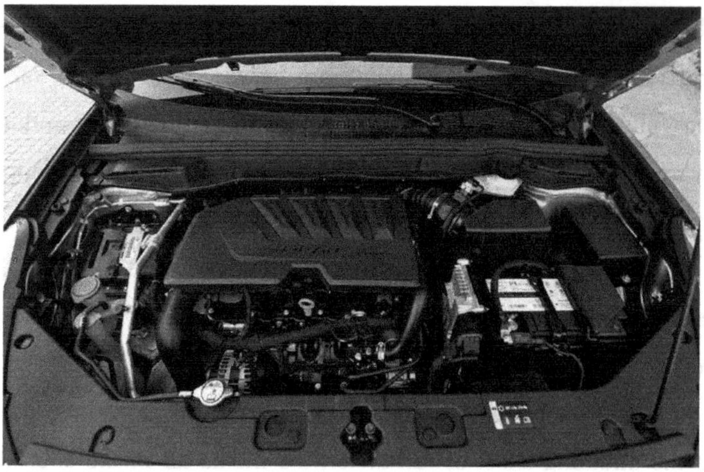

Figure 2-1-2　Great Wall Haval H6 Engine Compartment

(Ⅰ) Air supply system

The function of air supply system is to supply clean, adaptive-to-engine-load and metered fresh air to the gasoline engine so as to make the fresh air and the gasoline sprayed by the fuel injector form high-quality combustible mixture in an intake pipe or an air cylinder. The air supply system is composed of air filter, air flow sensor (intake pressure sensor), throttle body and throttle position sensor, power cavity and intake manifold, as shown in Figure 2-1-3.

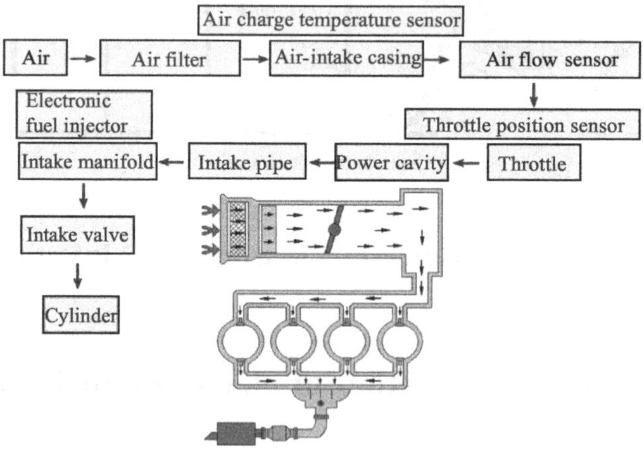

Figure 2-1-3　Air Supply System

1. Air metering device

The air quantity metering device is used for directly or indirectly measuring the quantity of fresh air sucked by an engine, converting the measured result into a voltage or frequency signal and transmitting the voltage or frequency signal to an ECU, and the ECU calculates the quality of the fresh air sucked in each working cycle according to an input signal and other parameters of the ECU. It adopts an air flow sensor to measure the volume flow or mass flow of air in a direct measuring mode. Indirect measurement methods mostly use the absolute pressure sensor of intake manifold to measure the absolute pressure of intake manifold.

1) Air flow sensor

The air flow sensor is a kind of sensor that directly measures the amount of air entering the intake port, and the electronic control system equipped with the air flow sensor is usually called L-type electronic control gasoline injection system. There are mainly four kinds of air flow sensors used in the engine, namely, vane type air flow sensor, Karman vortex air flow sensor, hot wire air flow sensor and hot film air flow sensor. Among them, the first three kinds have been basically eliminated. At present, passenger cars mainly used the hot film air flow sensor, and its structure is shown in Figure 2-1-4.

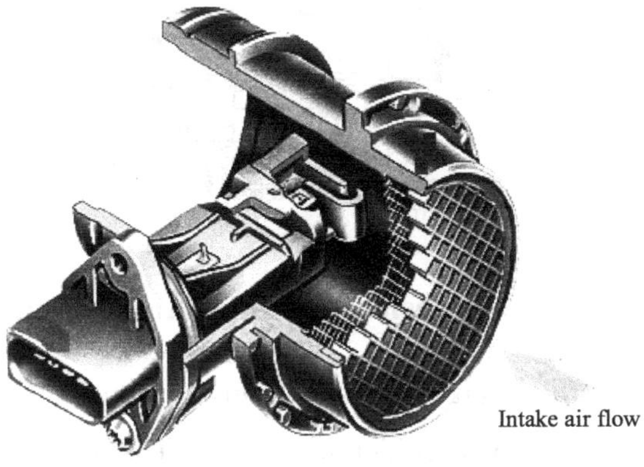

Figure 2-1-4 Hot film Air Flow Sensor

The working principle of hot film air flow sensor is shown in Figure 2-1-5. The difference between the temperature generated by energizing the hot wire (R_H) and the temperature of the entering air (R_T temperature) is maintained at 120 ℃. With the increase of air intake, R_H loses more heat and the temperature difference decreases. The control circuit increases the R_H current value (temperature difference is maintained at 120 ℃), R_S current value and signal voltage value U_S, which are sent to the ECU to increase the fuel injection amount.

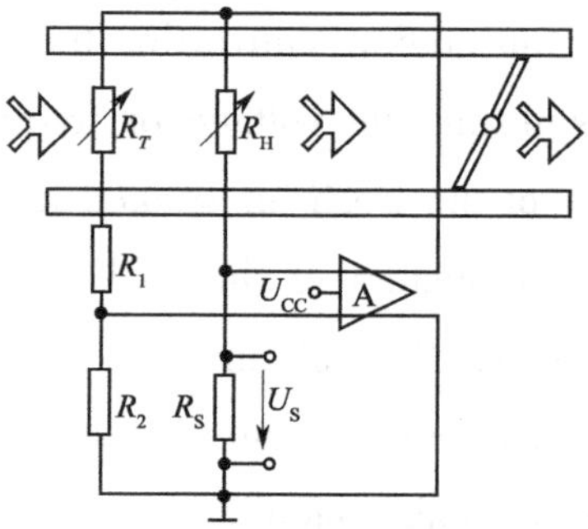

Figure 2-1-5 Working Principle of Thermal Air Flow Sensor

R_T–Temperature compensation resistor (intake air temperature sensor);R_H–resistance of heating element (hot wire or hot film); R_S–signal resistors;R_1,R_2–precision matching resistors;A–integrated control circuit

2) Intake pressure sensor

The intake pressure sensor is connected with the intake manifold by a vacuum tube, and senses the vacuum change in the intake manifold along with different rotating speeds and loads of the engine, and then converts the change of internal resistance of the sensor into a voltage signal for ECU to correct the fuel injection quantity and the ignition timing angle. The composition is shown in Figure 2-1-6.

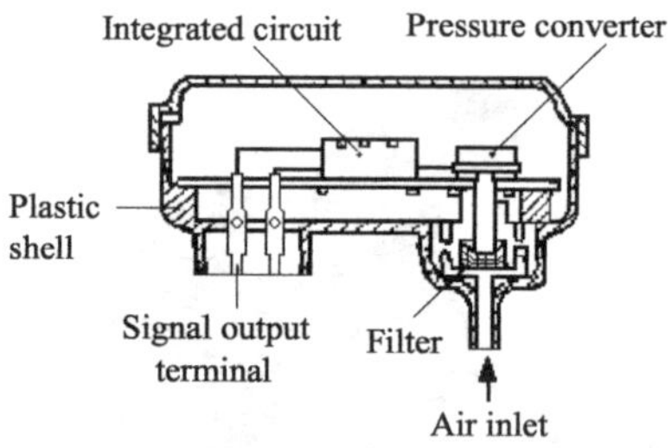

Figure 2-1-6 Composition of Inlet Air Pressure Sensor

In the EFI engine, the intake pressure sensor is used to detect the amount of intake air, which is called D-type injection system. The intake air pressure sensor is not directly detected as the intake flow sensor, but indirectly detected. At the same time, it is also affected by many factors, so its detection accuracy and response speed compared to the air flow sensor has a certain gap, has been gradually eliminated by the market. Figure 2-1-7 shows the installation position of the intake air pressure sensor on the real vehicle.

Figure 2-1-7 Installation Location of Inlet Air Pressure Sensor

2. Throttle body and throttle position sensor

1) Throttle body

The throttle body is installed on the intake pipe between the air flow meter and the engine intake manifold (for gasoline engine using air flow meter and electronic control), or between the air cleaner and the intake manifold (for gasoline engine with manifold absolute pressure sensor). The throttle body is generally composed of throttle valve, idle bypass air channel, idle adjustment screw, auxiliary air valve, etc. The throttle valve is connected with the accelerator pedal through a cable, and the driver controls the opening of the throttle valve through the accelerator pedal to make the output torque of the engine adapt to the required traction force. When the engine is idling, the throttle valve is completely closed. The air needed for idling is arranged in the main pipe through the bypass air duct. The idle adjustment screw is arranged on the idle bypass air duct. By screwing in or out of the idle adjustment screw appropriately, the section of the idle bypass air duct is changed, and the idle air volume is adjusted, which plays the role of adjusting the engine idle speed. In recent years, the electronic control gasoline engine produced in recent years has not adopted the structure of idle adjustment screw. A special electronic control idle speed system is used to adjust and control the idle speed of the engine. Figure 2-1-8 shows the throttle body of the Great Wall Haval H6.

Figure 2-1-8 Great Wall Haval H6 Throttle Body

3) Throttle position sensor (TPS)

In the electronic fuel injection system, the function of the throttle position sensor is to convert the opening of the throttle valve into an electric signal, and ECU corrects the actual fuel injection amount according to the output signal of the throttle position sensor. The throttle position sensor is installed on the throttle body and rotates synchronously with the throttle valve through the throttle shaft. There are three types of throttle position sensors used in electronic fuel injection system: linear output type, switch output type and adaptive cruise control (ACC) signal output type, among which linear output type is the most common.

Throttle position sensor working principle is shown in Figure 2-1-9. ① When the idle speed contact signal terminal IDL output $U = 0$, the throttle opening signal terminal VTA output $U_s = 0.5$ V; When the throttle valve is fully closed, the ECU determines the idle speed. ② When the idling contact signal terminal IDL output $U = +BV$, the output U_s of the throttle opening signal terminal VTA is slightly more than 0.5 V. When the throttle is partially open, the ECU determines a partial load. ③ When idling contact signal terminal IDL output $U = +BV$, the throttle opening signal terminal VTA output $U_s = +5$ V. When the throttle valve is fully opened, the ECU determines that the load is large.

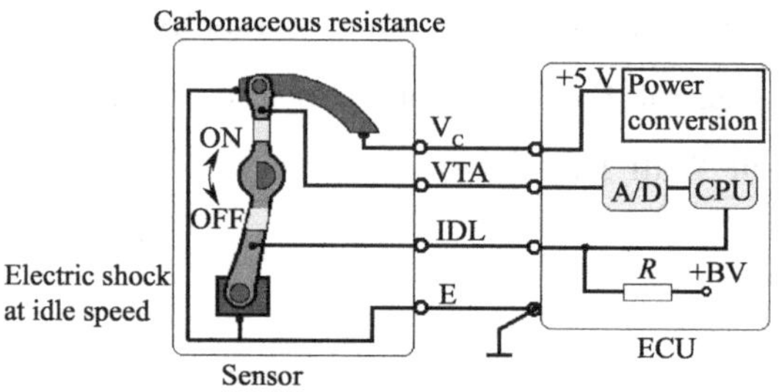

Figure 2-1-9 Linear Output Throttle Position Sensor Schematic

(Ⅱ) Fuel supply system

The task of the fuel supply system is to spray clean and well-atomized fuel into the engine intake manifold or intake manifold according to the determined pressure difference. As shown in Figure 2-1-10, the fuel supply system consists of fuel tank, electric fuel pump, fuel filter, smooth distribution pipe and injector pressure regulator. When the engine is working, the electric fuel pump sucks gasoline from the tank. After pressurization, the gasoline is pumped to the oil pipe, and the gasoline reaches the fuel distribution pipe through the oil pipe filter. Then it is distributed to each injector. The pressure regulator connected in series on the oil line regulates the oil pressure of gasoline, and the surplus gasoline flows back to the tank through the pressure regulator.

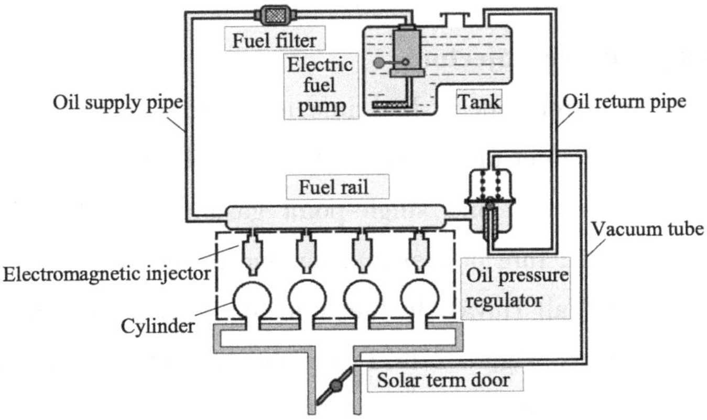

Figure 2-1-10 Composition of Fuel Supply System

1. Fuel pump (Figure 2-1-11)

(1) Action: pump oil to build up oil pressure.

(2) Structure: oil pump, permanent magnet motor, safety valve, check valve, shell, etc.

Oil pump is used to pump oil, roller type, gear type and turbine type.

Permanent magnet motor is used to pump oil, drive the oil pump and immerse it in the fuel oil for good cooling.

Safety valve is used to pump oil, prevent oil pressure from being too high.

Check valve is used to pump oil, prevent fuel from flowing back and to establish and maintain oil pressure.

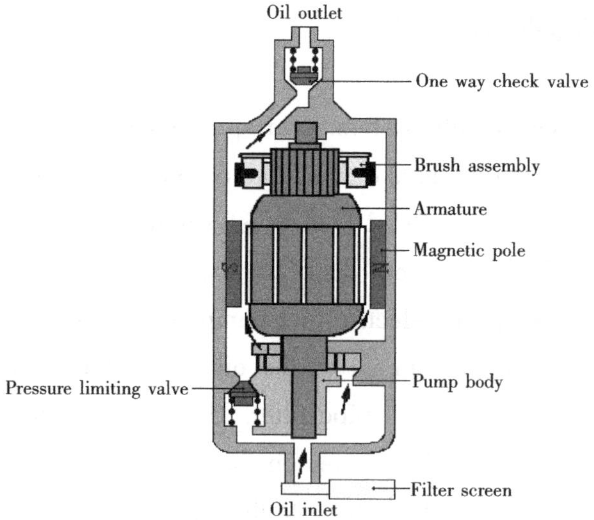

Figure 2-1-11 Electric Fuel Pump Structure

2. Electromagnetic fuel injector

The function of electromagnetic fuel injector is to inject well-atomized gasoline into the intake pipe or air inlet under the control of ECU. For electronic control multi-point gasoline injection system and single-point gasoline injection system, there are some differences in the structure of fuel injector due to the different injection positions and requirements. Great Wall Haval H6 fuel injector is shown in Figure 2-1-12, which uses ball valve fuel injectors. Figure 2-1-13 to Figure 2-1-15 are schematic diagrams of different types of fuel injectors.

Figure 2-1-12 Fuel Injector Physical

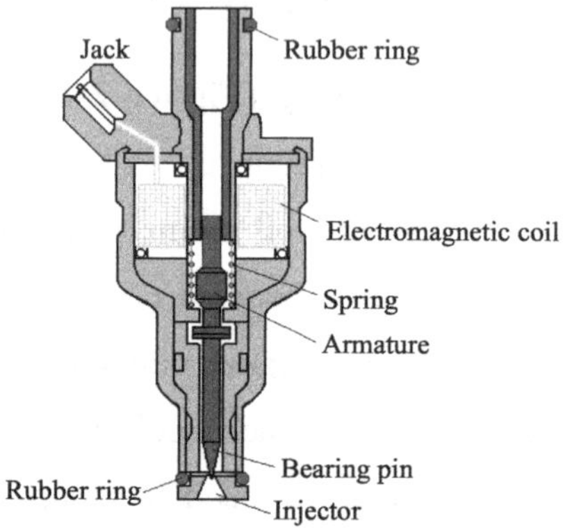

Figure 2-1-13 Pintle Type Fuel Injector

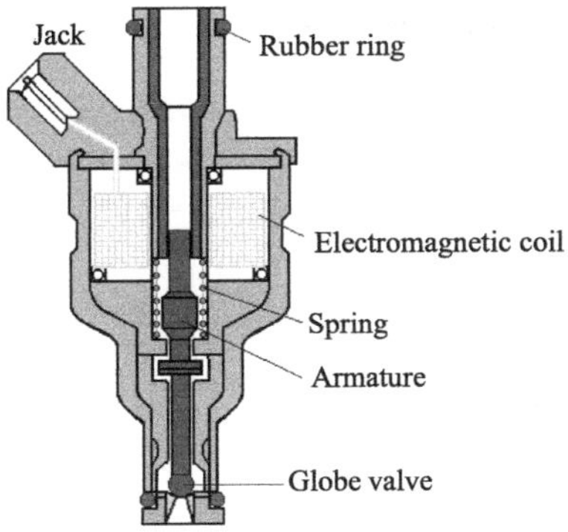

Figure 2-1-14 Ball Valve Injector

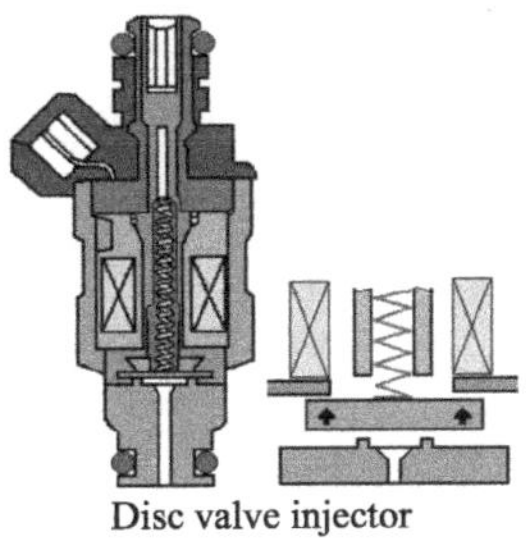

Figure 2-1-15 Reel Valve Injector

(Ⅲ) Electronic control system

Figure 2-1-16 shows the composition of the electronic control circuit.

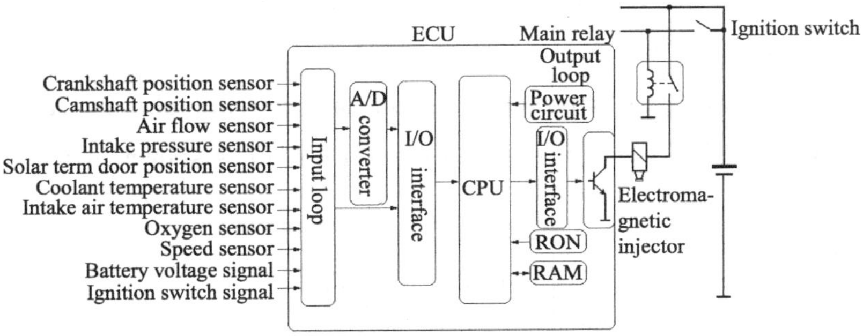

Figure 2-1-16 Electronic Control Circuit Composition

1. Oil pump switch control circuit

This control circuit is often used in injection systems where a vane type air flow sensor is installed. The oil pump switch is located in the air flow sensor.

Oil pump switch control circuit working principles are as follows.

(1) The ignition switch is energized, the open circuit relay is ON, and the oil pump is ON.

(2) After starting, ignition switch IG, oil pump switch ON, open circuit relay ON, oil pump ON.

(3) When the engine stops, the oil pump switch is OFF, the open circuit relay is OFF, and the oil pump is OFF.

L-Type Fuel Pump Control Circuit is shown in Figure 2-1-17.

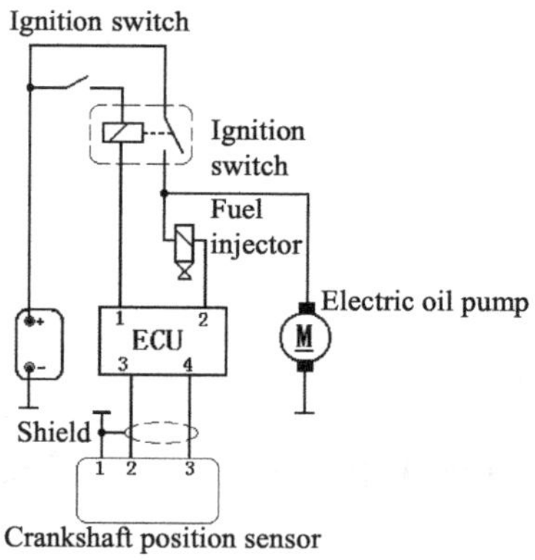

Figure 2-1-17 L-Type Fuel Pump Control Circuit

2. ECU control oil pump circuit

ECU control oil pump circuit working principles are as follows.

(1) The ignition switch is energized, the EFI relay is connected, the terminal 2 in the ECU is connected, the oil pump relay is connected, and the oil pump is ON.

(2) After starting, the ignition switch is ON, terminal 2 in ECU is ON, oil pump relay is ON and oil pump is ON.

(3) The engine stops, L1 is powered off, the open circuit relay is OFF, and the oil pump is off. Type D EFI system fuel pump control circuit is shown in Figure 2-1-18.

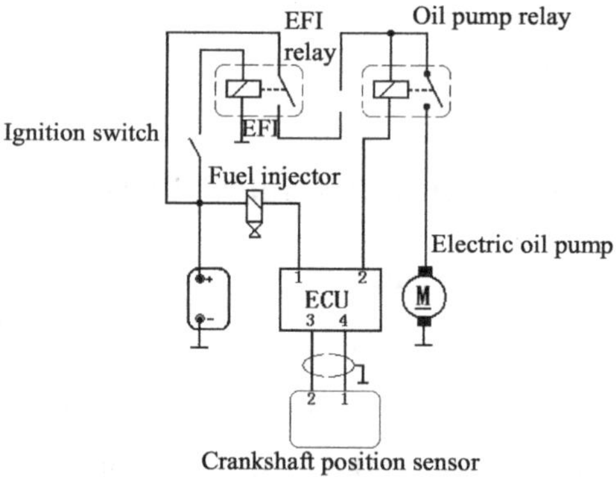

Figure 2-1-18 Type D EFI System Fuel Pump Control Circuit

3. Fuel pump speed control

1) Series resistance is used to control the oil pump speed.

When the engine runs at low speed or with medium and small load, the ECU controls the oil pump control relay B to be ON and A to be OFF, the resistor is connected in series, and the oil pump runs at low speed.

When the engine runs at high speed or heavy load, the ECU controls the oil pump control relay B to be OFF and A to be ON, the resistor is bypassed, and the oil pump runs at high speed.

Resistor Pump Speed Control Circuit is shown in Figure 2-1-19.

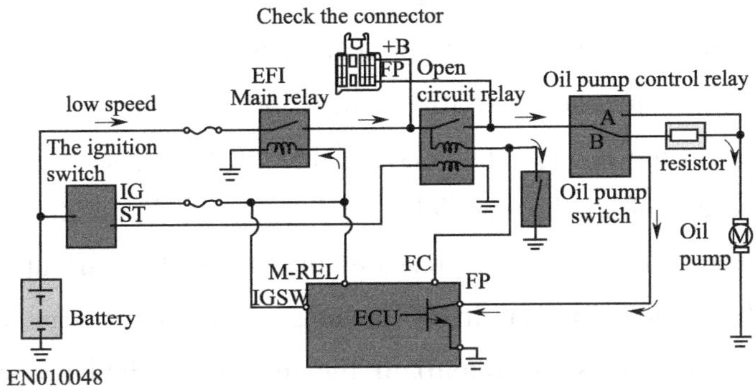

Figure 2-1-19 Resistor Pump Speed Control Circuit

2) The oil pump control module ECU is used to control the oil pump speed.

When the engine runs at low speed or medium and small load, the engine ECU inputs the low level to the FPC end of the oil pump ECU, and the FP end of the oil pump ECU provides 9 V low voltage to the oil pump, which runs at low speed.

When the engine starts, runs at high speed or heavy load, the engine ECU inputs the high level to the FPC end of the oil pump ECU, and the FP end of the oil pump ECU provides 12 V high voltage to the oil pump, and the pump runs at high speed.

Pump Control Module Control Pump Speed Circuit is shown Figure 2-1-20.

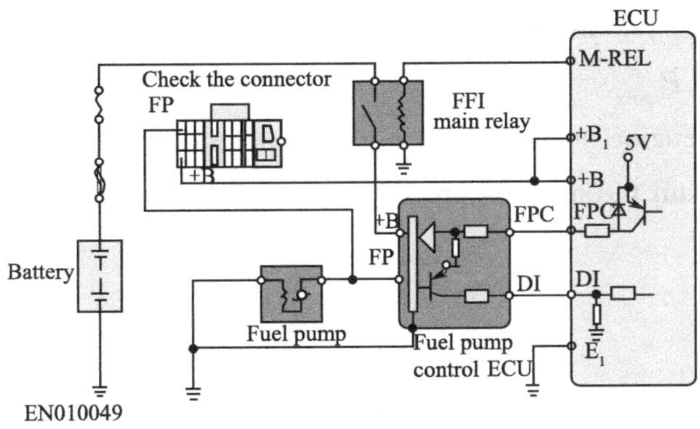

Figure 2-1-20 Pump Control Module Control Pump Speed Circuit

4. Pressure regulator

The main function of the fuel pressure regulator is to maintain a constant pressure difference between the fuel pressure in the fuel distribution pipe and the air pressure in the intake manifold. The difference depends on the type of engine. The pressure difference is generally 0.25-0.3 MPa.The constant pressure difference control method enables the ECU to control the fuel injection quantity simply and accurately with a single control parameter — the opening time of the fuel injector. This is because under the condition that the structural parameters of the fuel injector remain unchanged, the fuel injection quantity is not only related to the time when the maximum opening degree is kept, but also related to the pressure of fuel distribution pipe and the pressure of intake manifold. Under the condition that the full opening time of the injector and the oil pressure in the fuel distribution pipe remain unchanged, the fuel injection quantity will change with the change of back pressure (i.e. air pressure in the intake manifold). If the intake manifold pressure is high, the fuel injection quantity will decrease, otherwise it will increase. If the full open time of the fuel injector and the pressure of the intake manifold remain unchanged, the fuel injection quantity will change with the change of the oil pressure in the fuel distribution pipe, the oil pressure in the fuel distribution pipe will rise, and the fuel injection quantity will increase, contrarily, it will decrease. The pressure of the intake manifold varies with changes in engine speed and load. The fluctuation of the oil pressure in the fuel distribution pipe is related to factors such as the opening and closing of the fuel injector and the output characteristics of the electric gasoline pump. Pressure regulator principle is shown in Figure 2-1-21.

(1) When the pressure of the intake pipe increases, the opening of the oil return port decreases, and the oil return decreases, the oil pressure increases, $P_{oil}-P_{gas}$ is constant, $P_{oil}-P_{gas} = P_{spring}$.

(2) When the engine stops, the oil pump stops and the oil return port is closed to establish and maintain the oil pressure.

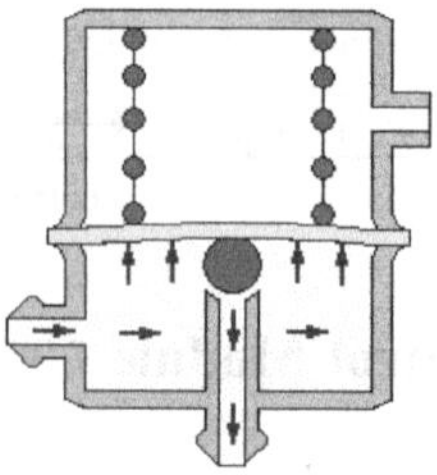

Figure 2-1-21 Pressure Regulator Principle

5. Speed and position sensor

The crankshaft position sensor is used to provide engine speed and crank angle signals to ECU. Engine speed is the main basis for ECU to judge engine operating conditions, select control programs and determine initial control parameters, and is also the necessary basic parameter for ECU to calculate the intake air volume of one engine working cycle. The purpose of the camshaft position sensor is to provide the ECU with a signal about the working stroke of the engine reference cylinder and the direction of piston movement, which is generally called the cylinder judgment signal.

In the electronic fuel injection system with sequential injection mode, the working stroke and piston position of the reference cylinder and the signal of judging cylinder are the only basis for ECU to control fuel injection timing and sequence. Therefore, the electronic fuel injection system with sequential injection mode must have a camshaft position sensor, while the electronic fuel injector system with group injection mode can be omitted. The crankshaft position sensor and camshaft position sensor used in electronic control gasoline injection system can be divided into three types according to their working principles: electromagnetic induction type, Hall effect type and photoelectric induction type. These three types of sensors can be combined in different ways to complete their respective parameter acquisition tasks. At present, magnetic induction position sensors are widely used, as shown in Figure 2-1-22.

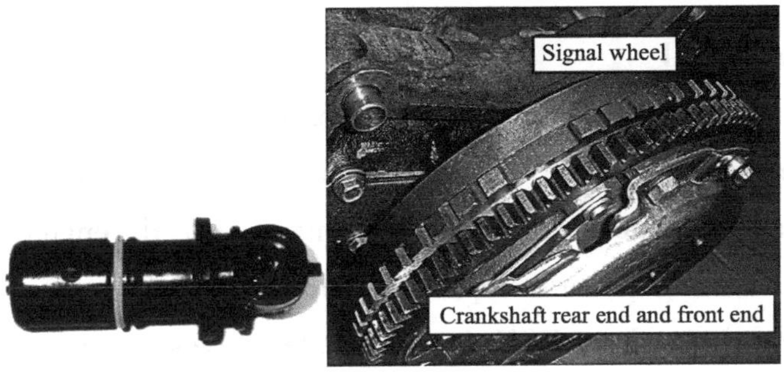

Figure 2-1-22 Magnetic Inductive Crankshaft Position Sensor

6. Temperature sensor

The function of the temperature sensor is to measure the temperature of the intake air, cooling water, fuel and so on of the engine, and convert the measured results into electric signals to be transmitted to the ECU. For all electronic control systems of gasoline engines, intake air temperature and cooling water temperature are two temperature parameters necessary for ECU control, while other temperature parameters vary with the type of electronic control system and control needs. Intake air temperature sensor is often installed in the air flow meter or air filter to the throttle body between the intake or air flow meter. The water temperature sensor is located in the engine cooling water pipeline, cylinder head or the appropriate location on the body. The sensors that can be used to measure the temperature include wire-wound resistance type, diffusion resistance type, semiconductor transistor type, metal core type, thermocouple type and semiconductor thermistor type. At present, the thermistor sensor is most widely used in the measurement of intake air temperature and cooling water temperature, which is mainly divided into single-terminal and two-terminal type, as shown in Figure 2-1-23.

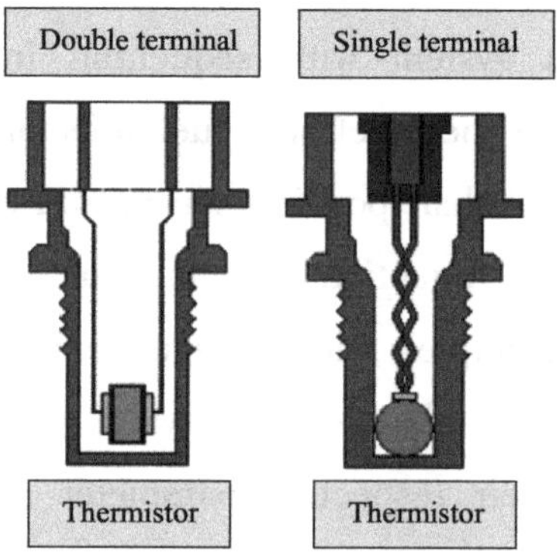

Figure 2-1-23 Common Thermistor Form

7. Switching signal

In order to realize the accurate control of engine operation, ECU needs some qualitative parameters indicating that the engine is in a certain state besides the quantitative parameters such as air intake, engine speed, engine load, air intake temperature and cooling water temperature detected by sensors. Such qualitative parameters are transmitted to ECU in the mode of yes or no, so they are called switching signals.

8. Electronic control unit

The Electronic control unit is the core of the engine electronic control system, which is mainly composed of four parts: input circuit, A/D converter, microcomputer and output circuit, as shown in Figure 2-1-24.

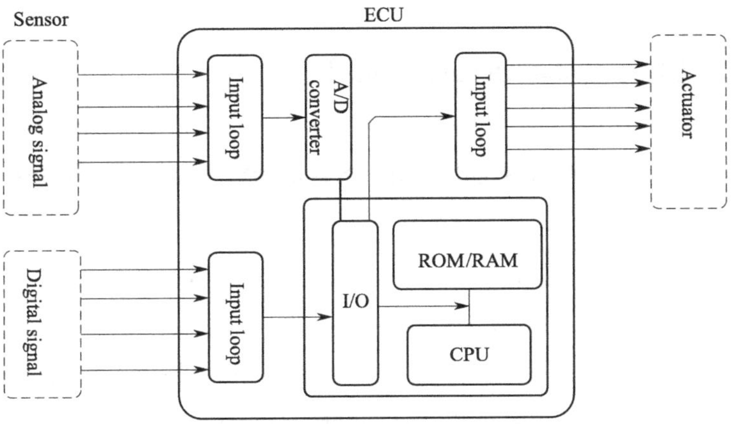

Figure 2-1-24 ECU Schematic

Figure 2-1-25 shows the ECU internal physical map. Its working process: when a car is running, the UCU is in a working state, some running programs or operating instructions from the memory (ROM) into the central processing unit (CPU). During program operation, all engine operating condition signals are provided by each sensor. When the sensor signal is input to the ECU, it enters the input circuit for processing. When an input signal is an analog signal, the analog signal is converted into a digital signal through an analog/digital (A/D) converter, and then the digital signal enters a CPU through an I/O interface; when the input signal is a digital signal, it can directly enter the CPU through the I/O interface. Most of the information is temporarily stored in the RAM, and is transferred from the RAM to the CPU according to an instruction. Then CPU introduces the set data stored in ROM, compares with the input signal of the sensor, calculates and judges, and sends out an instruction, outputs the instruction through an I/O interface, and controls the actuator to work.

Figure 2-1-25 Internal Structure of Harvard H6 ECU

【Knowledge Development】

(Ⅰ) Function and installation position of air flow sensor

Air flow sensor, also known as air flow meter (AFM), is one of the important sensors of the electronic fuel injection engine.

(1) Function: it converts the sucked air flow into an electric signal and sends it to the ECU, as one of the basic signals for determining fuel injection, it is a sensor for measuring the air flow sucked into the engine.

(2) Troubleshooting: inaccurate measurement of air intake, too rich or too thin mixture, ECU unable to correctly control the fuel injection of the engine, abnormal operation of the engine, excessive emissions and other issues.

(3) Installation position: on the intake pipe between the air cleaner and the throttle valve, as shown in Figure 2-1-26.

Figure 2-1-26 Installation Location of the Air Flow Sensor

(Ⅱ) Detection of Harvard H6 air flow sensor

The common faults of air flow sensor are short circuit, open circuit or abnormal air intake signal, which will make the computer unable to correctly measure the amount of air inhaled into the engine, thus being unable to normally control the fuel injection amount, resulting in too rich or too lean mixture and abnormal operation of the engine.

The air flow sensor is a high-precision component. In the process of maintenance and disassembly, care should be taken to avoid collision. Do not let dirt enter the flowmeter, and do not put tools or fingers into the flowmeter at will, so as to avoid damage. There are many types of air flow meters, and their structural principles are very different, so the maintenance methods are also different. Next, we take the hot film air flow sensor of Great Wall Harvard H6 as an example to conduct a typical practice exercise.

1. Power supply voltage detection

Turn on the ignition switch, set the digital multimeter at the DC voltage of 20 V, put the red probe on pin 2 of the air flow sensor, the black probe on the negative pole of the battery or the engine intake manifold housing, and when the starter is turned on, it should display 12 V; when the red probe is placed on the air flow sensor pin 4, and the black probe is placed on the battery negative pole or the engine intake manifold housing, it should display 5 V.

2. Signal voltage measurement

Signal voltage measurement is divided into single measurement and on-vehicle measurement.

1) Single measurement

Take an air flow sensor assembly component, apply battery voltage to pin 2 of air flow sensor electrical socket, apply 5 V voltage to pin 4 of air flow sensor electrical socket, set digital multimeter at DC voltage of 20 V, and measure the voltage of pin 3 and pin 5 of air flow sensor electrical socket, which should be about 1.5 V; Use a hair dryer to blow cold air or heated air from the side of the air flow sensor grille to the air flow sensor. Measure the pin 3 and pin of the air flow sensor electrical socket. The voltage should rise to 2.8 V and fall back. If the above conditions cannot be met, it can be judged that the air flow sensor is faulty.

2) On-vehicle measurement

Start the engine to the operating temperature, set the digital multimeter at the DC voltage 20 V gear, measure the feedback signal of pin 5 of the air flow sensor, with the red probe at pin 5 of the air flow sensor, and the black probe at pin 3 of the airflow sensor. The battery cathode or the intake manifold shell should display the voltage of about 1.5 V at idle speed 2.8 V change. If the above changes are not met, or the voltage drops instead, the air flow sensor can be judged to be damaged on the premise that the power supply voltage and reference voltage are in good condition and must be replaced.

3. Maintenance points of air flow sensor

1) Cleaning after the hot film is dirty

If the engine has a "backfire" fault, it often causes serious harm to the air flow sensor. Because the air flow of the engine reverses in the intake manifold (that is, "backfire"), which contains carbon particles, these carbon particles are easy to adhere to the sensing element of the air flow sensor, resulting in the following consequences: at idle, the signal of the air flow sensor is strong, while at acceleration and heavy load, the signal is weak.

To check whether the hot film has the self-cleaning ability, remove the air filter, and check the hot film from the air inlet of the air flow sensor. If you can't see the reddish glow of the hot wire for about 1 s after the engine shuts down for 5 s, it indicates that the self-cleaning ability of the hot film has been lost.

After the hot film is polluted, the filter screen of the air filter can be removed under the state of hot engine and idle speed, and the hot film can be directly sprayed with the carburetor cleaning agent to remove the carbon deposit adhered on it.

2) Treatment of damaged hot-film air flow sensor

The hot-film mass air flow sensor manufactured by BOSCH is adopted. Its core part consists of an integrated circuit (D/A conversion circuit) and a Wheatstone bridge. There is no voltage regulator circuit. Therefore, when the power supply voltage is too high or a transient high voltage occurs, the hot-film mass air flow sensor is easy to burn out. The peak voltage of the circuit is too high (more than 16 V). The reason is that the battery is vulcanized seriously, which reduces its capacity and can not absorb the peak voltage of the generator. Therefore, the battery vulcanization is one of the causes of damage to the hot film air flow sensor. The solution is to install a 7812 three-terminal voltage regulator integrated circuit in front of the hot film air flow sensor.

3) Blocking the entry way of air without metering

These include a broken intake manifold, a loose vacuum hose, and a loose seal between the intake manifold and the cylinder head. If any of these conditions exists, some of the air will enter the cylinders without being metered by the air flow sensor, resulting in a mismatched mixture in the engine.

【Thinking and Practice】

Ⅰ. Fill in the blanks

1. In the L-type electronic control fuel injection system, the intake air volume of the engine is measured by ____________.

2. According to different injection modes, the electronic fuel injection system can be divided into two modes, ____________ and ____________.

3. The electronic fuel injection system consists of ________, ________, ________.

4. The fuel injector is divided into two types, ____________ and ____________ according to the structure of the fuel injection port.

Ⅱ. Multiple choice

1. Which of the following is true regarding the idle adjustment screw on the air flow meter?____________

A. is used to adjust the fuel supply of the gasoline injector

B. is used to adjust the concentration of the mixture

C. All of the above is correct   D. None of the above is correct

2. When discussing EFI system, A said that ECU could provide appropriate air-fuel ratio by controlling fuel pressure; B said ECU could provide appropriate air-fuel ratio by controlling fuel injector pulse width. Who is correct?

A. A is correct.   B. B is correct.

C. Both of them are correct.   D. Both of them are incorrect.

Ⅲ. Short answer questions

1. Briefly describe the control principle of the electronic fuel injection system.

2. Briefly describe the function of the air flow sensor.

3. Briefly describe the maintenance points of the air flow sensor.

Section 2 Engine Electronic Ignition Control System

Ⅰ. The awareness of the ignition system

(Ⅰ) Requirements for engine electronic ignition system

(1) It can produce enough voltage to break down the spark plug gap. The voltage required for the spark plug electrode to break down and produce a spark is called the breakdown voltage. The secondary voltage generated by the ignition system must be higher than the breakdown voltage in order to make the spark plug jump.

(2) The spark should have enough energy. When the engine works normally, because the temperature of the mixture at the end of compression is close to its auto-ignition temperature, only 1-5 MJ of spark energy is needed. But if the mixture is too rich or too lean, when the engine starts, idles or the throttle valve opens sharply, higher spark energy will be needed. There is an urgent need to improve the spark energy. Therefore, in order to ensure reliable ignition. The high-energy electric ignition system should generally have a spark energy of 80-100 MJ, and should produce a spark energy of more than 100 MJ when starting.

(3) The ignition time should be adapted to the working conditions of the engine. First, the ignition system should fire according to the engine's working order. Second, the ignition must be carried out at the most favorable moment.

Since the combustion of the mixture in the cylinder takes a certain time, the mixture should not be ignited at the top dead center (TDC) of the compression stroke, but should be appropriately advanced so that when the piston reaches the TDC, the mixture has been fully burned, so that the engine can obtain greater power. That is, the crankshaft rotation during the period from the spark to the piston reaching the top dead center.

If the ignition is too late, ignition occurs when the piston reaches TDC, combustion of the mixture is completed mainly during the downward movement of the piston, that is, the combustion process is carried out under the condition of large volume, the contact area between the hot gas and the cylinder wall is large, so the heat converted into effective work is relatively reduced, the maximum combustion pressure in the cylinder is reduced, and the engine is overheated. If the ignition is too early, the combustion of the mixture is completely carried out in the compression process. The combustion pressure in the cylinder rises sharply, and reaches the maximum before the piston reaches the TDC, which makes the piston recoil and the engine do negative work, which not only reduces the power of the engine, but also may cause deflagration and unstable operation, and accelerate the damage of moving parts and bearings.

(Ⅱ) The role of the ignition system

The role of the ignition system in engine operation is to provide sufficient voltage at the right time at any engine speed and different engine loads, so that the spark plug can produce enough sparks to ignite the mixture in the cylinder, so that the engine can get the best combustion efficiency. The basic devices of ignition system include power supply (battery), ignition timing control device of ignition trigger device, high-voltage generator (high-voltage coil), high-voltage power distribution device (distributor), high-voltage wire and spark plug. The ignition advance of modern automobile engine has been controlled by engine management computer, the computer collects the signals of engine speed, intake manifold pressure or air flow, throttle position, battery voltage, water temperature, knock and so on, calculates the best ignition timing angle, and then sends out the ignition signal. The purpose of controlling ignition timing is achieved.

(Ⅲ) Classification of ignition system

1. Traditional ignition system

The working process of mechanical ignition system is that the crankshaft drives the distributor shaft to rotate, and the cam on the distributor shaft rotates, so that the secondary contact of the ignition coil is connected and closed to generate high-voltage electricity. This ignition high-voltage is supplied to the spark plug of each cylinder in sequence according to the working requirements of the engine through the distributor rotor on the distributor shaft. The spark plug emits the electric spark to ignite the gas in the combustion chamber. The distributor housing can be manually rotated to adjust the basic ESA (i.e. ESA during idling running). Additionally, there is a vacuum advance device, which provides different angles of advance according to the change of the vacuum degree in the intake pipe.

2. Microcomputer controlled ignition system

The electronic ignition system is completely different from the mechanical ignition system. It has an electronic control device for ignition. In the electronic ignition system, there is an ignition control curve map required by the engine under various working conditions. Through a series of sensors, such as engine speed sensor, intake pipe vacuum sensor (engine load sensor), throttle position sensor, crankshaft position sensor, etc., the working state of the engine can be judged. The ignition advance angle required by the engine in this working state can be found out on the curve chart, and the ignition can be carried out according to this requirement. Then according to the knock sensor signal, the above ignition requirements are modified to make the engine work at the best ignition time. Electronic ignition systems also have closed-loop control and open-loop control of the points: with knock sensors. The electronic control system that can correct the ignition advance angle in time according to whether the engine knocks or not is called the closed-loop control system. Without the knock sensor, the ignition advance control is only controlled according to the program set in the electronic control unit, which is called the open-loop control system. The principle of microcomputer controlled ignition system is shown in Figure 2-2-1.

(1) Breaker-triggered transistorized ignition (TI-B), which has been eliminated.

(2) Semiconductor ignition (SI) is available, as shown in Figure 2-2-2 to Figure 2-2-4.

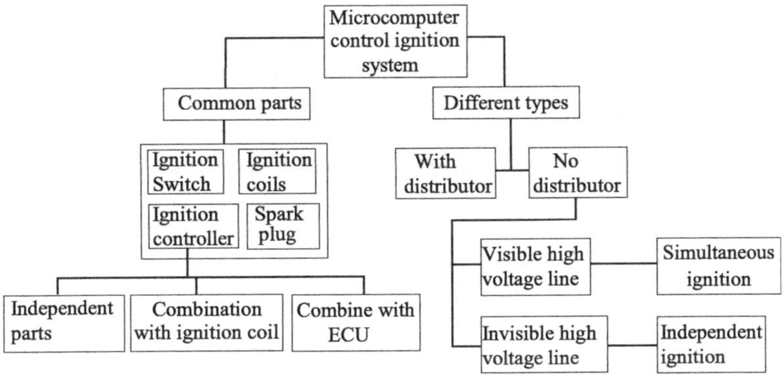

Figure 2-2-1 Principle of Microcomputer Controlled Ignition System

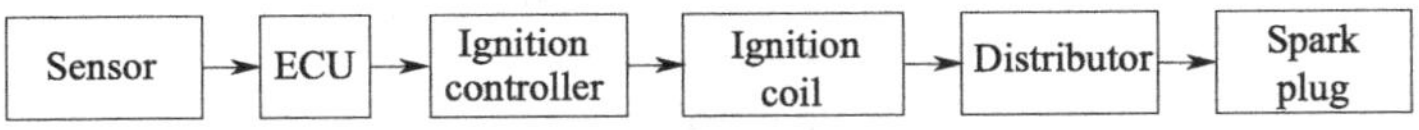

Figure 2-2-2 Control Schematic of Ignition System with Distributor

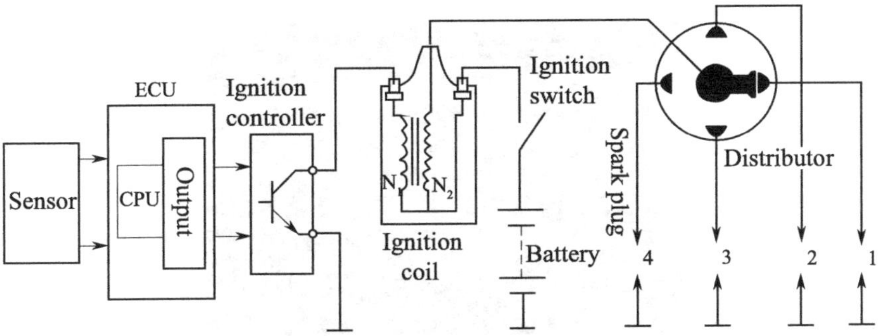

Figure 2-2-3 Ignition System with Distributor Circuit

Figure 2-2-4 Actual Vehicle with Distributor Ignition System

(3) Distributorless ignition system (DIS) without distributor is shown in Figure 2-2-5 to Figure 2-2-7.

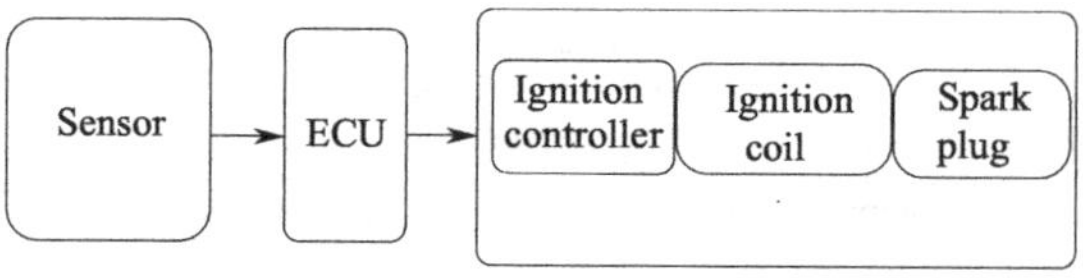

Figure 2-2-5　Control Schematic of Distributorless Ignition System

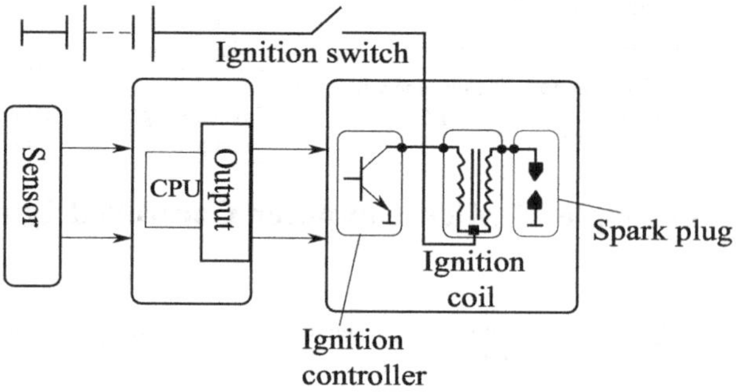

Figure 2-2-6　Distributorless Ignition System Circuit

Figure 2-2-7　Actual Vehicle with Distributorless Ignition System

Ⅱ. The composition and working principle of the automobile electronic ignition system

(Ⅰ) Composition of engine electronic ignition system

The engine electronic ignition system is mainly composed of low-voltage power supply, ignition coil, ignition controller, ignition signal generator, spark plug and sensor installed in the distributor, as shown in Figure 2-2-8.

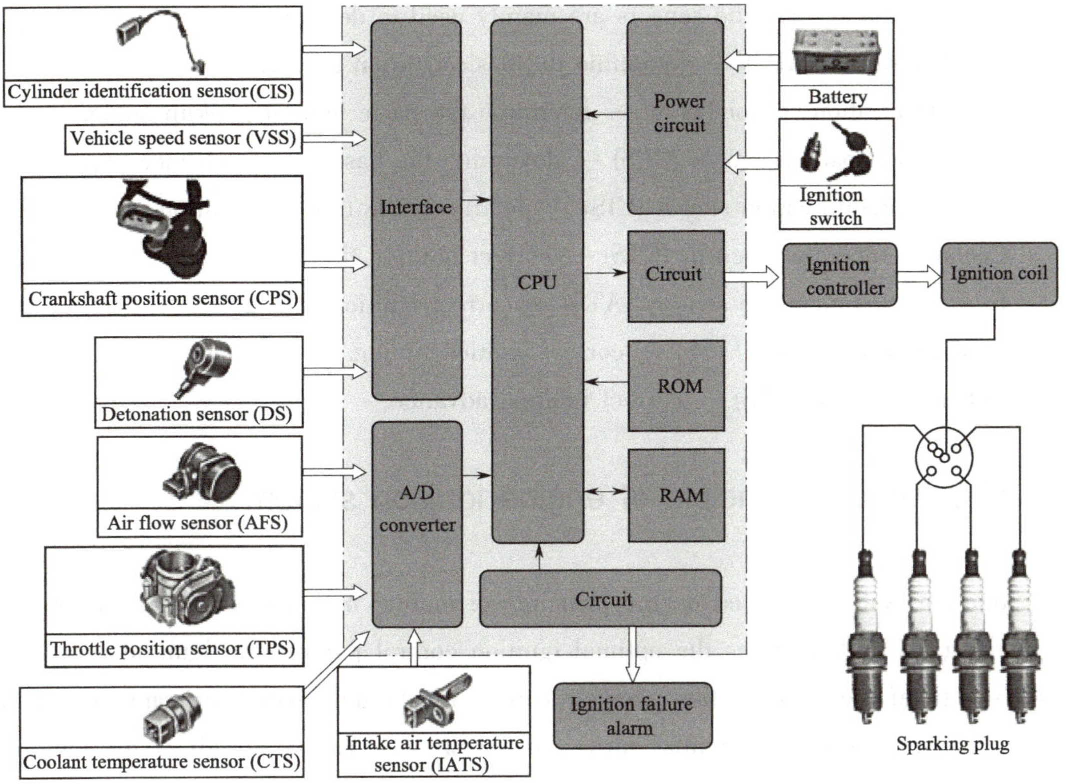

Figure 2-2-8 Composition of Electronic Control Ignition System

(1) The low-voltage power supply of the ignition system is a battery or an alternator, and the nominal voltage is generally 12 V. The function of the low-voltage power supply is to provide the required electric energy for the ignition system.

(2) The structure of ignition coil is similar to that of autotransformer, mainly composed of iron core, primary winding and secondary winding. Its function is to convert 12 V low voltage into 15-20 kV high voltage.

(3) Ignition controller is also called ignition electronic assembly or electronic igniter, which is composed of semiconductor devices and electronic switch circuit. Its main function is to connect and cut off the primary winding circuit of ignition coil according to the ignition pulse signal generated by ignition signal generator.

(4) The role of the spark plug is to introduce the high-voltage electricity generated by the secondary winding of the ignition coil into the combustion chamber of the cylinder, and generate electric sparks to ignite the combustible mixture.

(5) The ignition switch is used to control the primary circuit of the ignition system. Once the ignition switch is turned off, the engine will stop immediately.

(6) Sensors are the basic components of the electronic control system, and in the

electronic control system, the sensors are mainly used to determine the ignition timing.

Air flow sensor (AFS) — determine the basic ignition timing.

Throttle position sensor (TPS) — determine the basic ignition pickup angle.

Crankshaft position sensor (CPS) — determine the basic spark advance angle.

Cylinder identification sensor (CIS) — determine the time for ignition.

Coolant temperature sensor (CTS) — correct ignition timing.

Intake air temperature sensor (IATS) — correct ignition timing.

Vehicle speed sensor (VSS) — correct ignition timing.

Detonation sensor (DS) — correct ignition advance.

(Ⅱ) Working principle of engine ignition system

Ignition system is based on the principle of mutual inductance. When the engine is working, ECU determines the optimal ignition control parameters (ignition time and power-on time) according to the received sensor signals and related programs and data stored in the memory. The igniter turns on and off the primary circuit of the ignition coil according to the instructions of the ECU. When the circuit is on, current passes through the primary circuit of the ignition coil, and the ignition coil stores ignition energy in the form of a magnetic field. When the current in the primary circuit is cut off, a high induced electromotive force is generated in the secondary coil (15-20 kV). At this time, the distributor head rotating with the distributor shaft is just aimed at the side electrode of a certain cylinder on the distributor cap, and the high voltage power is sent to the spark plug by the high voltage line of the distributor cylinder. The ignition energy is instantaneously released by the spark plug to make the spark plug jump, and the generated electric spark ignites the mixture gas in the cylinder, so that the engine completes the process of the work process.

According to the above analysis, the working process of the ignition system can be divided into three stages: the primary circuit is turned on, the ignition energy is stored, the secondary circuit produces high-voltage electricity, and the spark plug electrode produces electric spark to ignite the mixture.

In addition, in the electronic control ignition system with deflagration control function, the ECU also judges whether the engine has deflagration or not and the intensity of deflagration according to the input signal of the detonation sensor, and controls the ignition advance angle in a closed-loop way.

【Knowledge Development】

There are many reasons for the failure of ignition. The first thing we need to consider is the supply of oil, liquid, gas and electricity, that is to say, we need to check the starting system and the fuel supply system. On the premise of confirming that there is no failure, we start to consider whether there is a problem with the ignition system. Circuit failure, component damage and so on will cause the failure of ignition or ignition difficulties. We will take the high-voltage circuit as an example to diagnose the fault of the ignition system, see Table 2-2-1.

Table 2-2-1 Detection of high voltage circuit

Serial Number	Graphic represent	Specific Content
1	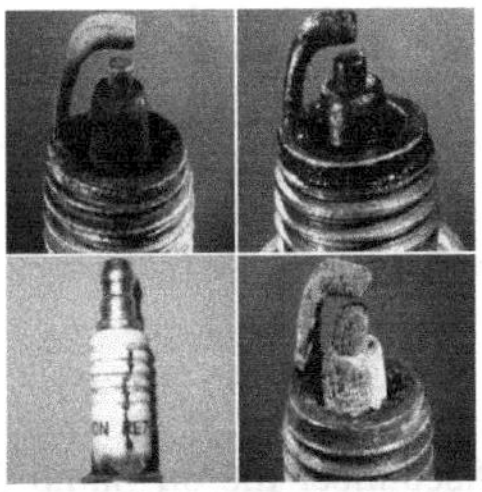	Check the appearance of the spark plus: 1. check the wear of the spark plug center electrode; 2. check the spark plug gap; 3. check the spark plug for carbon deposit; 4. check the spark plug ceramics for cracks
2	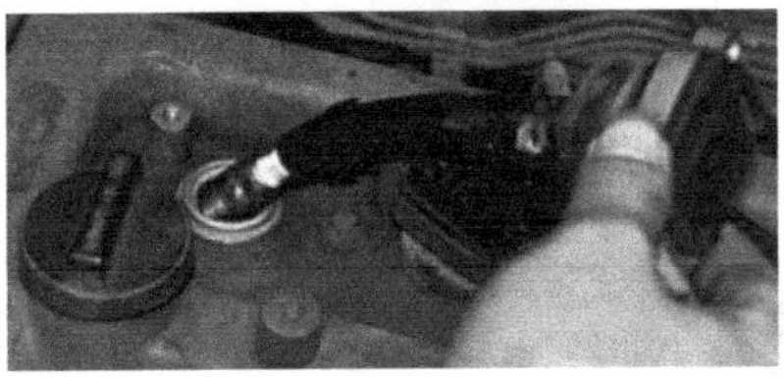 	Check the high-voltage wires: 1. check whether the spark plug and high-voltage wires are connected properly; 2. check whether the anti-interference plug and high-voltage wires are connected properly; 3. the spark plug, high-voltage wires and anti-interference plug shall be checked for cracks, corrosion and aging
3	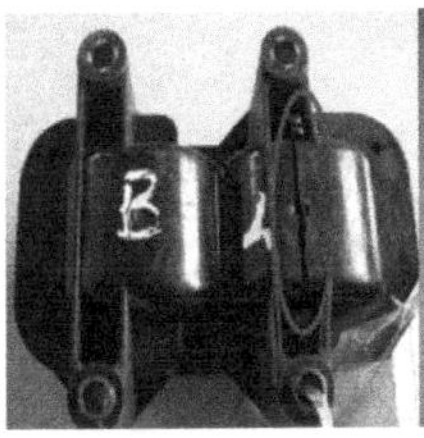 	Check ignition module: 1. check the ignition module for cracks; 2. check the ignition module for deformation; 3. the ignition module shall be checked for corrosion

Continued

Serial Number	Graphic represent	Specific Content
4	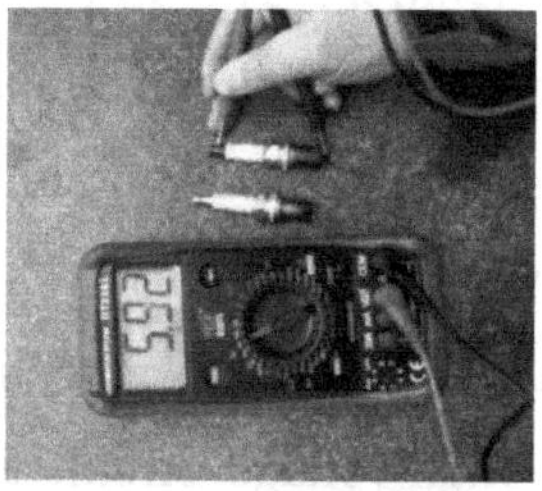	Check the Resistance of the Spark Plug Electrod: the normal value is 4-6 kΩ
5		Check the internal resistance of the ignition module: ignition module resistance 4-8 kΩ.
6		Disconnect the oil pump fuse
7	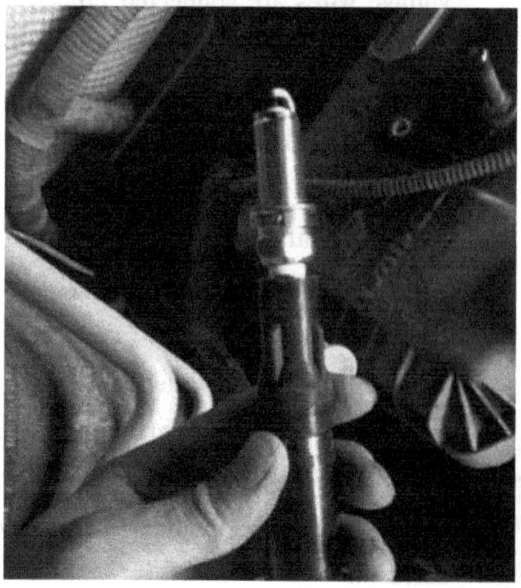	Pull out the high-voltage wires and fit the spark plus

Continued

Serial Number	Graphic represent	Specific Content
8	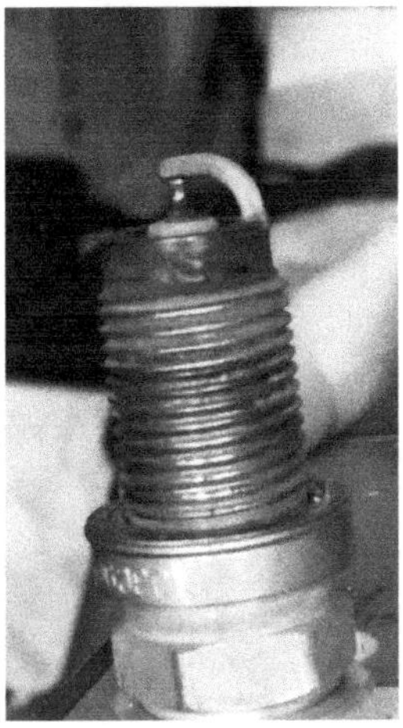	Start the engine and check for flashover

【Thinking and Practice】

1. Briefly describe composition of electronic control ignition system.

2. Briefly describe the advantages of electronic control ignition.

3. Briefly describe similarities and differences between distributor ignition system and non-distributor ignition system.

Chapter 3

Electronic Control System of Automobile Chassis

【Section Overview】

With the application of electronic control technology in automobile chassis, especially the high-speed development of large-scale integrated circuits and microcomputers, the degree of automobile electronization is getting higher and higher, and the electronic control technology is more and more widely used in automobiles. Modern automobile technology has realized the integration of mechanical, electrical, hydraulic, computer, network and other technologies, and the automobile chassis has also undergone significant changes. It has changed the traditional mechanical device of the automobile chassis, and added many new functions, making the driving of the car more simple and convenient, and the riding more comfortable and safe. It is very important to study and research the function, working principle, structure and inspection and repair method of chassis electronic control technology for engaging in the work of automobile. This chapter mainly introduces the electronic control hydraulic automatic transmission, automobile anti-skid control system, automobile driving and safety control system composition and working principle. It enables readers to have a comprehensive and systematic understanding of the electronic control system of automobile chassis.

Section 1 Electronic Control Hydraulic Automatic Transmission

The so-called automatic transmission refers to the automation of clutch operation and transmission operation in automobile driving, referred to as AT. Automatic transmission can change the transmission ratio according to the working conditions parameters such as engine load and speed, so that the car can obtain good power and fuel economy.

Ⅰ. Overview of automatic transmission

(Ⅰ) Classification of automatic transmission

Automatic transmissions can be classified according to the structure and control mode, vehicle driving mode and gear number.

1. According to the structure and control mode

According to the structure and control mode, automatic transmission can be divided into hydraulic automatic transmission, mechanical automatic transmission, continuously variable automatic transmission and stepped double clutch mechanical automatic transmission.

(1) Hydraulic automatic transmission (HAT) (Figure 3-1-1) is the most widely used and technologically mature automatic transmission at present. According to different control modes, hydraulic automatic transmission can be divided into hydraulic control hydraulic automatic transmission and electronic control hydraulic automatic transmission. At present, all cars use electronic control hydraulic automatic transmissions. According to the different transmission mechanism, hydraulic automatic transmission can be divided into planetary gear automatic transmission and non planetary gear automatic transmission, and the planetary gear automatic transmission can be divided into Simpson type and Lavina type.

Figure 3-1-1 Hydraulic Automatic Transmission

(2) Automatic mechanical transmission (AMT) (Figure 3-1-2) adds an electronic control system on the basis of the original common stepped manual gear transmission

to automatically control the engagement and separation of the clutch and the shift of the transmission gear. Because the original mechanical transmission structure of automatic mechanical transmission is basically unchanged, the inherent advantages of gear transmission, such as high transmission efficiency, compact structure and reliable operation, etc., are retained inherited because the original mechanical transmission structure is basically unchanged.

Figure 3-1-2 Automated Mechanical Transmission

(3) Continuously variable transmission (CVT) (Figure 3-1-3) uses the transmission belt and the driving and driven pulleys with variable working diameters to transmit power, which can realize the continuous change of transmission ratio. This is also a kind of automatic transmission with broad development prospects, which has been applied in some automobiles.

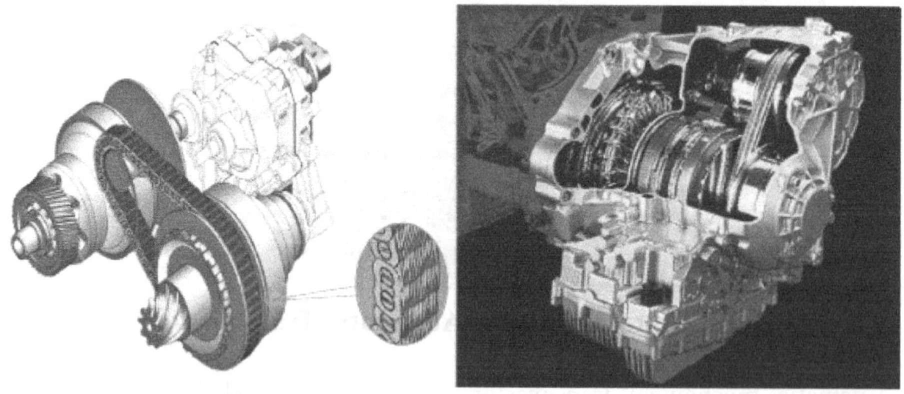

Figure 3-1-3 Continuously Variable Transmission

(4) Stepped dual clutch mechanical automatic transmission (DCT, DSG) (Figure 3-1-4) unlike the general automatic transmission system, which is based on manual transmission and belongs to automatic transmission, it has the flexibility of manual transmission and the comfort of automatic transmission, because it has two sets of clutches, which are responsible for the power transmission speed of different gears, so it can provide uninterrupted power output. The traditional manual transmission uses one clutch and when shifting and the driver must step on the clutch pedal to make the gears of different gears mesh. And the power is interrupted during the shift, which makes the output performance interrupted.

Figure 3-1-4 Stepped Dual Clutch Mechanical Automatic Transmission

2. According to the vehicle driving mode

Automatic transmission can be divided into automatic transmission with rear drive and automatic transmission with front drive according to different driving modes of vehicles. Automatic transmission with rear drive is used for the arrangement of engine front rear wheel drive, and the transmission is separated from final drive and differential. The front drive is used for that of the front wheel drive and the transmission, main reducer and differential are made into an assembly, as shown in Figure 3-1-5.

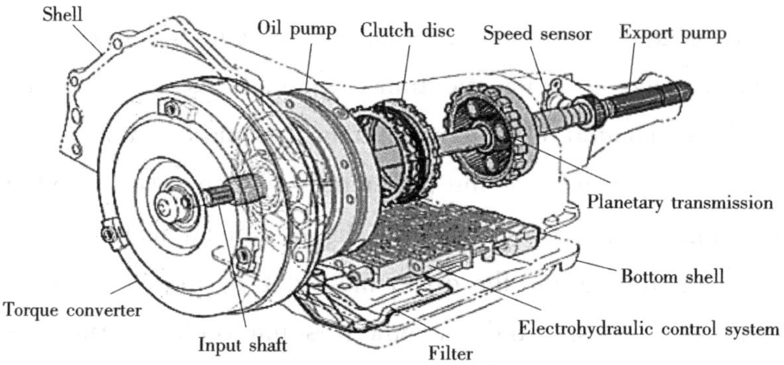

Figure 3-1-5 Composition of the Electronically Controlled Hydraulic Automatic Transmission

3. According to the forward gear of the automatic transmission

According to the different number of gears when the automatic transmission shift lever is placed in forward gear, it can be divided into 4th gear, 5th gear, 6th gear and so on.

(Ⅱ) The basic composition of the electronic control hydraulic automatic transmission

Electronic control hydraulic automatic transmission is mainly composed of four parts: hydraulic torque converter, planetary gear transmission mechanism, hydraulic control system and electronic control system.

1. Hydraulic torque converter

Hydraulic torque converter is a power transmission device through automatic transmission fluid (ATF), which can automatically and continuously change the torque ratio within a certain range to meet the requirements of different driving resistance. It also has the function of clutch. When the engine does not stop and the automatic transmission is in the power gear, the car can be in the parking state. The driver can control the output torque of the hydraulic torque converter by controlling the throttle opening, and gradually increase the output torque to realize the soft transmission of power.

2. Planetary gear transmission mechanism

Similar to the common gear-type manual transmission, the planetary gear transmission mechanism can form different transmission ratios and combine them into different gears of the electronic control transmission. It can increase the range of transmission ratio by 2-4 times on the basis of the hydraulic torque converter, so as to improve the driving adaptability of the automobile; in addition, the reverse gear transmission can also be realized.

3. Hydraulic control system

1) Shift actuator

The shift actuator of the electronic control hydraulic automatic transmission mainly includes brake, clutch and one-way clutch. Its function is similar to that of shift fork, combination sleeve and other shift elements of manual transmission, which can realize the shift of gear and transmission ratio.

2) Hydraulic control loop

The hydraulic control loop in the electronic control hydraulic automatic transmission mainly controls the work of the shift actuator, which is composed of hydraulic pump, various hydraulic control valves and hydraulic pipelines.

4. Electronic control system

The electronic control system is used together with the hydraulic control system, which is usually called the electro-hydraulic control system. The electronic control system mainly includes the electronic control unit, various sensors and actuators. The sensors and various control switches in the electronic control system transmit the signals of engine working conditions, vehicle speed and so on to the electronic control unit, which sends instructions to the actuators. The actuator and the hydraulic system control the shift actuator to work according to a certain rule, so as to realize the automatic shift of the electronic control hydraulic automatic transmission.

(Ⅲ) The control principle of the electronic hydraulic automatic transmission

Electronic control hydraulic automatic transmission (Figure 3-1-6) detects the running state of automobile and engine through sensors and various signal switches, receives the driver's instructions, converts the engine speed, throttle valve opening, vehicle speed, engine coolant temperature, hydraulic oil temperature of automatic transmission and other parameters into electric signals, and inputs them into ECU. According to these signals and the set shift schedule, ECU sends electronic control signals to shift solenoid valve, oil pressure solenoid valve, etc. Then the control signals sent out by the ECU are converted into hydraulic control signals by the shift solenoid valves and oil pressure solenoids. Each control valve in the valve plate controls the action of the shift actuating mechanism according to these hydraulic control signals, so as to realize automatic shift.

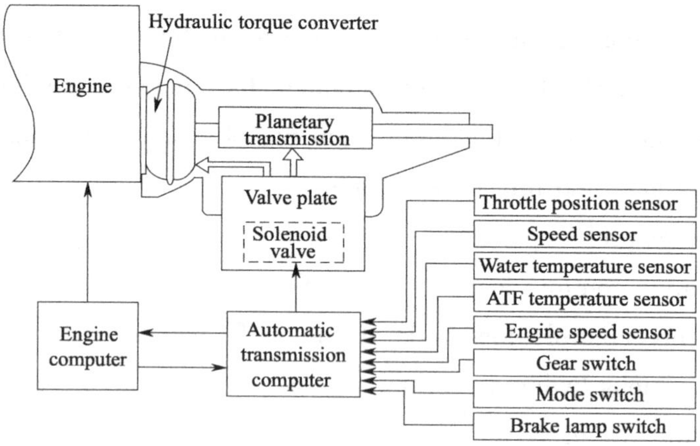

Figure 3-1-6 Control Principle of the Electronic Control Hydraulic Automatic Transmission

The Great Wall H6 uses a 7-speed wet dual clutch gearbox, and we will take the dual clutch gearbox as an example to illustrate.

Ⅱ. Maintenance of electronic dual clutch transmission

Dual clutch transmission (DCT) is unlike the traditional hydraulic automatic transmission, which is based on the development of manual transmission, and it should belong to one of the AMT mechanical automatic transmission. In addition to the flexibility of manual transmission and the comfort of automatic transmission, it can also provide uninterrupted power output. Compared with those equipped with manual transmission it has obvious advantages in power and 100 km acceleration, and its fuel consumption in urban and comprehensive conditions is similar to the vehicle equipped with manual transmission, lower than the vehicle equipped with ordinary torque converter AT. Now in the domestic market, some models such as FAW Volkswagen and SAIC are equipped with dual clutch transmission.

(Ⅰ) Structural composition of dual clutch transmission

The working principle of the dual clutch transmission is to arrange the transmission gears separately according to the odd and even numbers, connect with two clutches respectively, and complete the gear shifting action by switching the working conditions of the two clutches.

1. Overall structure composition

Dual clutch automatic transmission (Figure 3-1-7) is mainly composed of dual input clutches, electro-hydraulic control system and gear transmission system.

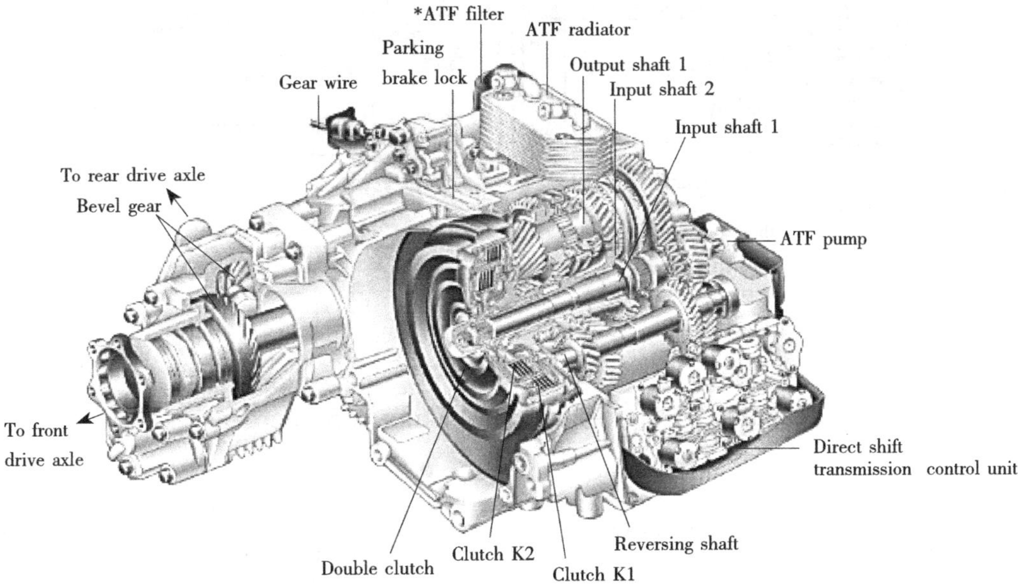

Figure 3-1-7 Dual Clutch Automatic Transmission

2. Gear speed change system

The gearshift system (Figure 3-1-8) is similar in construction to a manual transmission and is of the helical gear type, with two concentric input shafts and two parallel output shafts, as well as an intermediate shaft, also known as the reverse idler shaft.

(1) The front end of the transmission is equipped with a dual clutch device (K1 and K2) (Figure 3-1-9), which is assembled by two sets of clutch plates. The dual clutch is installed in a closed oil chamber filled with hydraulic oil, and the clutch plates are also filled with oil. Its transmission principle is the same as that of the wet multi-plate clutch in the ordinary AT. This "wet" structure has better adjustment ability and excellent thermal compatibility. Therefore, a relatively large torque can be transmitted.

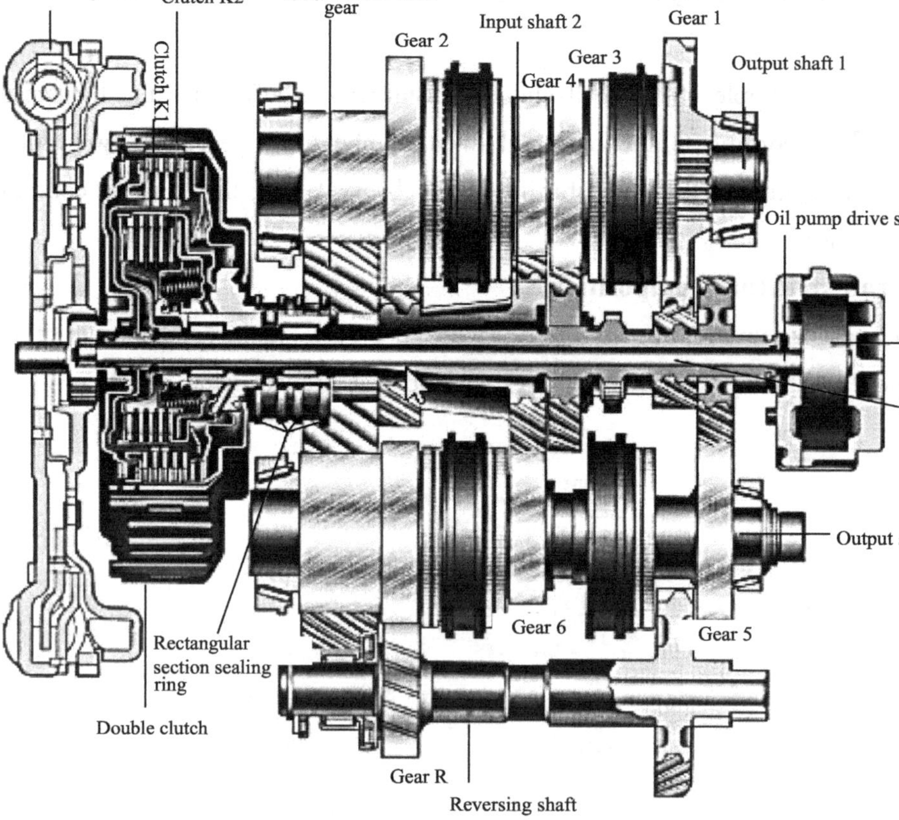

Figure 3-1-8　Gear Speed Change Structure

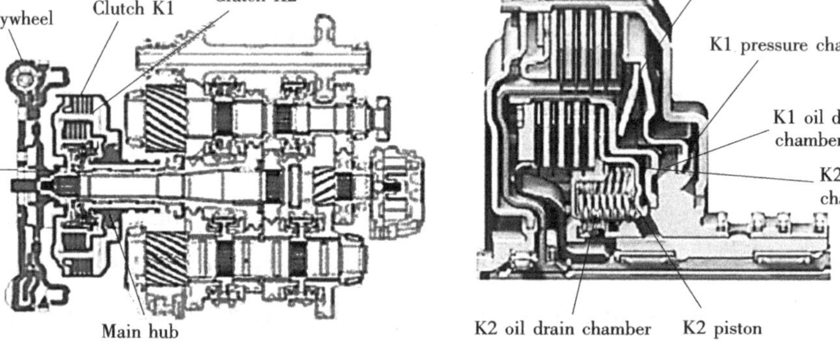

Figure 3-1-9　Dual Clutch

(a) Mounting position of double clutch　(b) Structure of double clutch

(2) Input shaft.

The dual transmission shaft mechanism that receives the power of the dual clutch device is composed of a solid shaft (input shaft 1) and its outer sleeve (input shaft 2).

The engagement of clutch K1 can transmit the engine power from the flywheel to the solid shaft [Figure 3-1-10 (a)], that is, input shaft 1. The input shaft 1 with the 1st gear/reverse gear, 3rd and 5th gear driving gears and the signal wheel of the input shaft 1 speed sensor G501, as shown in Figure 3-1-11. The input shaft 1 can realize the 1st, 3rd, 5th and reverse gears through gear transmission.

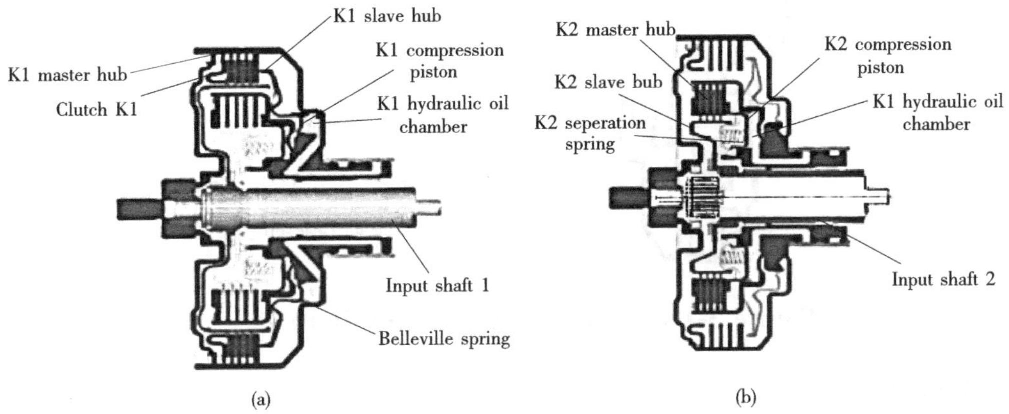

Figure 3-1-10 Structure of Clutches K1 and K2

(a) Clutch K1 (b) Clutch K2

Engagement of the clutch K2 can transfer the engine power from the flywheel to the input shaft 2. The input shaft 2 is a hollow sleeve sleeved on the input shaft 1 [Figure 3-1-10 (b)], which is connected with the clutch K2 through splines. There are driving gears of the 2nd gear, 4th gear/6th gear and signal wheel of the speed sensor of the input shaft 2, as shown in Figure 3-1-12. The input shaft 2 can realize the 2nd, 4th and 6th gear through gear transmission.

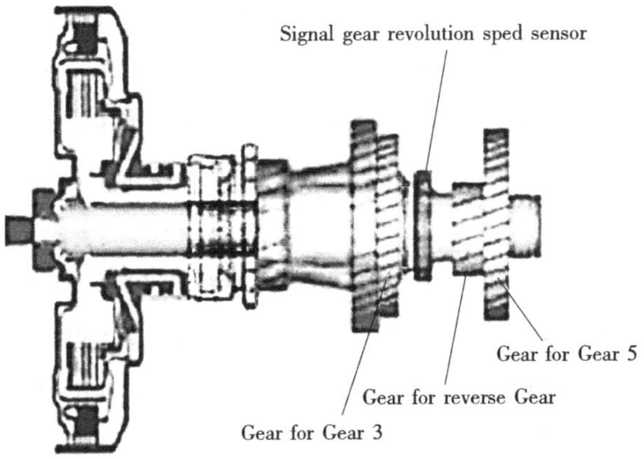

Figure 3-1-11 Structure of Input Shaft 1

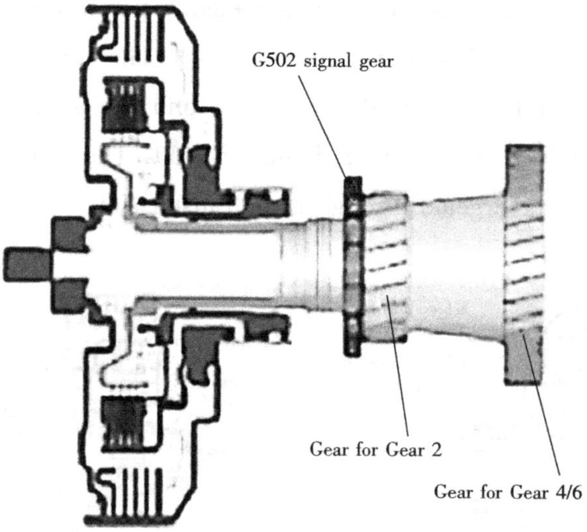

Figure 3-1-12 Structure of Input Shaft 2

(3) Output shaft.

The output gears of the two parallel output shafts are always meshed with the input gear of the final drive, and their relative installation positions are shown in Figure 3-1-13. The structure of output shaft 1 is shown in Figure 3-1-14 (a). As shown, the driven gears of the 1st, 2nd, 3rd and 4th gears are arranged on the shaft, and are respectively meshed with the driving gears of the 1st, 2nd, 3rd and 4th gears on the input shaft. There are shift coupling sleeve and synchronizer for the 1st and 3rd gear, shift coupling sleeve and synchronizer for the 2nd and 4th gear. The function of coupling sleeve and synchronizer is the same as that of manual transmission. In addition, output gear connected with differential is set on output shaft 1. The structure of output shaft 2 is shown in Figure 3-1-14 (b). The shaft has driven gears for the 5th, 6th and reverse gears, output gears connected to the differential and corresponding gear shifters.

(4) Reverse gear shaft.

Reverse gear idler gear 1 (large) and reverse gear idler gear 2 (small) are arranged on the reverse gear shaft, and are respectively meshed with the reverse gear driving gear on the input shaft 1 and the reverse gear driven gear on the output shaft 2, as shown in Figure 3-1-15.

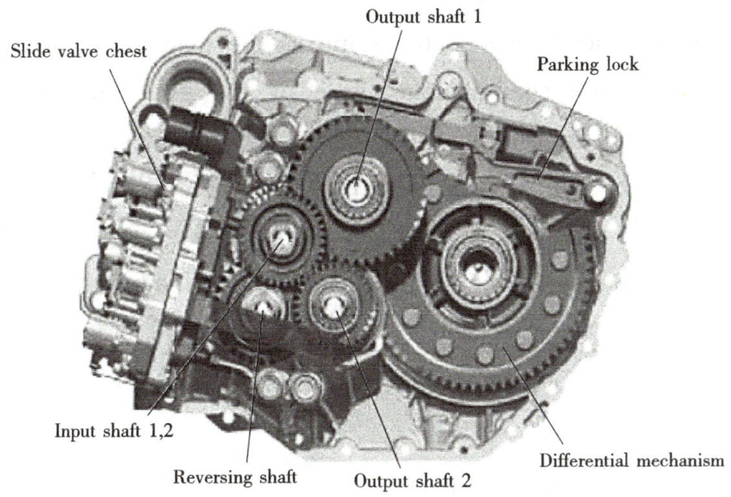

Figure 3-1-13 Installation Position of Output Shaft

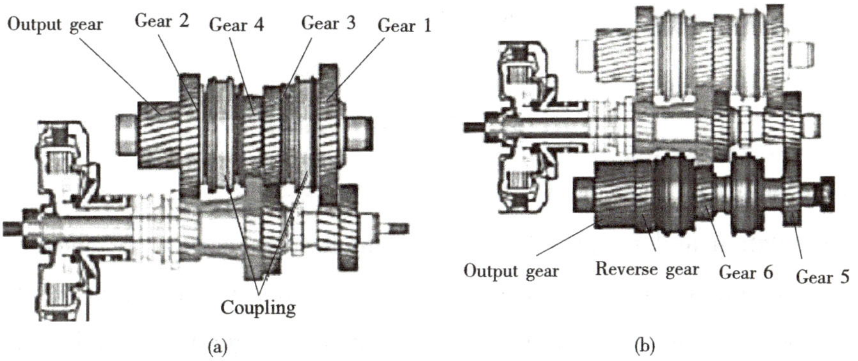

Figure 3-1-14 Output Shaft Structure of Transmission

(a) Output shaft 1 (b) Output shaft 2

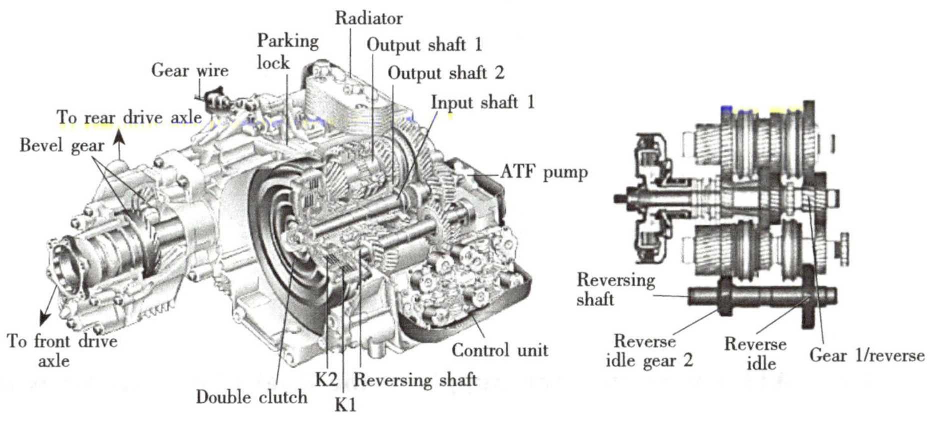

Figure 3-1-15 Structure and Installation Position of Reverse Gear Shaft

(5) Gear shifting mechanism.

The gear shifting mechanism is the same as the manual transmission, which is completed by pushing the combination sleeve by the gear shifting fork. However, different from the manual transmission, the dual clutch transmission no longer needs to push the shift fork by hand, but uses the hydraulic motor (or hydraulic servo mechanism) to push the shift fork to complete gear shifting, as shown in Figure 3-1-16. Each shift fork is driven by two hydraulic motors controlled by the electromechanical control system, and the travel sensor is used to detect the fork travel to determine whether the shift fork is in position.

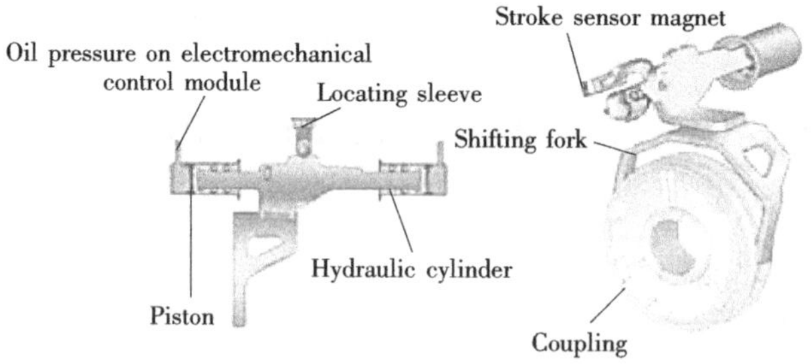

Figure 3-1-16 Shift Control

(6) Other auxiliary equipment.

ATF circulation and supply of the dual clutch transmission are shown in Figure 3-1-17. As the dual clutch transmission adopts wet design and uses single oil, the consumption of ATF oil is large, so the oil sump is designed, and it has a press oil filter, an oil cooler and an oil pump driven by crankshaft power.

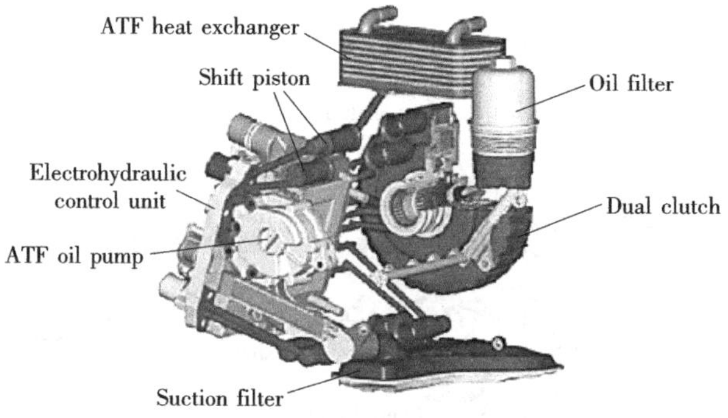

Figure 3-1-17 ATF Circulation and Supply of the Dual Clutch Transmission

(Ⅱ) Dual clutch automatic transmission working process

In both upshifts and downshifts of the dual clutch automatic transmission, 2 gears are engaged at the same time. In the upshift, one gear higher than the operating gear is engaged as a preselected gear. If 1st gear is operating, 2nd gear is engaged as the preselected gear; When downshifting, the gear lower than the operating gear is engaged as the preselected gear. If the working gear is the 6th gear, the 5th gear is engaged as the preselected gear. The upshift or downshift of the dual clutch transmission is determined by the transmission control unit (TCU): when the throttle pedal is pressed, TCU determines that it is an upshift process and prepares for upshift; when the brake pedal is pressed, TCU determines that it is a downshift process and prepares for downshift.

Generally speaking, the transmission upshift is always one gear and one gear, step by step, but the downshift often jumps. Dual clutch transmission can also jump downshift in manual mode, for example, from 6th gear to 3rd gear, continuously pressing the 3rd downshift button 3 times, the transmission will directly drop from 6th gear to 3rd gear, but if it drops from 6th to 2nd gear, the transmission will first drop to 5th gear, and then directly to 2nd gear. That is to say, when making the jump downshift, if the starting gear and the final gear are controlled by the same clutch, they must be changed over by the gear controlled by another clutch, and if the starting gear and the final gear are not controlled by the same clutch, they can jump directly to the set gear.

(Ⅲ) Electric control module

The electromechanical control module J743 of the dual clutch transmission is the core control unit of the transmission. In this module, the electronic control unit and the electro-hydraulic control unit are integrated into one unit. The electromechanical control block is connected to the transmission and is an independent and closed unit. It has an independent hydraulic oil circuit. It is completely isolated from the transmission oil circuit of the mechanical part of the transmission.

The advantages of a compact closed unit are:

(1) all sensors and actuators are integrated in the electromechanical control

module;

(2) The amount of hydraulic oil in the electromechanical module is specially determined according to the needs.

The independent oil supply system prevents debris from the mechanical part of the transmission from entering the module. Because the viscosity of the oil for the module does not have to meet the requirements of the transmission oil, the low temperature performance of the electromechanical control module is very good.

The electronic control unit of the electromechanical control module is the core control unit of the transmission (Figure 3-1-18 and Figure 3-1-19). This is where the signals from all the sensors and the signals from all the other control units come together, and where all the actions start and are monitored. Ten sensors are integrated in the ECU, and only the gearbox input speed sensor G182 is installed outside the control unit. The ECU hydraulically controls and regulates eight solenoid valves. These solenoid valves are used to shift the gears and control the clutches. The ECU matches the positions of the clutches and shift actuators when the gear is engaged and pays attention to the matching of these components during future operation.

The electro-hydraulic control unit is integrated in the electro-mechanical module (Figure 3-1-20). It generates the hydraulic pressure required for shifting and controlling the clutches.

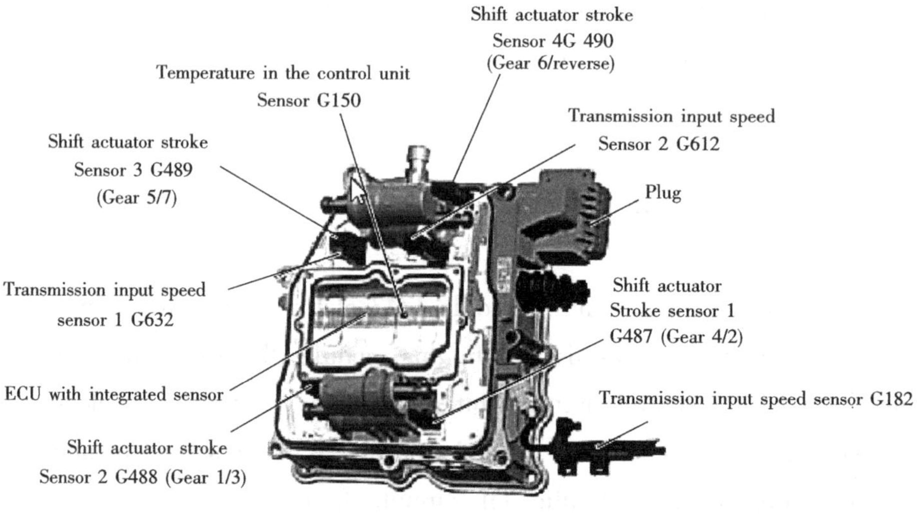

Figure 3-1-18 Electric Control Module 1

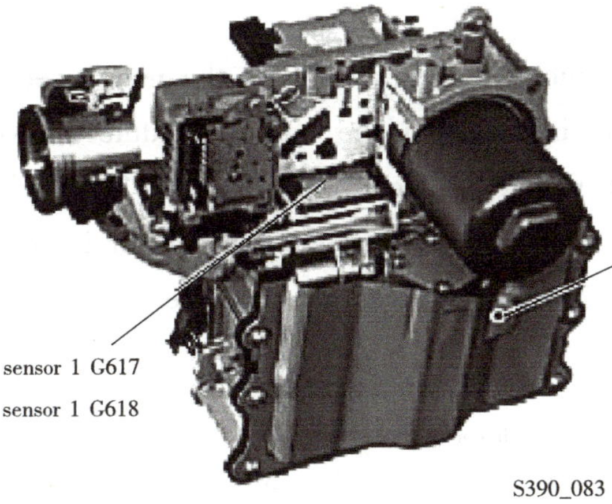

Figure 3-1-19 Electronic Control Module 2

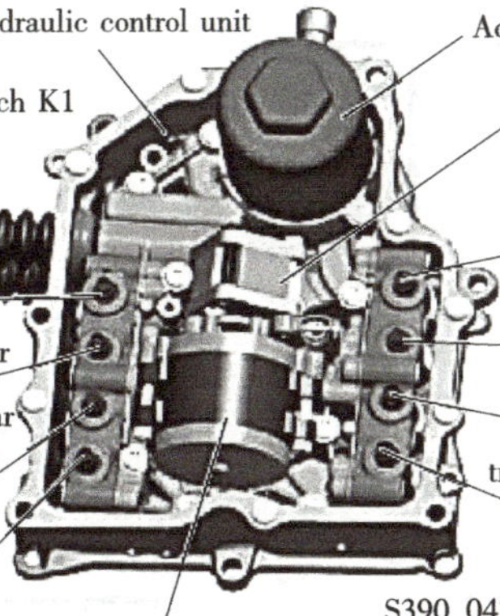

Figure 3-1-20 Electrohydraulic Control Unit

The hydraulic pressure is generated and controlled by the hydraulic pump motor and the hydraulic pump connected to it. The accumulator ensures that sufficient hydraulic pressure is always available on the solenoid valve.

There are two sets of independent oil circuits in the dual-clutch transmission, and the oil used in each circuit is different.

(1) Oil circuit of the mechanical part of the gearbox.

(2) Oil circuit of electromechanical control module.

The oil supply principle of the mechanical transmission is similar to that of the manual transmission, but the difference is that the control system is relatively complex. The hydraulic control module and the mechanical unit are isolated from each other, as shown in Figure 3-1-21.

The hydraulic pump assembly (Figure 3-1-22) is the main executive element of the control system, which is installed in the control module and consists of the hydraulic pump and the drive motor. The control unit controls the working state of the drive motor according to the shift demand, and the drive motor is connected with the hydraulic pump to control the hydraulic pressure in the pipe.

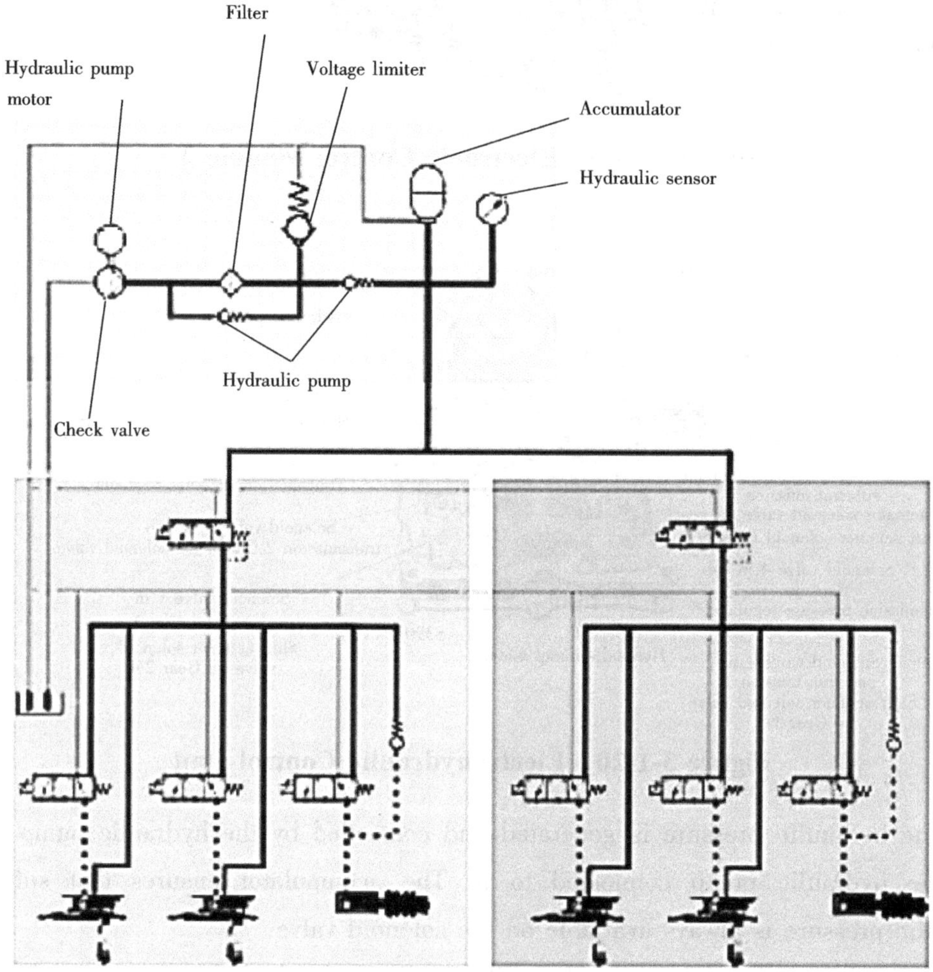

Figure 3-1-21 Oil Circuit

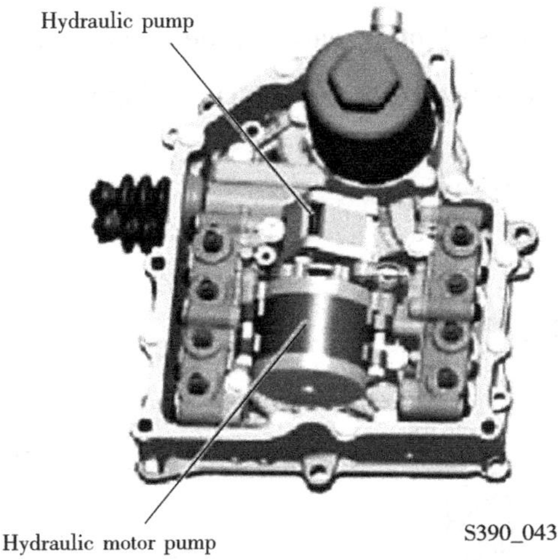

Figure 3-1-22 Hydraulic Pump

The hydraulic pump is meshed by two gears with the same radius. During rotation, the hydraulic oil on the suction side is continuously transmitted to the output side, so that a negative pressure is formed on the suction side, and then the hydraulic oil continuously enters the pump body according to the speed change, realizing the function of pressurizing the oil. The oil pressure on the output side can reach more than 80 bar, as shown in Figure 3-1-23.

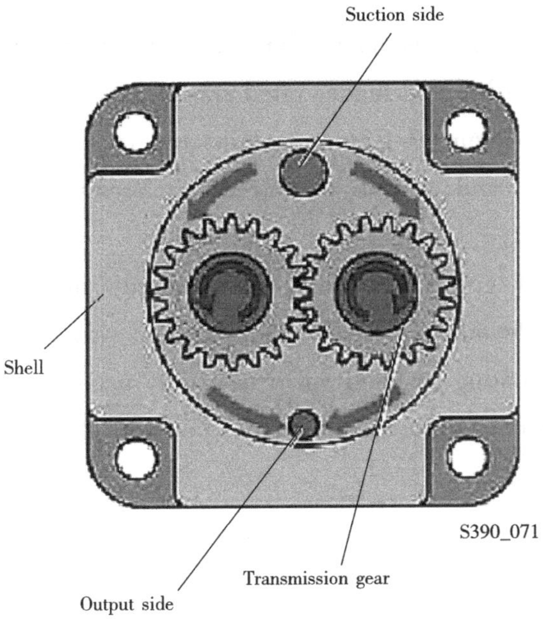

Figure 3-1-23 Working Principle of Hydraulic Pump

The hydraulic pump motor is a brushless DC motor, which is composed of stator and rotor. The rotor is composed of 6 pairs of permanent magnets and the stator is composed of 6 pairs of magnet windings, as shown in Figure 3-1-24.

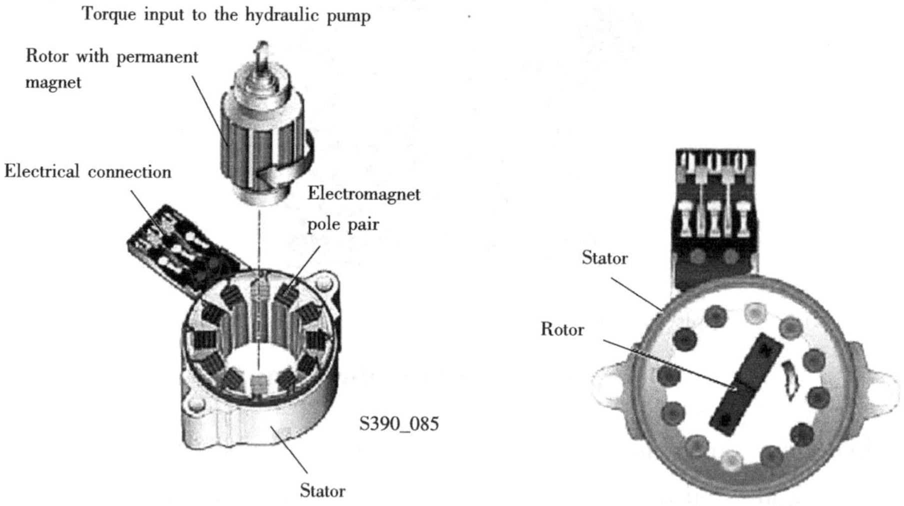

Figure 3-1-24 Hydraulic Pump Motor Structure

The brushless DC motor mainly changes the alternating frequency and waveform of the current wave input to its stator coil to form a magnetic field around the winding coil that rotates around the geometric axis of the motor. This magnetic field drives the permanent magnet on the rotor to rotate, and then the motor will rotate, as shown in Figure 3-1-25. Because there is no mechanical wear of the brush, the brushless DC motor has longer service life and higher rated speed.

The accumulator (Figure 3-1-26) maintains the pressure of the system by using the air as the medium, and provides the necessary pressure for the hydraulic system when it is turned off.

The hydraulic oil circuit (Figure 3-1-27) mainly includes pressure regulating solenoid valve, shift solenoid valve and clutch solenoid valve.

The pressure regulating solenoid valve is mainly used to regulate the oil pressure in the sub transmission to ensure the normal operation of each sub transmission, as shown in Figure 3-1-28.

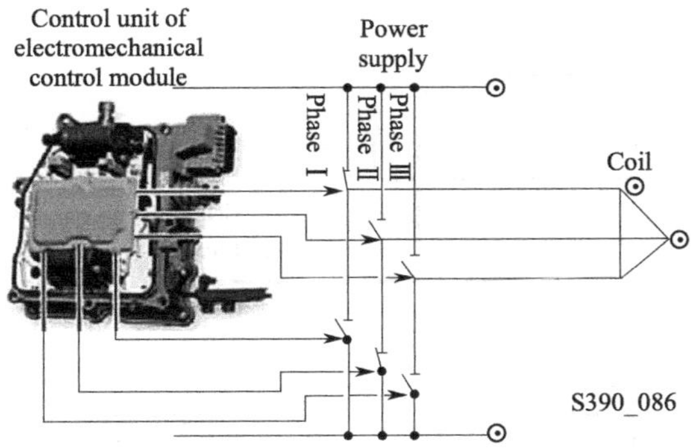

Figure 3-1-25 Electric Control Chart

Phase Ⅰ-switch on the positive pole; Phase Ⅱ-switch on the positive pole; Phase Ⅲ-swith off

Figure 3-1-26 Accumulator

The shift solenoid valve (Figure 3-1-29) is used to regulate the hydraulic oil volume delivered to the shift actuator. Each shift actuator can realize two gears. When no gear is engaged, the shift actuator stays in neutral under the action of oil pressure. When the gear is in the P gear and the ignition switch is turned off, the transmission is in the first gear.

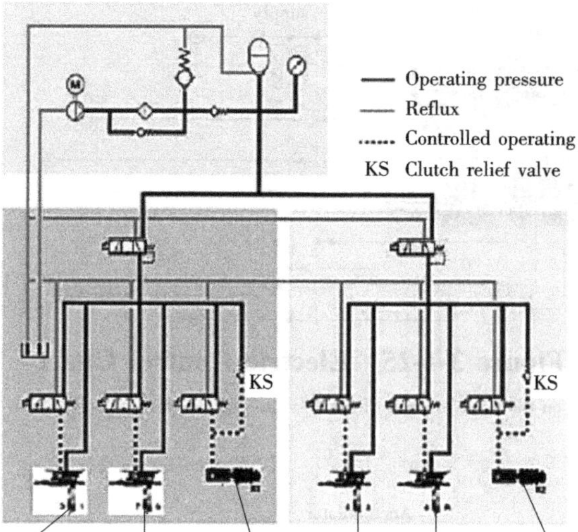

Figure 3-1-27 Hydraulic Oil Circuit

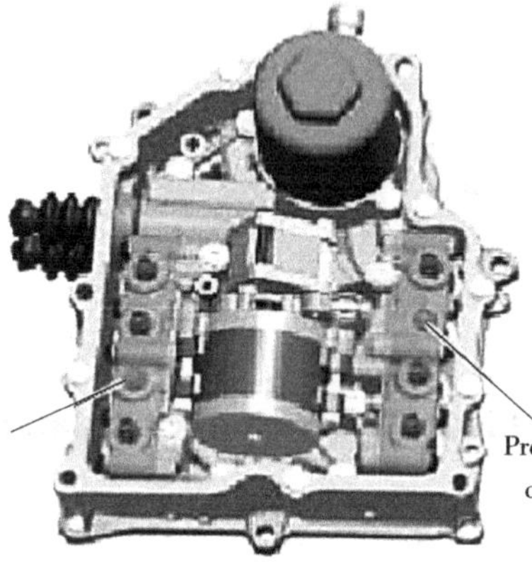

Figure 3-1-28 Hydraulic Oil Circuit Solenoid Valve

The clutch solenoid valve (Figure 3-1-30) is mainly used to regulate the hydraulic oil volume of the clutch actuator. When energized, the engagement and disengagement of the clutch are controlled by the clutch actuator. When de-energized, the solenoid valve and the clutch are in a disengaged state. In case of fault, the clutch relief valve can discharge the hydraulic oil to separate the clutch.

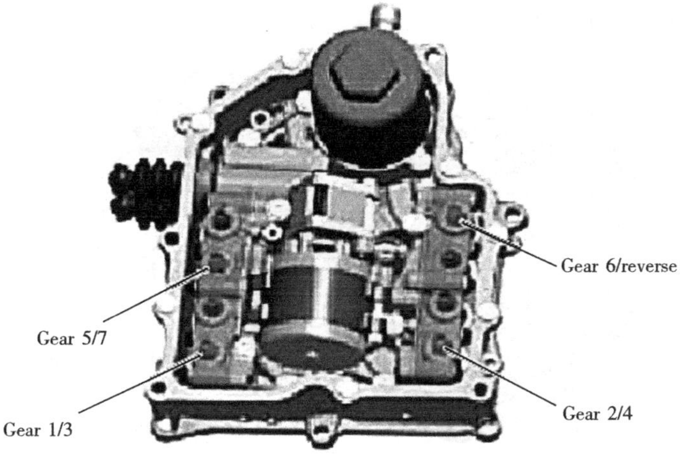

Figure 3-1-29 Shift Solenoid Valve

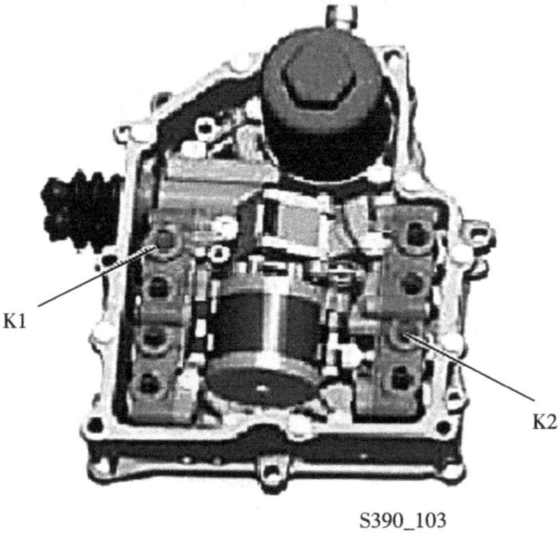

Figure 3-1-30 Clutch Solenoid Valve

The shift of the dual clutch transmission is driven by the shifting fork to move the coupling, so that the gears mesh with each other to realize the gear shifting. Each shifting fork (Figure 3-1-31) can control two gears, which are located on both sides of the transmission housing.

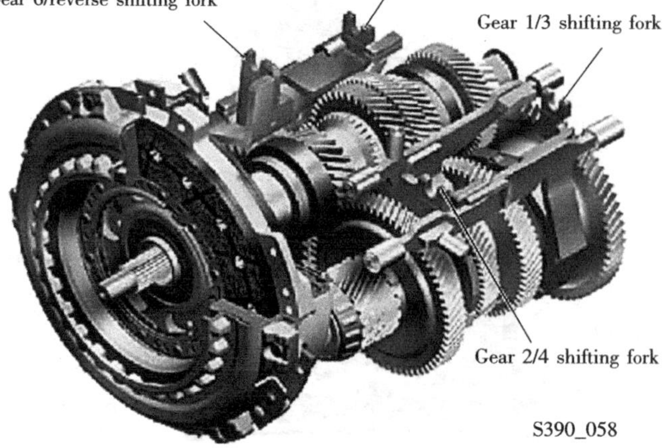

Figure 3-1-31 Shifting Fork

During gear shifting, the electromechanical control module controls the hydraulic pump to apply oil pressure to the piston of the shift actuator (Figure 3-1-32 and Figure 3-1-33). The piston pushes the shifting fork to move, drives the coupling and synchronizer to mesh the gears, and transmits power to realize gear shifting.

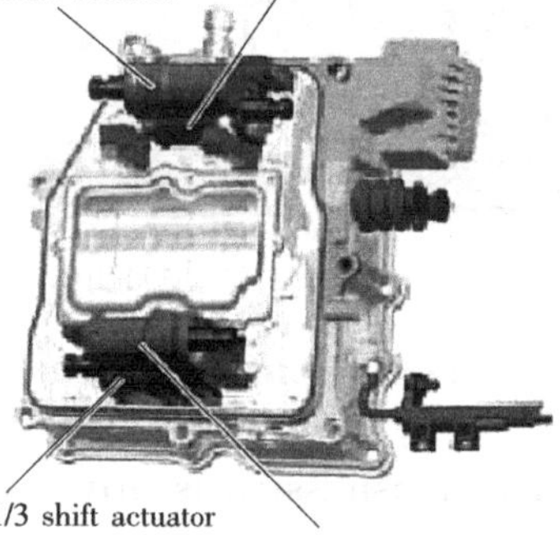

Figure 3-1-32 Electromechanical Control Module

In the initial position (Figure 3-1-34), the shift solenoid valve N433 is under the action of oil pressure, and the piston of the shift actuator is kept in the Gear N, and can be meshed in any gear. The No.4 solenoid valve N436 in the sub transmission 1 is used to regulate the oil pressure in the sub transmission 1.

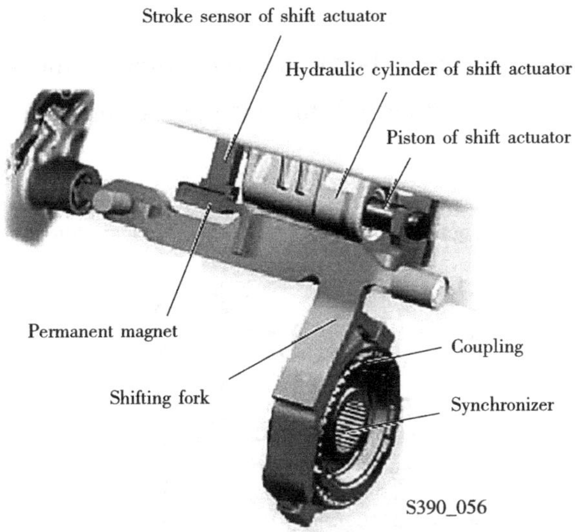

Figure 3-1-33 Sensor Location

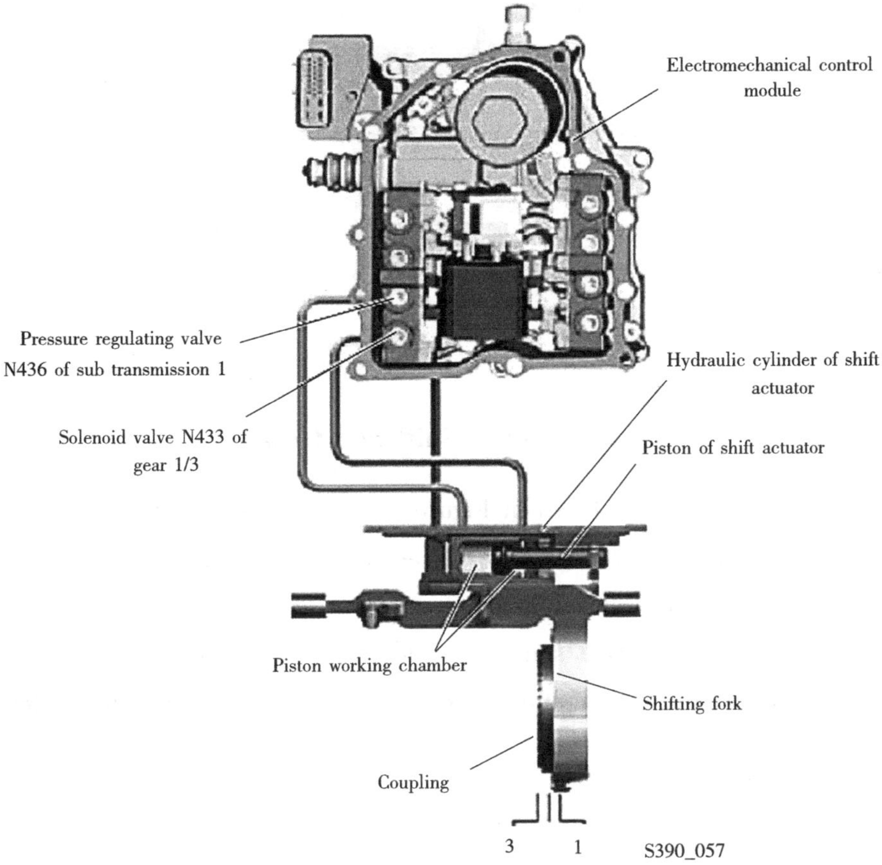

Figure 3-1-34 Initial Position

To shift into Gear 1, the shift solenoid valve increases the oil pressure of the left piston working chamber (Figure 3-1-35), and the piston of the shift actuator moves to the right, and connects the shifting fork to shift the transmission into Gear 1.

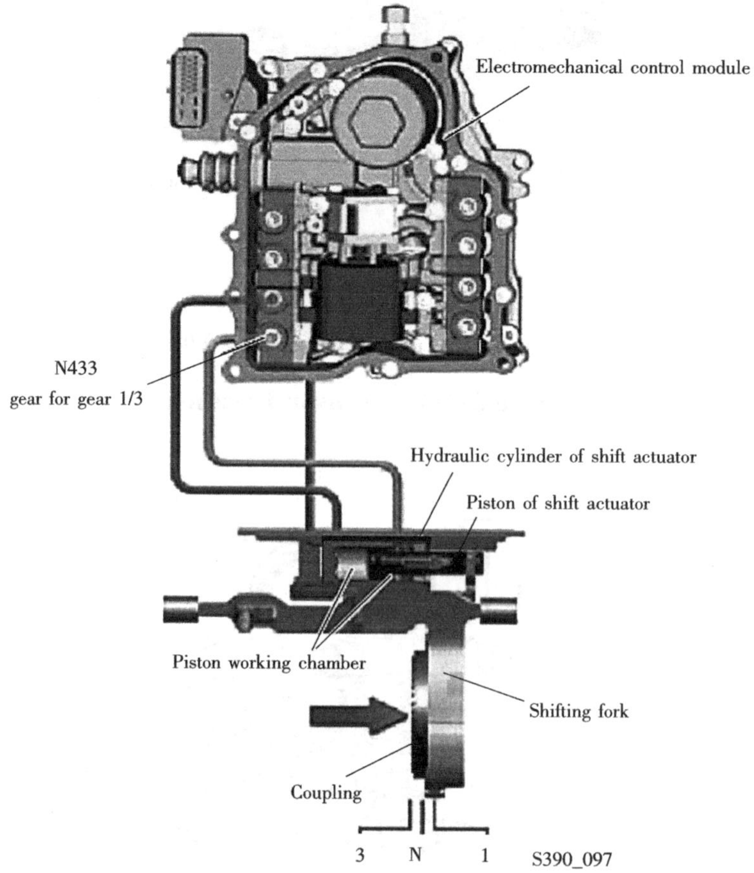

Figure 3-1-35 Shift into Gear 1

Clutches K1 and K2 are shown in Figure 3-1-36. The clutch fork is controlled by the piston of the clutch actuator to realize the engagement and disengagement of the clutch. In particular, there is a permanent magnet on the piston of the clutch actuator, through which the clutch stroke sensor can identify the piston position. In order to avoid affecting the identification effect, the hydraulic cylinder and the piston of the clutch actuator shall not be magnetic.

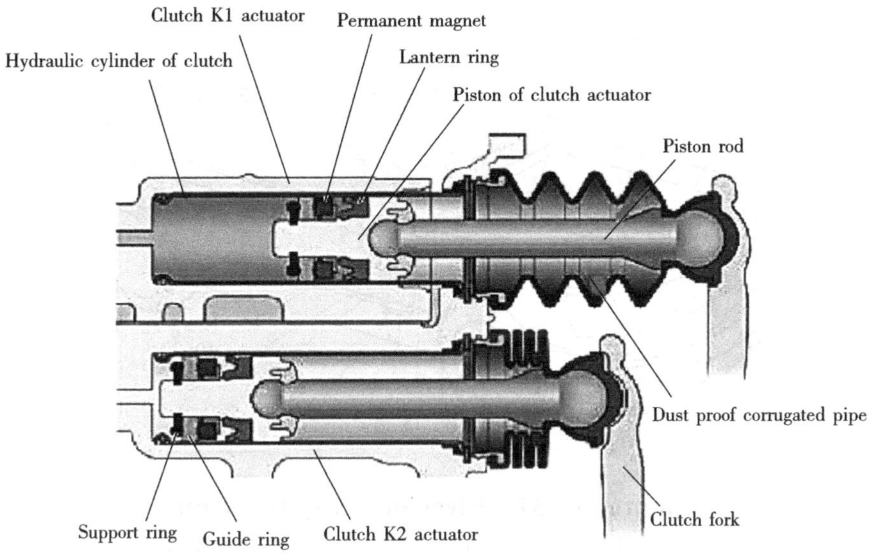

Figure 3-1-36 Clutch actuator

【Knowledge Development】

Ⅰ. Preparations

Practical vehicle (Toyota Corolla car); KT600, niversal meter, maintenance console, etc.; Maintenance manual and work order.

Ⅱ. Implementation steps

(Ⅰ) Locate the position of electronic control system elements

The position of each element, as shown in Figure 3-1-37.

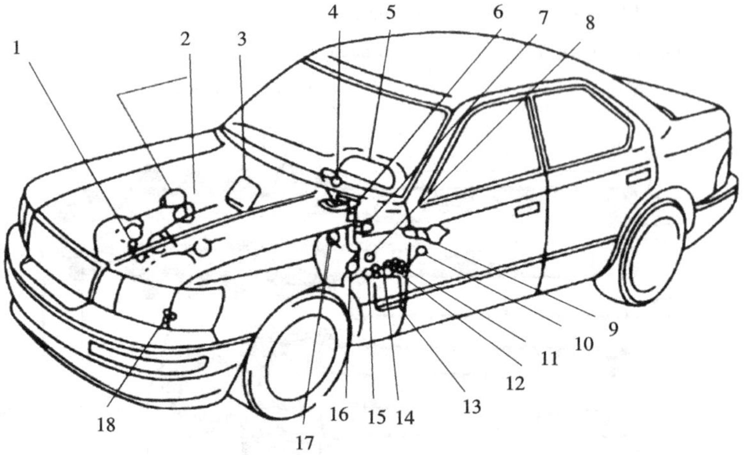

Figure 3-1-37 Electronic Control Unit

1-engine coolant temperature sensor; 2-throttle position sensor; 3-engine and transmission ECU; 4-Overspeed control switch; 5-O/D OFF indicator light; 6-driving mode selection switch; 7-brake lamp switch; 8-Overspeed clutch speed sensor; 9-No.1 speed sensor; 10-No.2 speed sensor; 11-No.1 solenoid valve; 12-No.2 solenoid valve; 13-cruise control ECU; 14-No.3 solenoid valve; 15-No.4 solenoid valve; 16-neutral start switch; 17-full throttle kickdown switch; 18-engine speed sensor

(Ⅱ) Understand the electronic control principle of A341E automatic transmission

The electronic control principle of A341E automatic transmission, as shown in Figure 3-1-38.

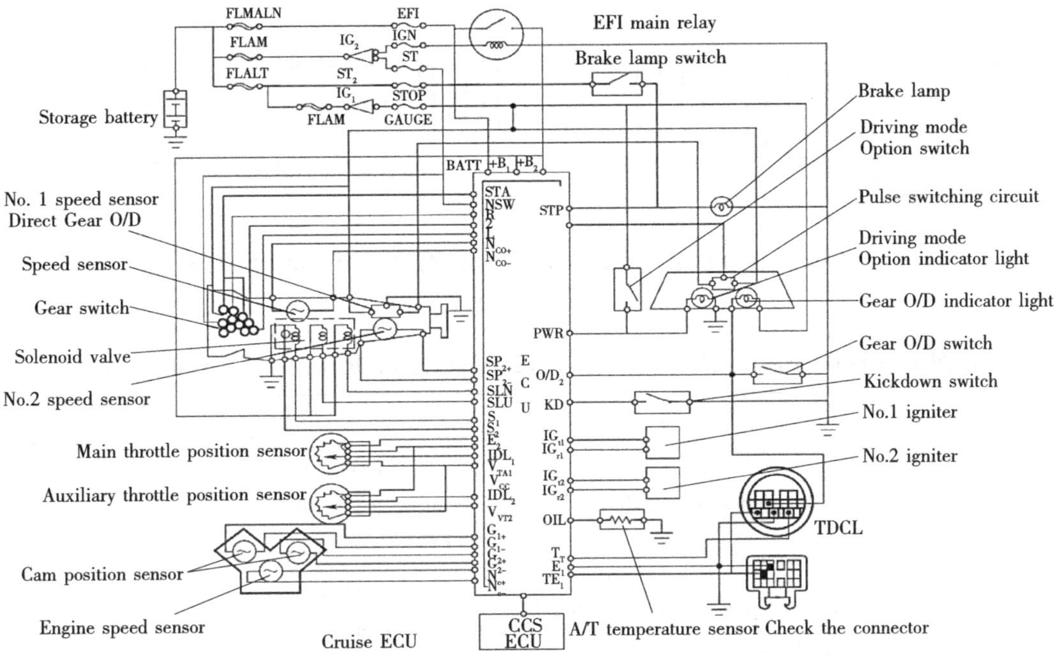

Figure 3-1-38 Electronic Control Principle of A341E Automatic Transmission

(Ⅲ) Read the fault code

When the computer detects that there is a fault in the electronic control system, it will store the fault code in the memory. Usually, the fault code can be called out manually or with the diagnostic instrument.

1. Read the fault code with a shorting stub

(1) Place the ignition switch and O/D switch at ON position.

(2) Jumper TDCL, or check TE and E_1 terminals of the connector (Figure 3-1-39).

(3) Read the fault code according to the flashing of the O/D OFF indicator light (Figure 3-1-40). See Table 3-1-1 for the meaning.

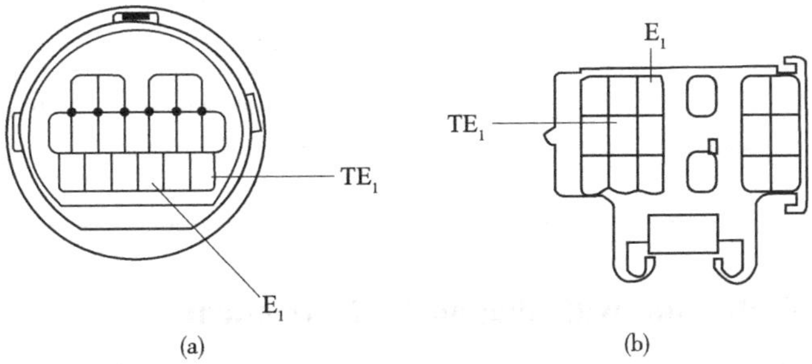

Figure 3-1-39 Toyota 17PIN Semicircular Fault Diagnosis Seat

(a) Normal code (b) Check the connector

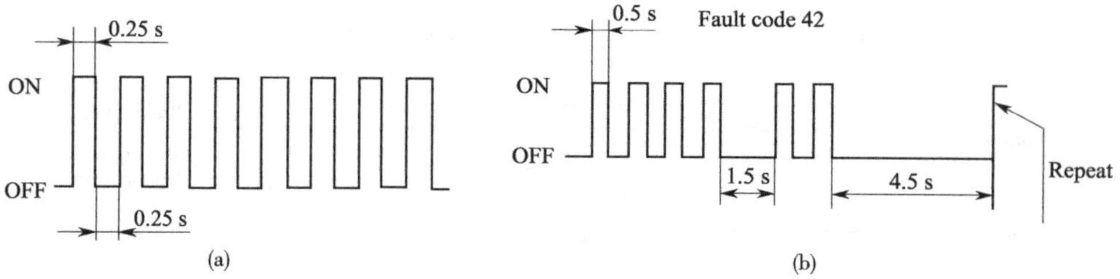

Figure 3-1-40 Normal Code and Fault Code of Toyota Car Series

(a) Normal code (b) Fault code

Table 3-1-1 Fault Code of Toyota A341E Automatic Transmission

Fault code	Meaning	Fault position
42	No.1 speed sensor fault	① No.1 speed sensor ② No.1 speed sensor harness or connector ③ ECU
46	No.4 solenoid valve short circuit or open circuit	① No.4 solenoid valve ② No.4 solenoid valve harness or connector ③ ECU
61	No.2 speed sensor fault	① No.2 speed sensor ② No.2 speed sensor harness or connector ③ ECU
62	No.1 solenoid valve short circuit or open circuit	① No.1 solenoid valve ② No.1 solenoid valve harness or connector ③ ECU
63	No.2 solenoid valve short circuit or open circuit	① No.2 solenoid valve ② No.2 solenoid valve harness or connector ③ ECU
64	No.3 solenoid valve short circuit or open circuit	① No.3 solenoid valve ② No.3 solenoid valve harness or connector ③ ECU
67	Gear O/D speed sensor fault	① Gear O/D speed sensor ② Gear O/D speed sensor harness or connector ③ ECU
68	KD switch short circuit	① KD switch short circuit ② KD switch short circuit harness or connector ③ ECU

2. Read the fault code with diagnostic instrument

(1) Select the test connector.

Select "Toyota-17" test connector for testing Toyota 17PIN semicircular TDCL model. Select "Toyota-17" test connector for testing Toyota 17PIN square TDCL model. Test the Toyota 16PIN square TDCL model and select OBD-Ⅱ test connector.

(2) Locate the TDCL.

The 17PIN semicircular TDCL is located at the lower left side of the instrument panel. The 17PIN rectangular TDCL is generally located in the engine chamber. The 16PIN square TDCL is generally under the steering column of the cab.

(3) Know the TDCL shape. The TDCL shape of Toyota model is shown in Figure 3-1-41.

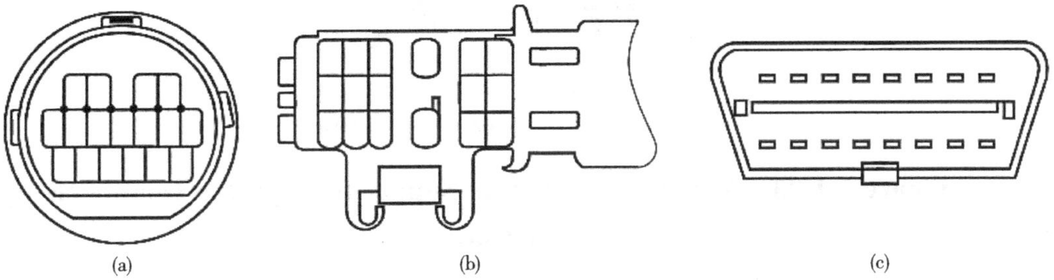

Figure 3-1-41 TDCL Shape of Toyota Model

(a) 17PIN semicircular (b) 17PIN rectangular (c) 16PIN square

(4) Test OBD-Ⅱ 16PIN square TDCL and connect KT600 diagnostic instrument, as shown in Figure 3-1-42.

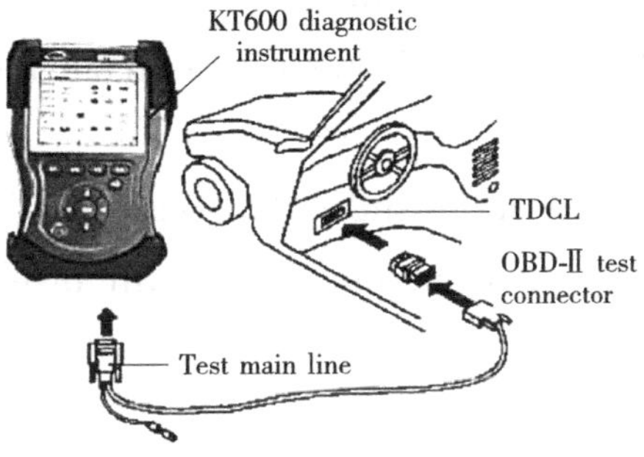

Figure 3-1-42 Connection of Diagnostic Instrument

Description: the 17PIN semicircular TDCL of Toyota cars does not have the power supply, which can be obtained by any of the following methods. ① Through the cigarette lighter. Take out the cigarette lighter, insert one end of the cigarette lighter cable into the hole of the cigarette lighter, and connect the other end to the power plug of the test main line of the KT600 diagnostic instrument. ② Through the double-clamp power cord. Clamp the power clamp of the double-clamp power cord on the positive and negative electrodes of the battery, and insert the other end into the power plug of the test main line of the KT600 diagnostic instrument, as shown in Figure 3-1-43.

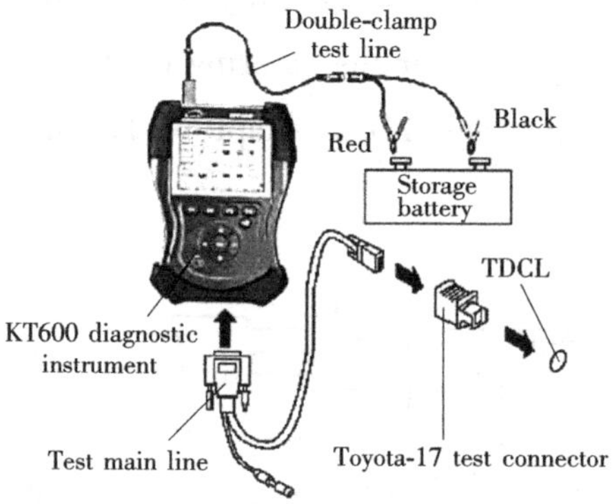

Figure 3-1-43 Access to the Power Supply through the Double-clamp Power Cord

(5) Place the ignition switch at ON position.

(6) Press the POWER key to start the KT600 diagnostic instrument. After starting, click the "Start" button and select "Diagnostic Program" → "Car Decoding Program"in the pop-up menu to enter the selection menu.

(7) Click the "OK" button after confirming that the correct test connector is selected and the instrument is connected.

(8) Click the "Read Fault Code" option to execute the function of reading fault code.

If the fault code is read successfully, the screen will display the test result. If there is a fault code in the system, the screen will display the fault code and its description.

(Ⅳ) Clear the fault code

1. Manually clear the fault code.

(1) The basic idea of clearing the fault code is to power off the ECU of ECT, and then the fault code stored in the memory will be cleared.

(2) Place the ignition switch at OFF position, and remove the EFI fuse for more than 10 s, as shown in Figure 3-1-44.

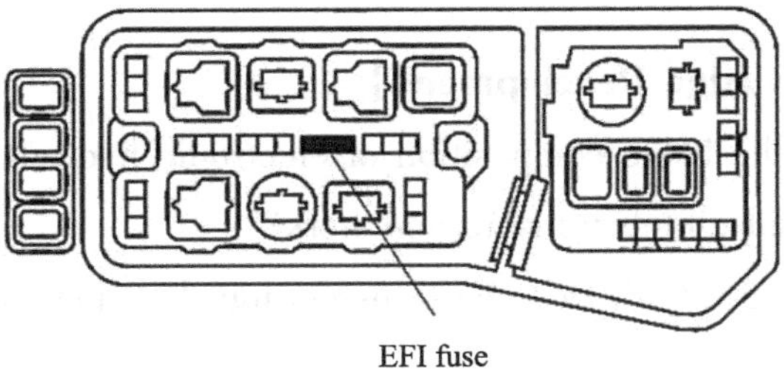

Figure 3-1-44 Fuse Location

2. Clear the fault code with the diagnostic instrument.

(1) Connect the diagnostic instrument to DLC3.

(2) Place the ignition switch at ON position.

(3) Operate the diagnostic instrument to clear the fault code.

Click the "Clear the Fault Code" option in the function menu, and press the "Yes" button to clear the fault code; click "No" to exit and return to the previous interface.

If the fault code is cleared successfully, the screen will display that the fault code is cleared successfully

(Ⅴ) Maintenance of electrical control system

When the fault code is read with the diagnostic instrument, the approximate range of most faults of the control unit can be found. However, to determine the specific location of the fault, the simple tools such as a universal meter, etc. must be used to test all parts according to the test methods, test steps and standard data specified in the maintenance manual. In addition, mechanical faults of some actuators (such as jamming, leakage, etc.) cannot be detected by ECU fault self-diagnosis circuit, and can only be found through actual detection.

(Ⅵ) Performance test

The performance test of the electronic automatic transmission is the basis for judging the fault. The fault type and location can often be judged through the corresponding performance test.

【Knowledge Development】

1. Briefly describe the basic composition of electronic hydraulic transmission
2. How does the dual clutch transmission work?
3. How to eliminate the fault that the transmission does not work in gear?

Section 2 Antiskid Control System

Automobile anti-skid control system mainly includes anti-lock braking system (ABS), acceleration slip regulation (ASR) and electronic stability program (ESP). The function of ABS system is to prevent the controlled wheel from locking by adjusting the braking pressure of the locked wheel adaptively and cyclically. ASR is to control the slip rate between the wheel and the road surface by using the controller. The automobile is prevent from skidding in that acceleration proces, especially preventing the idling of the driving wheels when the vehicle is on an asymmetric road surface or turning, so as to maintain the stability and maneuverability of the driving direction of the vehicle, maintain the best driving force of the vehicle and improve the smoothness of the car. ESP integrates the functions of ABS and ASR, and brakes each wheel separately. When understeering or oversteering occurs in emergency avoidance of obstacles or turning, the vehicle can avoid deviating from the ideal track. It can reduce the danger of sideslip in various occasions.

Ⅰ. Theoretical basis of anti-lock braking system

(Ⅰ) The braking ability of the car

In the process of driving, the ability of the car to decelerate forcibly to stop and maintain the stability of the driving direction is called the braking ability of the car.

The main evaluation indexes of braking performance are as follows.

(1) Braking efficiency: the braking efficiency refers to the capability of forced deceleration and even stop when the automobile is running, that is, the braking distance, braking time and braking deceleration when the automobile is braked to stop at a certain initial speed.

(2) Directional stability during braking: when braking, the automobile can still run in the specified direction, that is, no deviation, no sideslip and no loss of steering and this is called directional stability during braking.

(Ⅱ) Analysis of wheel force when the car is braking

Wheel stress analysis during automobile braking, as shown in Figure 3-2-1.

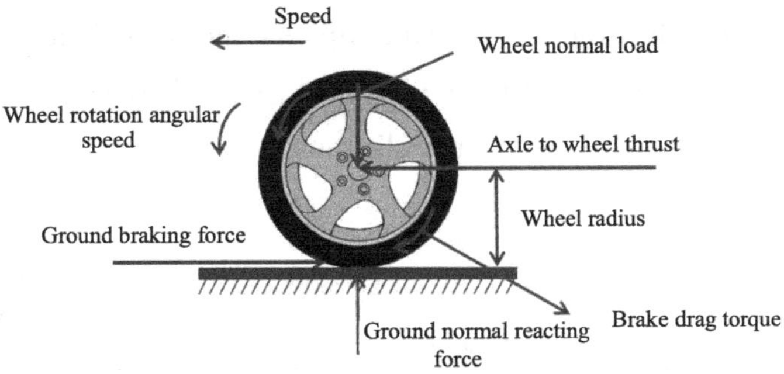

Figure 3-2-1 Analysis of Wheel Force During Automobile Braking

Shoe and brake drum (disc) pressure when the friction torque formed by the action of the wheels on the ground tangential force known as the brake braking force F_x. The tangential reacting force of the ground to the wheel during braking is called the ground braking force F_u.

The limit value of the tangential reaction force of the ground to the tire is called adhesion, which depends on the friction between the tire and the road and the shear strength of the road.

The relationship between ground braking force, brake braking force and adhesion is shown in Figure 3-2-2.

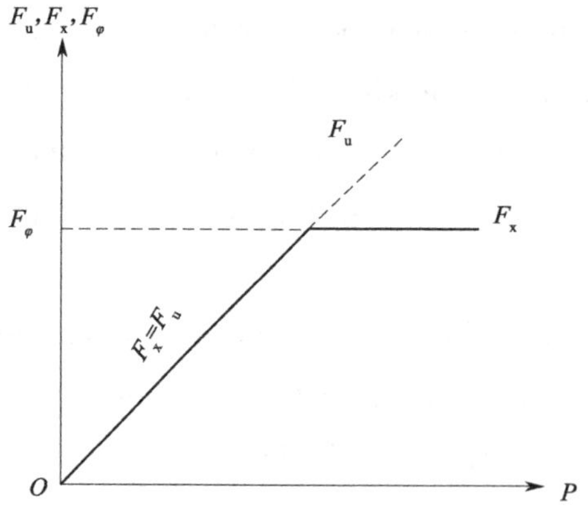

Figure 3-2-2 Relationship between Ground Braking Force, Brake Braking Force and Adhesion

It can be seen from Figure 3-2-2 that during normal braking, the ground braking force $F_u \leqslant$ adhesion F_φ, and the wheels are rolling at this time, if the ground braking force $F_u >$ adhesion F_φ, the wheels lock and slip. As shown in Figure 3-2-3, if the F_x needs to be increased, the F_φ must be increased. The F_φ depends on the adhesion coefficient φ, which is also affected by the slip rate S.

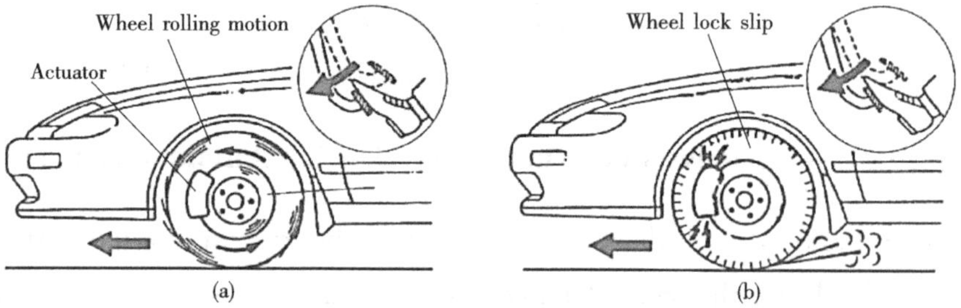

Figure 3-2-3 Relationship between F_u and F_φ

(a) $F_u \leqslant F_\varphi$ (b) $F_u > F_\varphi$

(Ⅲ) Relationship between adhesion coefficient φ and slip rate S

When braking, the motion form of the wheel on the road surface is slip, which indicates the degree of wheel slip and is expressed by slip rate S:

$$S = \frac{(v - \omega r)}{v} \times 100\%$$

In the formula S — slip rate of the wheel;

v — longitudinal speed of wheel center (m/s);

ω — angular speed of wheel rotation (rad/s);

r — free rolling radius of the wheel (m).

The relationship between adhesion coefficient φ and slip rate S is shown in Figure 3-2-4. From Figure, it can be seen that the peak adhesion coefficient of dry asphalt pavement and cement pavement is the largest, and it is smaller on ice. With the increase of slip rate S, longitudinal adhesion coefficient φ_S always decreases, transverse adhesion coefficient φ_B first increases and then decreases. When the slip rate S is about 20%, φ_B has a maximum value, φ_S is also larger, and the braking effect is good. At this time, the braking point is called the optimal braking point, and the adhesion coefficient is called the peak adhesion coefficient. Under the same circumstances, the larger the peak adhesion coefficient, the better the braking effect.

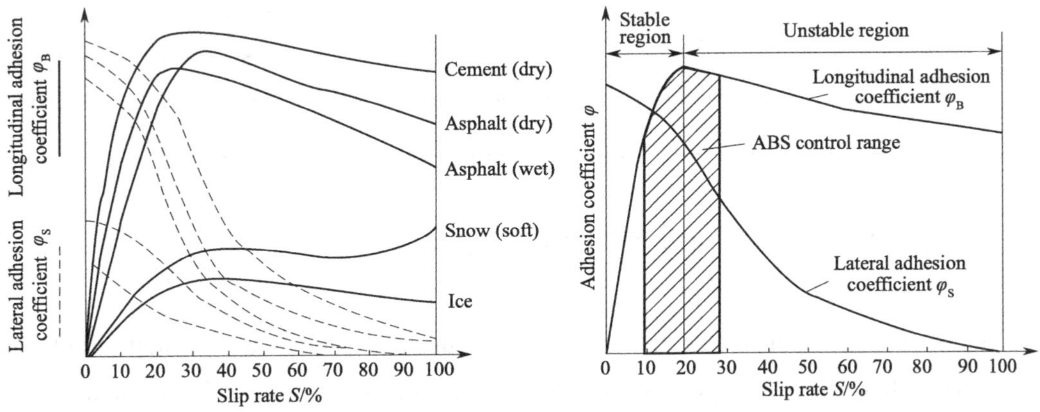

Figure 3-2-4 Relationship between adhesion coefficient and slip ratio

Through the analysis, it can be concluded that $S < 20\%$ is the braking stability region; $S > 20\%$ is the unstable braking area; if the wheel slip ratio S is controlled at about 20%, the maximum longitudinal adhesion coefficient and larger transverse adhesion coefficient can be obtained, which is the most ideal control effect.

Table 3-2-1 shows the relationship between wheel braking and ground impression of tire braking.

Table 3-2-1 Relationship between Wheel Braking and Ground impression of Tire Braking

Relationship between vehicle speed and wheel speed	Wheel motion state	Slip rate	Ground impression of tire braking
$\omega r = v$ (wheel speed = vehicle speed)	Pure rolling	$S = 0$	Ground impression is basically consistent with the tread pattern
$\omega r < v$ (wheel speed < vehicle speed)	While rolling and slippery	$0 < S < 100\%$	While rolling and slippery, the tire tread pattern can be recognized from the ground impression, but the tread pattern is gradually blurred
$\omega r = 0$ (wheel speed = 0)	Pure slip (full wheel lock slip)	$S = 100\%$	Slippery to hold and drag, and the ground impression are thick and black

(Ⅳ) The role of anti-lock braking system

Because ABS can make the controlled wheel obtain greater longitudinal and transverse adhesion, it can greatly improve the driving performance of the automobile, specifically in the following aspects.

(1) Shorten the braking distance. ABS can ensure that the automobile can obtain higher braking efficiency after rain, ice, snow and muddy roads, and prevent the automobile from sideslip and tail swing (except for loose sand and roads with deep snow).

(2) Keep the direction stability when the car is braking.

(3) Keep the steering control ability when the car is braking.

(4) Reduce the wear of tires during braking. ABS can prevent tires from dragging marks during braking and improve the service life of tires.

(5) Reduce the driver's fatigue intensity, especially the tension when the car is braking.

Ⅱ. Composition and working principle of anti-lock

(Ⅰ) Composition of braking system

Generally speaking, on the basis of traditional braking, the ABS adds a braking force regulation system, mainly including wheel speed sensors, ECU, actuators (brake pressure regulator) and ABS warning lamp, as shown in Figure 3-2-5.

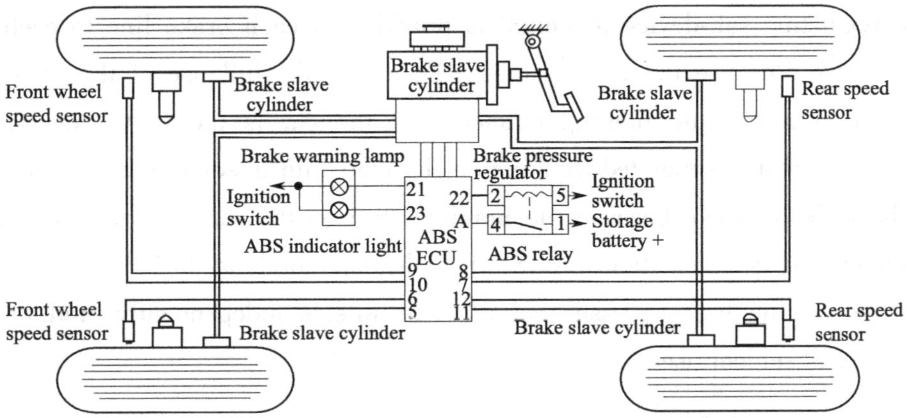

Figure 3-2-5 Composition of braking system

When braking, the ECU receives the signal from the sensor. When the wheel is about to be locked, the ECU sends out a control signal to control the braking force of the brake through the actuator so that the wheel will not be locked.

(Ⅱ) Classification of braking system

1. According to the control form

When ABS is in operation, the brake lines capable of independent brake pressure regulation are referred to as control channels. If each wheel occupies a separate control channel, it is referred to as independent control; if two wheels occupy the same control channel, it is called simultaneous control.

When the wheels are controlled at the same time, if the braking pressure is adjusted to ensure that the wheel with smaller adhesion coefficient does not slip, the two wheels are controlled according to the low selection principle, which is called low selection control (SL) for short; if the brake pressure is adjusted according to the principle of ensuring that the wheel with larger adhesion coefficient does not lock, then the two wheels are controlled according to the high selection principle, referred to as high selection control (SH) for short.

2. According to the number of control channels

ABS can be divided into four-channel ABS, three-channel ABS, two-channel ABS and single-channel ABS according to the number of control channels. The structure of four-channel ABS is shown in Figure 3-2-6. In order to control the brake pressure of four wheels independently, a wheel speed sensor is installed on each wheel. A brake-pressure regulating sub-device (channel) is provided in each brake line to each brake wheel cylinder. Because the four-channel ABS can make full use of the adhesion of each wheel to brake, the braking efficiency of the car is the best. But when the adhesion coefficient is separated (braking on the road with unequal adhesion coefficient of wheels on both sides), because the braking force on the same axle is unequal, the car produces a larger deflection torque, which leads to braking deviation. ABS usually does not adjust the brake pressure of the four wheels independently, and the four-channel ABS is seldom used.

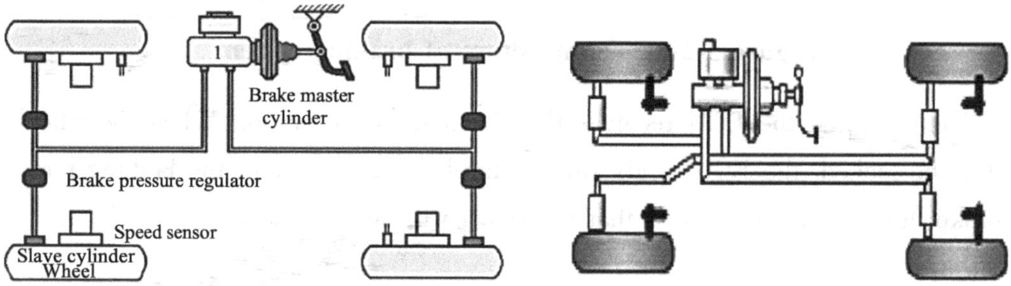

(a) (b)

Figure 3-2-6 Structure of Four-Channel ABS

(a) Four-sensor four-channel/four-wheel independent control corresponds to the H-shape (front and rear) arrangement of the dual brake links

(b) Four-sensor, four-channel/front wheel independent-rear wheel select control corresponds to a dual brake line, X-shaped (diagonal) arrangement

Most four-wheel ABS is three-channel ABS, and the three-channel ABS controls the brake pressures of the two front wheels independently, and controls the brake pressures of the two rear wheels together according to the principle of low selection, as shown in Figure 3-2-7. In this way, for rear-wheel drive vehicles, only one rotation speed sensor can be installed in the transmission or final drive to detect the average rotation speed of the two rear wheels. Because the three-channel ABS makes full use of the adhesion of the front wheels, the braking distance is short and has stable direction, and it is widely used.

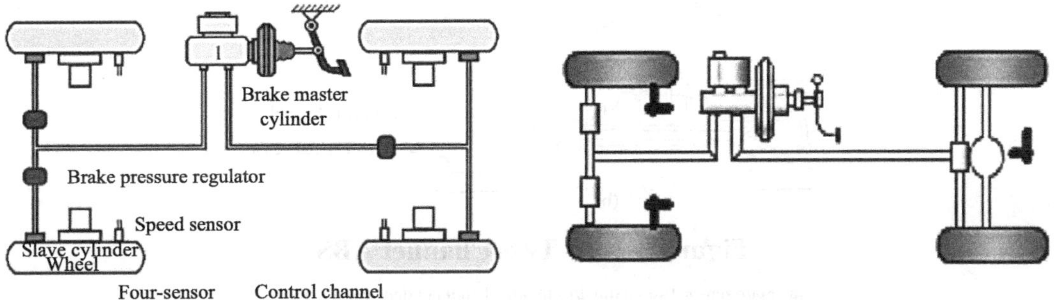

(a) (b)

Figure 3-2-7 Three-Channel ABS

(a) Four-sensor three-channel/front wheel independent-rear wheel low selection control model

(b) Three-sensor three-channel/front wheel independent-rear wheel low selection control model

The two-channel ABS is shown in Figure 3-2-8. The front and rear brake pipes are respectively provided with a brake pressure regulator, which controls the two front wheels and the two rear wheels together. The two front wheels can switch between high selection and low selection according to the attachment conditions, while the two rear wheels are controlled together according to the principle of low selection. Because it is difficult to take into account the directional stability, steering control ability and braking distance of two-channel ABS, it is rarely used at present.

Single-channel ABS is shown in Figure 3-2-9. All single-channel ABS is equipped with a brake pressure regulating device in the rear brake pipeline of the dual-pipeline brake system arranged front and rear. For rear-wheel drive vehicles, only one rotation speed sensor needs to be installed in the transmission system. Since the brake pressure of the front brake wheel cylinders are not controlled, the front wheels may still be locked. Therefore, the steering operation ability of the automobile during braking can not be guaranteed. However, single-channel ABS can significantly improve the direction stability of the automobile during braking, and has the advantages of simple structure and low cost, so it is widely used in light trucks.

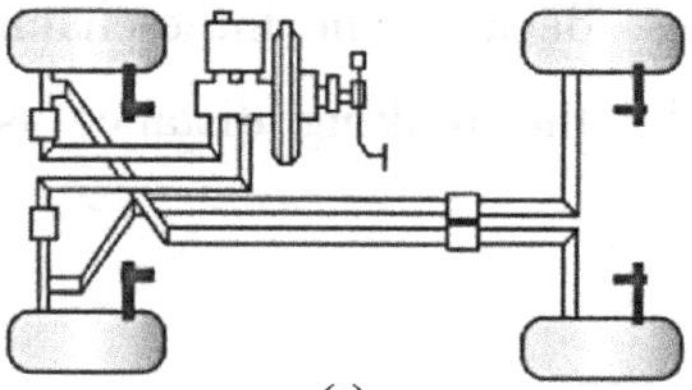
(a)

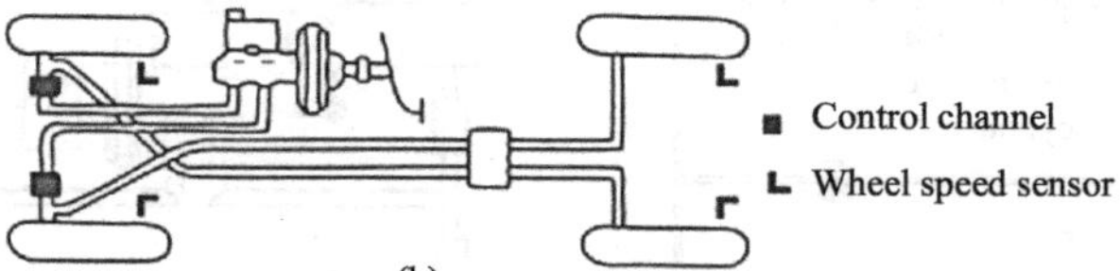

(b)

Figure 3-2-8 Two-Channel ABS

(a) Four-sensor two-channel/front wheel independent control model

(b) Four-sensor two-channel/front wheel independent-rear wheel low selection control model

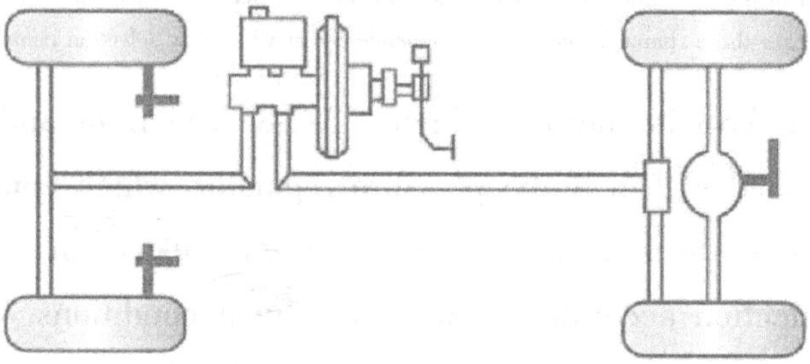

Figure 3-2-9 Single Channel ABS

(Ⅲ) Structure and working principle of main parts of ABS

1. Sensors

1) Wheel speed sensor

The wheel speed sensor is a sensor that transmits the wheel speed of the wheel to the electronic control unit in the form of electric signal during the driving process of the automobile, and determines whether to start the anti-lock braking control by judging the motion state of the wheel after processing. It is usually installed at the wheel, but it is also installed in the final drive or transmission. The outline and basic structure of the wheel speed sensor are shown in Figure 3-2-10.

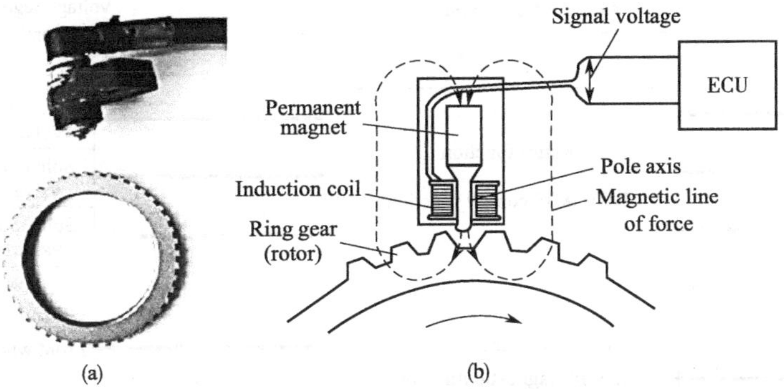

Figure 3-2-10 Shape and Basic Structure of Wheel Speed Sensor

(a) Shape (b) Basic Structure

2) Deceleration sensor

The function of the deceleration sensor is to obtain the deceleration signal of the automobile when the automobile is braked. When the automobile is braked on the road with high adhesion coefficient, the deceleration of the vehicle is great. When braking on the road with low adhesion coefficient, the deceleration of the vehicle is small. Therefore, after the signal is sent to ECU, the road surface can be distinguished and the road adhesion coefficient can be judged. When the vehicle is judged to be driving on a slippery road such as snow, ice, etc., corresponding control measures shall be taken to improve the braking performance. The deceleration sensor is mostly used in the four-wheel drive control system.

2. Electronic control unit

The electronic control unit is the control center of the ABS. It is actually a microcomputer, so it is often called the ABS computer. The ECU of ABS (Figure 3-2-11) is composed of input circuit, digital controller, output circuit and warning circuit. Its function is to receive the signals from the wheel speed sensor and other switches for amplification, calculation and comparison. After analysis and judgment according to specific control logic, the command is output to control the brake pressure regulator to adjust the brake pressure, as shown in Figure 3-2-11.

The ECU also has fault detection and fail-safe functions. When the ignition switch is turned on, the ABS warning lamp on the instrument panel flashes several times and then goes out, indicating that the ABS self-diagnosis is completed and the system is normal.

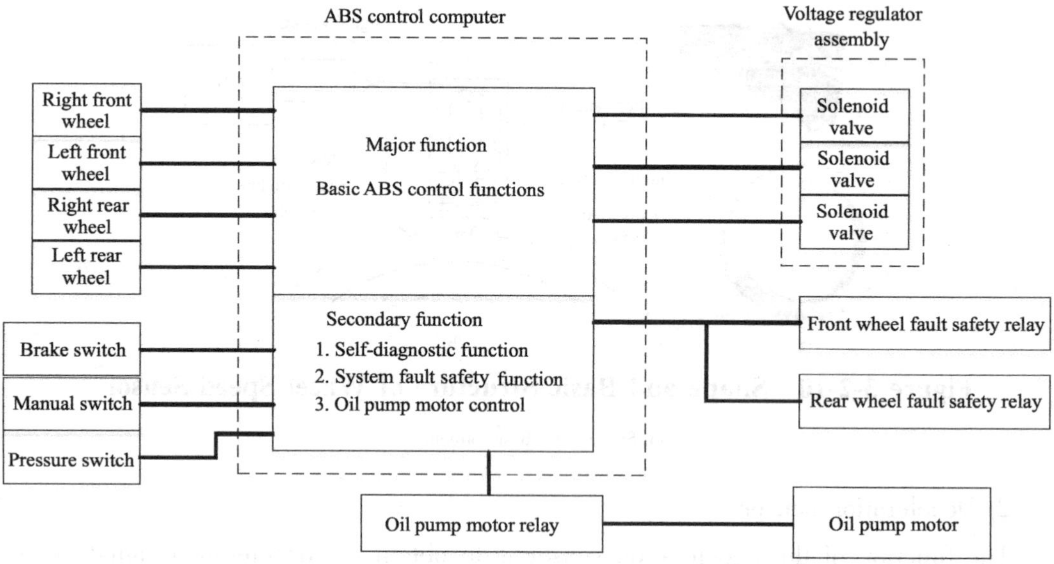

Figure 3-2-11 ECU Composition of ABS

3. Brake pressure regulator

The function of the brake pressure regulator is to receive the command from the ECU and realize the automatic adjustment of the brake pressure of the wheel brake through the action of the solenoid valve. The installation position and brake pipeline arrangement of the brake pressure regulator are different due to different vehicle models, but its structure and operation are basically the same. A brake pressure regulator is connected in series between that mast cylinder and the wheel cylinder, and directly or indirectly controls the brake pressure of the wheel cylinder through the solenoid valve. Usually, the regulator that directly controls the brake pressure of the wheel cylinder by the solenoid valve is called a circulating brake pressure regulator, and the regulator that indirectly controls the brake pressure is called a variable volume brake pressure regulator.

1) Circulating brake pressure regulator

The circulating brake pressure regulator (Figure 3-2-12) is a solenoid valve connected in series between the brake master cylinder and the brake wheel cylinder to directly control the brake pressure of the wheel cylinder. It is characterized by that the conventional brake oil circuit is connected with the ABS control pressure oil circuit, and the solenoid valve directly controls the brake pressure of the wheel cylinder. Three-position three-way solenoid valve and two-position two-way solenoid valve are mostly used. Under the control of ECU, make the solenoid valve in three positions of boosting, maintaining pressure and reducing pressure.

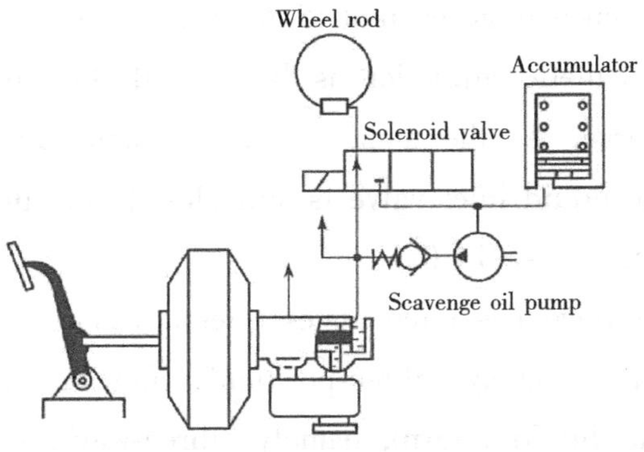

Figure 3-2-12 Recirculating Brake Pressure Regulator

(1) Three-position three-way solenoid valve consists of liquid inlet valve, liquid return valve, main spring, auxiliary spring, electromagnetic coil and armature sleeve, as shown in Figure 3-2-13.

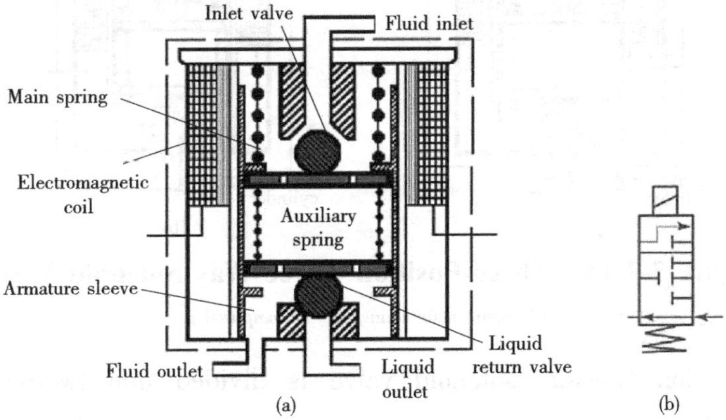

Figure 3-2-13 Structure and Symbol of Three-position Three-way Solenoid Valve

(a) Structure (b) Symbol

The working process of three-position three-way solenoid valve is as follows.

Pressurization: when the electromagnetic coil is not energized, under the action of the main spring tension, the liquid inlet valve is opened, the liquid return valve is closed, and the liquid inlet and outlet are kept unblocked.

Pressure maintaining: when a small current (2 A) is applied to the electromagnetic coil, the generated electromagnetic attraction is small, and the upward movement of the suction armature is small, but the main spring can be compressed properly to close the liquid inlet valve, and the auxiliary spring can be released. The liquid return valve is not opened, as shown in Figure 3-2-14 (a).

Decompression: when a large current (5 A) is applied to the electromagnetic coil, the generated electromagnetic attraction is large, and the upward movement of the suction armature is large. At the same time, the main and auxiliary springs are compressed, so that the liquid inlet valve is still closed, and the liquid return valve is opened, as shown in Figure 3-2-14 (b).

Since the solenoid valve has three States (pressurization, pressure maintaining, and decompression reducing), namely "three-position", and has three interfaces (liquid inlet, liquid outlet, and liquid return), namely "three-way", so the solenoid valve is called three-position three-way solenoid valve, which are often written as 3/3 solenoid valve.

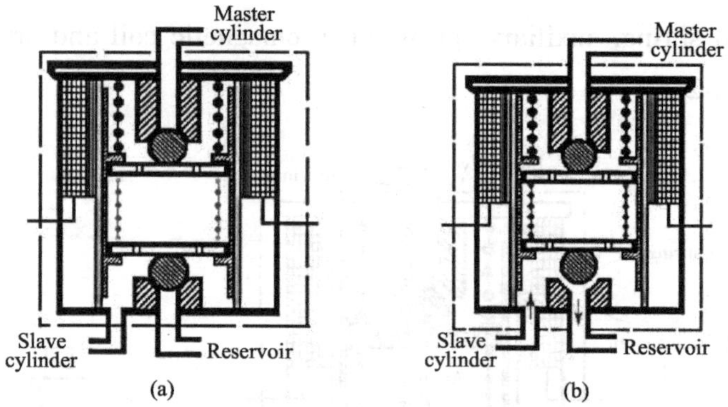

Figure 3-2-14 Three-Position Three-Way Solenoid Valve

(a) Pressure maintaining (b) Decompression

(2) Two-position two-way solenoid valve is divided into two-position two-way normally open solenoid valve and two-position two-way normally closed solenoid valve. Both of which are composed of valve armature, electromagnetic coil, return spring, etc.

Under normal conditions, the two-position two-way normally open solenoid valve opens under spring tension, and the two-position two-way normally closed solenoid valve closes under spring tension.

The structure and symbol of the two-position two-way solenoid valve are shown in Figure 3-2-15. The two-position two-way normally open solenoid valve is used to control the brake fluid path from the brake master cylinder to the brake wheel cylinder, and is also called the two-position two-way normally open fluid inlet solenoid valves. The 2-position 2-way normally closed solenoid valve is used to control the brake fluid circuit from the brake cylinder to the reservoir, also known as 2-position 2-way normally closed outlet solenoid valve. The two solenoid valves are used together to complete the task of brake pressure regulation in ABS work.

(3) Liguid return pump and accumulator

When the solenoid valve is in the process of decompression, the brake fluid flowing from the wheel cylinder is temporarily stored by the accumulator, and then pumped back to the master cylinder by the fluid return pump, as shown in Figure 3-2-16.

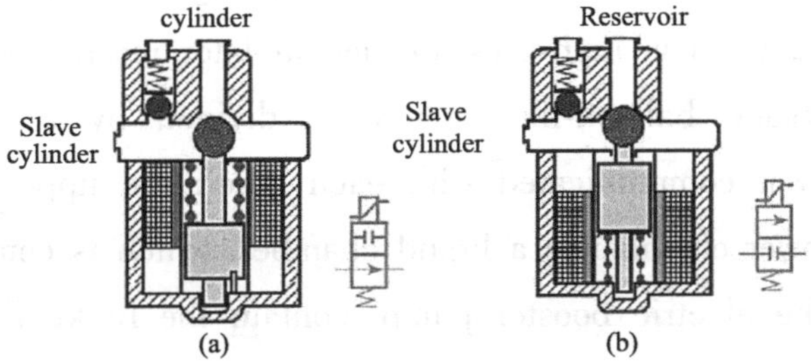

Figure 3-2-15 Structure and Symbol of Two-position Two-way Solenoid Valve

(a) Two-position two-way normally open solenoid valve (b) Two-position two-way normally closed solenoid valve

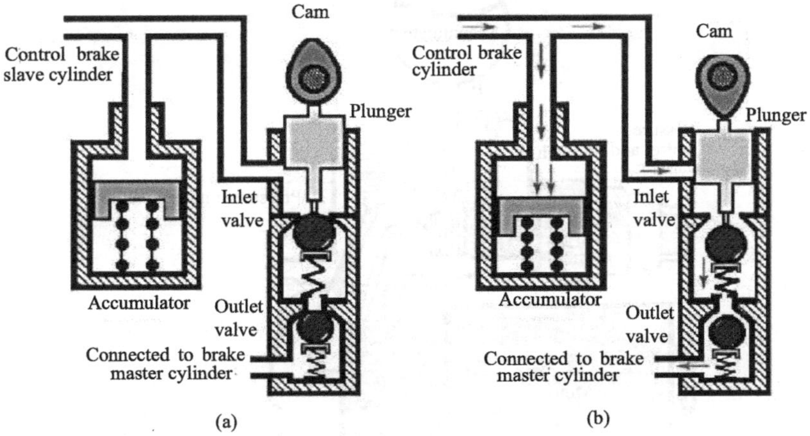

Figure 3-2-16 Accumulator and Liguid return Pump

(a) Liguid return pump does not start, no oil return (b) Liguid return pump starts, oil return

Accumulators are divided into low pressure accumulators and high pressure accumulators according to the pressure of stored brake fluid. They are configured in different forms of brake pressure regulation systems.

① The low-pressure accumulator is commonly called the liquid accumulator, which is used to receive the brake fluid returned from the brake wheel cylinder during the process of ABS decompression, and also has a certain attenuation effect on the pressure fluctuation of the returned brake fluid.

There is a piston and a spring in the accumulator. When pressure is reduced, the returning brake fluid compresses the piston to move downward against the spring tension, increasing the volume and temporarily storing the brake fluid. The accumulator in Figure 3-2-16 is the liquid accumulator.

The liquid return pump consists of DC motor and plunger pump. The plunger pump consists of plunger, liquid inlet and outlet valve and spring.

② The high-pressure accumulator and the electric booster pump are used to store the high-pressure brake fluid required during braking or during ABS operation, as shown in Figure 3-2-17. The high-pressure accumulator mostly uses a black balloon-like sphere. The black balloon-like sphere is divided by a diaphragm into two chambers that are not communicated with each other: the upper chamber is an air chamber, and the lower chamber is a liquid chamber, which is communicated with the liquid channel of the electric booster pump, contain the brake fluid pumped by the electric booster pump.

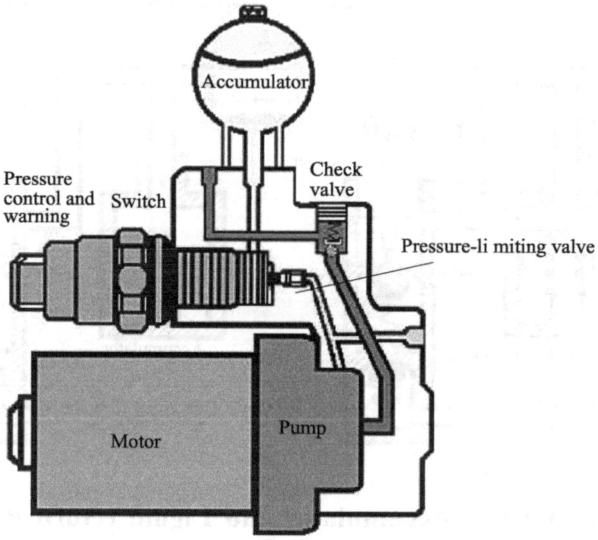

Figure 3-2-17 High-pressure Accumulator and Electric Booster Pump

At the lower end of the high-pressure accumulator, there are two pressure control switches, which are used to detect the brake fluid pressure in the lower cavity of the high-pressure accumulator. When the pressure is lower than 15 MPa, the switch closes, and the booster pump works; when the pressure reaches 18 MPa, the switch opens, and the booster pump stops working.

The electric booster pump is provided with a pressure warning switch. The pressure warning switch is provided with two pairs of switch contacts, one pair is normally open and the other pair is normally closed. When the brake fluid pressure in the lower cavity of the high-pressure accumulator is lower than 10.5 MPa, the normally open contacts closed and the red brake warning lamp is turned on; at the same time, the normally closed contacts open, and the signal is sent to the ECU to turn off the ABS and turn on the yellow brown ABS warning lamp.

2) Variable displacement brake pressure regulator

According to different control principles, variable volume brake pressure regulator can be divided into hydraulic control mode and DC motor control mode.

The hydraulic control variable volume pressure regulation mode (Figure 3-2-18) adds a set of hydraulic control device in the original brake system pipeline of the automobile, which is used to change the volume of the brake pipeline and realize the cyclic regulation of pressurization, pressure maintaining and decompression. The control hydraulic oil circuit of this brake pressure regulation system and the brake fluid oil circuit controlled by ABS are separated from each other.

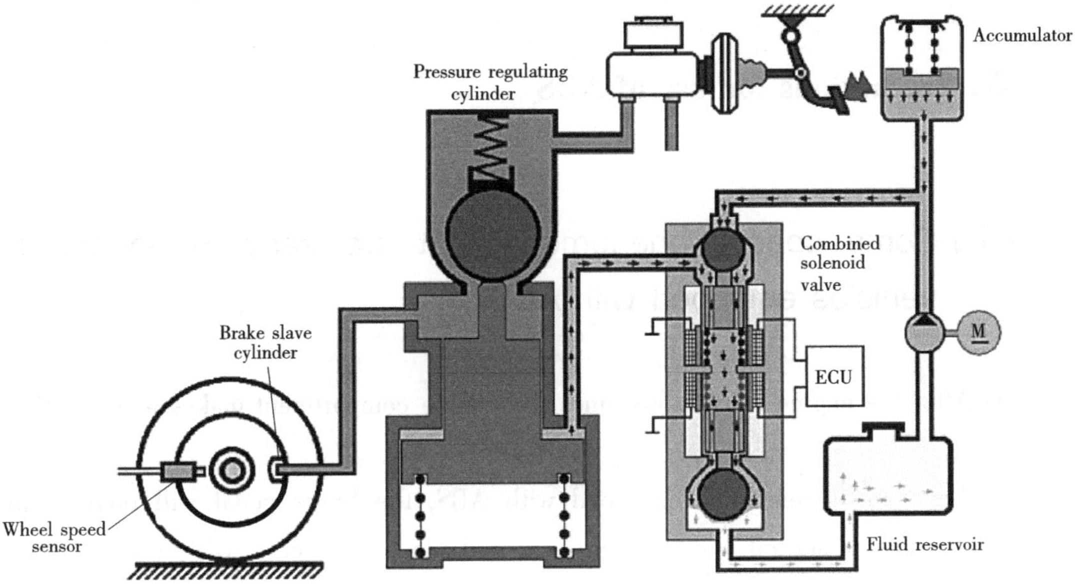

Figure 3-2-18 Hydraulic Control Variable Volume Pressure Regulation Mode

The working process of hydraulic control variable volume pressure regulation mode is as follows.

Conventional braking: input solenoid valve is de-energized and closed, output solenoid valve is de-energized and opened. The piston of pressure regulating cylinder moves upward under the action of spring, and the check valve is pushed open. The pressure of brake cylinder will increase with the increase of brake pedal force, as shown in Figure 3-2-19 (a).

Decompression: ECU supplies power to the two solenoid valves at the same time, the input solenoid valve is opened, the output solenoid valve is closed, and the high-pressure control fluid flows to the pressure-regulating piston cylinder through the input solenoids valve. The piston moves downward, the volume increases, and the brake pressure of the brake wheel cylinder decreases, as shown in Figure 3-2-19 (b).

Pressure maintaining: the input solenoid valve is de-energized and closed, the output solenoid valve is energized and closed, the piston position of the pressure regulating cylinder remains unchanged, and the brake fluid pressure of the brake wheel cylinder remains unchanged, as shown in Figure 3-2-19 (c).

Pressurization: the input solenoid valve is de-energized and closed, and the output solenoid valve is de-energized and opened. The pressure regulating cylinder piston moves upward under the action of the spring, the volume decreases, and the brake fluid pressure of the brake wheel cylinder increases, as shown in Figure 3-2-19 (d).

Ⅲ. Precautions for use of ABS

(Ⅰ) Some special phenomena that are easy to appear in vehicles equipped with ABS

(1) After the engine starts, sometimes the engine compartment makes a sound like impact.

(2) For some automobiles equipped with ABS, the brake pedal will bounce up when the engine is started and it is pressed, and the brake pedal will go down when the engine is stopped.

(3) Turn the steering wheel when braking, and you will feel a slight vibration of the steering wheel.

(4) When braking, the brake pedal may sink slightly or vibrate slightly, which is caused by the frequent extrusion of high-pressure brake fluid when the brake cylinder is retracted and released at high speed.

(5) When driving at high speed and making a sharp turn or driving on the icy road, the brake warning light will sometimes light up.

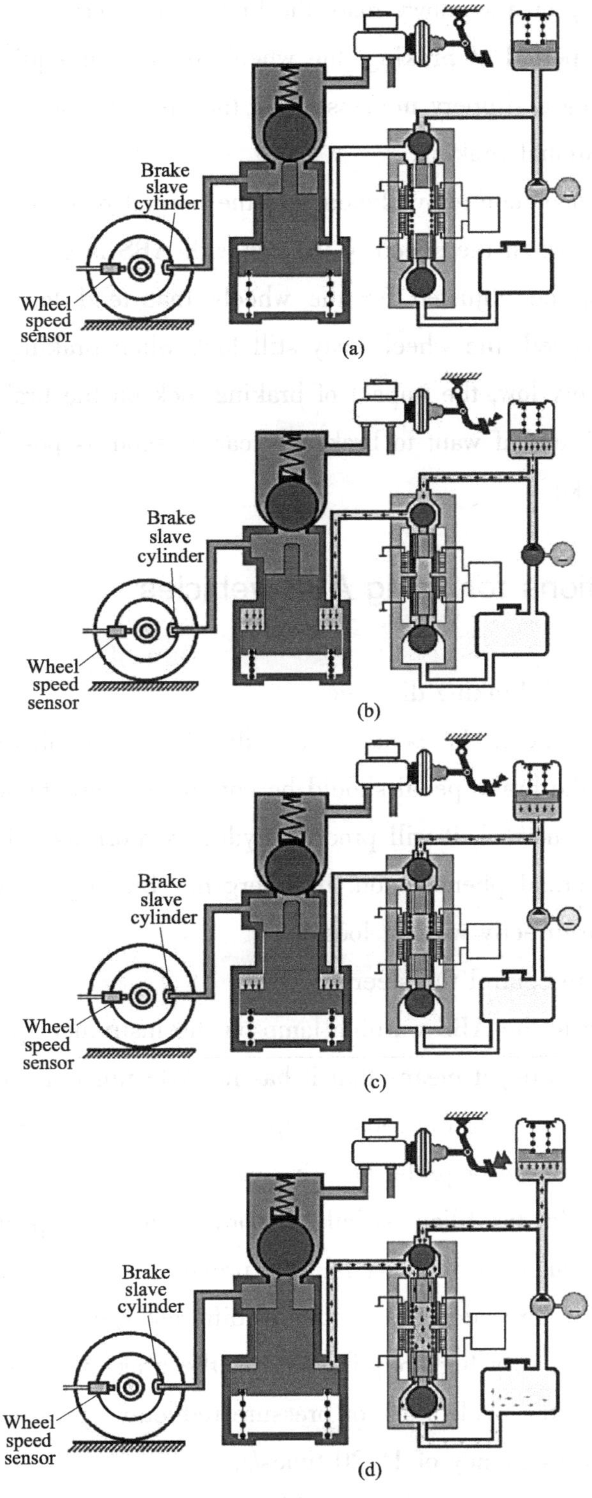

Figure 3-2-19 Working Process of Hydraulic Control Variable Volume Pressure Regulation

(a) Conventional braking (b) Decompression (c) Pressure maintaining (d) Pressurization

(6) When braking on the snowy road, the braking distance will sometimes longer.

(7) In the later period of braking, the wheels of the car equipped with ABS will also be locked, leaving a slippery impression on the ground, but it is different from the impression of conventional braking.

The special phenomenon above belongs to the normal reaction of ABS.

In addition, only when the speed of the car with ABS is greater than 5 km/h, will the anti-lock braking be adjusted for the wheels that tend to lock in the braking process. Below this speed, the wheels may still lock when braking, because when the speed of the car is very low, the impact of braking lock on the braking performance of the car is very small, and if want to brake the car as soon as possible, it is necessary to lock the wheel brake.

(Ⅱ) Precautions for using ABS vehicles

(1) Maintain enough braking distance.

(2) Do not press the brake pedal repeatedly. When the brake pedal is pressed, the force exerted on the brake pedal should be continuous and stable.

(3) When ABS is normal, it will produce hydraulic working noise and brake pedal chatter, which is a normal phenomenon. In emergency braking, brake pedal should be pressed to the bottom directly without loosening.

(4) Don't forget to control the steering wheel.

(5) Pay attention to the ABS warning lamp on the instrument panel during driving. If it flashes or is always on, it means that it has no ABS function, but the conventional brake system still works. Go to the repair shop for repair as soon as possible.

(6) Keep the wheel sensor probe and ring gear clean.

(7 The air should be filled strictly according to the specified tire pressure standard, and the balance of the coaxial tire pressure should be maintained at the same time. It is strictly forbidden to use tires of different specifications.

(8) The ABS has a very high requirement on the brake fluid, so as to ensure that the ABS can carry out the cycle work of pressure reduction, pressure maintenance and pressure increase at a frequency of 15-20 times/s.

Requirements of the brake fluid are as follows: ① high boiling point ensures no "air lock" during braking; ② the kinematic viscosity should be low to ensure timely response during braking; ③ no corrosion to metal rubber; ④ it can be stored for a long time and has stable performance; ⑤ the boiling point of moisture absorption should be high.

When adding or replacing the brake fluid, it should be in strict accordance with the requirements of the vehicle manual, and it is forbidden to mix different types of brake fluid.

Ⅳ. The theoretical basis of the anti-skid regulation system

Acceleration slip regulation (ASR) system is mainly used in European cars. Other Japanese cars like Toyota, which are Traction Regulation Control (TRC) . Hyundai, Kia and other Korean cars, are mainly use TCS (Traction Control System).

ASR system is a set of anti-skid control system adopted after ABS, which is a further development and an important supplement to the functions of ABS. ASR system and ABS are closely related and usually used together to form an active safety system for automobile driving. Therefore, the main components of ASR system and ABS can be common or shared.

(Ⅰ) The harm to the car when the car wheel slips

When the automobile runs on the road with low adhesion coefficient (such as muddy road or ice and snow road), because the reaction torque exerted by the ground on the wheels is very small, the driving wheels will slip when starting or accelerating, especially on smooth roads such as ice and snow, and there will be a danger of out of control, as shown in Figure 3-2-20.

Figure 3-2-20 Drive Wheel Slip

When the vehicle is running under off-road conditions, if a driving wheel is on the road with low adhesion coefficient, the vehicle will not be able to move forward, and most of the power output by the engine is consumed on the wheel slip, which not only wastes fuel, accelerates tire wear, but also reduces the passing performance and maneuverability of the vehicle.

(Ⅱ) The function of ASR

The ASR system can reduce the output torque of the engine when the wheels begin to slip, and control the braking system to reduce the torque transmitted to the driving wheels to achieve appropriate driving force, so that the starting and accelerating of the automobile can achieve rapid and stable results, as shown in Figure 3-2-21. Its main purpose is to prevent the driving wheels from slipping during acceleration (especially on special roads with less friction such as rain, snow, hail, road frost, etc.). When the car accelerates, the slip rate is controlled within a certain range, so as to prevent the driving wheel from sliding rapidly. Its function is to improve traction as well as to keep the car stable.

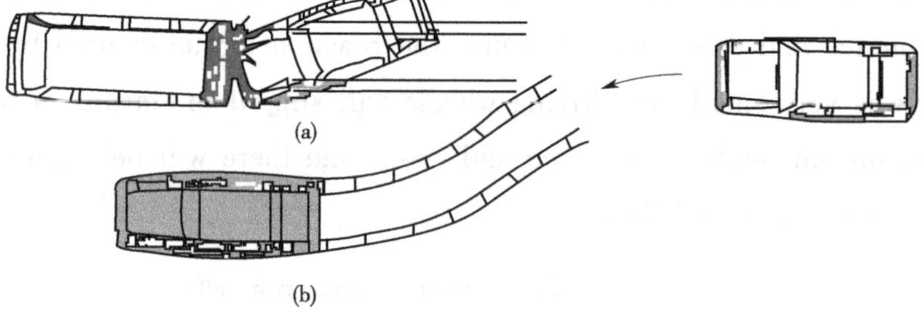

Figure 3-2-21 Function of ASR

(a) Vehicles not equipped with ASR system (b) Vehicles equipped with ASR system

The degree of slip of the driving wheels is usually expressed in slip rate S_d. Its formula is as follows:

$$S_d = \frac{v_c - v}{v_c} \times 100\%$$

In the formula v_c — the circumferential speed of the wheel;

v — the instantaneous speed of the vehicle body.

The relationship between slip rate and adhesion coefficient is shown in Figure 3-2-22.

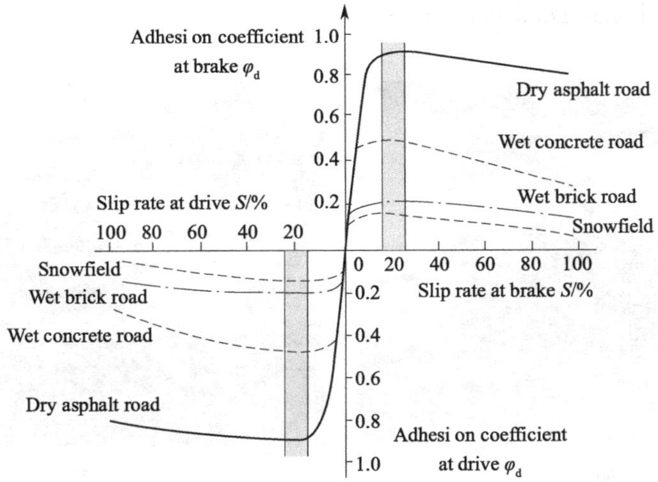

Figure 3-2-22 Relationship Between Slip Rate and Adhesion Coefficient

(1) The adhesion coefficient varies greatly with the road surface.

(2) On various roads, when S_d is about 20%, the adhesion coefficient reaches the peak.

(3) The trend above is almost the same whether braking or driving.

In the actual control process of the driving wheel, because each part of the device has a certain delay and lag, it can not accurately control the slip rate at the best braking point (about 20%). Meanwhile, to prevent the wheel from being worn too fast due to the excessive slippage rate, the slippage rate of the wheel is usually controlled at 5%-15%.

(Ⅲ) Control method of ASR

1. Engine output power control

When the vehicle starts and accelerates, the ASR controller outputs control signals to control the output power of the engine to restrain the slip of the driving wheel. The common methods are auxiliary throttle opening adjustment, ignition parameter adjustment and fuel supply adjustment.

1) Auxiliary throttle opening adjustment

Auxiliary throttle opening adjustment means that an auxiliary throttle valve is connected in series in the original throttle pipeline, and its opening is controlled by the transmission mechanism, so as to change the air intake and adjust the output torque, as shown in Figure 3-2-23. This control method has poor handling stability and poor traction, but it has good comfort.

(a) (b)

Figure 3-2-23 Engine Auxiliary Throttle Opening Adjustment

(a) Auxiliary throttle partially open (b) Auxiliary throttle fully open

2) Ignition parameter adjustment

The ignition parameter adjustment is to control the ignition advance angle or to control whether to ignite. The output torque can be moderately reduced by reducing the ignition advance angle.

3) Fuel supply adjustment

Fuel reduction and fuel pauses reduce torque, which is an easier control mode in modern drive slip control systems. This control is often combined with electronic fuel control.

2. Drive wheel brake control

Directly brake the idling driving wheel, and the reflection time is the shortest. The hydraulic control system combining ASR and ABS is generally used, and the solenoid valve and regulator are added to the ABS, thus increasing the driving control function, as shown in Figure 3-2-24.

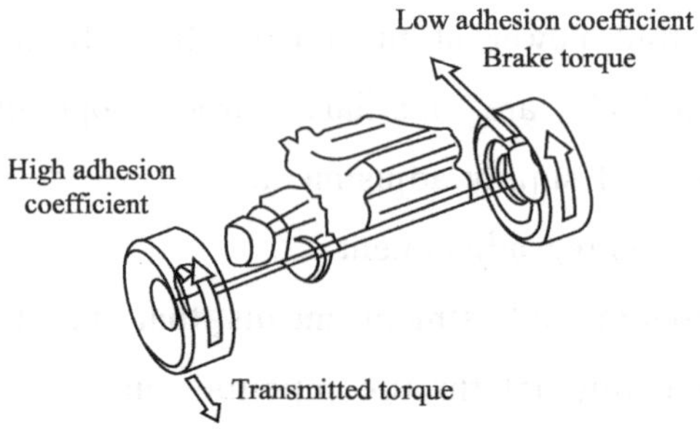

Figure 3-2-24 Driving control of driving wheel

3. Control the output power of the engine and the braking force of the driving wheel at the same time

The control signal simultaneously activates the ASR brake pressure regulator and the auxiliary throttle regulator, applying braking force to the driving wheels while reducing the output power of the engine to achieve the desired control effect.

4. Limited-slip-differential (LSD) control

LSD can control the locking device of the differential to make the locking range from 0% to 100%. When the driving wheel slips unilaterally, the controller outputs a control signal to make the differential lock and the brake pressure regulator act to control the slip rate of the wheel. At this time, the non-slipping wheel still has normal driving force, so as to improve the starting and accelerating ability of the automobile on the slippery road surface and the stability of driving direction.

5. Integrated control of differential lock and engine output power

The control system combining the differential lock brake control with the engine output power control can take corresponding control according to the engine condition and the actual situation of wheel slip, so as to achieve the most ideal control effect.

(Ⅳ) Composition and working principle of ASR

The ASR system mainly consists of sensors (wheel speed sensor and throttle position sensor), ESP controller assembly/automatic transmission controller, engine ECU communication and actuators (brake pressure regulator and throttle drive).

1. Sensors

(1) Wheel speed sensor: shared with ABS system.

(2) Throttle opening sensors: including primary and secondary throttle position sensors, which are shared with the engine electronic control system.

In addition, you can manually control the switch of the ASR system. It has a control knob, if you want to manually control, you can turn off the system at the right time. When the ASR selector switch is turned off, ASR will not work.

2. ECU

The ECU of ASR is also composed of microprocessor as the core, input and output circuits and power supply, etc. Because some signal inputs and processing of ASR and ABS are the same, in order to reduce the number of electronic devices, ASR controller and ABS electronic control unit are often combined together, as shown in

Figure 3-2-25.

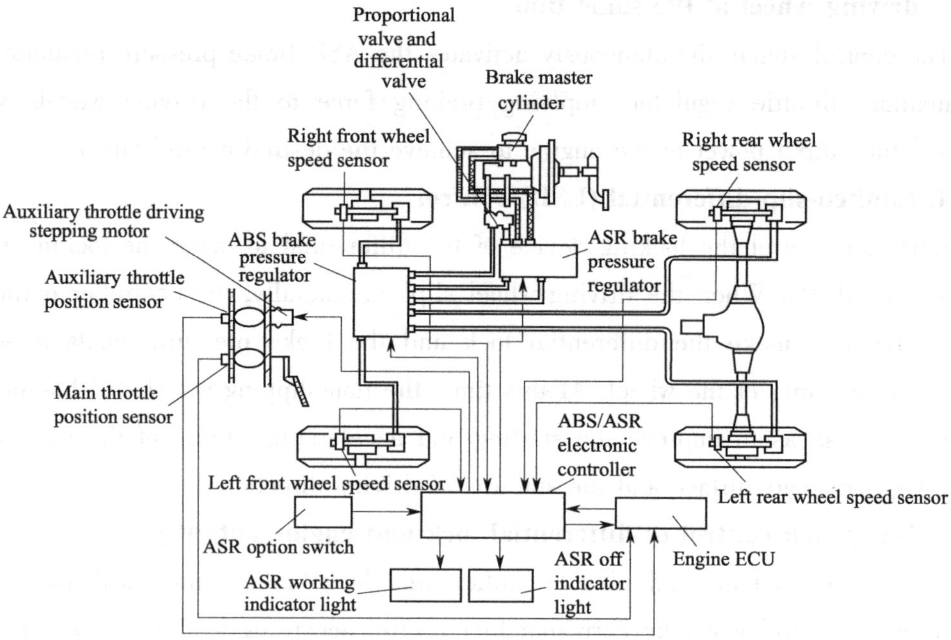

Figure 3-2-25 ASR System Composition

ASR relies on an electronic sensor to detect when the speed of the driven wheel is lower than that of the driving wheel (which is the characteristic of slippage), and a signal will be sent to adjust the ignition time, reduce the valve opening, reduce the throttle, downshift or brake the wheel, so that the wheel slippage can no longer occur.

Another function of the ECU is to give an alarm or store and display fault codes.

3. Actuator

ASR brake pressure regulator has two kinds of structure forms: independent and combined. The former refers to the structure form of ASR and ABS brake pressure regulator separated from each other, which is more suitable for ASR as an optional system of vehicles, the arrangement is more flexible, but the structure is not compact, with many connection points, and easy to leak; the latter is a structural form of combining two sets of pressure regulating devices into one, which is opposite to the independent structure.

1) Independent adjustment

The working process of ASR system is the same as that of the ABS. During the braking process, it is also divided into three stages: pressurization, pressure maintaining and decompression. During normal braking, ASR system does not work, the solenoid valve is not energized, the valve is in the left position, and the piston of the pressure regulating cylinder is pushed to the right limit position by the reset spring.

When starting or accelerating, if the driving wheel slips and needs to be braked, the ASR system energizes the solenoid valve to the right position, and the brake fluid in the pressure accumulator pushes the piston to move left.

When maintaining pressure, the solenoid valve is half energized, the valve is in the neutral position, and the pressure regulating cylinder is isolated from the reservoir chamber and the accumulator, so the piston remains at its original position and the brake pressure remains unchanged.

When pressure is reduced, the solenoid valve is de-energized, and the valve returns to the left position, so that the right chamber of the pressure regulating chamber is isolated from the accumulator and connected with the liquid storage chamber, so the pressure of the right chamber of the pressure regulating cylinder decreases, and the brake pressure decreases.

2) Combined adjustment

When the ASR system does not work, the solenoid valve Ⅰ is not energized, and the ABS performs the braking function and regulates the braking pressure through the solenoid valve Ⅱ and Ⅲ. When the driving wheel slips, the ASR controller energizes the solenoids valve Ⅰ and moves the valve to the right position. The solenid valves Ⅱ and Ⅲ are not energized, and the valve is still in the left position. Then the pressure oil of the pressure accumulator passes through the driving wheel brake pump and the braking pressure increases.

When maintaining pressure, the ASR controller makes the solenoid valve Ⅰ half-energized, the valve to the neutral position, to isolate the pressure accumulator and brake master cylinder access, driving wheel brake cylinder pressure remains unchanged.

When the pressure is reduced, the ASR controller energizes the solenoid valve Ⅰ and the solenoid valve Ⅱ, and the valve moves to the right position to connect the brake wheel cylinder and the channel of the reservoir, so the brake pressure decreases.

The ASR system controls the output power of the engine by changing the opening of the auxiliary throttle valve of the engine. The throttle valve driving device consists of a stepping motor and a transmission mechanism. The stepping motor rotates the specified angle according to the control pulse output by the ASR controller, and drives the auxiliary throttle valve to rotate through the transmission mechanism.

The control process is as follows: when ASR system does not work, the auxiliary throttle valve is in the full open position. When the engine driving force needs to be reduced to control the wheel slip, the ASR controller outputs a signal to make the auxiliary throttle valve drive mechanism work and change the opening degree of the auxiliary throttle, as shown in Figure 3-2-26.

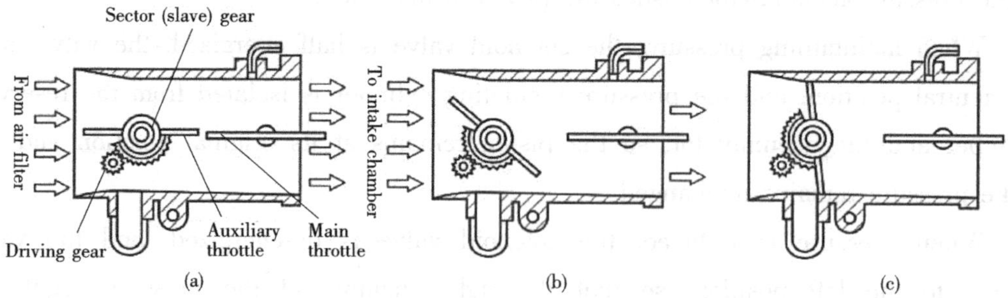

Figure 3-2-26 Operation of the Auxiliary Throttle

(a) Fully open position (b) Half-open position (c) Fully closed position

(Ⅴ) The difference between ASR and ABS

Both ASR and ABS control the slip rate of the wheels and the road surface so that the adhesion force between the wheels and the ground will not decrease. Therefore, the two adopt the same technology. They are closely related and are often used together. They control the movement of the wheels by sharing many electronic components and common system components to form a driving safety system. The differences between ASR and ABS are shown in Table 3-2-2.

Table 3-2-2 Differences between ASR and ABS

Control item	Control system	
	ABS	ASR
General control objective	Control the sliding of wheels relative to the ground at brake	Control the sliding of wheels relative to the ground at drive
Expected result	Improve braking effect to ensure braking safety	Improve starting, acceleration and traction on slippery roads to ensure driving stability
Controlled object	Four wheels	Driving wheel
Work time	It doesn't work when the speed is very low	It doesn't work when the speed is very high

V. Theoretical basis of electronic stability program (ESP) system

(I) The role of ESP

ESP system belongs to the active safety technology of vehicles, and it is used in Volkswagen, Audi and Mercedes-Benz models. In other models, the system with the same or similar function adopts different names, for example, BMW calls it DSC. Toyota calls it VSC, while Honda calls it VSA.

ESP system is a vehicle auxiliary control system developed on the basis of ABS and ASR, which integrates the basic functions of ABS and ASR, and greatly expands its functional scope. Its specific role is mainly manifested in the following three aspects.

1. Real-time monitoring

ESP system is a real-time monitoring system, which monitors the driver's control, road reaction and vehicle movement state all the time, and constantly issues instructions to the engine and braking system.

2. Active intervention

ESP system actively regulates the speed of the engine and adjusts the driving force and braking force of each wheel to correct the oversteering and understeering of the car.

3. Early warning

ESP system also has a real-time warning function, when the driver operates improperly and the road is abnormal, it will warn the driver with warning lights.

Vehicles with ESP system and without ESP system will have great differences when running on different roads with different ground adhesion, as shown in Figure 3-2-27.

Figure 3-2-27 Comparison of Driving with and without ESP system

(Ⅱ) Composition of ESP

ESP system is based on ABS and consists of sensors, electronic control unit and actuators, as shown in Figure 3-2-28. Most components of ESP system can be shared with ABS and ASR. Yaw rate sensor, steering angle sensor, lateral acceleration sensor and brake pressure sensor for detecting the state of the vehicle are added. The electronic control unit of ESP system is generally integrated with the electronic control units of ABS and ASR, which is called ABS/ASR/ESP electronic control unit. The actuator of ESP is on the basis of ABS/ASR actuators, improved the hydraulic passage to each wheel, and added ESP warning lamp and ESP buzzer, as shown in Figure 3-2-29.

(Ⅲ) ESP System Working Principle

During driving, the angle sensor can sense the driver's turning direction and angle; the speed sensor can sense the vehicle speed, throttle opening and speed torque; the brake sensor can sense the braking force; the pivot angle sensor can sense the vehicle's inclination and roll velocity. After knowing such information, ECU judges the difference between the normal & safe driving and the driver´s intention to control the automobile through calculation, and then sends instructions to adjust the engine speed and the braking force on the wheels, so as to correct the oversteer or understeer, thus avoiding the automobile from slipping, oversteer, understeer and locking, and ensuring the driving safety. Strictly speaking, ESP system has the functions of ABS and TCS (traction control system), but it is not a simple superposition of the two systems. The main difference between them is that ABS and TCS can only react passively, while ESP can detect and analyze the vehicle conditions and correct driving errors to provide against possible trouble. Its working principle is shown in Figure 3-2-30.

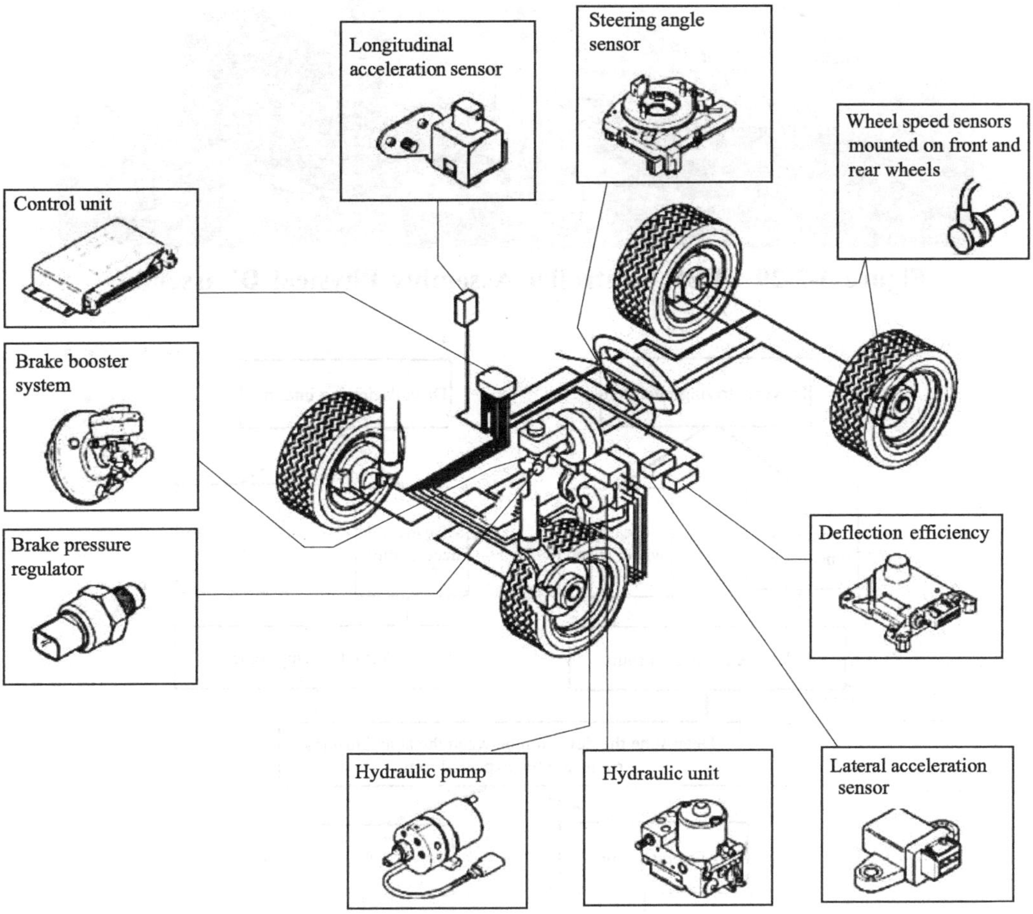

Figure 3-2-28 Composition and Installation Position of ESP

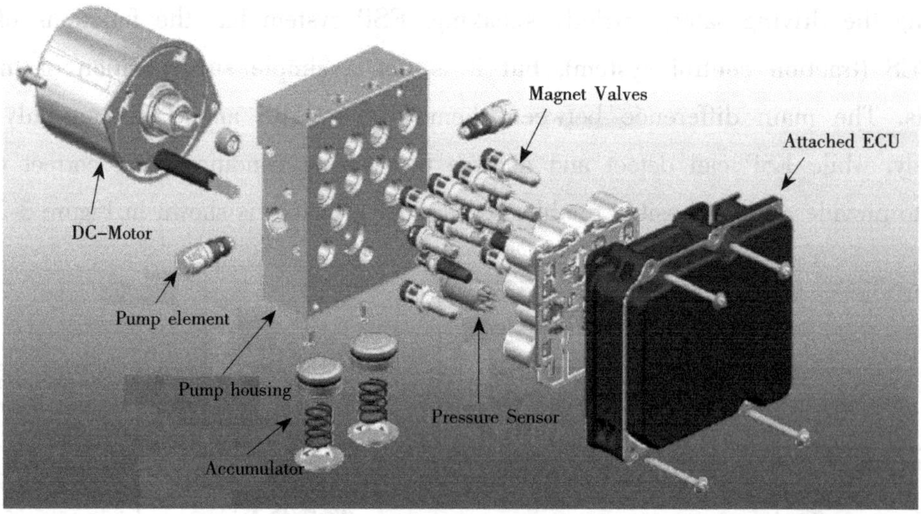

Figure 3-2-29 ESP Controller Assembly Physical Disassembly

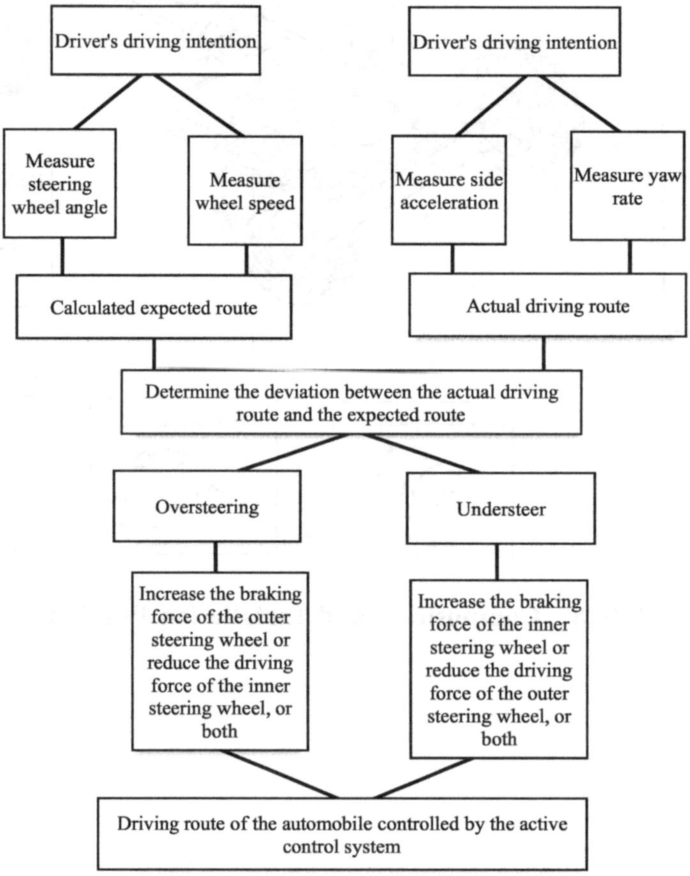

Figure 3-2-30 ESP System Working Principle

ESP system regulates the system pressure through the process of boosting, maintaining and reducing pressure, and has reached the optimal braking pressure, as shown in Figure 3-2-31. The system adopts an X-shaped arrangement, including 1 motor, 2 reflux pumps, 2 accumulators and 12 solenoid valves (see Table 3-2-3 for the abbreviations of the parts). The difference between ESP and ABS is that ABS has only 8 valves and ESP has 12 valves. This is because ESP needs to form a closed hydraulic circuit during active control. In addition, two valves (HSV) are added on the basis of the ABS circuit. The other two valves (USV) are opened when ESP system is working, so that the motor pump can pump oil from the reservoir to the brake wheel cylinder, achieving traction control and stability control functions.

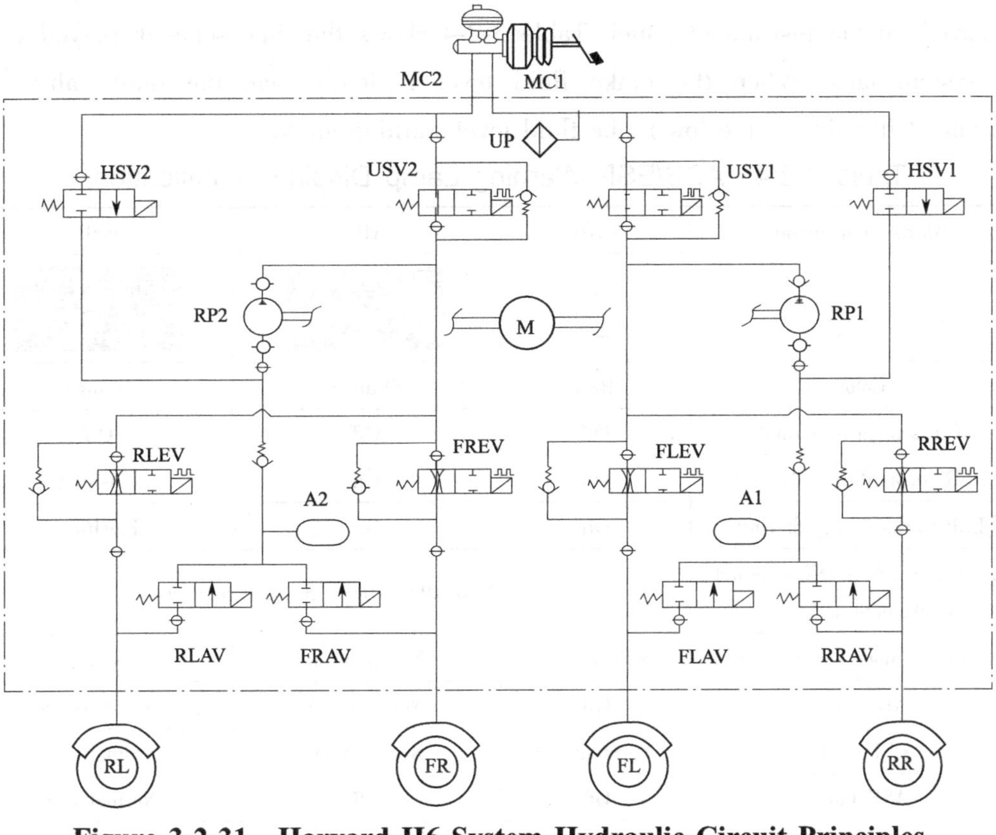

Figure 3-2-31 Harvard H6 System Hydraulic Circuit Principles

Table 3-2-3 Harvard H6 System Hydraulic Circuit Component Name Abbreviation

MC1	Brake master cylinder first circuit	FLEV	Left front wheel inlet valve
MC2	Brake master cylinder secondary circuit	FLAV	Left front wheel delivery valve
M	Motor	FREV	Right front wheel inlet valve
RP1	Return pump 1	FRAV	Right front wheel delivery valve
RP2	Return pump 2	RLEV	Left rear wheel inlet valve

Continued

A1	Accumulator 1	RLAV	Left rear wheel delivery valve
A2	Accumulator 2	RREV	Right rear wheel inlet valve
FL	Left front wheel	RRAV	Right rear wheel outlet valve
FR	Right front wheel	HSV1	High pressure switching valve 1
RL	Left rear wheel	HSV2	High Pressure Switch Valve 2
RR	Rear right wheel	USV1	Circuit control valve 1
UP	Pressure transducer	USV2	Circuit control valve 2

When the Harvard H6 brake system module fails, the ABS/ESP warning lamp is displayed on the instrument panel. Table 3-2-4 shows the time scale displayed when the system fails. When the brake fluid level is lower than the limit value, the instrument illuminates the low brake fluid level warning mark.

Table 3-2-4 ABS/ESP Warning Lamp Display Identification

Alarm lamp name	EBD	ABS	ESP
Symbol shape			
Color	Red	Orange	Orange
The system is normal	Off	Off	Off
ASR works during driving	Off	Off	Flashing
ESP works during driving	Off	Off	Flashing
Ignition switch is ON; conduct instrument self-test	Normally on for 2.5 s and then off		
Diagnostic mode (brake ystem)	Normally on	Normally on	Normally on
ABS fault	Off	Normally on	Normally on
EBD fault	Normally on	Normally on	Normally on
ASR fault	Off	Off	Normally on
ESP fault	Off	Off	Normally on
Turn off ESP function	Off	Off	Normally on
No CAN network signal received (Braking system) more than 500 ms	Normally on	Normally on	Normally on

【Knowledge Development】

Overhaul of ESP system

1. Problem

Turn on the ignition of Harvard H6 vehicle , the system self-test is complete, and the warning lamp remains on.

2. Preliminary inspection

Before diagnosing the ESP system, inspect the easily accessible components that may cause the ESP system to malfunction. Visual and visual inspection procedures quickly identify the malfunction, eliminating the need for further diagnosis.

(1) Ensure that only the recommended sizes of tires and wheels are installed on the vehicle. The tread pattern and depth of the same axle tires must be the same.

(2) Check whether there is leakage at the ESP hydraulic regulator, brake pipeline and connection.

(3) Check the fuses of the ESP system to make sure that the fuses are not burnt and the type is correct. There are three fuses in the 38 pin ESP system, namely: pump motor fuse (40 A), solenoid valve fuse (40 A), electronic control unit fuse (5 A). There are three fuses in ESP system, namely: pump motor fuse (40 A), solenoid valve fuse (40 A), electronic control unit fuse (40 A).

(4) Check the battery voltage, check whether the battery terminal is corroded or loose. The normal working voltage range of ESP system is 9 to 16 V.

(5) Check whether the grounding point of ESP system grounding wire is loose and whether the grounding position is changed.

(6) Perform visual inspection and visual inspection of the following electrical components: whether the wiring harness and connector of relevant parts of ESP system are correctly connected, pinched or cut; whether the wiring harness wiring is too close to high-voltage or high current devices, such as high-voltage electricity or components, generator and motor, stereo amplifier installed after sales, ESP components are sensitive to electromagnetic interference (EMI). If intermittent fault is suspected, check whether the anti-theft device, lamp or mobile phone installed after the sale is installed correctly.

3. The overhaul process of ESP system

The overhaul process of ESP system is shown in Figure 3-2-32.

4. No-code fault maintenance

If there is a fault in the brake system but no codes are stored in the ESP system, such a fault is referred to as a no-code fault. A no-code fault is generally caused by a fault in the base brake system.

(1) Brake fluid leakage, may cause the brake to be too soft, the brake pedal travel too long, and serious to cause brake failure.

(2) Use of inferior brake fluid, will corrode the brake pipeline and the internal components of the ESP hydraulic regulation module, and even lead to brake failure in serious cases.

(3) There is air in the brake pipeline, which may cause the brake to be too soft, or even brake failure.

(4) The brake pipeline is blocked, which may cause the brake to be too hard, the brake to deviate, or even brake failure.

(5) Excessive wear of the brake disc, may cause the brake to be too soft and the brake pedal travel to be too long.

(6) Booster failure, may cause brake too hard or too soft, brake pedal stroke too long, serious to lead to brake failure.

(7) Brake line connection error, may cause ESP system performance to decrease, tail swing, long braking distance, etc. For the correct installation method, please refer to the identification near the oil hole on the ESP hydraulic regulating module: MC1 means No.1 master cylinder oil pipe; MC2 represents No.2 master cylinder oil pipe; FL represents left front wheel cylinder oil pipe; FR represents right front wheel cylinder oil pipe; RL represents left rear wheel cylinder oil pipe; RR represents right rear wheel cylinder oil pipe.

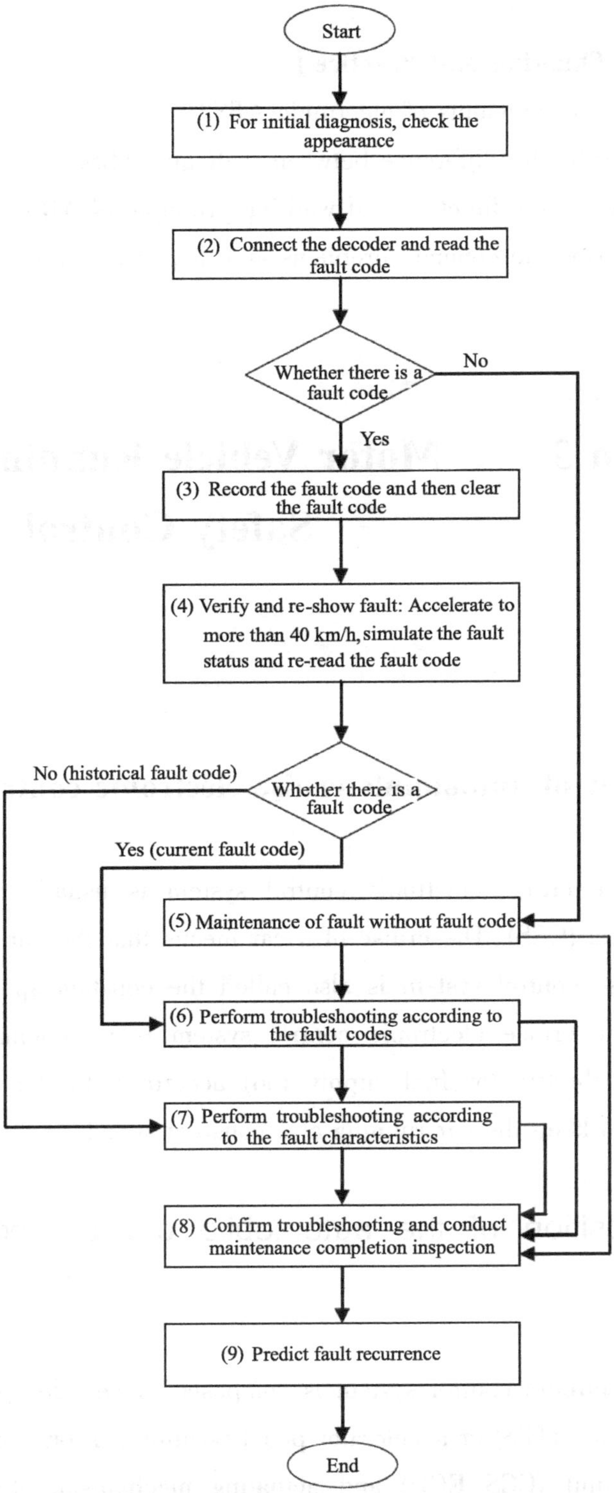

Figure 3-2-32 Maintenance Process of Harvard H6 ESP System

【Thinking and Practice】

1. What are the components of electronic ABS?
2. Briefly describe the difference between ASR and ABS.
3. Briefly describe the function and working principle of ABS.
4. Briefly describe the common problems and diagnosis process of ESP.

Section 3 Motor Vehicle Running and Safety Control

Ⅰ. Overview of automobile cruise electronic control system

The automobile cruise electronic control system is usually referred to as the cruise control system (CCS). The cruise of a car means that the car runs at a constant speed, so the cruise control system is also called the constant speed control system. The function of the cruise electronic control system is to automatically adjust the opening of engine throttle (or fuel supply rod) according to the change of vehicle driving resistance to keep the car running at a constant speed.

(Ⅰ) Composition of the automobile cruise electronic control system

The cruise electronic control system is composed of vehicle speed sensor (VVS), throttle position sensor (TPS) or accelerator pedal position sensor, cruise control system electronic control unit (CCS ECU) and actuating mechanism, etc. The installation positions of CCS control components of a certain vehicle type are shown in Figure 3-3-1.

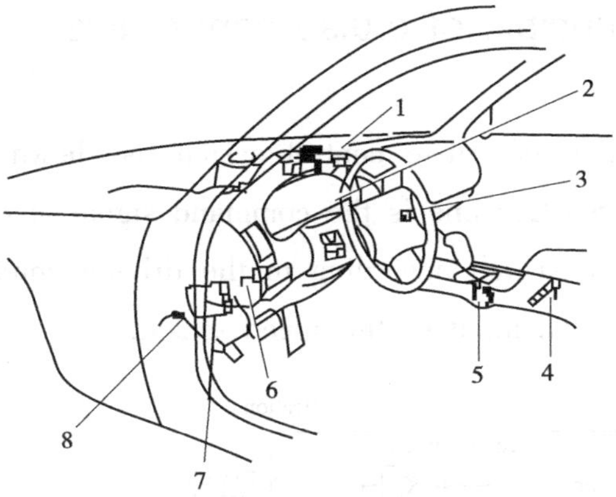

Figure 3-3-1 Installation Positions of CCS Control Components of a Certain Vehicle

1-actuator; 2-cruise indicator; 3-cruise switch; 4-speed sensor; 5-neutral start switch;6-brake light switch; 7-CCS ECU; 8-parking brake switch

The vehicle speed sensor, throttle position sensor, or accelerator pedal position sensor of the cruise control system can be common to the engine control system or to the electronic control automatic transmission system, or can be set separately.

Control switches mainly include cruise switch, brake lamp switch, parking brake switch, ignition switch, clutch switch (only for vehicles with manual transmission) or neutral start switch (for vehicles with automatic transmission), etc. The function of cruise switch is to input command signals such as constant speed, acceleration or deceleration, recovery of original speed and cancellation of cruise driving into CCS ECU. The function of the other switch is to input various status information into the CCS ECU, so that the CCS ECU can determine whether to perform the constant speed control.

CCS ECU is the control core of the cruise control system, which has the functions of mathematical calculation, logic judgment, memory storage, fault self-diagnosis and so on.

The actuator is divided into pneumatic type and electric type. Pneumatic type is mainly composed of speed servo device and solenoid valve; electric type is mainly composed of motor (permanent magnet or stepping motor), deceleration mechanism and electromagnetic clutch. The function of actuator is to adjust the opening of engine throttle through throttle cable (steel cable) or electronic throttle controller according to CCS ECU instruction, keep the speed constant.

(Ⅱ) Control principle of cruise control system

The control principle of cruise control system is shown in Figure 3-3-2. Two signals are input to CCS ECU: one is the command signal of cruise speed set by the driver through the cruise switch according to the driving condition; the other is the actual speed feedback signal input by the speed sensor.

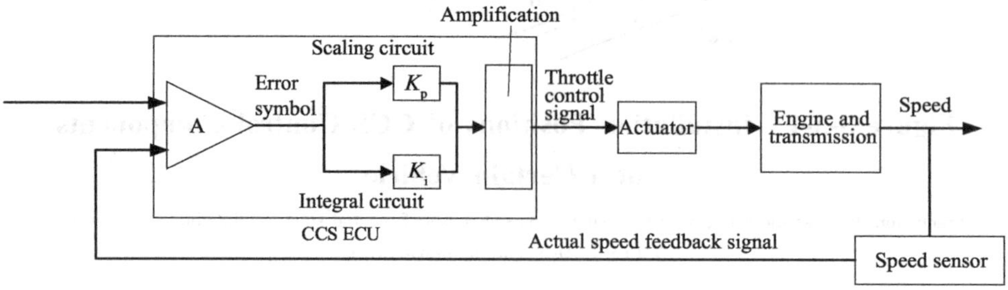

Figure 3-3-2 The Control Principle of Cruise Control System

When the cruise vehicle speed command signal and the actual vehicle speed feedback signal are input into the CCS ECU, the difference between the two signals can be obtained by the comparator A of the CCS ECU through comparing and calculating, which is called as an error signal. After the error signal is proportional and integrated, and then amplified, the control signal controlling the throttle opening can be obtained. The CCS ECU send a control instruction to an actuator, the actuator can actuate that throttle cable (or electronic throttle control). By adjusting the throttle opening, the actual vehicle speed can be quickly adjusted to the value set by the driver, so as to realize cruise control (constant speed control). In the control process, when the actual speed is lower than the cruising speed set by the driver, CCS ECU will send an instruction to the actuator to increase the throttle opening, so that the actual speed increases to the cruising speed. Conversely, when the actual speed is higher than the cruising speed set by the driver, CCS ECU will send an instruction to the actuator to reduce the throttle opening. The actual vehicle speed is reduce to that cruising speed. As a result, the actual speed basically remains unchanged at the cruise speed value set by the driver.

(Ⅲ) Control mode of cruise speed

When the car is on a flat road at the set cruise speed v_a when driving, set the throttle opening is θ_a. If CCS ECU sends a command to the actuator to keep the throttle valve opening unchanged, the vehicle will set the cruise speed v_a. However, when the vehicle is running on a slope or in the wind and headwind, the speed will be reduced to v_b due to the increase of the slope resistance or wind resistance. It is not possible to set the cruise speed v_a. Therefore, the CCS ECU must send a command to the actuator to increase the throttle opening (That is, the throttle rotation angle increases $\Delta\theta°$), so as to make the vehicle speed v_a close to the set cruise speed (i.e. the actual speed is lower than the cruise speed v_a Δv). Similarly, when the vehicle is driving downhill or downwind, the throttle rotation angle will be reduced by and the actual speed v_a will be higher than the cruise speed v_a Δv.

Therefore, in order to make the vehicle cruise speed not affected by the change of driving resistance, the control line controlled by the internal integral operation amplifier circuit of the CCS ECU should reduce the range of vehicle speed change as much as possible, so when the vehicle is driving on an uphill or downhill road and wind resistance and other factors lead to the change of driving resistance, the control system only needs to adjust the throttle opening. The change of vehicle speed can be limited to a small range of $\pm\Delta v$.

(Ⅳ) Advantages of cruise control system

The cruise control system mainly has the following advantages.

1. Reduce the driver's labor intensity and improve the driving safety

When the vehicle speed reaches a certain value (more than 40 km/h) during driving, as long as the driver operates the cruise switch to set a desired constant speed, the CCS ECU can automatically control the opening of the engine throttle valve to keep the vehicle running at the set speed without stepping on the accelerator pedal.

2. The driving speed is stable, and the ride comfort is improved

In the process of cruising, no matter the car is running on the uphill or downhill road, or on the flat road or in the case of wind speed change, as long as the engine power is within the allowable range, the car speed will remain unchanged.

3. Save fuel consumption, improve fuel economy and emission performance

Practice has proved that under the same driving conditions, the use of cruise driving can save about 15% of the fuel.

Ⅱ. Structural principle of electronic control system for automotive cruise

(Ⅰ) Cruise control switch

The master switch of the cruise control switch is generally a lever switch, which is installed on the steering column where the driver can easily access, or a combination switch, which is designed on the steering wheel. Most switches have three gears: SET/COAST, CANCEL, and RES/ACC. Normally, when the speed exceeds 40 km/h, the vehicle will remember the current speed and keep running at a constant speed as long as the SET key is pressed. The constant speed running will stop immediately when the CANCEL key is pressed. The "RES/ACC" gear is used for braking or shifting to make the vehicle drive at the set speed again after the circuit is disconnected. When the vehicle is under automatic cruise control, the speed can be increased by pressing the ACC key or decreased by pressing the COAST key, as shown in Figure 3-3-3.

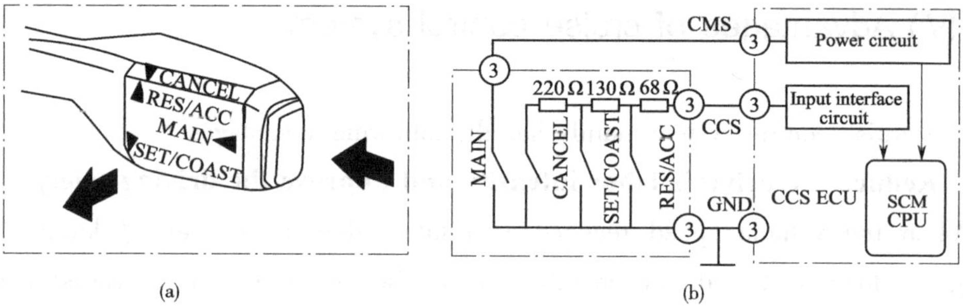

Figure 3-3-3 Configuration and Internal Circuit of Cruise Switch Control Handle

(a)Joystick outline structure (b)Cruise switch internal circuit

(Ⅱ) CCS ECU

CCS ECU is also called the electronic cruise controller, which is the center of the cruise control system. It is used to receive the signals of the speed sensor, cruise control switch, brake lamp switch, etc., and output the control signal after calculation, memory, amplification and conversion to drive the actuator to act. The electrical block diagram is as shown in Figure 3-3-4.

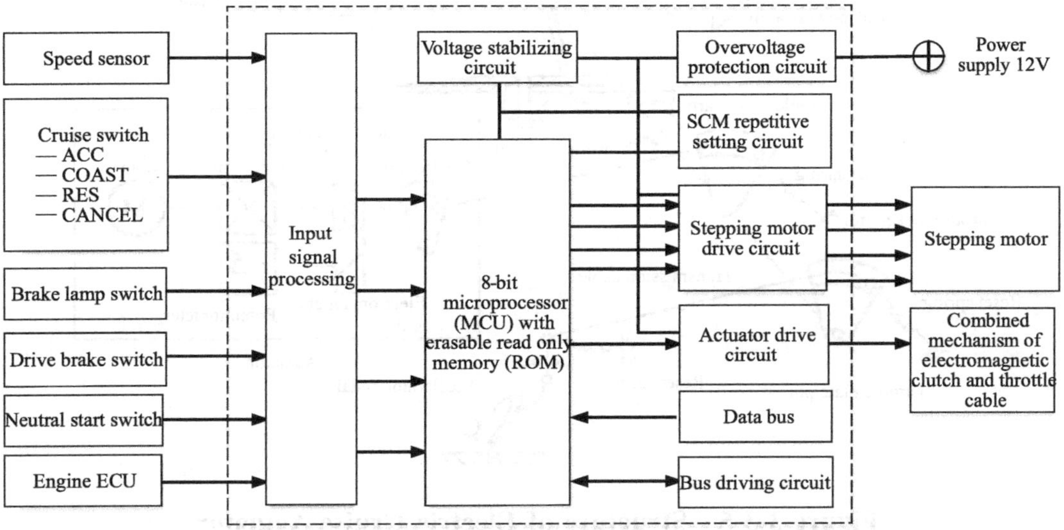

Figure 3-3-4 Electrical Block Diagram of Motorola Digital CCS ECU

(Ⅲ) Cruise actuator

The CCS actuator is also called speed servo device, which is used to convert the current or voltage signal output by the ECU into mechanical motion according to the control command of CCS ECU, so as to control the throttle opening and control the speed. There are two types of actuators: electric and pneumatic. The structure of cruise actuator is shown in Figure 3-3-5.

The electric cruise actuator is to use the rotation of the motor and drive the swing of the control rocker arm to change the throttle opening. It mainly includes electromagnetic clutch, DC motor or stepping motor. The DC motor operates continuously, and its speed is related to the average voltage supplied by ECU; its operation or stop is determined by the voltage ("Yes" or "No") output by ECU; its operation direction is determined by the direction of the voltage output by ECU. The stepping motor is to rotate the motor shaft at a certain angle when it is powered on.

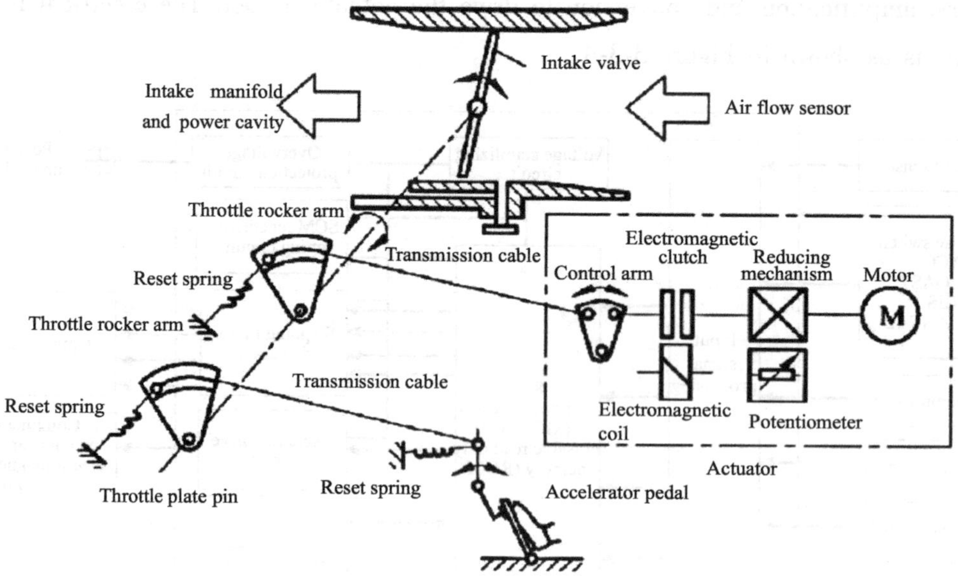

Figure 3-3-5 Structure of Electric Cruise Actuator

The electromagnetic clutch is to combine the motor shaft and the throttle control rocker arm when it is powered on, and separate the motor shaft and the throttle control rocker arm when it is powered off, so that the throttle is controlled by the motor and the secondary clutch, achieving reliable operation.

Ⅲ. CCS control process

CCS generally adopts closed-loop control mode for control. The cruise control process is shown in Figure 3-3-6.

Ⅳ. Automobile electronic modulated suspension (EMS).

(Ⅰ) Composition of automobile EMS

1. Function of automobile EMS

The automobile EMS can: automatically adjust the body height, suspension stiffness and shock absorber damping when the road surface, speed and load of the vehicle change, improving the ride comfort. Damping refers to the phenomenon that the amplitude decreases correspondingly when the energy of vibrating objects or oscillating circuits decreases gradually.

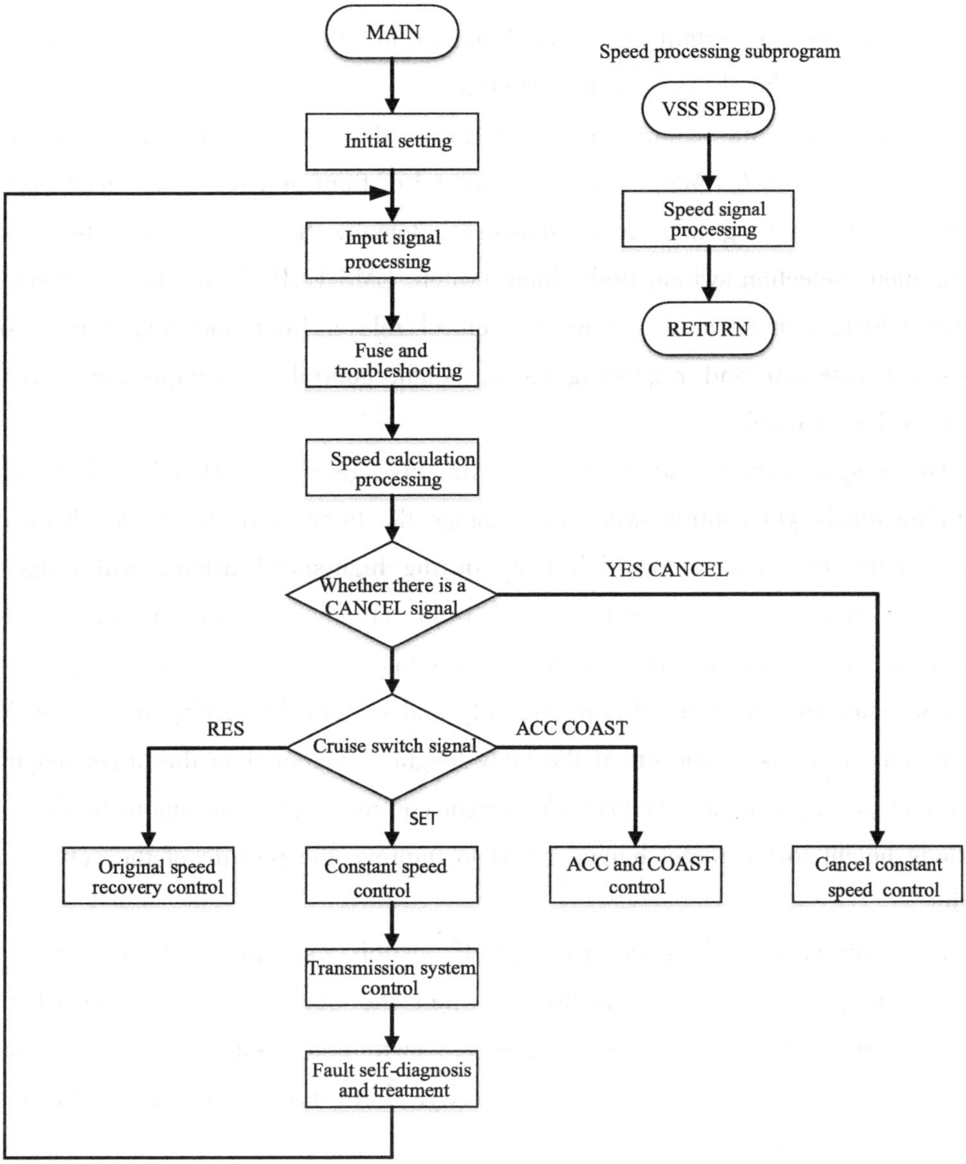

Figure 3-3-6 Cruise Control Process

2. Composition of automobile EMS

EMS mainly consists of front and rear body height sensors, steering wheel steering and angle sensors, throttle position sensor and speed sensor, control switch, EMS ECU and actuator. The body height sensor collects the height signals from the front and rear bodies; the steering wheel steering and angle sensor collects the driving direction signals; the throttle position sensor collects the driver's acceleration or deceleration signals; the vehicle speed sensor collects the driving speed signals; the sensor and control switch input the body and running status information to EMS ECU; the EMS actuator generates a certain mechanical action to change the body height, the air spring stiffness or the shock absorber damping.

The functions and components of EMS of different vehicles are different. As shown in Figure 3-3-7, EMS is mainly composed of front and rear body height sensors, steering wheel steering and angle sensors, automatic height control cut-off switch, driving mode selection switch, brake lamp switch, EMS ECU, front and rear suspension control actuators, front and rear height control relays, front and rear height control valves, air reservoir and regulating valve, height control air compressor, dryer and exhaust valve assembly.

The height control switch is set with two gears of "High" and "Normal". Operating the height control switch can change the target body height to "Normal" or "High" state. However, a too high body during high-speed driving will reduce the stability, so when the height control switch is in "High" gear and the speed reaches a certain value, the height control system can automatically reduce the body height to "Normal" state to ensure the driving stability and reduce the driving resistance. When the ignition switch is turned off, if the body height is higher than the target height due to the change of passengers or load, the height control system can automatically reduce the body height to the target height, so as to improve the posture of the vehicle when parking.

The automatic height control cut-off switch can turn off the air spring suspension system to prevent accidents when the body is too high or when the trailer is towed. The driving mode selection switch is used to select the working mode of shock absorber damping. Generally, there are "automatic", "hard" and "soft" working modes.

When the driver steps on the brake pedal, the brake lamp switch signal will be sent to the EMS ECU, which will control the front air spring stiffness and shock absorber damping to become "hard" state, so as to suppress the braking nose dive and minimize the change of vehicle attitude.

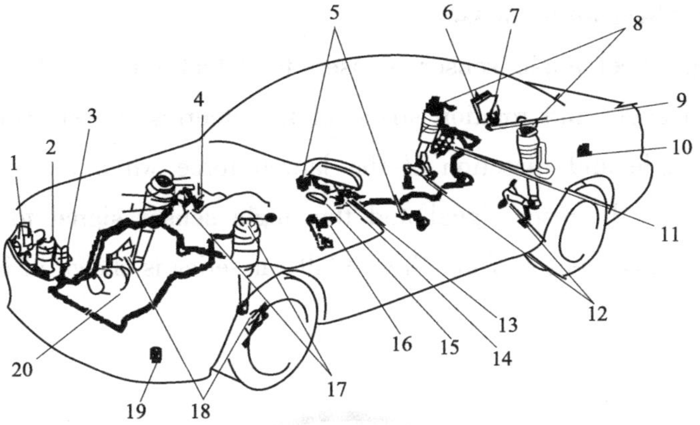

Figure 3-3-7 Composition of EMS

1–dryer and exhaust valve assembly; 2–height control air compressor; 3–No.1 height control valve; 4–main throttle position sensor; 5–door control switch; 6–EMS ECU; 7–No.2 height control relay; 8–rear suspension control actuator; 9–height control connector; 10–automatic height control cut-off switch; 11–No.2 height control valve and relief valve; 12–rear height sensor; 13–driving mode selection switch; 14–height control switch; 15–steering wheel steering and angle sensors; 16–brake lamp switch; 17–front suspension control actuator; 18–front height sensor; 19–No.1 height control relay; 20–air reservoir and regulating valve

3. Classification of electronic modulated suspension system (TEMS)

According to the different functions, the TEMS currently adopted mainly includes the following types:

(1) Body height electronic control system (i.e. electronic modulated variable height air spring suspension system);

(2) Electronic modulated variable stiffness air spring suspension system (i.e. suspension stiffness electronic control system);

(3) Electronic modulated variable damping shock absorber suspension system (i.e. suspension damping electronic control system);

(4) Electronic modulated variable height and variable stiffness air spring suspension system (i.e. suspension height and stiffness electronic control system)

(5) Electronic modulated variable height, variable stiffness air spring and variable damping shock absorber suspension system (i.e. suspension height, stiffness and damping electronic control system)

(Ⅱ) EMS sensors

The main EMS sensors include height sensor, steering wheel angle sensor, speed sensor, height control sensor, door control switch, etc.

1. Steering wheel angle sensor

The steering wheel angle sensor is used to detect the middle position, rotation direction, rotation angle and rotation speed of the steering wheel. The electronic unit judges the magnitude and direction of the lateral force when the vehicle is turning according to the speed sensor signal and the angle sensor signal to control the roll. The steering wheel angle sensor of the Great Wall car series is shown in Figure 3-3-8.

Figure 3-3-8 Steering Wheel Angle Sensor of Great Wall H6

There are a certain number of narrow grooves on the blanking disc pressed into the steering shaft. Both ends of the blanking disc are equipped with photoelectric elements, generally two LEDs and two phototriodes, forming two pairs of photocouplers (signal generators). When the steering wheel is turned, the steering shaft drives the blanking disc to rotate. When it is turned to the narrow groove, the phototriode will sense the light emitted by LED and output the "ON" signal; When the blanking disc is turned to other positions except for the narrow groove, the phototriode will output the "OFF" signal because it cannot sense the light emitted by LED. With the rotation of the steering wheel, the output terminals of the two photocouplers will form an "ON/OFF" conversion, as shown in Figure 3-3-9.

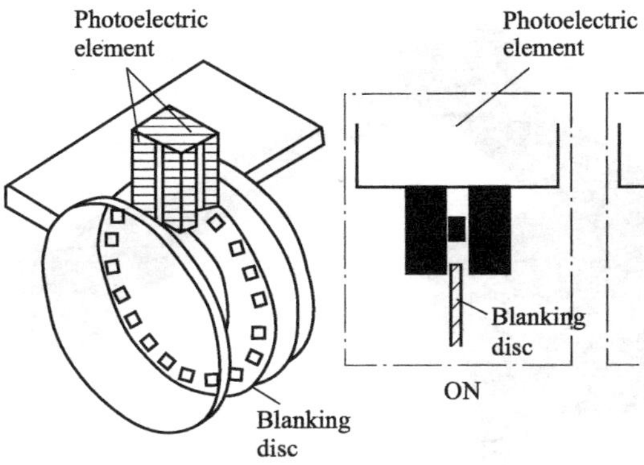

Figure 3-3-9 Working Principle of Photoelectric Steering Wheel Angle Sensor

2. Speed sensor

The speed sensor is usually used with the automatic transmission system. The rotor of the speed sensor is driven by the transmission output shaft through gears. For each revolution of the rotor shaft, the sensor generates 20 pulse signals and sends them to the combination instrument, which converts such signals into 4 pulse signals. The signals are sent to ECU for calculating the speed. Great wall H6 speed sensor is shown in Figure 3-3-10.

Figure 3-3-10 Great Wall H6 Speed Sensor

3. Height control sensor

The body height control sensor detects the change of the body height during driving. There are two common types: photoelectric and variable resistance, as shown in Figure 3-3-11.

Figure 3-3-11 Photoelectric Height Control Sensor

For general cars, there are four body height control sensors. The photoelectric sensor has a rotating shaft driven by a connecting rod, on which there is a disc with many narrow grooves. Four groups of photoelectric couplers are installed on both sides of the disk. When the body height changes, the connecting rod can drive the rotation of the rotating shaft, so the four groups of photocouplers can sense four groups of pulse signals. Through different combinations of the four groups of pulse signals, the body height range can be reflected, as shown in Figure 3-3-12.

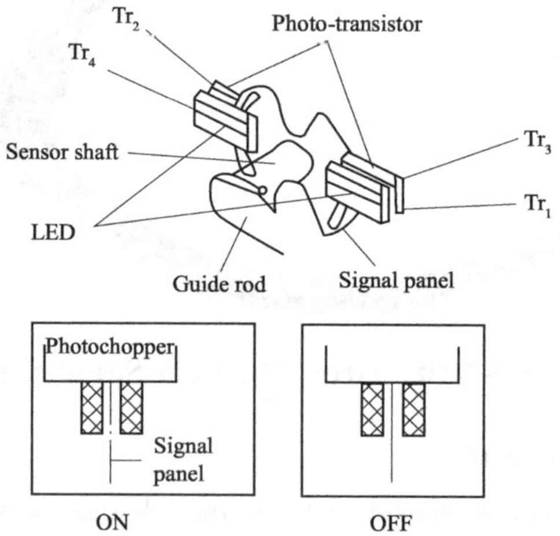

Figure 3-3-12 Working Principle of Photoelectric Height Control Sensor

4. Door control switch

The door control switch is used to detect whether the door is open. After the vehicle stops, the suspension system automatically controls the vehicle body to reduce the height. If ECU detects that the door is open at this time, the automatic height control must stop to avoid danger, as shown in Figure 3-3-13.

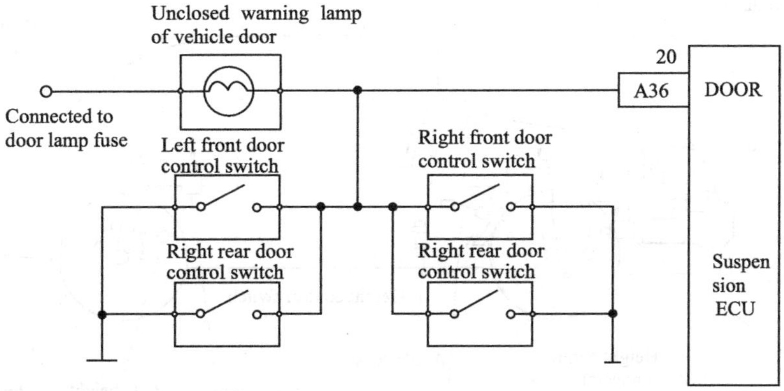

Figure 3-3-13 Door Control Switch Control Circuit

(Ⅲ) EMS control unit

The EMS control unit is referred to as suspension ECU or EMS ECU, which is mainly composed of central processing unit (CPU), random access memory (RAM), read only memory (ROM), input / output interface (I/O), analog/digital (A/D) converter, etc. Various sensors and actuators communicate with each other through I/O interface circuit. ROM stores various programs for calculating suspension control and data necessary for calculation. CPU processes the information according to the inherent program of the memory, and sends the control signals to actuators to control the operation of actuators, as shown in Figure 3-3-14.

(Ⅳ) EMS actuator

The control actuator is mainly composed of front suspension control actuator, generator voltage regulator, suspension control actuator, body height actuator, air compressor, etc., which mainly affect the height, stiffness and other parameters of EMS, as shown in Figure 3-3-15.

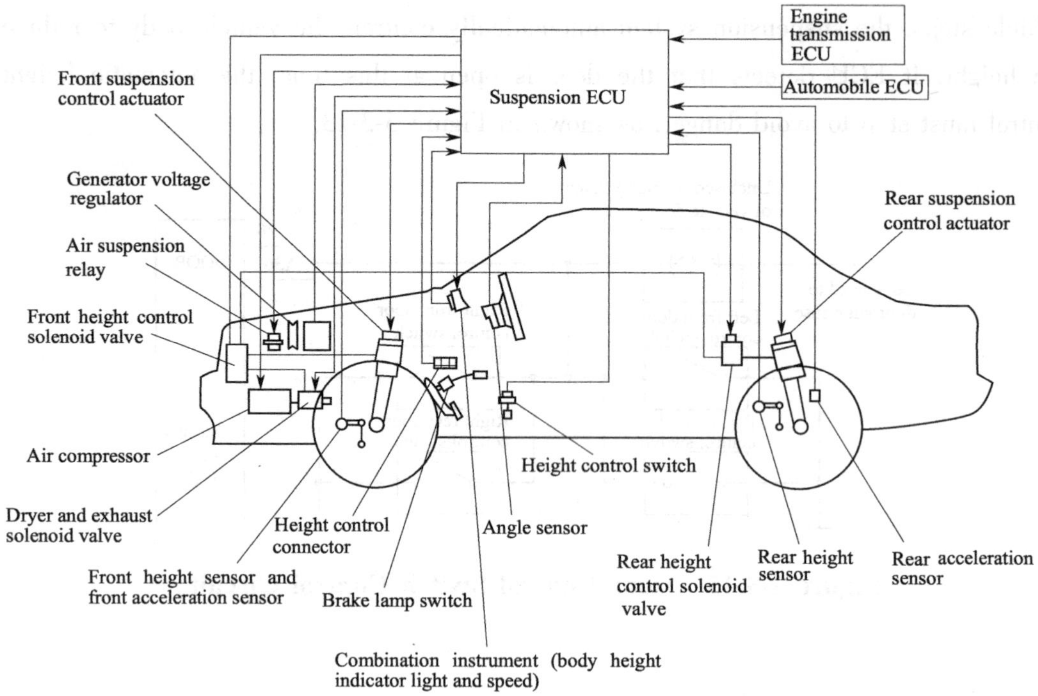

Figure 3-3-14 Composition of EMS

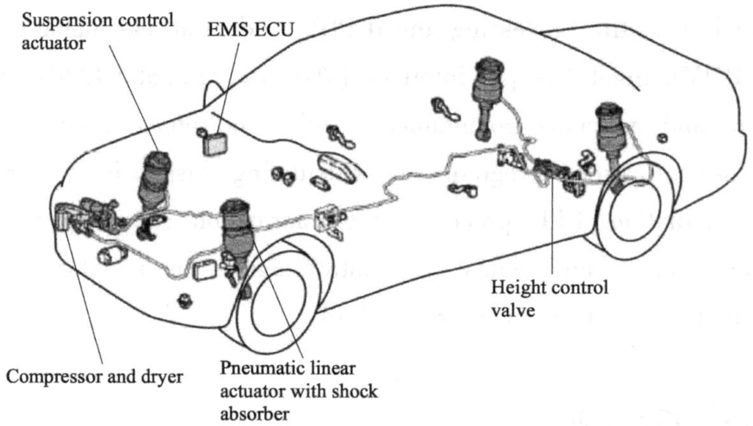

Figure 3-3-15 EMS Actuator

【Knowledge Development】

Brief Introduction of Autopilot System

"Great Wall car is expected to achieve Level 5 automatic driving by 2025," said Wang Fengying, President of Great Wall Motor. Due to the rapid technical development, in case of visualizing the Level 5 automatic driving in the concept, the car is a means of transportation with human perception, decision-making and control. Strictly speaking, to realize an autopilot system, it needs to be divided into perception layer, information fusion layer, decision-making and planning layer and control layer.

1. Perception layer

Automobile perception is similar to human eyes capturing things, while autonomous vehicles need to use sensors to sense things, as shown in Figure 3-3-16. To drive safely, autonomous vehicle needs to understand the surrounding driving environment through the sensors. At present, the main sensors carried by autonomous vehicle include cameras, laser radar, millimeter wave radar and ultrasonic radar, as shown in Table 3-3-1.

Figure 3-3-16 Automatic Driving Perception Layer

Currently, CMOS image sensors are widely used in cameras to capture clear images and help autonomous vehicle input data parameters. Many autonomous vehicles in the market use 3-6 cameras to ensure data integrity. Such cameras are extremely sensitive to light. If there is strong or weak light, the images captured by ordinary cameras cannot be directly used or unrecognized, which is extremely fatal to autonomous vehicles. Therefore, autonomous vehicles in the market generally adopt image sensors with a dynamic range of more than 130 dB.

Table 3-3-1 Comparison of Advantages and Disadvantages of Four Sensors

Performance	Sensor			
	Camera sensor	Laser radar sensor	Millimeter wave radar sensor	Ultrasonic radar sensor
Distance	6-50 m	100-200 m	> 200 m	0.1-3 m

Continued

Performance	Sensor			
	Camera sensor	Laser radar sensor	Millimeter wave radar sensor	Ultrasonic radar sensor
Advantages	Low cost, panoramic parking: ability to identify the shape of obstacles (size, distance and category)	High ranging accuracy, clear directionality, fast response speed, and real-time building of three-dimensional model for surrounding environment	Long detection distance, not affected by weather	Strong penetration, low cost and convenient testing
Disadvantages	High light requirements, unable to accurately measure distance	High cost, easily affected by the weather	Weak pedestrian reflection wave, difficult to identify	Small test angle, needing to install more than one

The radar mainly measures three parameters, namely, position, speed and azimuth. Laser radar is a new star in the automobile industry and is also regarded as one of the most core sensors in the future of autonomous vehicles. It mainly calculates the distance between the target and the vehicle according to the time of flight (TOF) after the laser encounters the obstacle by sending the linear laser beam (non radio wave), as shown in Figure 3-3-17. Laser radar is unique in accuracy, information volume and safety performance, but number of the laser radar beam needs to be increased to obtain more accurate measurement data. At present, 8, 16 and 32 lines of laser radar products are common in the market, and 64 lines are relatively few, which is also positively related to the cost (the more the laser beam is, the higher the cost will be). Although domestic and foreign technology companies such as Velodyne and Quangery, etc. have been developing low-cost and small-size laser radar, it is difficult to achieve mass production due to the high cost.

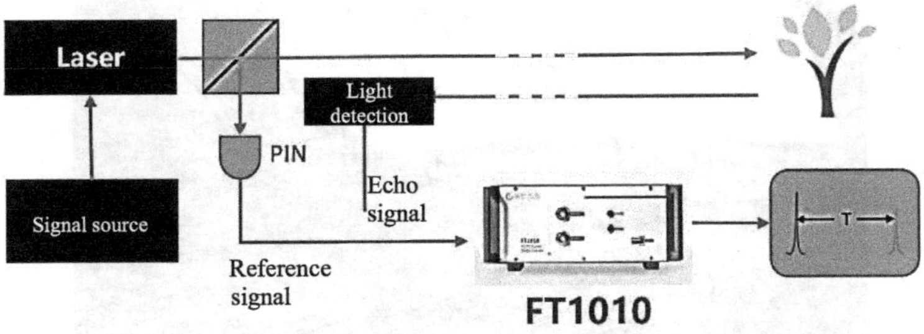

Figure 3-3-17 Working Principle of Radar

Millimeter wave radar, as its name implies, is a detection radar operating in the millimeter wave band (wavelength: 1-10 mm, frequency: 30-300 GHz). Different from the emitting mode of laser radar, millimeter wave radar can emit cone-shaped electromagnetic wave. Its working principle is to calculate the distance according to the echo time difference. It cannot be affected by weather conditions and achieve ultra far ranging, and the radar frequency band is positively correlated with ranging. Now, there are two kinds of main radars in the market: 24 GHz and 77 GHz. With the technical level improvement and the cost reduction, this sensor is gradually applied to ADAS.

Just as bats emit ultrasonic waves to detect the distance of objects, autonomous vehicles also use ultrasonic waves to find obstacles. Ultrasonic wave is a kind of mechanical waves, which is easily affected by propagation media, such as different weather and different propagation speeds, etc. Therefore, in order to make full use of the advantages of ultrasonic radar, such as strong penetration, convenient distance measurement and low cost, some automobile enterprises put a large number of ultrasonic radars around the vehicle body. For example, the number of ultrasonic radars used in L2-L3 Tesla, Audi and other cars is as high as 12.

2. Information fusion layer.

The information fusion layer is quite critical. Autonomous vehicles are equipped with multiple sensors such as cameras, laser radars and millimeter wave radars, through which we can sense and capture data. When the vehicle travels to a certain distance from the target, and the camera and the laser radar detect the target, it is necessary to analyze and compare the multi-sensor data to obtain the same target detected by the two sensors. If they are the same, information fusion will be carried out to tell the vehicle that there is a target in front of it, as shown in Figure 3-3-18

Figure 3-3-18 Automatic Driving Information Fusion Layer

Information fusion is a process of data processing, and when the data size is large, the time delay of the information fusion will be prolonged. It should be noted that if the vehicle is moving forward and the target in front is stationary, the distance traveled by the vehicle in the detection time from the sending of the detection wave to the return of the detection wave is not included in the actual distance. Therefore, when calculating the time delay, it is necessary to consider the speed in the process of time delay and the time difference between the system sending and receiving the test data.

In addition, the emitting frequency will also be affected by the environment. For example, in high and low temperature environment, the processing performance may be diffcrent. Different frequencies will also lead to different time delays, so in the calculation process, there will be certain errors when using the initial (rated) frequency to calculate the time delay. For autonomous vehicles, time means safety. If the calculation result is wrong, even 1 s, it will produce fatal results for vehicles running at high speed.

3. Decision-making and planning layer.

The decision-making and planning layer (Figure 3-3-19) is to make task planning and decision-making according to the driving demand based on the fused data. There are many views in the industry on this point. Here, only two macro views are introduced.

(1) Global planning; This method needs to use map information to select the best route according to the needs of passengers.

(2) Local planning; The autonomous vehicle is required to plan the optimal route according to the global planning and local environmental information.

This concept is equivalent to a framework, which requires that the autonomous vehicle plans their routes in advance based on big data. This is also one of the important indicators to judge the intelligence of autopilot system.

Figure 3-3-19 Automatic Driving Decision-making and Planning Layer

4. Control layer.

The control layer (Figure 3-3-20) of the autonomous vehicle is to replace human operation, and implement the decision-making and planning based on the information and data obtained, that is, real-time operation. This requires the control system to cooperate with the decision-making system, and enable the vehicle to correctly accelerate, decelerate, brake, turn, change lanes and overtake according to the requirements, as shown in Figure 3-3-20.

Figure 3-3-20 Automatic Driving Control Layer

It can be seen that the perception layer, information fusion layer, decision-making and planning layer mentioned above are all the basis for the control layer, which can ultimately make actions.

5. Conclusion.

In fact, automatic driving is to reflect the process of manual driving with hardware and software technology, and replace human or achieve the completely automatic driving in some processes. For the driver, the cooperation between the body and the car is very natural in the driving process of driving. The same is true for automatic driving, except that all its information acquisition and judgment are not through the eyes and brain, but through the "eyes" and "brain" of the car itself, which liberates the driver.

The concept of automatic driving is easy to understand, but it is difficult to realize. As Wei Dong, President of the AutoNavi Business Department, said, it must be step by step from ordinary navigation to semi-automatic auxiliary driving, to higher automatic auxiliary driving, and then to automation and full automatic driving.

【Thinking and Practice】

1. What are the main components of the cruise control system?

2. Briefly describe the functions of various components of the cruise control system.

3. What are the classifications of air bag restraint systems?

4. What are the main components of the automobile EMS?

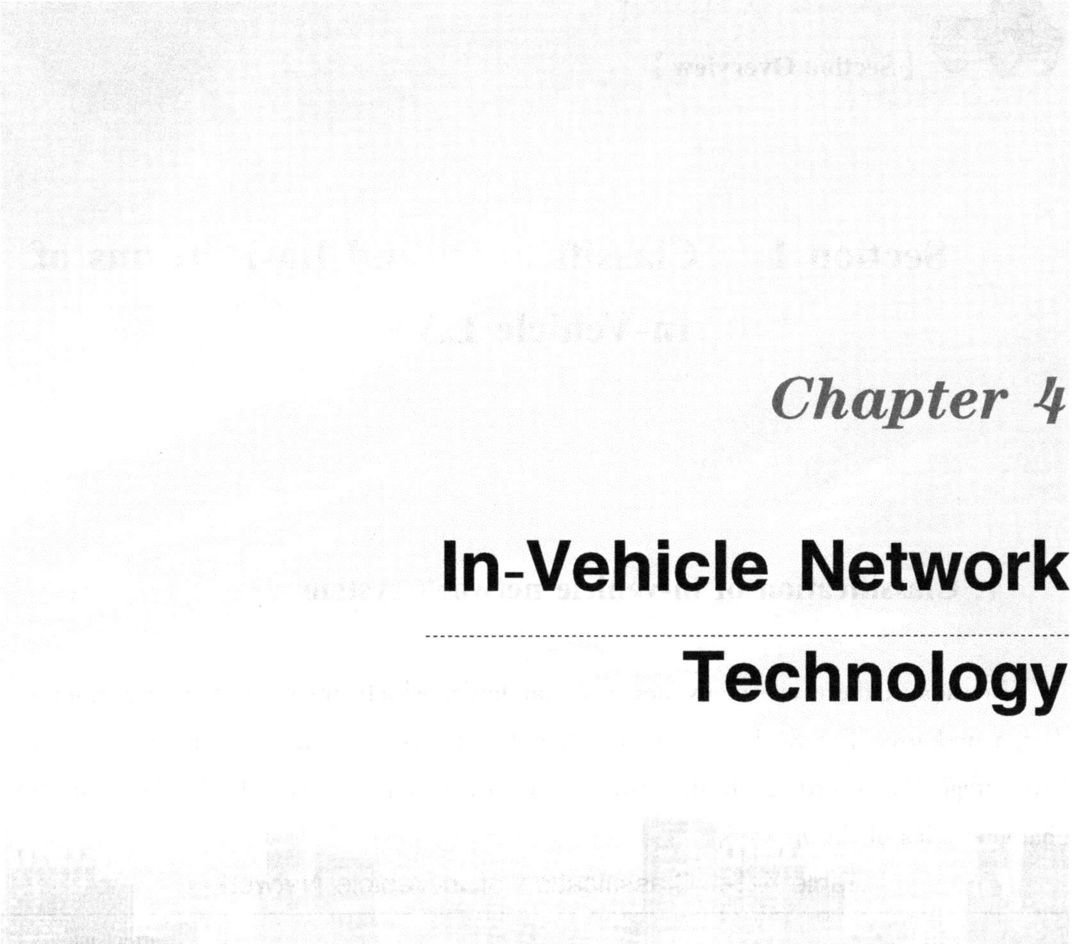

Chapter 4

In-Vehicle Network Technology

【Section Overview】

Section 1 Classification and Basic Terms of In-Vehicle LAN

Ⅰ. Classification of in-vehicle network system

Nowadays, there are many network standards, which are convenient for research, design and use. The Society of Automotive Engineers classifies vehicle networks into five categories according to the rate: A, B, C, D and E. See Table 4-1-1 for the characteristics of the networks

Table 4-1-1 Classification of In-Vehicle Network

Category	Rate	Application scope	Current main networks
A	1-10 kbit/s	For sensors and actuators, mainly used for controlling the power doors and windows, seat adjustment, lighting, etc.	TIP/A、I/LIN
B	10-100 kbit/s	For data sharing among independent modules, mainly used in vehicle information center, fault diagnosis, instrument display and other systems	Low-speed CAN J1850
C	125 kbit/s-1 Mbit/s	For real-time control, mainly used for systems related to vehicle safety and with high real-time requirements, such as power system	High-speed CAN、TIP/C、FlexRay

Continued

Category	Rate	Application scope	Current main networks
D	250 kbit/s-400 Mbit/s	For multimedia and navigation systems, mainly used for the vehicle network of entertainment and multimedia information exchange	MOST
E	10 Mbit/s	For passenger safety system, mainly used in the field of vehicle passive safety	Byteflight

At present, most passenger vehicles use four types of networks (A, B, C and D) for the communication. A relatively mature multi-network vehicle-carried communication system has been built, as shown in Figure 4-1-1.

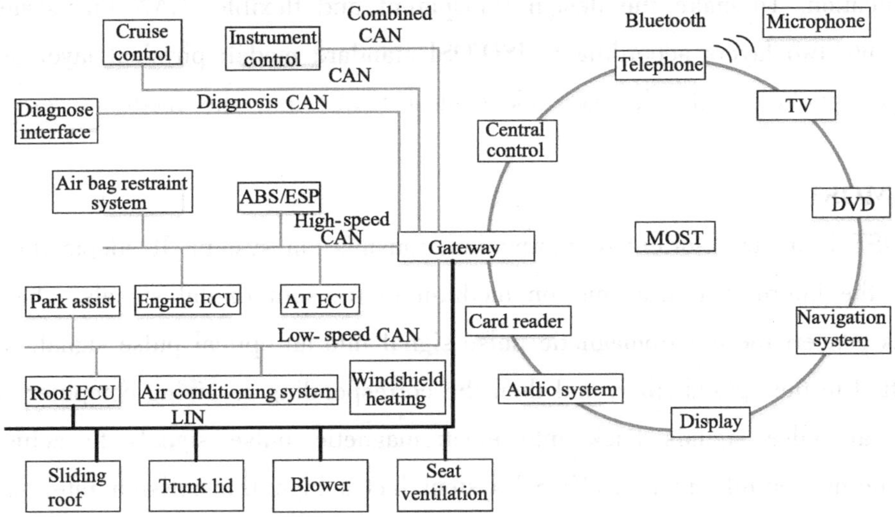

Figure 4-1-1 Schematic Diagram of In-vehicle Network System

1. LIN

LIN (Local Interconnect Network) is a kind of low-cost serial communication network, which is used to realize the distributed electronic system control for the automobiles. LIN is to provide auxiliary functions for existing automobile networks, so LIN bus is a kind of auxiliary bus network. In the occasions where the bandwidth and multifunction of CAN bus are not required, for example, in case of communication between intelligent sensors and braking devices, LIN bus can greatly save the cost.

LIN communication, based on SCI (UART) data format, adopts the mode of single master controller/multiple slave devices. Only one piece of 12 V signal bus and one node synchronization clock line without a fixed time reference are used.

This low-cost serial communication mode is to reduce the cost for automobile manufacturers and suppliers in developing and applying operating systems. It is mainly used for the information transmission that does not have high requirements for network bandwidth, performance or fault-tolerant function.

2. CAN

CAN (Controller Area Network, CAN) was developed by BOSCH, which is famous for R&D and production of automobile electronic products, and finally became an international standard (ISO 11898). It is one of the most widely used field buses in the world. CAN belongs to bus-based serial communication network. Due to the adoption of many new technologies and unique design ideas, compared with similar products, CAN bus has the advantages of reliability, real time and flexibility in data communication. To make the design transparent and flexible, CAN bus structure is divided into two layers according to ISO/OSI standard model: physical layer and data link layer (including the logical link control (LLC) and the media access control (MAC).

3. MOST

MOST is a media-oriented information transmission system. It adopts the optical fiber as the information transmission medium to transmit digital signals. The control elements convert the electromagnetic pulse signal into an optical pulse signal, which is transmitted to the optical fiber, and then the corresponding receiving computer converts the optical pulse signals back into electromagnetic pulse signals to achieve the corresponding control function. MOST system has a high transmission rate, so it can transmit multiple signals at the same time with only two optical fibers. However, MOST is facing elimination due to the rapid development of intelligent vehicles, the wide application of Ethernet in high-speed transmission of large data size, and the incomparable interoperability of Ethernet in multi equipment and multi fields.

Ⅱ. Basic terms of in-vehicle network

There are many special terms in the in-vehicle network. To better understand the in-vehicle network technology, some common terms are introduced below.

1. Frame

The physical memory is divided into fixed-size blocks, called frames. A "frame"consists of two parts: frame header and frame data. The frame header includes the location of the physical address of the receiving host and other network information. The frame data area contains a datagram. To ensure that the computer can interpret the data in the data frame, the two computers use a common communication protocol.

2. CAN data frame

CAN data frame is the protocol data unit of data link layer, which can control the physical link between adjacent systems, and ensure the reliable data communication between adjacent nodes on the basis of transmitting "bit" information. To ensure the reliable data transmission, the user data is encapsulated into frames. The ordered bit fields necessary to constitute the CAN protocol frame for data transmission start with the start of frame (SOF) and end with the end of frame (EOF).

3. Standard frame

The arbitration field of the standard frame is continuous 11 bits, and 2^{11} types of messages can appear, that is, the range of the frame ID is 000-7FF.

4. Extended frame

The arbitration field of the standard frame is continuous 29 bits, and 2^{29} types of messages can appear. There is a gap on the data link (transparent to the operator). The range of frame ID is 0000 0000-1FFF FFFF.

5. Packet

A single message is divided into multiple data blocks, which are called packets. The packet contains the address information of the sender and receiver. These packets are then transmitted in one or more networks along different paths and recombined at the destination. A single CAN data frame is a packet. When the data length of a message containing parameter groups is less than or equal to 8 bytes, such a message is also called a packet.

6. Address

The address is an 8-bit field, which is used to determine the message source (or destination).

7. Message

The message refers to one or more CAN data frames with the same PGN.

8. Bit stuffing

The bit stuffing refers to a handler used to ensure that messages are sent or received with a minimum number of dominant or recessive bit transitions to achieve correct synchronization of the bit stream in the CAN data frame.

9. Idle state

The idle state refers to the CAN bus state when no node transmits or attempts to transmit data.

10. Preferred address

The preferred address refers to the address that ECU first attempts to use when declaring the address.

Section 2 Mechanism and Principle of Automobile Multiplex Transmission System

Automobile network multiplex transmission system is a kind of technical circuit or device which can transmit multiple signals in the same channel at the same time without mutual interference. Multiplex transmission is wired or wireless transmission of many information at the same time, such as data information. Multiplex transmission technology makes the current automobile network control possible, and the use of multiplex transmission technology can save a lot of electrical equipment. Wires and connectors to reduce mass, save space, and improve reliability.

Ⅰ. Technical characteristics of multiplex transmission system (SWS)

(1) The module has become a digital equipment with the central processing unit as the core. They are connected to each other by bus topology through transmission

media (twisted pair, coaxial cable or optical fiber). The bus controller of the multiplex transmission system can access data from multiple operating stations, sensors and actuators on the bus.

(2) It has the advantages of high reliability, good stability, strong anti-interference ability, fast communication rate, system safety, low cost and low maintenance cost.

(3) The transfer rate of a data bus is usually expressed in terms of the bit rate, which is either kilobits per second (kbit/s) or megabits per second (Mbit/s). The data transfer rate is affected by the bandwidth, and 32 bit data transfer is four times faster than 8 bit data transfer.

(4) Interoperability. On the premise of abiding by the same communication protocol, field equipment products from different manufacturers can be configured to form the required network.

(5) Open interconnection structure. Which can be connected with the same layer network, and can also be connected with the control level network or management information level network through network interconnection equipment.

Ⅱ. Composition of multiplex transmission system

The multiplex transmission system is mainly composed of modules, data bus, network architecture, communication protocol and gateway, as shown in Figure 4-2-1.

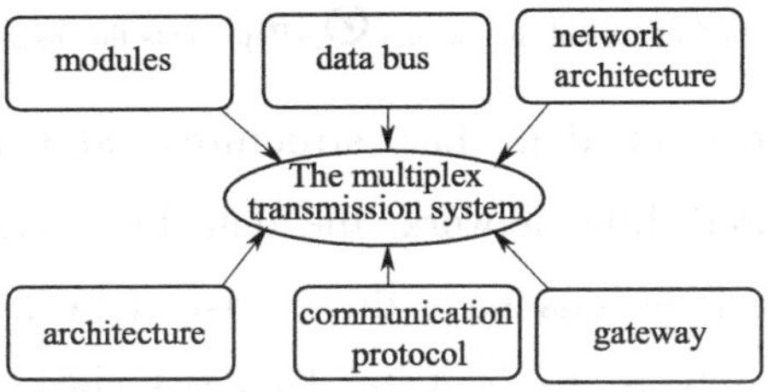

Figure 4-2-1 Multiplex System Topology

1. Module

A module is an electronic device. A simple one, such as temperature and pressure sensors, or a complex one, such as a computer (central processing unit). Sensor is a modular device that generates different voltage signals according to temperature and pressure. These voltage signals are converted into digital signals at the input interface of the computer (a digital device). Some simple modules in the computer multiplexing system are also called nodes, as shown in Figure 4-2-2 and

Figure 4-2-3.

Figure 4-2-2 Central Processing Unit

Figure 4-2-3 Sensor

2. Data bus

Data bus is a digital, bidirectional and multi-branch communication network connecting intelligent field devices and automation systems. It is a channel for operating data between modules. Its key sign is that it can support bidirectional multi-node, bus-type full digital communication. If the module can send and receive data, such a data bus is called bidirectional data bus. The data bus is shown in Figure 4-2-4.

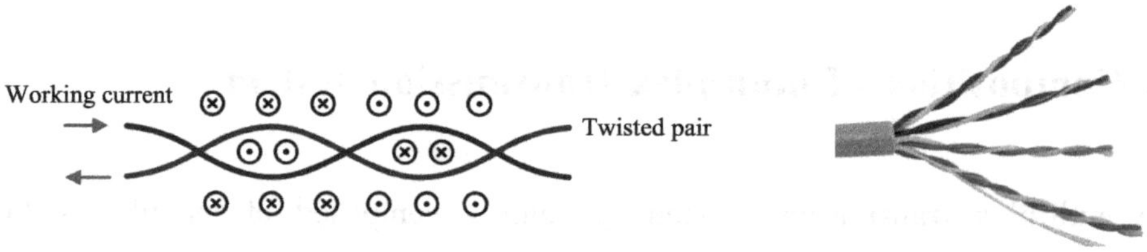

Figure 4-2-4 Schematic Diagram of Twisted Pair

⊙ –Represents the magnetic line of force our of the paper; ⊗ –Represents the magnetic line of force through the paper

There are many types of data bus structures, and different structures have different prices. In the automobile network, the data bus must avoid unnecessary high speed and complexity. Most designs have three basic types: low speed type、medium speed type and high speed type. Table 4-2-1 lists the class classification of multiplex transmission system recommended by the society of automotive engineers (SAE).

Table 4-2-1 Classification of SAE Recommended Automobile Multiplex Communication System

System level	Signal types	Response speed/ms
A	Body control system: lamps, relays, electric doors and Windows, electric seats	20-50(low speed)
B	Dynamic information system: navigation, telephone, fault diagnosis	5-50(middle speed)

Continued

System level	Signal types	Response speed/ms
C	Real-time control system: engine, drive system, brake system, suspension control system	1-5(high speed)

3. Network

The network is to connect multiple data buses together for information sharing, or to regard the data buses and modules as a system. The new LS430 has 29 modules for exchanging information among several data buses, as shown in Figure 4-2-5. Several data buses connect 29 modules, and the buses are connected to the local area network, including 3 junction box computer(Two as front end modules, one as back end module), which is used to provide diagnostic support (including easy to plug connectors and test points). In a physical sense, many modules and data buses on the car are in close proximity, so it is called a local area network (LAN). A smart body auxiliary device network designed by MOTOROLA is called local interconnect network(LIN)。

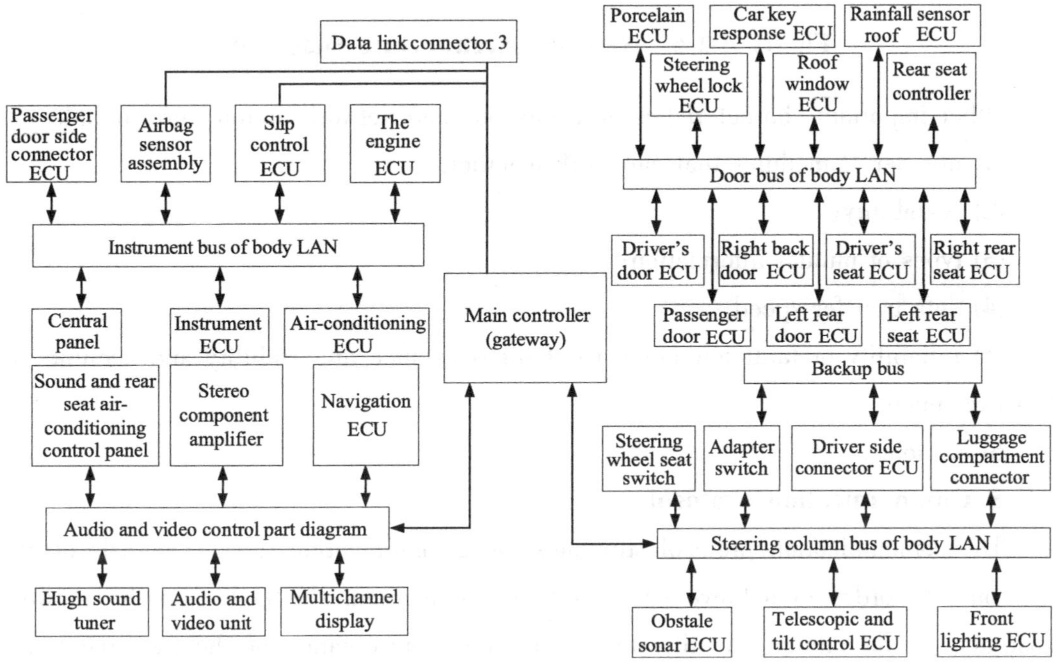

Figure 4-2-5 Multiplex Network

4. Architecture

An architecture is a configuration of an information highway with inputs and outputs that specify what information can come in and what information can come out, as shown in Figure 4-2-6. An architecture typically consists of one or two wires, with two wires where the transfer of data is based on the voltage difference between the two wires. When one of the wires is transferring data, it has a reference voltage to ground. The architecture requires a specific communication protocol.

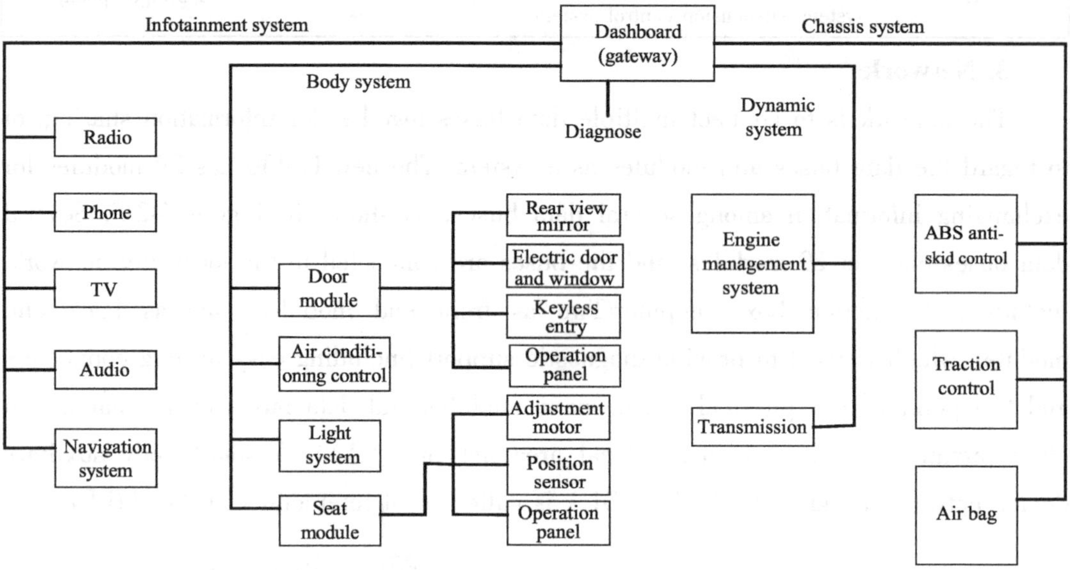

Figure 4-2-6 Network Architecture Diagram

Other important characteristics of a data bus and network architecture include:

(1) number of modules that can work together;

(2) scalability;

(3) types of mutual information;

(4) data transfer speed;

(5) reliability or fault tolerance, i.e. fault resistance and stability and accuracy of data exchange;

6) economy.

5. Communication protocol

The communication protocol stipulates the communication rules of signals on the data bus. In order to achieve successful communication, the nodes on the network must accept the mutual identification and mutual acceptance of the agreement and rules, and establish a common standard for communication between ECUs.

Communication protocols are classified as follows.

(1) Direct type: point-to-point link direct communication, without intermediate information processing protocol.

(2) Indirect type: a communication protocol for information exchange through a

switched communication network or two or more networks.

(3) Structure-optimized protocols: as needed, they are divided into different layers, lower-level functions are implemented at lower layers, and they provide services to higher-level entities. It is a composite of protocols at different layers.

6. Gateway

Usually a vehicle is equipped with multiple buses and networks, so a way must be found to share them and not cause conflicts between the protocols. For example, the engine control module needs to wake up when the door of the vehicle is opened. In order to achieve error-free data transmission between data buses of different protocols and speeds, a computer with special functions must be used. This computer is called a gateway.

1) The role of the gateway

The gateway is actually a module, whose quality, function and performance determine the quality of communication between different buses, modules and networks. For incompatible buses and networks that need to communicate with each other, the gateway plays the role of a bridge. If information can not be transmitted, it is not necessarily a problem of the gateway, but maybe failure of communication link equipment such as, modules. In short, the role of the "gateway" in the new automobile network control system is as follows:

(1) it can transform the data on the LAN into OBDII diagnostic data language that can be recognized, so as to facilitate diagnosis;

(2) it can realize the information sharing of low speed network and high speed network;

(3) it is the same as the gateway in the computer, which is responsible for receiving and sending information;

(4) activate and monitor the working state of the local area network;

(5) synchronization of vehicle data is realized;

(6) translate the message identifier.

2) Arrangement of the gateway.

If the two CAN network actuators are two independent chips (Figure 4-2-7), and the central controller (single-chip microcomputer) is used as the gateway, then the CAN Chip is read and written by the gateway like a smart random memory. Once the information is received, the gateway executes the external reading operation of the CAN chip, and then executes the logic instruction of converting the information. Then execute the external write operation to program the CAN chip of the second network for transmission.

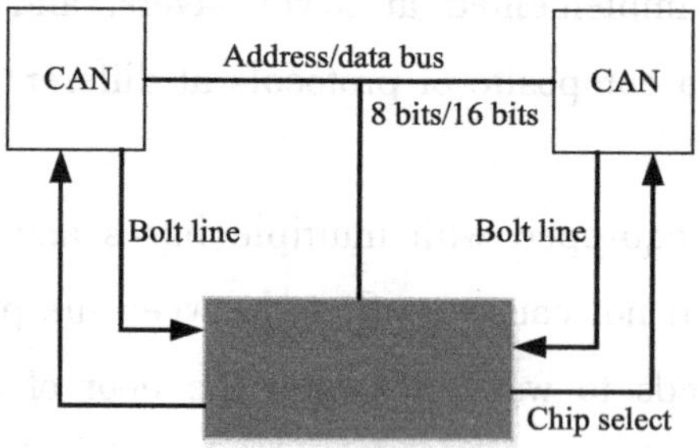

Figure 4-2-7 Schematic Layout of Gateway Hardware

Therefore, the gateway mainly performs external read/write operations and converts message identifiers, and the important technical condition for performing read/write operations is time, and the time required for reading and writing depends on the timing characteristics of the gateway and CAN chip interface.

3) Communication protocol standard of multiplex transmission system

To Solve the problems of system priority, flexibility, expansibility, diagnosis interface, independence and data sharing, several generations of communication protocols have been developed in the past decade, among which SAE standards based on serial bus such as SAE J1708, SAE J1587 and SAE J1922 were developed earlier. The transmission rate of serial protocol is low and the definition of code is troublesome. Except for some applications in diagnostic systems, it has been basically replaced. Up to now, the typical network standards for automotive applications are LIN, CAN, J1850, MOST, TTCAN, TTP, Flex Ray, J2284 and so on. The topology structure is mainly bus type, such as LINCAN, J1850, TTCAN. A plurality of ECU share one transmission line in that bus type network, the channel utilization rate is high, simple structure, easy wiring, easy to add nodes, each system has the same right to the bus, multi-master work mode, only one node can send messages at the same time, network extension distance, limited network nodes. ISO 7498 divides the network communication system into seven layers of structure, that is, the seven layer model of open system interconnection (OSI), including physical layer, data link layer, network layer. transport layer session layer, presentation layer, application layer (Figure 4-2-8). See Table 4-2-2 for the role of each layer. Automobile network protocols generally define only the bottom protocols in the OSI structure, that is, the physical layer and the data link layer.

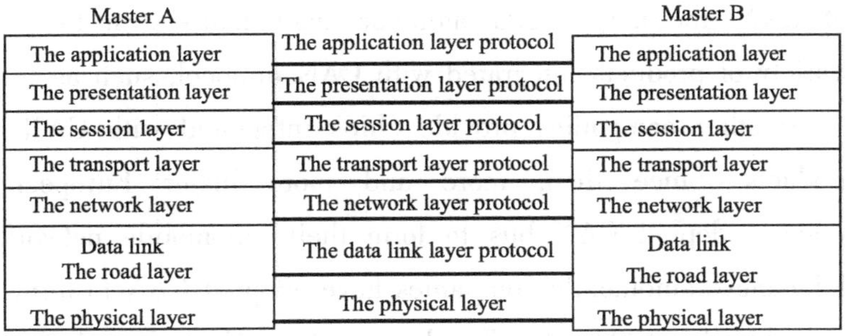

Figure 4-2-8 OSI Seven Layer Model as defined by ISO 7498

Table 4-2-2 Role of Layers in OSI Open Systems Interconnection Model

No.	Layar Name	Function
7	Application layer	The highest level, used for information exchange between users, software, network terminals, etc., such as DeviceNet
6	Presentation layer	Convert information from two systems using different data formats into a commonly understood format
5	Session layer	The data can be effectively transmitted by the communication function of the lower layer
4	Transport layer	Control of data transmission between two communication nodes, such as data retransmission and data error recovery
3	Network layer	Protocols that specify the establishment, maintenance, and teardown of network connections, such as routing and addressing
2	Data link layer	Defines the arrangement and organization of data bits transmitted on a medium, such as data checks and framing
1	Physical layer	Defines the physical properties of the communication medium, such as electrical characteristics and signal exchange

LIN bus is a typical class a network, issued by the LIN association, is a low-cost single-bus low-end network, also known as the economic CAN network. LIN is based on the widely used universal asynchronous receiver/transmitter (UART). Basic definition, physical layer is based on ISO 9141, generally used for vehicle body system with low transmission speed and low real-time requirement, adopts single master/multi-slave communication mode, network node is divided into master node and slave node, master node executes master control sending task, decides when and which frame will be transmitted on the bus, the length of information frame is variable, data length can be 2, 4 or 8 byte. At present, LIN protocol has been applied to a certain extent in the body system independently developed in our country.

CAN bus was proposed by German BOSCH company in the mid-1980s. After the introduction of CAN, the major semiconductor manufacturers in the world quickly introduced a variety of products integrated with CAN protocol, such as Intel, Motorola, NEC, Philips and other companies provide chips integrated with CAN protocol and CAN bus products. Since then, more and more major European automobile manufacturers have adopted CAN bus to form their automobile networks, and later American and Japanese automobile companies have adopted CAN to form their B-level or C-level networks. In 1994, the Truck and Bus Control and Communications Subcommittee of SAE in the United States selected CAN bus as the J1939 standard. (A foundation for high-speed networking standards for trucks and buses, with the addition of higher-level protocols). CAN is the only internationally standardized protocol that includes the high-speed ISO 11898 (Class C Net) and the low-speed ISO 11519 (Class B Net). CAN works in multi-master mode, any node on the network can actively send information to other nodes on the network at any time, regardless of master and slave, nodes on the network can be divided into different priorities according to different real-time requirements, when two nodes transmit information to the network at the same time, the node with low priority actively stops data transmission. While nodes with a higher priority can continue to transmit data without being affected. With the function of point-to-point, point-to-multipoint and global broadcast data transmission, the communication rate can reach 1 Mbit/s, the number of data bytes in each frame is 8, in the case of heavy errors, the node can automatically cut off its connection with the bus, so that other communications on the bus will not be affected. CAN Protocol defines two communication formats, i.e. standard information frame and extended information frame. Both of them have 7 bit fields. There is a difference in their arbitration fields. The identification code of the standard frame is 11 bits and that of the extended frame is 29 bits. CAN can use a variety of physical media, such as twisted pair, optical fiber, etc. The most commonly used is twisted pair, the signal is transmitted by differential voltage, and the two signal lines are called CAN H and CAN L. With the continuous reduction of the cost of CAN controller, a large number of products are available to support CAN-based systems. The cost of adopting the CAN control system is further reduced. Therefore, CAN is the most widely used automobile network at present.

There are usually two or three independent can buses in a vehicle. The high-speed CAN is used for engine and chassis control system, and the low-speed CAN is used for comfort systems such as sunroof, seat, air conditioner, etc. The high-speed

CAN And low-speed CAN constitute the whole vehicle network through the gateway. In some vehicles, the low-speed CAN is replaced by LIN network and connected to the CAN bus through the gateway. SAE J1850 bus was initially proposed by three major American automobile companies. It is mainly developed on the basis of Class 2 protocol of General Motors and SCP protocol of Ford, which belongs to the typical Class B network. This standard has been implemented for many years and has been widely accepted and adopted. Many American models adopt J1850, which is a relatively mature protocol. The current OBDI diagnostic system is defined in J1850. Due to the low communication rate. It is only suitable for body control system and diagnostic system. At present, it is gradually replaced by CAN in the United States.

MOST is a network protocol using optical fiber and used for intelligent transportation and multimedia, the transmission rate can reach 22 Mbit/s, TTCAN is based on time-triggered network, CAN bus and time-triggered mechanism of the combination. The main difference between it and CAN Protocol based on event triggering is that: different information on the bus defines different time slots. It avoids the uncertainty of information transmission time caused by bus arbitration, improves the real-time performance of CAN bus, and can meet the needs of increasing message transmission density. ISO 11898-4 defines the TTCAN protocol.

FlexRay is a flexible communication system that can meet the needs of advanced automotive high-speed control applications in the future, and can complement major network standards such as CAN, LIN and MOST. SAE2284 is a high-speed CAN network based on time-triggered, up to 500 kbit/s, mainly used in cars. Automobile network protocols include TTP/A, TTP/C, VAN, etc. Up to now, there is no protocol that can fully meet the cost and performance requirements of future automobiles, and the future automobile network will still have a variety of protocols. But at present, CAN or LIN is the best choice. See Table 4-2-3 for the basic information of the main in-vehicle network.

Table 4-2-3 Basic Information of Main In-Vehicle Network

Name of the in-vehicle network	Synopsis	Communication Speed
CAN	LAN protocol for body/powertrain legacy system control	1 Mbit/s
J1850	LAN protocol for body system control, US-centric	10.4 kbit/s
LIN	LAN protocol for body system control, dedicated to hydraulic component	20 kbit/s

Continued

Name of the in-vehicle network	Synopsis	Communication Speed
TTCAN	Safety, LAN protocol for control by application, CAN for time synchronization	1 Mbit/s
Byteflight	Secure, Control by Purpose LAN Protocol, general time division multiplexing	10 Mbit/s
FlexRay	Control LAN protocol with emphasis on security and classification by application	5 Mbit/s
MOST	Information systems communications protocol, Europe-centric	22.5 Mbit/s
IEEE 1394	Information system communication protocol	100 Mbit/s

【Knowledge Development】

Overhaul of Harvard H6 anti-theft system

1. Components and circuit diagram of Harvard H6 anti-theft system

Components of Harvard H6 anti-theft system are shown in Figure 4-2-9.

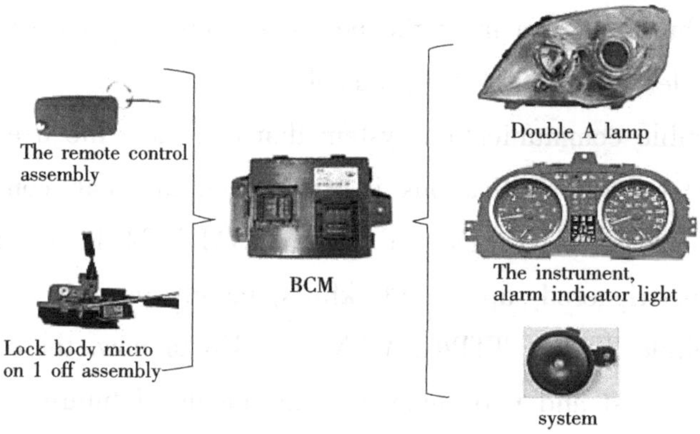

Figure 4-2-9 Composition of Harvard H6 Anti-theft system

Circuit diagram of Harvard H6 anti-theft system is shown in Figure 4-2-10.

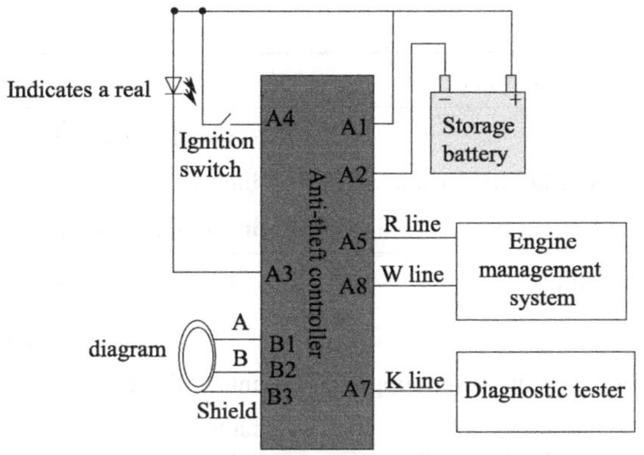

Figure 4-2-10 Circuit Diagram of Harvard H6 Anti-theft system

2. Common fault phenomena and fault Reason

Common fault phenomena and fault Reason are shown in Table 4-2-4.

Table 4-2-4 Common Fault Phenomena and Fault Reason

Common fault symptom	Possible cause of fault	Elimination method and idea
Key not detected	1. Key mismatch 2. Theft coil fault 3. Theft controller fault 4. Theft converter accessory error or damage	1. Read the data stream to see the key status 2. Troubleshoot the immobilizer coil 3. Troubleshoot the immobilizer 4. Troubleshoot the key
Immobilizer does not communicate with engine ECU	1. W line fault 2. Immobilizer power line and IG position fault 3. Engine ECU power line and IG position fault 4. Immobilizer fault 5. Engine ECU fault	1. Check whether the W-line is normal 2. Check the matching state of the immobilizer and the engine ECU 3. Check whether the power supply of the immobilizer and the engine ECU is normal 4. Rematch the immobilized immobilizer or engine ECU, and replace it if it can not be excluded

3. Meaning of common fault code

Meaning of common fault code are shown in Table 4-2-5.

Table 4-2-5 Meaning of Common Fault Code

Fault Code	Fault Name	Possible fault
B1000	Internal fault of anti-theft device	Check and consider replacing the immobilizer or immobilizer coil and connecting the wiring harness. This DTC does not normally exist on its own, eliminate other DTCs

Continued

Fault Code	Fault Name	Possible fault
B3040	Communication failure on line W	Check the harness connected to the immobilizer W wire and replace the immobilizer or engine ECU
B3042	W-line grounding	Check the immobilizer wire W for grounding
B3043	W line short circuit power supply	Check the connection harness of the immobilizer W wire and the ignition terminal, battery positive terminal pin
B3045	LED short to ground or open, LED is not working properly	Check the connection harness between led and immobilizer, and replace LED or immobilizer
B3048	LED short to power	Check the connection harness between LED and immobilizer, and replace the LED

【Thinking and Practice】

1. What are the components of the multiplex system?
2. How many layers are there in the network communication system? What are they?
3. What are the compositions of CAN data bus transmission system?
4. Briefly describe the data transmission process of CAN bus.

鲁班工坊汽车工程专业系列丛书

汽车电子控制系统构造与维修

石剑飞 主编

天津大学出版社
TIANJIN UNIVERSITY PRESS

图书在版编目（CIP）数据

汽车电子控制系统构造与维修：汉文、英文 / 石剑飞主编. -- 天津：天津大学出版社, 2022.6

（鲁班工坊汽车工程专业系列丛书）

ISBN 978-7-5618-7196-6

Ⅰ. ①汽… Ⅱ. ①石… Ⅲ. ①汽车－电子控制－控制系统－系统结构－职业教育－教材－汉、英②汽车－电子控制－控制系统－车辆修理－职业教育－教材－汉、英 Ⅳ. ①U472.41

中国版本图书馆CIP数据核字(2022)第088916号

组稿编辑　胡小捷
责任编辑　胡小捷
装帧设计　逸　凡

QICHE DIANZI KONGZHI XITONG GOUZAO YU WEIXIU

出版发行　天津大学出版社
地　　址　天津市卫津路92号天津大学内(邮编:300072)
电　　话　发行部:022-27403647
网　　址　www.tjupress.com.cn
印　　刷　北京盛通数码印刷有限公司
经　　销　全国各地新华书店
开　　本　787mm×1092mm　1/16
印　　张　20
字　　数　580千
版　　次　2022年6月第1版
印　　次　2022年6月第1次
定　　价　60.00元

前言

汽车的电子化、智能化、网络化是现代汽车发展的重要标志。随着消费者对汽车功能和性能要求的日益提高，汽车已经由机械系统向电子系统转换。在本书编写过程中，编者认真总结了全国交通职业院校多年来的专业教学经验，采用先进的职业教育理念和方法，积极推进课程改革和教材建设，力求为职业教育教学和培训提供更加丰富多样和实用的教材，更好地满足职业教育改革与发展的需求，并紧密结合目前汽车维修行业实际需求，参照相关行业岗位技能鉴定规范，供职业院校汽车维修类专业教学使用。

本书针对马达加斯加鲁班工坊项目编写，难易适度，图文并茂，深入浅出，通俗易懂。每个项目都是完整独立的教学模块，可根据学校实际情况和用人单位需求，合理、灵活地安排教学内容和进程。本书共四章，内容包括：汽车电子控制系统概述、汽车发动机电控系统、汽车底盘电控系统、车载网络技术。其特色可以概括如下。

（1）专业培养目标设计基本指导思想是以行业关键技术操作岗位和技术管理岗位的岗位能力要求为核心，确定专业知识的培养目标，并为毕业生在其职业生涯中能顺利进入汽车运用工程师行列奠定良好发展基础。

（2）在内容的选择上，注重汽车后市场职业岗位对人才的知识、能力要求，力求与相应的职业资格标准衔接，并较多地反映了新知识、新技术、新工艺、新方法、新材料的内容。

本书根据人才培养方案的要求，每一章节都以实际的维修项目作为课程的拓展学习，以提高学生和培训者在实际生产中的知识应用能力。本书适合于各类职业院校汽车运用技术、汽车电子技术、汽车检测与维修等相关专业使用，还可供汽车修理工、驾驶员、汽车行业工程技术人员阅读参考。

本书由天津市机电工艺技师学院石剑飞担任主编，天津市机电工艺技师学院刘焱超、李琦参与编写。

本书在编写过程中参阅了许多国内外公开出版与发表的文献，在此表示感谢。

限于编者经历及水平，内容难以覆盖各地的实际情况，也难免有不妥和错误之处，恳请读者提出宝贵意见和建议，以便再版修订时改正。

编者

目录

第1章

汽车电子控制系统概述

【章节概述】

中国式现代化的本质要求之一就是实现高质量发展，这也是全面建设社会主义现代化国家的首要任务。社会主义的现代化，离不开汽车产业的现代化。回望党的十八大以来的十年间，不断强大起来的中国现代汽车产业，在国民经济中的地位越来越重要，在国际上的影响力越来越大。

随着汽车工业与电子工业的不断发展，汽车电子技术在现代汽车上的应用越来越广泛。汽车上原有的机械控制装置逐渐被电子控制（简称电控）装置所取代，使汽车的性能、技术水平不断趋于完善。汽车电控系统是汽车的重要组成部分，其性能直接影响汽车的动力性、经济性、排放性、舒适性等。特别是大规模集成电路和微处理器的应用，使汽车对各工作过程的控制内容由传统的机械手段转变为电子控制手段，从而提高了控制精度，增加了控制内容。

汽车电子控制系统基本由传感器、电子控制器（ECU）、执行器和控制程序软件等部分组成，与车上的机械系统配合使用（通常与动力系统、底盘系统和车身系统中的子系统融合），并利用电缆或无线电波互相传输信息，即所谓的“机电整合”，如电子燃油喷射系统、制动防抱死系统、防滑控制系统、电子控制悬架系统、电子控制自动变速器、电子助力转向等。汽车电子控制系统大体可分为四个部分：发动机电子控制系统、底盘电子控制系统、车身电子控制系统、信息传递装置。

第 1 节　汽车电子技术的发展背景

一、汽车电子技术的发展历程

汽车电子技术顾名思义是现代汽车技术与电子技术的结合，涉及两个技术领域。汽车电子技术的出现是汽车发展过程中一次重要的革命性事件，并且成为衡量现代汽车发展水平的一个重要技术标志。纵观汽车技术发展史，汽车电子技术的发展主要有以下四个阶段。

第一阶段，从 20 世纪 50 年代初到 70 年代初，主要开发由分立元件和集成电路组成的汽车电子产品，代替传统机械部件，例如集成电路调节器、电子点火器等。电子

管收音机和晶体管收音机相继在汽车上安装，这是电子技术在汽车上应用的开始。

第二阶段，从 20 世纪 70 年代中期到 80 年代中期，主要发展专用独立系统，电子装置用于机械装置所无法解决的复杂控制功能方面，例如电子控制汽油喷射系统、巡航控制系统、制动防抱死系统（ABS）等。

第三阶段，从 20 世纪 80 年代中期到 90 年代中期，主要开发多种功能的综合系统及各种车辆的微机控制，汽车上的电子装置不仅能自动承担基本控制任务，而且能处理外部和内部的各种信息，例如集发动机控制与自动变速器控制为一体的动力传动控制、制动防抱死与防滑转控制等。

第四阶段，从 20 世纪 90 年代中期开始，主要研究车辆的智能控制技术，模拟人的思维和行为进行控制，例如汽车自动驾驶系统、汽车自动导航系统等。智能化集成传感器和智能执行机构也已付诸实用，数字式信号处理方式用于声音识别、安全碰撞、适时诊断、导航系统等。

二、汽车电子技术的应用现状

汽车电子技术经过较长时间的积累后，已经进入全面快速发展阶段，具有功能多样化、技术一体化的特征。目前，电子技术的应用几乎深入汽车的所有系统。按对汽车行驶性能作用的影响，可把汽车电子产品归纳为两类：一类是汽车电子控制装置；另一类是车载汽车电子装置。目前较多见的成熟的汽车电子控制系统主要有：发动机电子控制、底盘电子控制、车身电子控制、信息传递装置等。

（一）发动机电子控制

1. 电子控制喷油装置（EFI）

现代汽车上，机械式或机电混合式燃油喷射系统趋于淘汰，电控燃油喷射系统因其性能优越而得到普及。电控燃油喷射系统是 20 世纪 60 年代末开始发展起来的，与传统的化油器供油系统相比，其突出优点在于空燃比的控制更为精确，可实现最佳空燃比；且电喷技术提高了汽油的雾化、蒸发性能，提升了加速性能，发动机功率和转矩得以显著提高。这样能使发动机一直在最优工作条件下运行，并使发动机的综合性能得到提高。

2. 电子点火提前装置（ESA）

早在 20 世纪初，点火系统在汽车发动机上便已开始应用。如今，点火系统已从有触点式、普通无触点式、集成电路式发展到了微机控制电子点火系统。微机控制电子点火系统可控制并维持发动机点火提前角（ESA）在最佳范围以内，使汽油机的点火时刻更接近于理想状态，从而进一步挖掘发动机的潜能。微机控制电子点火系统中，目

前出现了一种无分电器点火系统（DLI）。它取消了普通微机控制点火系统中的分电器，改由 ECU 内部控制各缸配电。这样点火线圈产生的高压电，不需经过分电器分配，直接送到火花塞发生点火。无分电器点火系统可消除分火头与分电器盖边电极的火花放电现象，减少电磁干扰。

3. 怠速控制系统（ISC）

怠速性能的好坏是评价发动机性能优越与否的重要指标。怠速性能差将导致油耗增加、排污严重，因此需进行必要的控制。现代轿车中一般都有怠速控制系统，由 ECU 控制并维持发动机怠速在某一稳定范围内。怠速控制通常是指怠速转速控制，实质是对怠速工况时的进气量进行调节（同时配合喷油量及点火提前角的控制）。

目前，除了怠速转速的稳定性控制之外，怠速控制还可实现起动控制、暖机控制、负荷变化控制等功能，这样多种功能的集中，不仅简化了机构，而且也提高了怠速控制的精确性。

4. 其他控制系统

除此之外，发动机利用电子技术的内容还有废气再循环（EGR）、电动燃油泵、发电机输出、冷却风扇、发动机排量、节气门正时、二次空气喷射、发动机增压、油气蒸发、系统自我诊断功能等，它们在不同的车型上或多或少都有应用。

（二）底盘电子控制

1. 电控自动变速器（ECAT）

电控自动变速器可以根据发动机的载荷、转速、车速、制动器工作状态及驾驶员控制的参数，经过计算机的计算和判断后自动实现换挡，从而实现变速器换挡的最佳控制，即可得到最佳挡位和最佳换挡时间。其优点是加速性能好、灵敏度高、能准确反映行驶负荷和道路条件等。不仅能明显简化汽车操作，而且能实现最佳的行驶动力性和安全性。

2. 防抱死制动系统（ABS）

防抱死制动系统是一种开发时间长、推广应用迅速的重要的安全性部件。它可以通过控制汽车制动时车轮的抱死来保证车轮与地面达到最佳滑移率（15%~20%），而使汽车在各种路面上制动时，车轮与地面都能达到纵向的峰值附着系数和较大的侧向附着系数，以保证车辆制动时不发生抱死拖滑、失去转向能力等不安全工况，提高汽车的操纵稳定性和安全性，减少制动距离。驱动防滑系统（ASR）也叫牵引力控制系统（TCS 或 TRC），是 ABS 的完善和补充，它可以防止起动和加速时的驱动轮打滑，既有助于提高汽车加速时的牵引性能，又能提高操作稳定性。

3. 电子转向助力系统

电子转向助力系统是用一台直流（DC）电动机代替传统的液压助力缸，用蓄电池

和电动机提供动力的系统。这种微机控制的转向系统和传统的液压系统比起来具有部件少、体积小、重量轻的特点，其最优化的转向作用力和转向回正特性大大提高了汽车的转向能力和转向响应特性，提高了汽车低速行驶时的机动性以及高速行驶时的稳定性。

4. 自适应悬挂系统

自适应悬挂系统能根据悬挂装置的瞬时负荷，自动适时调节悬架弹簧的刚度和减震器的阻尼特性，适应当时的负荷，保持悬挂的既定高度。这样就能极大地改进车辆行驶的稳定性、可操作性、乘坐舒适性。

5. 自适应巡航控制系统（ACC）

自适应巡航控制系统是一种智能化的自动控制系统，是在早已存在的巡航控制技术的基础上发展而来的。在车辆行驶过程中，安装在车辆前部的车距传感器（雷达）持续扫描车辆前方道路，同时轮速传感器采集车速信号。当与前车之间的距离过小时，ACC 控制单元可以通过与防抱死制动系统、发动机控制系统协调动作，使车轮适当制动，并使发动机的输出功率下降，以使车辆与前方车辆始终保持安全距离。

（三）车身电子控制

1. 汽车空调控制

汽车空调控制是根据设置在车内外的各种温度传感器输出的信号，由 ECU 中的微机计算出经过空调热交换器后进入车内应该达到的出风温度。对混合气调节器开度、风扇驱动电动机转速、冷却器风门（或加热器风门）、压缩机等进行控制，自动将车内温度保持在设定的温度范围内，使车内的温度、湿度始终处于最佳值，为驾驶员和乘员提供舒适的乘坐环境。

2. 信息显示系统

信息显示系统正处于发展和完善阶段，由车况监测部件、车载计算机、电子仪表三部分组成。车况监测是传统机械式仪表板报警功能的改进和发展，通过液位、压力、温度、灯光等传感器监测发动机、制动系统、电源系统及车灯的故障。车载计算机提供的信息能提高行车安全性、燃油经济性、乘坐舒适性。电子仪表为驾驶员提供汽车行驶时最基本的操作信息，且这些信息连续在仪表板上显示。

3. 安全气囊控制系统

安全气囊控制系统是一种被动安全保护装置，由触发装置、气体发生器、气囊三部分组成。触发装置包括传感器、电子控制装置、储备电源、监控装置，由电子控制系统接收加速度传感器发出的信号，并进行分析，以判定是否发生碰撞事故。若发生了碰撞，则对气体发生器发出指令，迅速吹胀气囊，整个过程约需 0.03 s。触发装置中的监控装置可连续自我监控，确保整个气囊系统在任何时刻都处于准备工作状态。

4. 汽车电子灯光控制系统

汽车电子灯光控制系统可根据光传感器检测到的车外天气光亮情况的信号自动将后灯和前照灯接通或切断，以提高汽车使用的便利性和行驶的安全性。

（四）信息传递装置

1. 信息显示与报警

信息显示与报警系统可将发动机的工况和其他信息参数通过微机处理后输出对驾驶员有用的信息，并用数字、线条显示或声光报警。显示的信息除水温、油压、车速、发动机转速等常见参数外，还有瞬时耗油量、平均耗油量、平均车速、行驶里程、续驶里程、车外温度等。监视和报警的信息主要有：燃油温度、水温、油压、充电、尾灯、前照灯、排气温度、制动液量、手制动、车门未关严等。当出现不正常现象或自诊断系统测出有故障时，立即由声光报警。

2. 语音信息

语音信息系统包括语音警告和语音控制。语音警告是在汽车出现不正常情况（包括水温、水位、油位不正常，制动液不足，蓄电池充电值偏低等情况）时，电子控制单元经过逻辑判断，输出信息至扬声器，发出模拟人的声音向驾驶员报警，多数还能同时用灯光报警。语音控制是用驾驶员的声音来指挥和控制汽车的某个部件或设备进行动作。

3. 车用导航

车用导航系统可在城市或公路网范围内定向选择最佳行驶路线，并能在屏幕上显示地图，显示汽车行驶中的位置以及目的地的方向和距离。

三、现代汽车电子技术应用的发展趋势

20 世纪 90 年代，汽车电子技术进入了优化人 - 汽车 - 环境的整体关系的阶段，向着超微型磁体、超高效电机、集成电路的微型化方向发展，并为汽车上的集中控制提供基础（例如制动、转向、悬架的集中控制，以及发动机和变速器的集中控制）。汽车电子技术成就汽车工业的未来，未来汽车电子技术将有下列发展趋势。

（一）传感器技术

车用传感器的多样化和使用数量的增加，使得传感器朝着多功能化、集成化、智能化、微型化方向发展。未来的智能化集成传感器不仅能提供用于模拟和处理的信号，

而且能对信号做放大等处理；还能自动进行时漂、温漂、非线性的自校正，具有较强的抵抗外部电磁干扰的能力，保证传感器信号的质量不受影响，即使在特别严酷的使用条件下，仍能保持较高的精度；它还应有结构紧凑、安装方便的优点，从而免受机械特性的影响。现在汽车制造商为开发自动行驶汽车，正加紧研制各种传感器，包括车辆位置传感器、后方障碍物传感器、侧方障碍物传感器、前方障碍物传感器、车间距离传感器、路面传感器、防撞检测传感器、车速传感器、加速传感器、防火检测传感器、驾驶盘角度传感器、驾驶员状态传感器等。

（二）电子控制器（ECU）技术

将 ECU 应用到汽车发动机的控制系统之后，汽车电子控制系统进入新的高速发展阶段；随后 ECU 被应用到动力传动、车身、安全等控制系统中。由于车用 ECU 对可靠性、信息处理能力、实时控制能力及成本的特殊要求，基于通用芯片开发出的 ECU 已经很难满足汽车电子控制系统的要求，因此，开发多路同步实时控制、自带模 / 数（A/D）与数 / 模（D/A）转换器、自我诊断、高输入 / 输出等功能的汽车专用 ECU 系统具有很高的现实意义。随着控制日趋集中化，ECU 需要处理的信息量不断增加，因此，16 位和 32 位 ECU 将成为未来汽车用 ECU 的首选。预计今后几年需求量将增加 50% 以上，并逐步成为车用 ECU 的主流。

（三）执行器

目前，汽车上用的执行器主要有电磁式、电动式、气动 / 液动式执行器。电磁式和电动式的执行器是以电为动力的操作机构，具有体积小、重量轻、响应快、耗能小的特点，但输出驱动能力不足，无法满足未来汽车控制领域大驱动输出的需要。随着新材料、新工艺、新机构的采用，电磁式和电动式执行器将逐渐取代气动 / 液动执行器，尤其是在未来汽车普遍更换 42 V 新型电源系统之后，输出驱动能力将大幅度提升，完全可以取代传统的气动 / 液动系统。

（四）控制策略

目前，汽车电子控制系统中广泛采用的比例 - 积分 - 微分（PID）控制理论，是用于单输入 / 单输出、线性定常系统的经典控制理论。由于汽车中的控制对象往往具有很强的时变和非线性特点，控制的输入和输出参数越来越多，采用以状态空间为基础，用于多输入 / 多输出、非线性时变系统的现代控制理论已成必然，例如最优控制、自适应控制、模糊控制等。

（五）总线技术

利用总线技术将汽车中各种电子控制单元、智能传感器、智能仪表等连接起来，从而构成汽车内部局域网，实现各系统间的信息资源共享，其优点主要有：

（1）大大减少线束数量、连接点及体积，提高系统的可靠性和可维护性；

（2）采用通用传感器，达到数据信息共享的目的；

（3）改善系统的灵活性，即通过系统的软件实现系统功能的变化。

根据侧重功能的不同，美国汽车工程师学会（SAE）将总线划分为 A、B、C 三类。A 类是面向传感器和执行器的一种低速网络，主要用于后视镜调整、灯光照明控制、电动车窗控制等，目前 A 类的主流是 LIN。B 类是用于独立模块间的数据共享的中速网络，主要用于汽车舒适网络、故障诊断、仪表显示、四门中央控制等，目前 B 类的主流是低速 CAN。C 类是面向高速、实时闭环控制的多路传输网络，主要用于发动机、ABS 和自动变速器、安全气囊等的控制，目前 C 类的主流是高速 CAN。随着下一代高速、具有容错能力的时间触发方式“X-by-Wire”线控技术的发展，其将逐渐代替高速 CAN 在 C 类中的位置，力求在未来 5~10 年内使传统的汽车机械系统变成通过高速容错通信总线与高性能 CPU 相连的百分之百的电子控制系统，完全不需要后备机械系统的支持，其主要代表有 TTP/C 和 FlexRayo，而在多媒体与通信系统中，MOST、IDB-1394、蓝牙技术成为今后的发展主流。再者，光纤凭借其高传输速率和抗干扰能力，越来越广泛地被用作高速信号传输介质。

（六）安全技术

未来汽车电子控制的重要发展方向在汽车安全领域，主要有：

（1）利用雷达技术和车载摄像技术开发各种自动避撞系统；

（2）利用近红外技术开发各种能监测司机行为的安全系统；

（3）高性能的轮胎综合监测系统；

（4）自适应自动驾驶系统；

（5）驾驶员身份识别系统；

（6）安全气囊、ABS/ASR 和车身动态控制系统。

（七）多媒体娱乐与智能通信系统

随着第三代移动通信技术和计算机网络技术的发展，未来汽车正朝着移动办公室、家庭影院方向发展，为司机和乘客提供行进中的实时通信和娱乐信息，并把汽车和道路及其他远程服务系统结合起来，构建未来的智能交通系统（ITS）。其具体功能有：

（1）提供丰富的多媒体设施环境，利用全球定位系统（GPS）、全球移动通信系统（GSM）网络实现导航、行车指南、无线因特网以及汽车与家庭等外部环境的互动。

（2）具备远程汽车诊断功能，紧急时能够引导救援服务机构赶到故障或事故地点。

【思考与练习】

1. 汽车电子控制技术分为哪几个阶段？

2. 未来汽车电子控制技术的发展趋势是什么？

3. 目前汽车上现有的电子控制技术有哪些（至少说出五个）？

第 2 节　汽车电子控制技术的基础知识

一、发动机电控系统组成及各部分功能

（一）发动机电控系统简介

发动机电控系统，也称发动机管理系统（EMS）、发动机集中控制系统，就是将多项目控制集中在一个动力控制模块（PCM）或发动机控制单元（ECU）上完成，共用传感器，主要由传感器、ECU 和执行器组成。

（二）发动机电控系统组成

1. 传感器

传感器是一种信号采集装置，安装在汽车的各个部位，用于检测发动机运行参数，并转换成电信号输送至控制单元。传感器数量越多，检测越精确；执行器数量越多，功能越强。发动机电控系统的主要传感器及执行器如图 1-2-1 所示。

2. 电子控制单元（ECU）

电子控制单元（ECU），又称行车电脑、车载电脑等，从用途上讲是汽车专用微机

控制器，也叫汽车专用单片机。它和普通的单片机一样，由微处理器（CPU）、存储器（ROM、RAM）、输入/输出（I/O）接口、模/数（A/D）转换器以及整形、驱动等大规模集成电路组成。ECU 实物如图 1-2-2 所示。

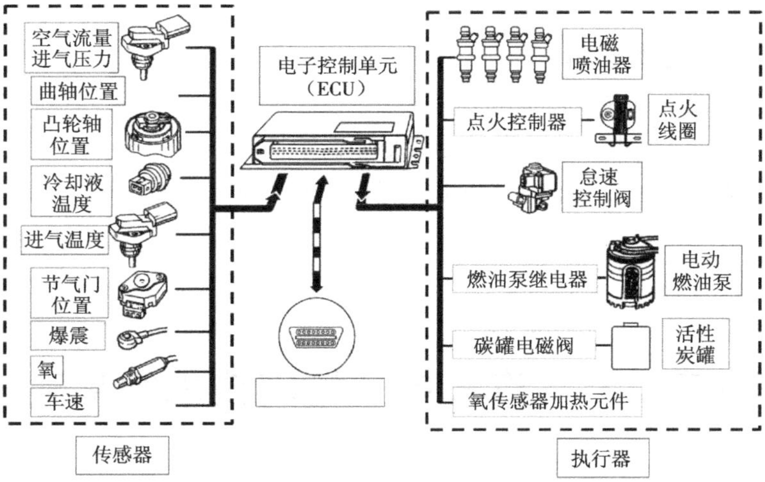

图 1-2-1　汽车发动机电控系统的主要传感器及执行器

图 1-2-2　哈弗 H6 发动机 ECU

ECU 的电压工作范围一般为 6.5~16 V（内部关键处有稳压装置）、工作电流在 0.015~0.1 A、工作温度在 -40~80 ℃。能承受 1 000 Hz 以下的振动，因此 ECU 损坏的概率非常小，在 ECU 中 CPU 是核心部分，具有运算与控制功能，发动机在运行时，采集各传感器的信号，进行运算，并将运算的结果转变为控制信号，控制被控对象的工作。它还实行对存储器（ROM、RAM）、输入/输出（I/O）接口和其他外部电路的控制；存储器 ROM 中存放的程序以经过精确计算和大量实验的数据为基础，这个固有程序在发动机工作时，不断与采集来的各传感器的信号进行比较和计算。用比较和计算的结果控制发动机的点火、空燃比、怠速、废气再循环等。它还有故障自诊断和保护功能，当系统产生故障时，还能在 RAM 中自动记录故障代码并采用保护措施从上述的固有程序

中读取替代程序来维持发动机的运转，使汽车能维持基本的速度行驶到维修场所。

电子控制单元 ECU 的主要功能如下。

（1）接收控制信息，主要指接收操作人员的各种控制指令，如油门指令。

（2）系统参数的采集处理功能，应用单片机丰富的接口资源采集发动机的工况和状态参数，之后加以转换处理。

（3）在控制软件的管理下，完成各种控制功能，根据采集的系统参数进行工况判断，实现喷油量控制和喷油定时控制。

（4）输出驱动功能，根据系统处理后所得的控制信息进行信号输出放大，驱动油量控制机构和定时控制机构。

（5）系统自诊断功能，如果检测到故障，则启用后备功能。

（6）与监控系统进行实时通信的功能。

ECU 的安装：注意防水、防振、防热、防过电压、防磁保护，一般将其安装在仪表板、杂物箱或控制台中其他零部件、座椅、滤清器的下面或后面，如图 1-2-3 所示。

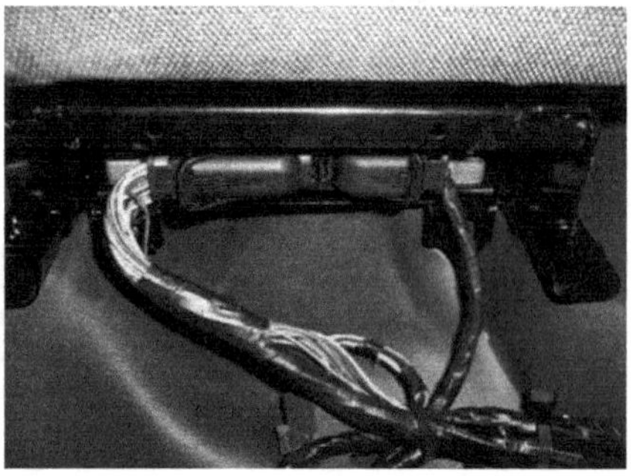

图 1-2-3　ECU 的安装位置

3. 执行器

执行器受 ECU 的控制，接收控制单元的输出信号，产生执行动作，实现各种控制，是具体执行某种控制功能的装置，一般是由 ECU 控制执行器电磁线圈的搭铁回路，也有的是由 ECU 控制的某些电子控制电路，如电子点火控制器等。发动机主要执行器如图 1-2-1 所示。发动机电控系统组成如图 1-2-4 所示。图 1-2-5 为长城哈弗 H6 的喷油器。

总结：电子控制发动机由空气供给系统、燃油供给系统和电子控制系统三部分组成，其中，电子控制系统由传感器、ECU、执行器等组成。传感器是“情报员”，ECU 是“司令部”，执行器是“工作机构”或“作战部队”，仅当三个方面相互协作时，才能确保发动机正常工作。

ECU 控制发动机正常工作，需要的“情报”有曲轴位置与转速、凸轮轴位置、空气流量、节气门位置、水温等，因而发动机会装设多个传感器；另外，维持发动机正常工作所需要的“工作机构”有喷油、点火、燃油供给、怠速控制系统等，因而发动机还会装设多个执行器。

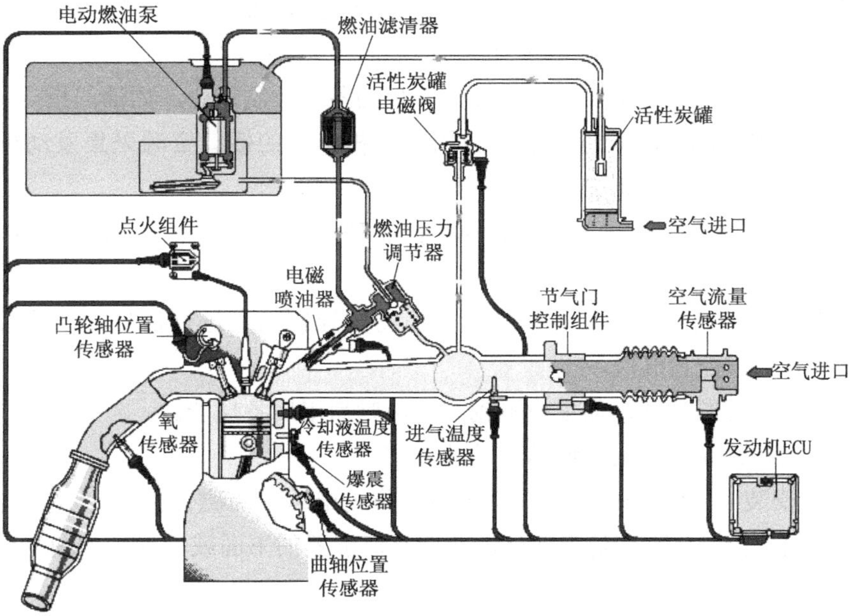

图 1-2-4　发动机电控系统组成

图 1-2-5　长城哈弗 H6 的喷油器

（三）发动机电控系统各部分功能

1. 电控燃油喷射系统（EFI）

电控燃油喷射系统（简称电喷系统）是 20 世纪 60 年代末开始发展起来的，与早期普遍使用的化油器供油系统相比，其突出优点在于空燃比的控制更为精确，可实现最佳空燃比；而且电喷技术提高了汽油的雾化、蒸发性能，加速性能更好，发动机功率和扭矩显著升高。目前，电喷系统主要采用开环与闭环控制（反馈控制）相结合的方式。按照喷油器安装位置的不同，电喷系统可分为三种：单点喷射（SPI）、多点喷射（MPI）和缸内直接喷射。

电控燃油喷射系统功用：根据进气量确定基本喷油量，再根据其他传感器（如冷却液温度传感器、节气门位置传感器等）信号等对喷油量进行修正，使发动机在各种运行工况下均能获得最佳浓度的混合气，从而提高发动机的动力性、经济性和排放性。

2. 电子点火控制系统（ESA）

早在 20 世纪初，点火系统在汽车发动机上便已开始应用，从有触点式、普通无触点式、集成电路式，发展到现今的微机控制电子点火系统。微机控制电子点火系统可控制并维持发动机点火提前角在最佳范围内，使汽油机的点火时刻更接近于理想状态，进一步挖掘发动机的潜能。

在微机控制电子点火系统中，目前出现了一种无分电器点火（DLI）系统，它取消了普通微机控制电子点火系统中的分电器，改由 ECU 内部控制各缸配电。这样点火线圈产生的高压电不需经过分电器分配，直接就送至火花塞发生点火。在发动机的点火控制中，同样采用了开环和闭环相结合的控制形式。

电子点火控制系统功用：根据各相关传感器信号，判断发动机的运行工况和运行条件，选择最理想的点火提前角点燃混合气，从而改善发动机的燃烧过程，以实现提高发动机动力性、经济性和降低污染排放的目的。

3. 怠速控制系统（ISC）

怠速性能的好坏是评价发动机性能优越与否的重要指标，怠速性能差将导致油耗增加，排污严重，因此，需进行必要的控制。怠速控制通常是指怠速转速控制，其实质就是对怠速工况时的进气量进行调节（同时配合喷油量及点火提前角的控制）。怠速控制的基本原理是 ECU 根据冷却水温、空调负荷、空挡信号等计算目标转速，并与实际转速相比较，同时检测节气门全关信号及车速信号，判断是否处于怠速状态，确认后则按目标转速与实际转速之间的差值来驱动执行器调整控制进气量。

怠速控制系统功用：在发动机怠速工况下，根据发动机冷却液温度、空调压缩机是否工作、变速器是否挂入挡位等，通过怠速控制阀对发动机的进气量进行控制，使发动机随时以最佳怠速转速运转。

4. 排气再循环电控系统（EGR）

国外的早期研究发现，将少量的排气（5%~20%）再次循环进入汽缸与新鲜可燃混合气混合后燃烧，可有效抑制 NO_x 的产生。事实上，除了可采用气门重叠产生排气回流的内部 EGR 方式外，更常用的措施是用专门的管道将部分排气引至进气管，由 ECU 控制 EGR 阀改变流通截面来调节排气量，实现再循环排气率的变化。

排气再循环电控系统功用：对发动机排放控制装置的工作实行电子控制。

排放控制的项目主要包括：废气再循环（EGR）控制、活性炭罐电磁阀控制、氧传感器和空燃比闭环控制、二次空气喷射控制等。

5. 进气控制系统

进气控制系统功用：根据发动机转速和负荷的变化，对发动机的进气进行控制，以提高发动机的充气效率，从而改善发动机动力性。

6. 增压电控系统

发动机中增压电控系统的安装日渐增多，通常增压器是为与发动机低速小负荷工

况相匹配而设计的，其目的是提高进气效率。目前，应用较普遍的是电控废气涡轮增压系统。

增压电控系统功用：对发动机进气增压装置的工作进行控制。在装有废气涡轮增压装置的汽车上，ECU 根据检测到的进气管压力，对增加装置进行控制，从而控制增压装置对进气增压的强度。

7. 故障自诊断系统

目前轿车发动机的电控系统中，ECU 一般都带有故障自诊断系统，自行监测、诊断发动机控制系统各部分的故障。故障自诊断系统时刻监测各控制系统的工作情况，当出现故障时，一般轿车仪表板上的故障指示灯可闪烁报警，同时将故障信息以代码的形式保存在微机的存储器中，维修时不仅可以通过故障指示灯间断闪烁来显示，也可以通过专用的检测仪器以数字的形式显示故障代码，以便进一步通过手册查出故障原因。自诊断系统很好地解决了复杂电控系统难以判断故障的问题。

故障自诊断系统功用：提示驾驶员发动机有故障，同时，系统将故障信息以设定的数码（故障码）形式储存在存储器中，以帮助维修人员确定故障类型和范围。

8. 故障保险系统及故障备用控制系统

当自诊断系统检测出传感器及其电路故障后，ECU 中的故障保险系统随之自动启动发挥作用。故障保险系统会用程序设定的数据取代故障部分输入的非正常信号，进行直接控制。故障保险系统一般通过软件编程来实现。

故障保险系统及故障备用控制系统功用：当控制系统电脑发生故障时，自动启用备用系统（备用集成电路），按设定的信号控制发动机转入强制运转状态，以防车辆停驶在途中。

9. 巡航控制系统

巡航控制系统功用：设定巡航控制模式后，ECU 根据汽车运行工况和运行环境信息自动控制发动机工作，使汽车自动维持一定的行驶车速。

10. 其他电控系统

（1）进气涡流电控系统：进气涡流可以促进汽油蒸发以及与空气的均匀混合，提高燃烧效率。

（2）可变进气控制系统：从增加进气量、提高进气效率的角度出发来改善发动机动力性能。实践证明，可变进气控制系统可增强发动机的动力性和经济性。

（3）进气温度预热控制系统：通过调节低温起动时的进气温度来促进汽油蒸发，改善排放性能。

（4）燃油蒸发电控系统：用来降低燃油箱中汽油蒸气排向大气所造成的污染。目前，活性炭罐蒸发电控系统得到了广泛应用，这样可有效防止汽油蒸气的外逸，降低碳氢化合物（CH）的排放污染。

（5）曲轴箱强制通风电控系统：将汽缸中经活塞环间隙渗入曲轴箱内的气体再次循环进入进气管中，以减少该部分气体直接排向大气造成的污染。

（6）二次空气喷射系统：二次空气喷射作为早期控制污染物排放的措施之一，目前与催化转换器配合使用。

二、汽车底盘电控系统

汽车底盘电控系统主要包括以下几个部分。

1. 电控自动变速器

自动变速器的优点：驾驶省力、起步加速平稳、避免过载和发动机熄火，提高了发动机和传动系的寿命。

自动变速器主要有以下三种类型。

1）电控机械式自动变速器

电控机械式自动变速器由传统的离合器与手动齿轮变速器采用电控进行自动变速。它与手动齿轮变速器的零部件有一定通用性，保留了传动效率高的优点，目前在重型货车上选用较多。

2）电控液力 - 机械式自动变速器

电控液力 - 机械式自动变速器由液力变矩器、机械式自动变速器和液压 - 电子控制系统三部分组成。目前技术成熟，应用最广。在发达国家轿车上的装车率已达 80%~90%。

3）电控机械式无级变速器（CVT）

电控机械式无级变速器（CVT）由 V 形金属钢带与可调半径的带轮得到无级变速。它与发动机之间还要有自动离合器，如图 1-2-6 所示。

图 1-2-6　电控机械式无级变速器

2. 防抱死制动系统（ABS）

ABS 的作用就是在汽车制动时，自动控制制动器制动力的大小，使车轮不被抱死，处于边滚边滑的状态，以保证车轮与地面的附着力在最大值。ABS 工作示意如图 1-2-7 所示。

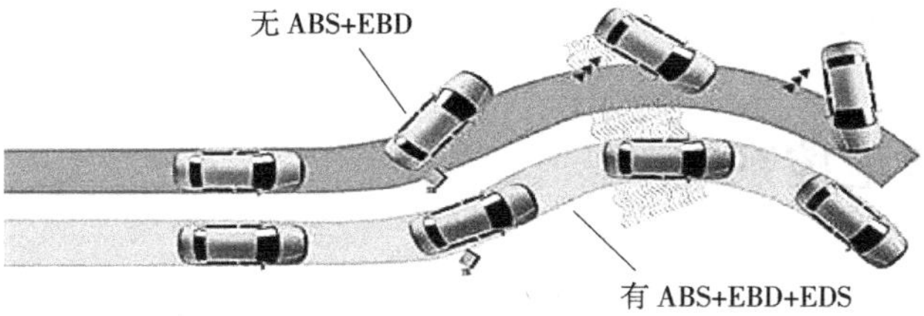

图 1-2-7　ABS 工作示意

EBD—电子制动力分配；EDS—电子差速锁

防抱死制动系统的作用如下。

（1）缩短制动时间和距离。

（2）防止紧急制动时车辆侧滑和甩尾。

（3）在紧急制动时可操纵方向。

（4）减少轮胎的磨损。

3. 驱动防滑系统

驱动防滑系统是在车轮出现滑转时，通过对滑转车轮施以制动力或控制发动机的动力输出来抑制车轮的滑转，以避免汽车牵引力和行驶稳定性的下降。驱动防滑系统示意如图 1-2-8 所示。由于驱动防滑系统通常是通过调节驱动车轮牵引力来实现驱动车轮滑转控制的，因此也被称为牵引力控制系统（TCS）。

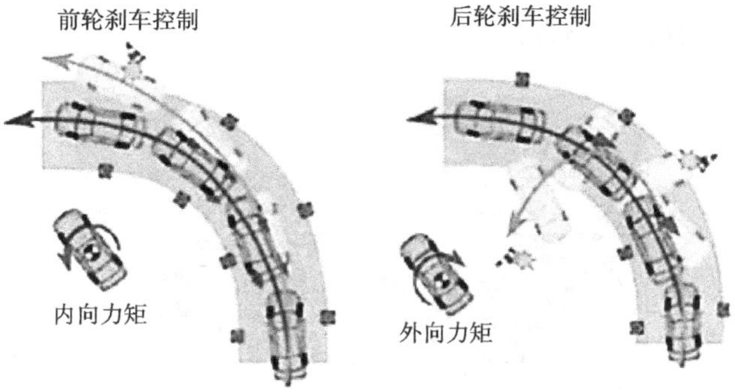

图 1-2-8　驱动防滑系统示意

4. 电控悬架系统

电控悬架系统是连接车身和车轮之间全部零件和部件的总称，主要由弹簧（如板簧、螺旋弹簧、扭杆等）、减振器和导向机构三部分组成，如图 1-2-9 所示。它可以有效抑制、降低车体与车轮的动载和振动，从而保证汽车行驶的平顺性和操纵稳定性。汽车行驶的平顺性和操纵稳定性是衡量悬架性能好坏的主要指标，理想的悬架应在不同的使用条件下具有不同的弹簧刚度和减振器阻尼，既能满足平顺性要求又能满足操纵

稳定性要求。

图 1-2-9　电控悬架系统

汽车电子控制悬架的作用：通过控制调节悬架的弹簧刚度和减振器阻尼，突破被动悬架的局限区域；使汽车的悬架特性与行驶的道路状况相适应，保证平顺性和操纵稳定性两个相互排斥的性能要求都能得到满足。

主动悬架检测系统运动的状态，将信号反馈到电控单元，电控单元发出指令给主动力发生器，构成闭环控制，由外部提供能量产生的主动控制力作用于系统进行控制。主动悬架除了控制振动，还可以控制汽车的姿态和高度。

5. 四轮转向控制系统

四轮转向控制系统（4WS）的后轮与前轮一起参与转向，是一种提高车辆反应性和稳定性的关键技术。四轮转向控制系统示意如图 1-2-10 所示，把后轮与前轮同相位转向，可以减小车辆转向时的旋转运动（横摆），改善高速行驶的稳定性；把后轮与前轮逆相位转向，能够改善车辆中低速行驶的操纵性，提高快速转向性。

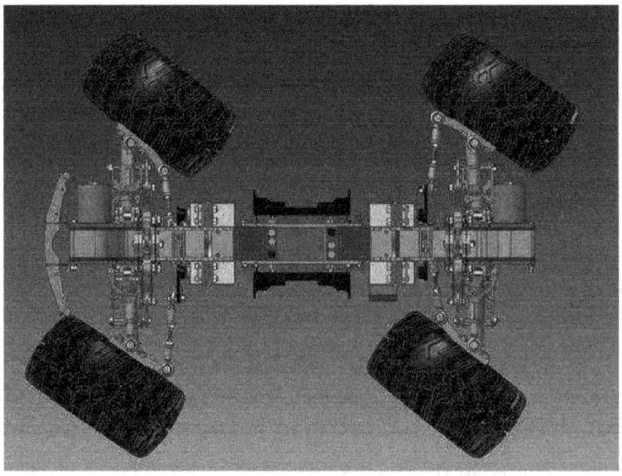

图 1-2-10　四轮转向控制系统示意

6. 汽车电子稳定（ESP）系统

ESP 系统能够帮助驾驶者避免车辆出现不稳定状态。电子稳定程序属于车辆的主动安全程序，汽车电子稳定系统示意如图 1-2-11 所示。ESP 系统能够识别车辆的不稳

定状态，并通过对制动系统、发动机管理系统和变速箱管理系统实施控制，来有针对性地弥补车辆滑动。

图 1-2-11　汽车电子稳定系统示意

ESP 系统是在 ABS 的基础上开发出来的。ESP 系统能够识别诸如驾驶员慌乱反应这样的紧急驾驶工况并通过对单个车轮施加制动和干预发动机控制系统来保持车辆的稳定性。这个软件能够综合理想转向角、横摆角度、侧向力和轮速差异等信号，很快判别出汽车失去控制的时刻，然后不管驾驶员是对车辆施加制动还是加速，ESP 系统都会开始发挥作用使汽车稳定下来。

三、汽车车身电控系统

汽车车身电子控制技术所涉及的内容很多，如汽车的视野性、方便性、舒适性、娱乐性、通信功能等。汽车车身电子控制主要包括：安全控制（电控安全气囊、电控安全带、车辆碰撞安全系统等）、舒适性控制（中央电动门锁系统、防盗报警系统、巡航控制系统等）、仪表控制（电子仪表、多功能综合屏幕显示、辅助电气系统等）。

（一）安全控制

1. 安全气囊系统（SRS）

安全气囊是汽车上一种常见的被动安全装置。撞车时，由 ECU 提供电流，引爆安放在转向盘中央及仪表板（杂物箱）后面等处气囊中的氮化合物，使其像“火药”般迅速燃烧而产生大量氮气，在瞬间充满气囊（气袋），整个过程约在 0.02 s 内完成。这样，在驾驶员与转向盘之间、副驾驶员与仪表板（杂物箱）之间立刻形成一种缓冲的软垫，避免硬性撞击而发生严重的伤害。现在越来越多的车辆将其定为标准配置。

2. 电控安全带

为确保乘员的安全，除了车身结构设计中应考虑有效吸收撞击能量，确保车内具有有效的乘员生存空间外，作为乘员约束装置之一的座椅安全带，要求当汽车发生碰撞和翻车事故时可让乘员免受大的减速度，同时约束乘员防止二次冲撞，减轻乘员伤害程度。当安全带结构性能的改进与座椅结构和安全气囊相配合时，可达到较理想的乘员保护效果，进一步降低乘员的伤害指数。

3. 车辆碰撞安全系统

车辆碰撞安全系统包括预防碰撞安全系统、防追尾碰撞系统、倒车防撞报警系统等。预防碰撞安全系统可以在发生碰撞之前收缩前座椅安全带的松弛部分，并使制动控制系统进入制动辅助等状态，以减少对驾驶员和乘客造成的伤害。防追尾碰撞系统又叫自动制动控制的防追尾碰撞系统，这是一种主动安全新技术。倒车防撞报警系统又称为倒车雷达系统或声纳测距系统，可以防止车辆在倒车过程中发生碰撞。

（二）舒适性控制

1. 中央电动门锁系统

采用中央电动门锁系统的车辆，当驾驶员锁住驾驶员车门时，其他几个车门（包括后车门、行李箱门等）能同时自动锁住；当打开驾驶员车门时，其他几个车门能同时打开；乘客仍可用各车门的机械或弹簧锁开关车门。

2. 防盗报警系统

为了防止车辆被盗，许多汽车公司已经将汽车防盗装置作为汽车的标准配置。防盗报警系统通常与汽车中控门锁系统配合工作，当汽车处于防盗报警功能状态时，若有人企图强行进入汽车或打开发动机罩、行李箱门时，防盗报警系统一方面发出报警，如灯光闪烁、喇叭鸣叫，另一方面阻止车辆运行，如切断点火电路、起动电路及供油电路等。

3. 巡航控制系统

汽车巡航控制系统根据其特点又称为恒速控制系统、车速自动控制系统等。该系统无须驾驶员操纵油门踏板即可将汽车车速自动控制在驾驶员设定的目标车速上。该系统将根据行车阻力自动增减节气门开度，使汽车行驶速度保持一定，省去了驾驶员频繁踩加速踏板的动作。在行驶中，驾驶员只要掌握转向盘就可以轻松驾驶。当路况发生变化时，驾驶员可以重新操纵汽车，如加减速、停靠等，从而使整个驾驶过程变得简便、轻松和舒适。

4. 汽车空调

空调是空气调节器的简称。汽车空调用于对汽车驾驶室和车厢内空气的温度、湿度、流速和清洁度等参数进行调节，并预防或去除风窗玻璃上的雾、霜和冰雪，保障

乘员的身体健康、视野和行车安全。汽车空调是由制冷剂循环流动实现制冷的，液体制冷剂于蒸发器中在低温下吸取被冷却对象的热量而汽化，使被冷却对象降温，然后又在高温下把热量传给周围介质而冷凝成液体。如此不断循环，借助于制冷剂的状态变化，达到制冷的目的。

（三）仪表控制

1. 电子仪表

传统的仪表对车速、发动机转速、燃油消耗等信息进行监测、传递和显示。随着汽车工业的发展，人们对汽车行驶过程中各系统工作状态的信息需求量显著增加，即对汽车仪表功能的要求越来越高。因此，传统的汽车仪表逐渐被电子仪表所取代。它采用微处理器采集处理不同传感器信号，控制、显示如车速、发动机转速、燃油消耗和行车里程等多种信息。

2. 多功能综合屏幕显示

随着汽车电子技术的飞速发展，汽车仪表的电子显示系统从简单地显示传感器信息，发展成为可以对各种信息进行分析计算、加工处理的综合信息系统。综合信息系统能够从大量的信息中选择出驾驶员所需要的各种信息，包括电子行车地图、维修、后视镜等方面的信息，还可以显示电视、广播、电话等方面的信息。

3. 辅助电气系统

汽车辅助电气系统主要包括电动车窗系统、电动座椅系统、风窗玻璃刮水系统等。

电动车窗系统实质上是在手动玻璃升降系统的基础上，增设玻璃升降驱动电动机和减速器。驾驶席侧面的总开关可以控制全部车门玻璃的升降，各车窗升降开关可以单独控制各自车门玻璃的升降。电动座椅系统又称为座椅位置（座位）调节系统，通过操纵座位控制开关，可以调整座位的前后滑移，前垂直、后垂直位置，靠背和头枕的倾斜位置以及腰垫的位置。风窗玻璃刮水系统的功用是刮除挡风玻璃上的雨水、积雪、尘土和污物，为驾驶人提供良好的视野，以确保行车安全。

四、信息通信系统

汽车信息通信系统作为汽车技术革新的关键环节，是科技创新和社会发展的产物，也是人类文明进步的体现。它不仅能够提高汽车的性能和安全性，还能够促进人与人、人与社会、人与自然的和谐相处。汽车信息通信系统是指汽车与外界进行通信的一种装置，主要包括车载多媒体系统、驾驶员信息系统、语言系统、智能交通系统（ITS）、全球定位系统（GPS）、计算机网络通信系统、车载短距离无线通信系统、状态监测与故障诊断系统等。

汽车信息通信系统的部件主要有漫游器、移动电话、电子邮件和国际互联网终端、视频或电子游戏中控台等。一个比较齐全的信息通信系统，具有协助驾驶员、连接汽车与外界以及协调整车各部件的电子控制功能，使驾驶员能得到很大的信息量，从而提高驾驶员操作的舒适性和车辆行驶的安全性。

（一）导航系统

随着科学技术的发展，汽车导航系统也得到快速发展，目前已发展为比较先进的具有汽车导航功能、防盗功能、调度功能、汽车主要工况的监测报警功能等的综合系统。从设备上看，目前已发展成为利用“3C 技术”，即计算机、通信及控制技术结合的全球卫星定位系统，建立了具有行车导航、控制等功能的综合系统，而且民用精度已达到米级。

（二）车载网络系统

20 世纪 90 年代以来，汽车上的电控装置越来越多，例如电子燃油喷射装置、防抱死制动装置（ABS）、安全气囊装置、主动悬架等，因此电子控制区域网络（CAN）应运而生。它通过不同的编码信号表示不同的开关动作，信号解码后，根据指令接通或断开对应的用电设备（前照灯、刮水器、电动座椅等）。这样，就将过去一线一用的专线制改为一线多用制，减少了汽车上电线的数量，缩小了线束的直径。

【知识拓展】

一、设备准备

长城哈弗 H6 一辆；举升机一台；通用工具一套；发动机舱防护罩一套；“三件套”（座椅套、转向盘套、脚垫）一套。

二、实训步骤

（1）打开车门，铺好“三件套”，拉动发动机舱盖手柄。

（2）打开发动机舱盖，铺好发动机舱防护罩，拆下发动机护板。

（3）找出空气滤清器、进气管道，并观察其结构及布置。

（4）找出空气流量计（或进气压力传感器）、进气温度传感器节气门及节气门位置

传感器、曲轴位置传感器、爆震传感器、氧传感器，如图 1-2-12 至图 1-2-17 所示，并观察其各自的位置。

图 1-2-12　空气流量计

图 1-2-13　进气温度传感器

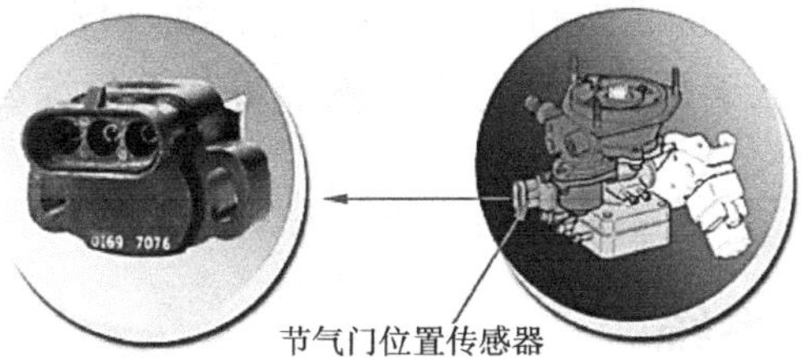

图 1-2-14　节气门位置传感器

图 1-2-15　曲轴位置传感器

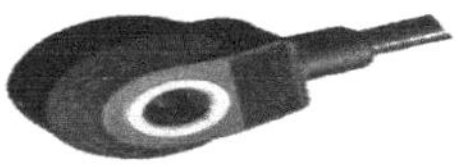

图 1-2-16　爆震传感器

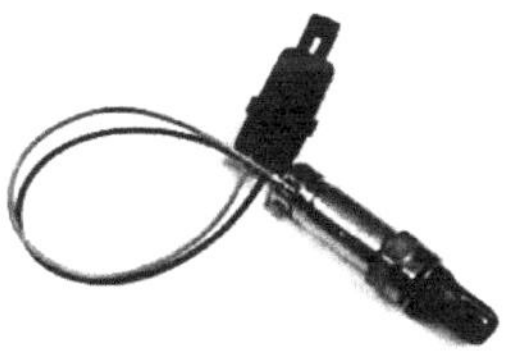

图 1-2-17　氧传感器

（5）找出各喷油器、怠速阀、点火模块，并观察其各自的位置。

（6）找出发动机舱内（或驾驶室仪表板下方）的配电盒（或称继电器盒），打开盖板，观察各继电器、熔断器（俗称熔断丝）的位置。

（7）找出发动机舱内（或驾驶室仪表板下方）的 ECU，观察其安装位置。

（8）打开汽车行李舱，拆下行李舱底部的燃油箱盖板，观察燃油箱及电动燃油泵。

（9）按照举升机的操作要求采取相应的安全防护措施，用举升机举起汽车。

（10）按照相反的顺序将汽车及举升机复位，并检查复位状况是否良好。

三、实训要求

（1）能够熟练找出各传感器、执行器、ECU、电动燃油泵、继电器盒。

（2）习惯性使用“三件套”、发动机舱防护罩等汽车防护物品，养成良好职业习惯。

（3）养成“采取安全防护措施”的习惯。

（4）养成工具、零部件、油液“三不落地”的职业习惯，工具及拆下的零部件等都应整齐地放置在工具车及零件盘中。

【思考与练习】

1. 汽车防抱死系统的英文简称是什么？
2. 汽车电子控制系统可分为哪三大部分？
3. 汽车发动机电子控制系统的辅助系统都有哪些？
4. 检测发动机工况的传感器都有哪些？
5. 说出至少三个执行器的名称及其作用。

第 2 章

汽车发动机电控系统

【章节概述】

高端半导体全产业链的自主可控是国家走向科技强国的必经之路，是实现民族复兴进程中一件举足轻重的大事。国产替代依旧是我国高端半导体产业发展的主要趋势，未来替代速度将逐年提升，尤其是在国产化率较低的半导体材料以及生产设备等领域。

汽车发动机电控系统是半导体领域在汽车中的典型应用，其主要包括电控燃油喷射系统、电子点火系统以及辅助控制系统三大部分。其中核心环节是电控燃油喷射系统和电子点火系统。随着电子技术的高速发展，越来越多的先进技术应用在发动机电控系统中，这其中很大一部分表现在辅助控制系统的控制项目、控制精度与复杂程度上。本章主要围绕电控燃油喷射系统、电子点火系统展开学习，对于辅助控制系统以介绍为主。

第 1 节　电控燃油喷射系统

一、电控燃油喷射系统的作用

燃油供给系统的功用是用电动汽燃油泵向喷油器提供足够压力的汽油，喷油器根据来自 ECU 的控制信号，向进气歧管内进气门上方喷射定量的汽油，即对喷油正时、喷油量、燃油停供及燃油泵进行控制。

二、电控燃油喷射系统的优点

电控燃油喷射系统应用各种传感器来检测发动机工况和汽车行驶状态。发动机 ECU 根据传感器检测的发动机工况信息进行喷油正时和喷油量控制。电控燃油喷射系统的基本组成如图 2-1-1 所示。与传统化油器式发动机相比，电控燃油喷射系统有如下优点。

（1）根据工况配给不同浓度的混合气。

（2）安装三元催化装置，进行空燃比闭环控制，减少 HC、CO 和 NO_x 排放。

（3）喷射压力高、雾化好。

（4）根据大气压力和温度变化对喷油进行补偿控制。
（5）具有减速断油功能，降低油耗。
（6）无化油器节流作用，利用惯性进气，动力性强。
（7）具有暖机怠速控制，快速暖机。

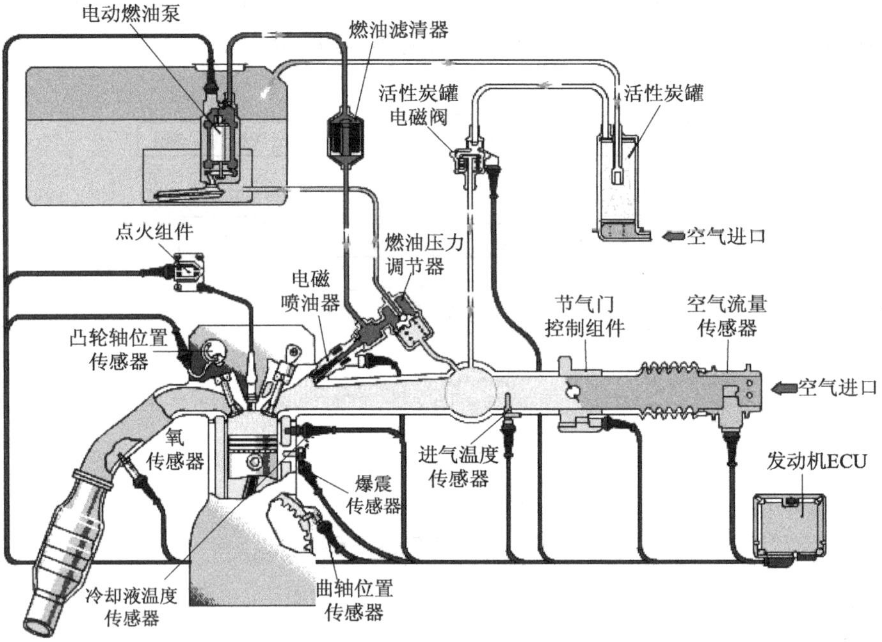

图 2-1-1　电控燃油喷射系统组成

三、电控燃油喷射系统的组成及功能

一个完整的电控燃油喷射系统通常由空气供给系统、燃油供给系统和电子控制系统三个子系统构成。图 2-1-2 所示为长城哈弗 H6 发动机舱。

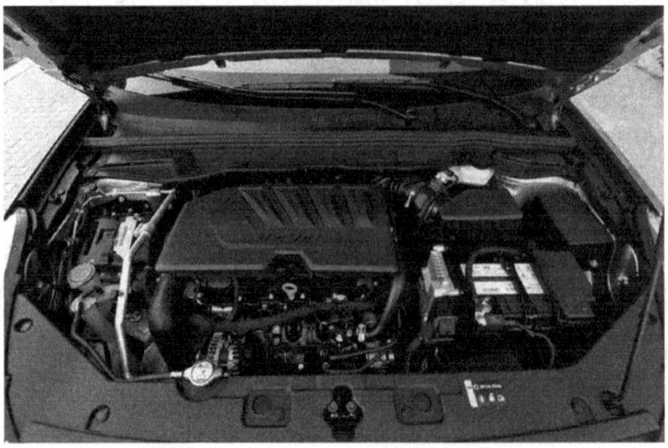

图 2-1-2　长城哈弗 H6 发动机舱

（一）空气供给系统

空气供给系统的任务是向汽油机提供清洁的、与发动机负荷相适应的、经过计量的新鲜空气，使它们在进气管或汽缸内与喷油器喷出的汽油形成质量好的可燃混合气。空气供给系统由空气滤清器、空气流量传感器（进气压力传感器）、节气门体和节气门位置传感器、动力腔、进气歧管等组成，如图 2-1-3 所示。

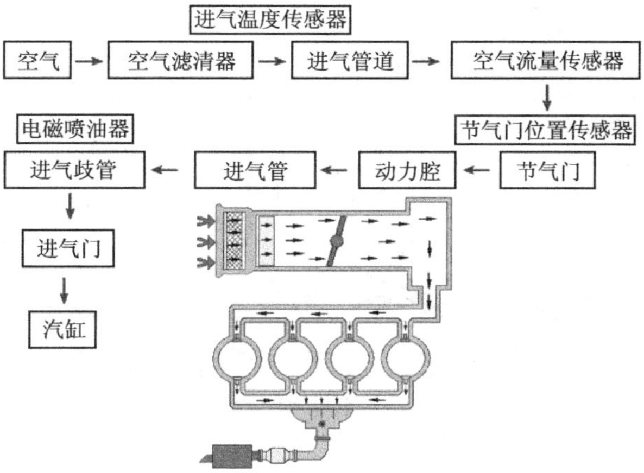

图 2-1-3　空气供给系统

1. 空气量计量装置

空气量计量装置的作用是对发动机吸入的新鲜空气量进行直接或间接的测量，并把测量结果转换成电压或频率信号输送到 ECU，ECU 根据输入信号及其他参数计算出每一工作循环吸入的新鲜空气质量。直接测量方式采用空气流量传感器测量空气的体积流量或质量流量，间接测量方式大都采用进气歧管绝对压力传感器测量进气歧管的绝对压力。

1）空气流量传感器

空气流量传感器是直接测量进入进气道内空气量的一种传感器类型，装有空气流量传感器的电控系统通常称为 L 型电控燃油喷射系统。发动机中使用的空气流量传感器主要有翼片式空气流量传感器、卡门旋涡式空气流量传感器、热线式空气流量传感器和热膜式空气流量传感器四种。其中前三种基本已经被淘汰，目前主要采用热膜式空气流量传感器，其结构如图 2-1-4 所示。

热膜式空气流量传感器工作原理如图 2-1-5 所示。热丝（R_H）通电发热产生的温度与进入的空气温度（R_T 温度）之差维持在 120 ℃。进气量增加，R_H 失热多，温差减小，控制电路使通过 R_H 的电流值增大（温差维持在 120 ℃），流过信号电阻 R_S 的电流值增大，信号电压值 U_S 增大，送至 ECU 控制增加喷油量。

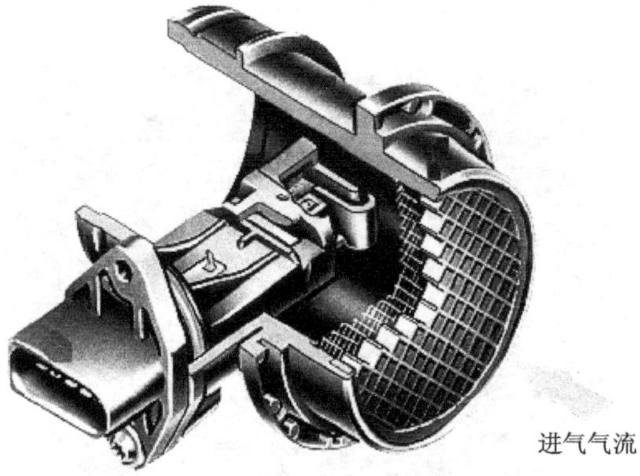

图 2-1-4　热膜式空气流量传感器

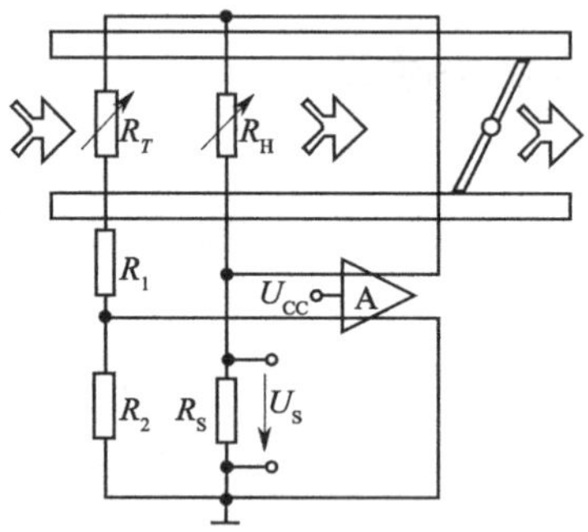

图 2-1-5　热膜式空气流量传感器工作原理

R_T—温度补偿电阻（进气温度传感器）；R_H—发热元件电阻（热丝或热膜）；
R_S—信号电阻；R_1、R_2—精密匹配电阻；A—集成控制电路

2）进气压力传感器

进气压力传感器以真空管连接进气歧管，通过发动机转速负荷的变化，感应进气歧管内的真空变化，再将感知器内部电阻的改变转换成电压信号，供 ECU 修正喷油量和点火正时角度。其组成如图 2-1-6 所示。

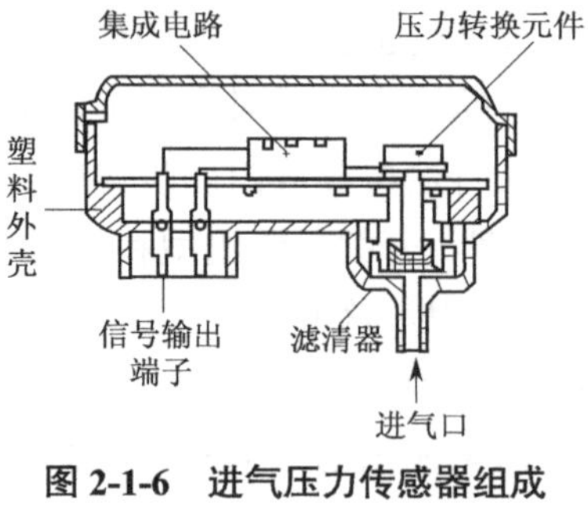

图 2-1-6　进气压力传感器组成

电喷发动机中采用进气压力传感器来检测进气量的系统称为 D 型喷射系统。进气压力传感器检测进气量不是像空气流量传感器那样直接检测，而是采用间接检测，同时它还受诸多因素的影响，因此其检测精度和响应速度对比空气流量传感器都有一定

的差距，目前已逐渐被市场淘汰。图 2-1-7 为进气压力传感器在实车上的安装位置。

图 2-1-7　进气压力传感器安装位置

2. 节气门体和节气门位置传感器

1）节气门体

节气门体安装在空气流量计和发动机进气总管之间的进气管上（对于采用空气流量传感器进气和电控的汽油机），或者安装在空气滤清器与进气总管之间（对于使用进气歧管绝对压力传感器的汽油机）。节气门体一般由节气门、怠速旁通气、怠速调整螺钉、辅助空气阀等组成。节气门通过拉索与油门踏板相连，驾驶员通过油门踏板控制节气门开度，使发动机的输出扭矩与所需的牵引力相适应。对于设置怠速旁通气道的节气门体，怠速旁通气道布置在主进气通道一侧，发动机怠速运转时，节气门完全关闭，怠速所需要的空气经旁通气道布置在气道进入总管。怠速调整螺钉布置在怠速旁通气道上，通过适当旋进或退出怠速调整螺钉改变怠速旁通气道截面，调整怠速空气量，起到调整发动机怠速的作用。近年来生产的电控燃油机已不采用怠速调整螺钉的结构，而是采用专门的电控怠速系统对发动机的怠速进行调整和控制。图 2-1-8 为长城哈弗 H6 的节气门体。

2）节气门位置传感器（TPS）

在电控燃油喷射系统中，节气门位置传感器的作用是把节气门的开度转换为电信号，ECU 根据节气门位置传感器的输出信号对实际喷油量进行修正。节气门位置传感器安装在节气门体上，通过节气门轴与节气门同步旋转。在电控燃油喷射系统中应用的节气门位置传感器有线性输出型、开关量输出型和带自适应巡航控制（ACC）信号输出型三种形式，其中线性输出型使用最普遍。

节气门位置传感器工作原理如图 2-1-9 所示。①当怠速触点信号端子 IDL 输出 $U = 0$，节气门开度信号端子 VTA 输出 $U_s = 0.5$ V，节气门全闭时，ECU 则判定为怠速；②当怠速触点信号端子 IDL 输出 $U = +BV$，节气门开度信号端子 VTA 输出 $U_s > 0.5$ V，节气门部分打开时，ECU 则判定为部分负荷；③当怠速触点信号端子 IDL 输出 $U = +BV$，节气门开度信号端子 VTA 输出 $U_s = +5$ V，节气门全开时，ECU 则判定为大负荷。

图 2-1-8　长城哈弗 H6 节气门体

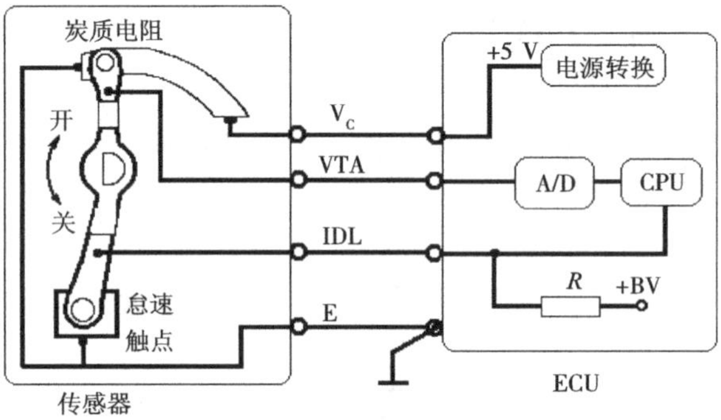

图 2-1-9　线性输出型节气门位置传感器工作原理

（二）燃油供给系统

燃油供给系统的任务是以确定的压力差，向发动机进气总管或进气歧管内喷入清洁、雾化良好的燃油。如图 2-1-10 所示，燃油供给系统由油箱、电动燃油泵、燃油滤清器、光滑分配管、喷油器压力调节器等组成，发动机工作时，电动燃油泵从油箱吸入汽油，加压后泵送到供油管，汽油经供油管、滤清器到达燃油分配管，然后分送到各个喷油器。串联在油路上的油压调节器对汽油的油压进行调节，多余的汽油经油压调节器流回油箱。

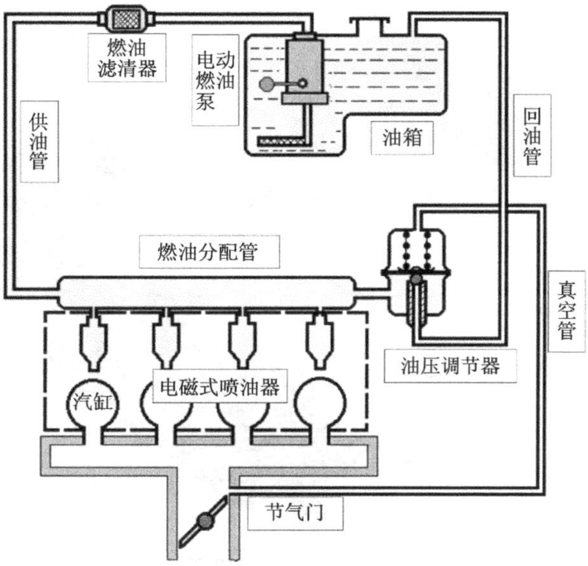

图 2-1-10　燃油供给系统组成

1. 电动燃油泵（图 2-1-11）

（1）作用：泵油，建立油压。

（2）结构：泵体、永磁电动机、限压阀、单向止回阀、外壳等。

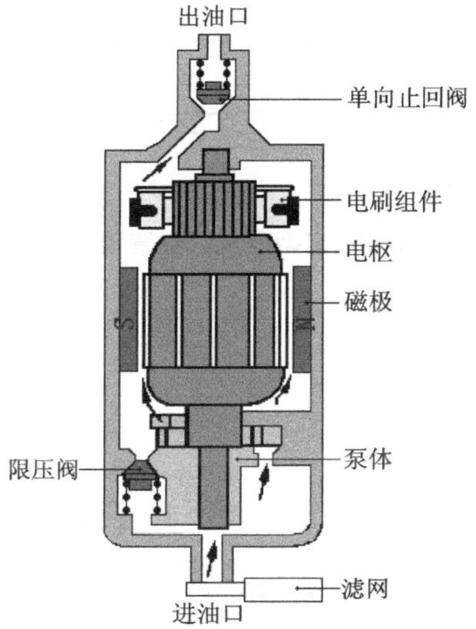

图 2-1-11　电动燃油泵结构

2. 电磁式喷油器

电磁式喷油器的作用是在 ECU 的控制下，把雾化良好的汽油喷入进气管或进气道。对于电控多点汽油喷射系统和单点汽油喷射系统，由于喷射位置和要求的不同，喷油器的结构存在一些差异。长城哈弗 H6 喷油器如图 2-1-12 所示，其采用球阀式喷油器。图 2-1-13 至图 2-1-15 为不同类型喷油器的示意图。

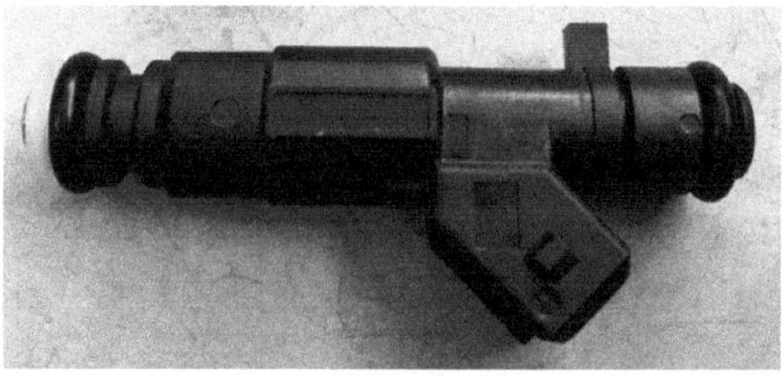

图 2-1-12　喷油器实物

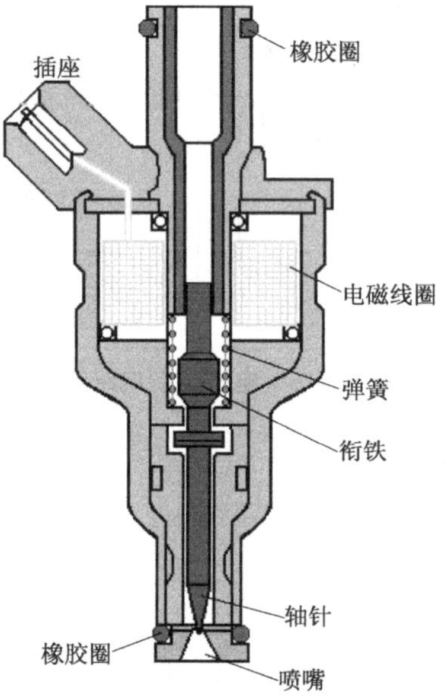

图 2-1-13　轴针式喷油器

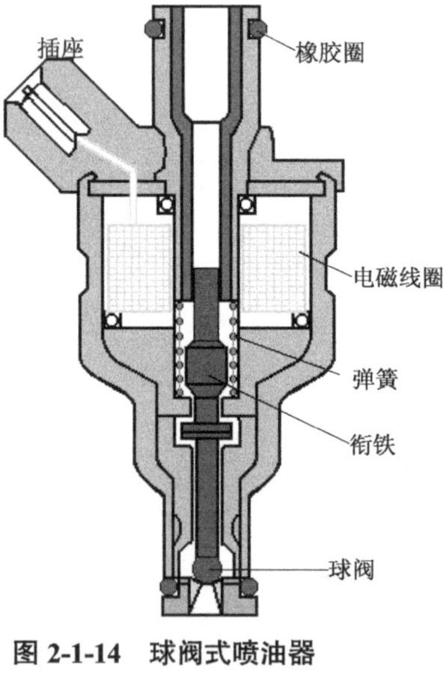

图 2-1-14　球阀式喷油器

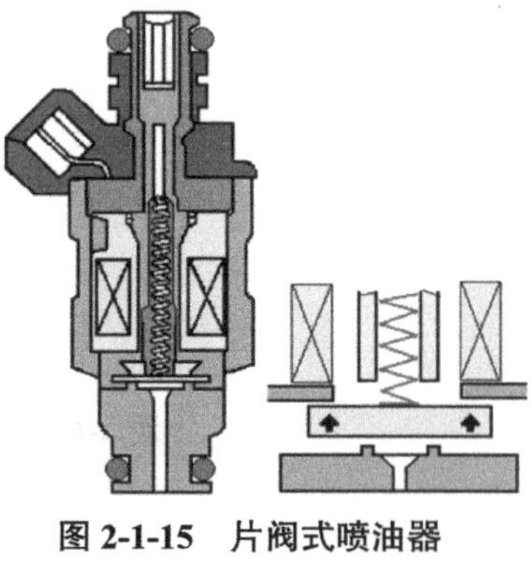

图 2-1-15　片阀式喷油器

（三）电子控制系统

图 2-1-16 为电子控制电路的组成。

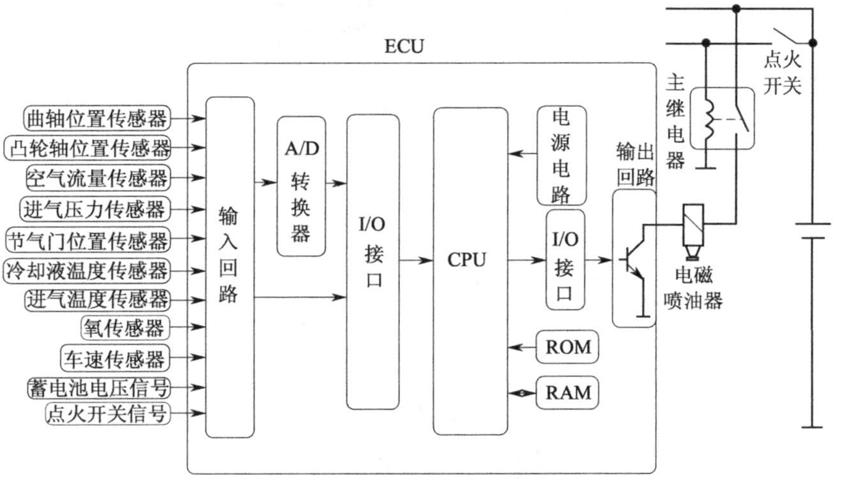

图 2-1-16 电子控制电路组成

1. 燃油泵开关控制电路

安装叶片式空气流量传感器的喷射系统中，常采用此控制电路。燃油泵开关设在空气流量传感器内。

燃油泵开关控制电路工作原理如下。

（1）点火开关通电，开路继电器 ON，燃油泵 ON。

（2）起动后，点火开关 IG，燃油泵开关 ON，开路继电器 ON，燃油泵 ON。

（3）发动机停转，燃油泵开关 OFF，开路继电器 OFF，燃油泵 OFF。

L 型燃油泵控制电路如图 2-1-17 所示。

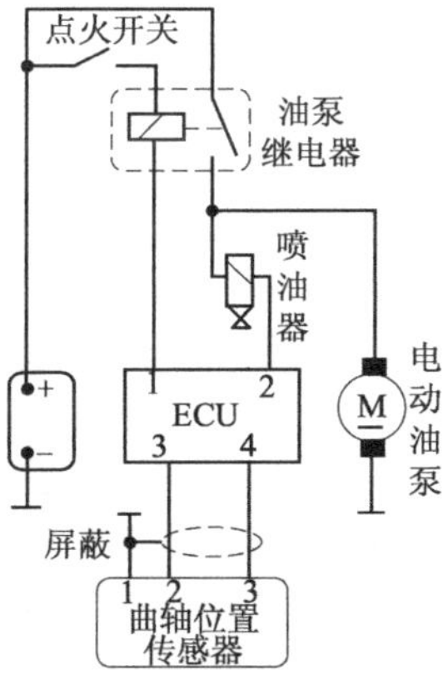

图 2-1-17 L 型燃油泵控制电路

2.ECU 控制燃油泵电路

ECU 控制燃油泵电路工作原理如下。

（1）点火开关通电，EFI 继电器通路，ECU 中的端子 2 导通，燃油泵继电器导通，燃油泵 ON。

（2）起动后，点火开关导通，ECU 中的端子 2 导通，燃油泵继电器 ON，燃油泵 ON。

（3）发动机停转，点火开关断电，EFI 继电器 OFF，燃油泵继电器 OFF。

D 型 EFI 系统燃油泵控制电路如图 2-1-18 所示。

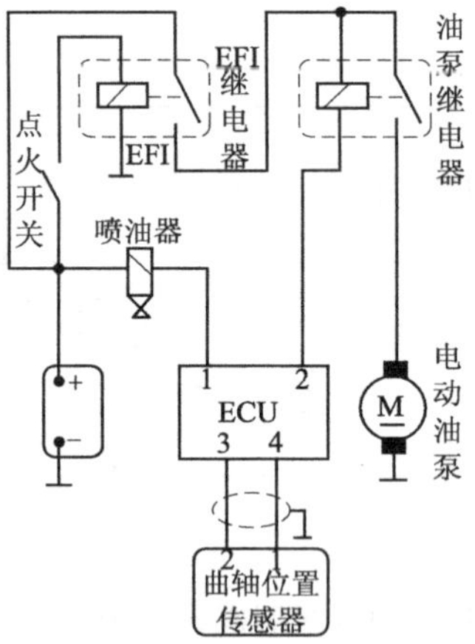

图 2-1-18　D 型 EFI 系统燃油泵控制电路

3. 燃油泵转速的控制

1）利用串联电阻控制燃油泵转速

发动机低速或中小负荷运转时，ECU 控制燃油泵控制继电器 B 接通、A 断开，电阻串入，燃油泵低速运转。

发动机高速或大负荷运转时，ECU 控制燃油泵控制继电器 B 断开、A 接通，电阻被旁路，燃油泵高速运转。

电阻式燃油泵转速控制电路如图 2-1-19 所示。

2）利用燃油泵控制模块 ECU 控制燃油泵转速

发动机低速或中小负荷运转时，发动机 ECU 向燃油泵 ECU 的 FPC 端输入低电平，燃油泵 ECU 的 FP 端向燃油泵提供 9 V 低电压，燃油泵低速运转。

发动机起动、高速或大负荷运转时，发动机 ECU 向燃油泵 ECU 的 FPC 端输入高电平，燃油泵 ECU 的 FP 端向燃油泵提供 12 V 高电压，燃油泵高速运转。

燃油泵控制模块控制燃油泵转速电路如图 2-1-20 所示。

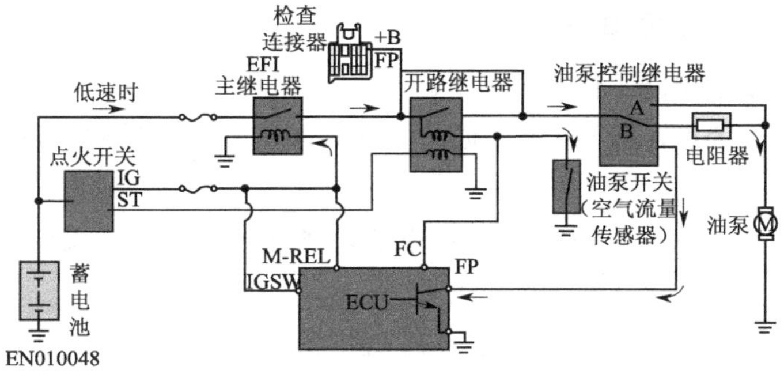

图 2-1-19　电阻式燃油泵转速控制电路

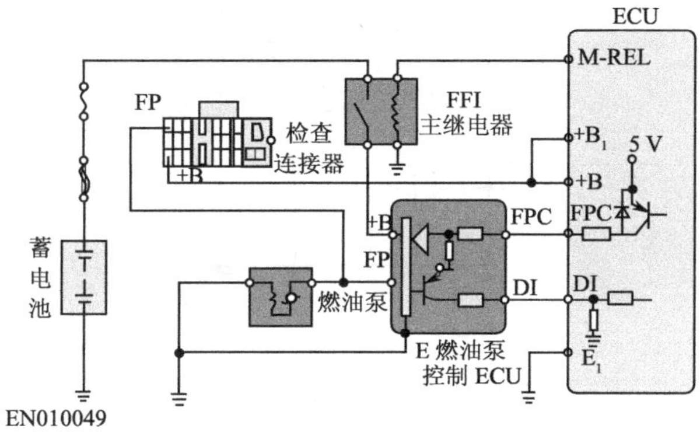

图 2-1-20　燃油泵控制模块控制燃油泵转速电路

4. 压力调节器

燃油压力调节器的主要功用是保持燃油分配管内油压与进气歧管内气压的压差不变，差值依发动机的类型而异，一般为 0.25~0.3 MPa。采用压力差恒定的控制方法，使 ECU 能够用单一控制参数——喷油器开启时间，对喷油量进行既简单又精确的控制。因为在喷油器结构参数不变的情况下，喷油量不仅与喷油器保持最大开度的时间有关，还与燃油分配管的压力、进气歧管的压力有关。在喷油器全开时间和燃油分配管内油压不变的条件下，喷油量将随背压（即进气歧管内气压）的变化而变化，进气歧管压力高，喷油量减少，反之则增加。若喷油器全开时间和进气歧管的压力保持不变，则喷油量将随燃油分配管内油压的变化而变化，燃油分配管内油压升高，喷油量增加，反之则减少。实际发动机运转时，进气歧管的压力随发动机转速及负荷的变化而变化，燃油分配管内油压的波动与喷油器的开、关及电动燃油泵的输出特性等因素有关。压力调节器原理如图 2-1-21 所示。

（1）进气管压力 $P_{气}$ 增大，回油口开度减小，回油减少，油压 $P_{油}$ 增大，$P_{油}-P_{气}$ 恒定，$P_{油}-P_{气}=P_{簧}$。

（2）发动机停机时，燃油泵停转，回油口关闭，建立保持油压。

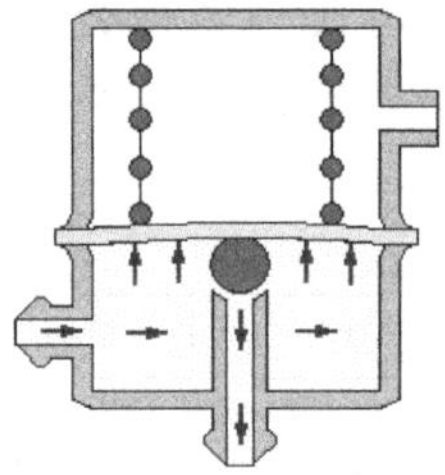

图 2-1-21　压力调节器原理

5. 转速及位置传感器

曲轴位置传感器的作用是向 ECU 提供发动机的转速和曲轴转角信号。发动机转速是 ECU 判断发动机运行工况、选择控制程序和确定初始控制参数的主要依据，也是 ECU 对发动机一个工作循环吸入空气量进行计算所必需的基本参数。凸轮轴位置传感器的作用是向 ECU 提供关于发动机基准汽缸所处的工作行程和活塞运动方向的信号，一般称为判缸信号。

在采用顺序喷射方式的电控燃油喷射系统中，表明基准汽缸所处工作行程和活塞位置的判缸信号是 ECU 进行喷油正时和顺序控制的唯一依据，因此顺序喷射方式的电控燃油喷射系统中必须有凸轮轴位置传感器，对于采用分组喷射方式的电控燃油喷射系统则可省略。电控燃油喷射系统中使用的曲轴位置传感器和凸轮轴位置传感器，按它们的工作原理有电磁感应式、霍尔效应式和光电感应式三种类型，这三种类型的传感器可以不同的组合方式，完成各自承担的参数采集任务。目前磁感应式位置传感器应用较为广泛，如图 2-1-22 所示。

图 2-1-22　磁感应式曲轴位置传感器

6. 温度传感器

温度传感器的作用是测量发动机的进气、冷却水、燃油等的温度，并把测量结果转换为电信号输送到 ECU。对于所有的汽油机电控系统，进气温度和冷却水温度是 ECU 进行控制所必需的两个温度参数，而其他的温度参数则随电控系统的类型及控制需要不尽相同。进气温度传感器常安装在空气流量计或空气滤清器到节气门体之间的进气道或空气流量计中，水温传感器则布置在发动机冷却水路、汽缸盖或机体上的适当位置。可以用来测量温度的传感器有绕线电阻式、扩散电阻式、半导体晶体管式、金

属芯式、热电偶式和半导体热敏电阻式等多种类型，目前在进气温度和冷却水温度测量中应用最广泛的是热敏电阻式传感器，主要分为单端子式和两端子式，如图 2-1-23 所示。

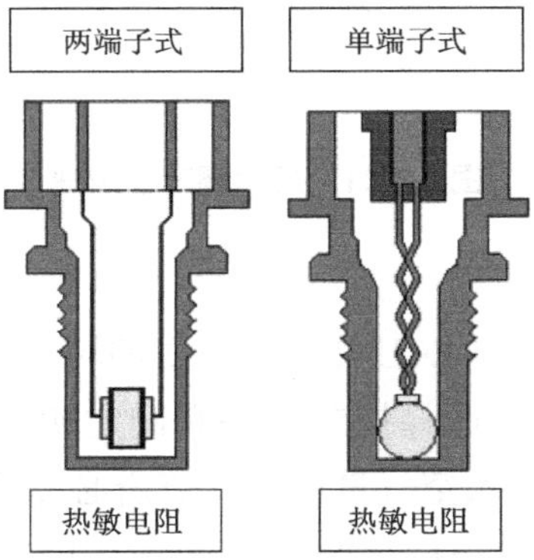

图 2-1-23　常见热敏电阻式传感器

7. 开关量信号

ECU 要实现对发动机运行的精确控制，除了需要传感器检测进气量、发动机转速、发动机负荷、进气温度和冷却水温度等定量参数外，还需要一些表明发动机处于某种状态的定性参数，这种定性参数以是或否的方式传输到 ECU，故称为开关量信号。

8. 电子控制单元

电子控制单元（ECU）是发动机电控系统的核心，电控单元主要由输入回路、 A/D 转换器、微型计算机和输出回路四部分组成，如图 2-1-24 所示。

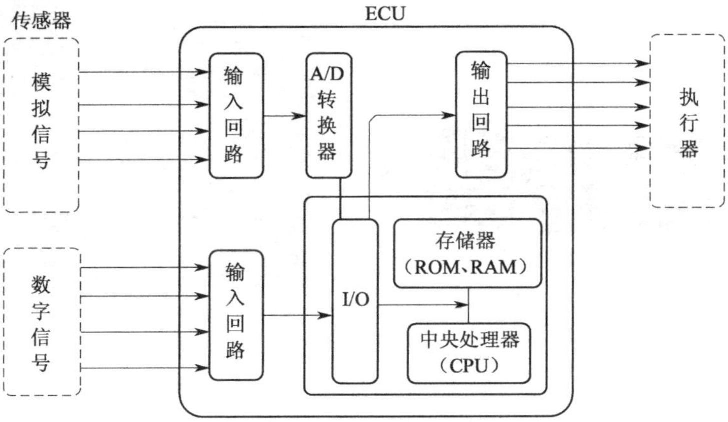

图 2-1-24　ECU 原理图

图 2-1-25 为哈弗 H6 ECU 内部结构。其工作过程：汽车一运转，ECU 就处于工作状态，某些运行程序或操作指令从存储器（ROM）中调入中央处理器（CPU）。在程序运行过程中，所有发动机工况信号由各传感器提供。当传感器信号输入 ECU 后，首先进入输入回路进行处理。当输入信号为模拟信号时，先经过模 / 数（A/D）转换器转换

成数字信号后，再经过 I/O 接口进入 CPU；当输入信号是数字信号时，可直接经 I/O 接口进入 CPU。多数信息暂时存储在 RAM 中，根据指令再从 RAM 中输送到 CPU。接着 CPU 将存储在 ROM 中的设定数据引入，与传感器输入信号进行比较、运算后作出断定，并发出指令，经 I/O 接口输出，控制执行器工作。

图 2-1-25　哈弗 H6 ECU 内部结构

【知识拓展】

（一）空气流量传感器的功用及安装位置

空气流量传感器，又称为空气流量计（AFM），是电喷发动机的重要传感器之一。

（1）作用：将吸入的空气流量转换成电信号送至 ECU，作为决定喷油的基本信号之一，是测定吸入发动机的空气流量的传感器。

（2）故障表现：进气量测量不准确，混合气会过浓或过稀，ECU 无法正确控制发动机的喷油量，出现发动机运转不正常、排放超标等问题。

（3）安装位置：在空气滤清器和节气门之间的进气管路上，如图 2-1-26 所示。

图 2-1-26　空气流量传感器的安装位置

（二）哈弗 H6 空气流量传感器的检测

空气流量传感器的常见故障是线路短路、断路或进气量信号异常，它的故障会使电脑不能正确测定吸入发动机的空气量，从而不能正常进行喷油量的控制，造成混合气过浓或过稀，使发动机运转不正常。

空气流量传感器是一种高精度的部件，在检修、拆卸过程中，应小心谨慎，切忌碰撞，不要让污物进入流量传感器内，也不要随意将工具或手指伸入流量传感器内，以免造成损坏。空气流量传感器有多种类型，其结构原理有很大的不同，因此检修方法也各不相同。下面以长城哈弗 H6 的热膜式空气流量传感器为例进行典型实践演练。

1. 电源电压检测

打开点火开关，将数字万用表设置在直流电压 20 V 挡，红色表笔置于空气流量传感器针脚 2，黑色表笔置于电瓶负极或发动机进气歧管壳体，打开起动机时应显示 12 V；红色表笔置于空气流量传感器针脚 4，黑色表笔置于电瓶负极或发动机进气歧管壳体，应显示 5 V。

2. 信号电压测量

信号电压测量分单件测量和就车测量。

1）单件检测

取一空气流量传感器总成部件，将蓄电池电压施加在空气流量传感器电器插座针脚 2 上，将 5 V 电压施加在空气流量传感器电器插座针脚 4 上，将数字万用表设置在直流电压 20 V 挡，测量空气流量传感器电器插座针脚 3 和针脚 5，应有 1.5 V 左右的电压；使用电吹风从空气流量传感格栅一端向空气流量传感器吹入冷空气或加热的空气，测量空气流量传感器电器插座针脚 3 和针脚，电压应顺势上升至 2.8 V 后回落。若不能满足上述条件，可以判定空气流量传感器有故障。

2）就车检测

起动发动机至工作温度，将数字万用表设置在直流电压 20 V 挡，测量空气流量传感器针脚 5 的反馈信号，红色表笔置于空气流量传感器针脚 5，黑色表笔置于空气流量传感器针脚 3、蓄电池负极或进气歧管壳体，怠速时应显示电压 1.5 V 左右；急踩加速踏板时应显示 2.8 V。若不符合上述规律，或电压反而下降，则在电源电压与参考电压无误的前提下，可以判定空气流量传感器损坏，必须进行更换。

3. 空气流量传感器维修要点

1）热膜脏污后的清洗

如果发动机存在“回火”故障，往往会对空气流量传感器造成严重危害。由于发动机的气流在进气歧管内逆向流动（即“回火”），其中含有炭颗粒，这些炭颗粒容易黏附在空气流量传感器的感应元件上，并产生如下后果：在怠速时，空气流量传感器的信号偏大，而在加速及大负荷时信号偏小。

热膜是否具有自洁能力的检查方法是：拆下空气滤清器，从空气流量传感器的进气口处察看热膜，若发动机熄火 5 s 后看不到热线发出微红的辉光约 1 s，说明热膜的自洁能力已经丧失。

热膜污染后，可以在热机、怠速状态下拆下空气滤清器的滤网，采用汽化器清洗剂直接喷射热膜，以清除黏附在其上的积炭。

2）热膜式空气流量传感器损坏后的处理

采用 BOSCH 公司生产的热膜式空气流量传感器，其核心部分由一块集成电路（数 / 模转换电路）和惠斯登电桥组成，没有设置稳压电路。因此，当电源电压过高或者出现瞬间高电压时，这种热膜式空气流量传感器容易烧坏。而电路峰值电压过高（超过 16 V）的原因往往是蓄电池硫化严重，使其容量下降，无法吸收发电机的峰值电压，所以蓄电池硫化是导致热膜式空气流量传感器损坏的原因之一。解决办法是：在热膜式空气流量传感器的前端加装一个 7812 三端子稳压集成电路。

3）堵住空气不经过计量的进入途径

这些不正常途径包括：进气管破裂、真空软管松脱、进气歧管与汽缸盖密封不严。如果存在以上情况。部分空气将不经过空气流量传感器的计量而直接进入汽缸，最终导致发动机混合气失调。

【思考与练习】

一、填空题

1. 在 L 型电控燃油喷射系统中，由 ________ 测量发动机的进气量。
2. 电控燃油喷射系统按喷射方式不同可分为 ________ 和 ________ 两种。
3. 电控燃油喷射系统由 ________、________、________ 组成。
4. 喷油器按喷油口的结构不同，分为 ________ 和 ________ 两种。

二、选择题

1. 关于空气流量传感器上的怠速调整螺钉，以下哪项正确？ ______

A. 是用来调节汽油喷射器的供油量的　　B. 是用来调节混合气的浓度的

C. 以上都正确　　D. 以上都不正确

2. 讨论 EFI 系统时，甲说，ECU 通过控制燃油压力提供合适的空燃比；乙说，ECU 通过控制喷油器脉冲宽度提供合适的空燃比。试问谁正确？ ______

A. 甲正确　B. 乙正确　C. 两人均正确　D. 两人均不正确。

三、简答题

1. 简述电控燃油喷射系统的控制原理。
2. 简述空气流量传感器的作用。
3. 简述空气流量传感器的维修要点。

第 2 节　发动机电子点火控制系统

一、点火系统的认知

发动机电子点火系统是工程技术的重要组成部分，也是人类智慧的结晶。它不仅能够提高发动机的性能和效率，还能够减少污染物的排放，保护生态环境。它体现了社会主义核心价值观中的创新、绿色、和谐的理念，也符合习近平新时代中国特色社会主义思想中的科技创新、生态文明、人与自然和谐共生的要求。因此，我们应该积极学习和掌握发动机电子点火系统的相关知识和技能。

（一）发动机电子点火系统的要求

（1）能产生足以击穿火花塞间隙的电压。火花塞电极击穿而产生火花时所需要的电压称为击穿电压。点火系统产生的次级电压必须高于击穿电压，才能使火花塞跳火。

（2）火花应具有足够的能量。发动机正常工作时，由于混合气压缩终了的温度接近其自燃温度，仅需要 1~5 MJ 的火花能量。但在混合气过浓或是过稀，发动机启动、怠速或节气门急剧打开时，则需要较高的火花能量。并且随着现代发动机对经济性和排气净化要求的提高，都迫切需要提高火花能量。因此，为了保证可靠点火，高能电子点火系统一般应具有 80~100 MJ 的火花能量，启动时应产生高于 100 MJ 的火花能量。

（3）点火时刻应适应发动机的工作情况。首先，点火系统应按发动机的工作顺序进行点火。其次，必须在最有利的时刻进行点火。

由于混合气在汽缸内燃烧占用一定的时间，所以混合气不应在压缩行程上止点处

点火，而应适当提前，使活塞达到上止点时，混合气已得到充分燃烧，从而使发动机获得较大功率。点火时刻一般用点火提前角来表示，即从发出电火花开始到活塞到达上止点为止的一段时间内曲轴转过的角度。

如果点火过迟，当活塞到达上止点时才点火，则混合气的燃烧主要在活塞下行过程中完成，即燃烧过程在容积增大的情况下进行，使炽热的气体与汽缸壁接触的面积增大，因而转变为有效功的热量相对减少，汽缸内最高燃烧压力降低，导致发动机过热，功率下降。如果点火过早，由于混合气的燃烧完全在压缩过程中进行，汽缸内的燃烧压力急剧升高，在活塞到达上止点之前即达最大，使活塞受到反冲，发动机做负功，不仅使发动机的功率降低，并有可能引起爆燃和运转不平稳现象，加速运动部件和轴承的损坏。

（二）点火系统的作用

点火系统在发动机运转时所扮演的角色是在任何发动机转速及不同的发动机负荷下，均能在适当的时机提供足够的电压，使火花塞能产生足以点燃汽缸内混合气的火花，让发动机得到最佳的燃烧效率。点火系统的基本装置包含电源（电瓶）、点火触发装置点火正时控制装置、高压产生器（高压线圈）、高压电分配装置（分电盘）、高压导线及火花塞。现代汽车发动机的点火提前装置则已改由发动机管理电脑控制，电脑收集发动机转速、进气歧管压力或空气流量、节气门位置、电瓶电压、水温、爆震等信号，算出最佳点火正时提前角度，再发出点火信号，达到控制点火正时的目的。

（三）点火系统的分类

1. 传统点火系统

传统点火系统工作过程是由曲轴带动分电器轴转动，分电器轴上的凸轮转动，使点火线圈次级触点接通与闭合，从而产生高压电。这个点火高压电通过分电器轴上的分火头，根据发动机工作要求按顺序送到各个汽缸的火花塞上，火花塞发出电火花点燃燃烧室内的气体。分电器壳体可以手动转动来调节基本的点火提前角（即怠速运转时的点火提前角），同时还有真空提前装置，它根据进气管内真空度的变化提供不同的提前角。

2. 微机控制点火系统

微机控制点火系统与传统点火系统完全不同，它有一个点火用电子控制装置，内部有发动机在各种工况下所需的点火控制曲线图。通过一系列传感器如发动机转速传感器、进气管真空度传感器（发动机负荷传感器）、节气门位置传感器、曲轴位置传感器等来判断发动机的工作状态，在曲线图上找出发动机在此工作状态下所需的点火提

前角，按此要求进行点火，然后根据爆震传感器信号对上述点火要求进行修正，使发动机工作在最佳点火时刻。电子点火系统也有闭环控制与开环控制之分：带有爆震传感器，能根据发动机是否发生爆震及时修正点火提前角的电控系统称为闭环控制系统；不带爆震传感器，点火提前控制仅根据电控单元内设定的程序进行控制的称为开环控制系统。微机控制点火系统原理如图 2-2-1 所示。

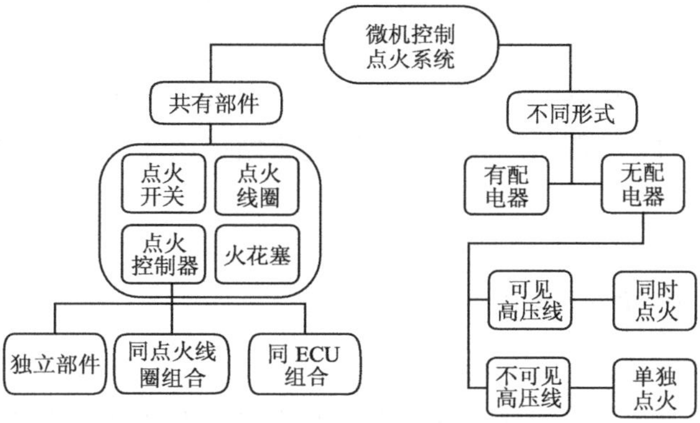

图 2-2-1　微机控制点火系统原理

（1）晶体管点火系统（TI-B），此种点火系统已经被淘汰。

（2）有分电器点火系统（SI），如图 2-2-2 至图 2-2-4 所示。

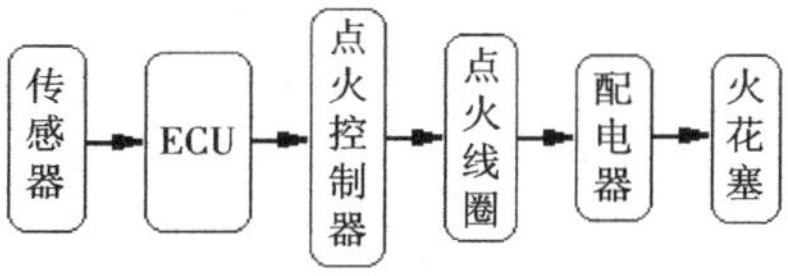

图 2-2-2　有分电器点火系统控制原理

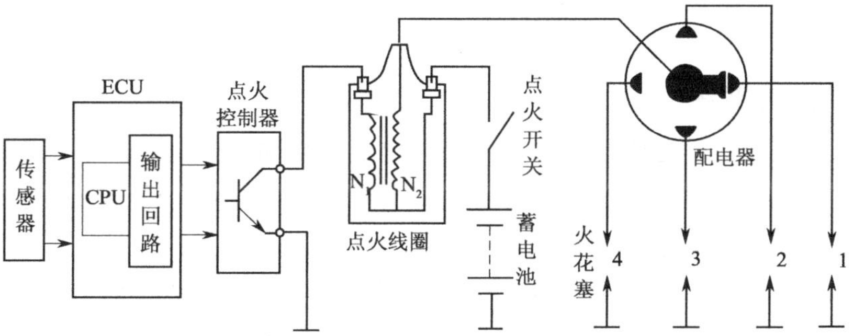

图 2-2-3　有分电器点火系统电路

图 2-2-4　有分电器点火系统实车

（3）无分电器点火系统（DIS），如图 2-2-5 至图 2-2-7 所示。

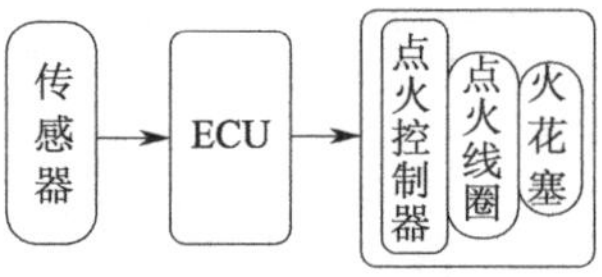

图 2-2-5　无分电器点火系统控制原理

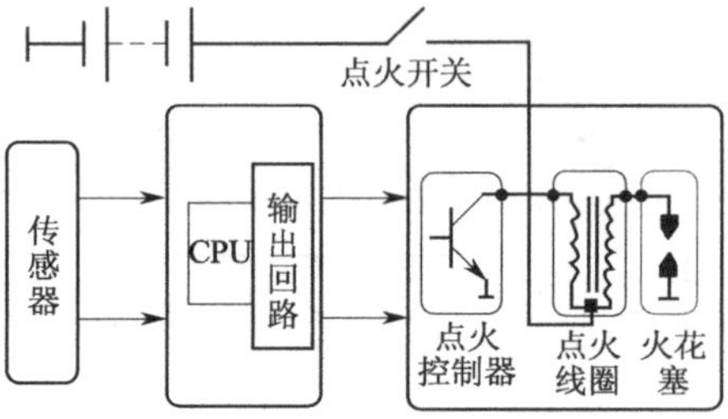

图 2-2-6　无分电器点火系统电路

图 2-2-7　无分电器点火系统实车

二、汽车电子点火系统的组成及工作原理

（一）发动机电子点火系统的组成

发动机电子点火系统主要由低压电源、点火线圈、点火控制器和安装在分电器内部的点火信号发生器、火花塞、传感器等组成，如图 2-2-8 所示。

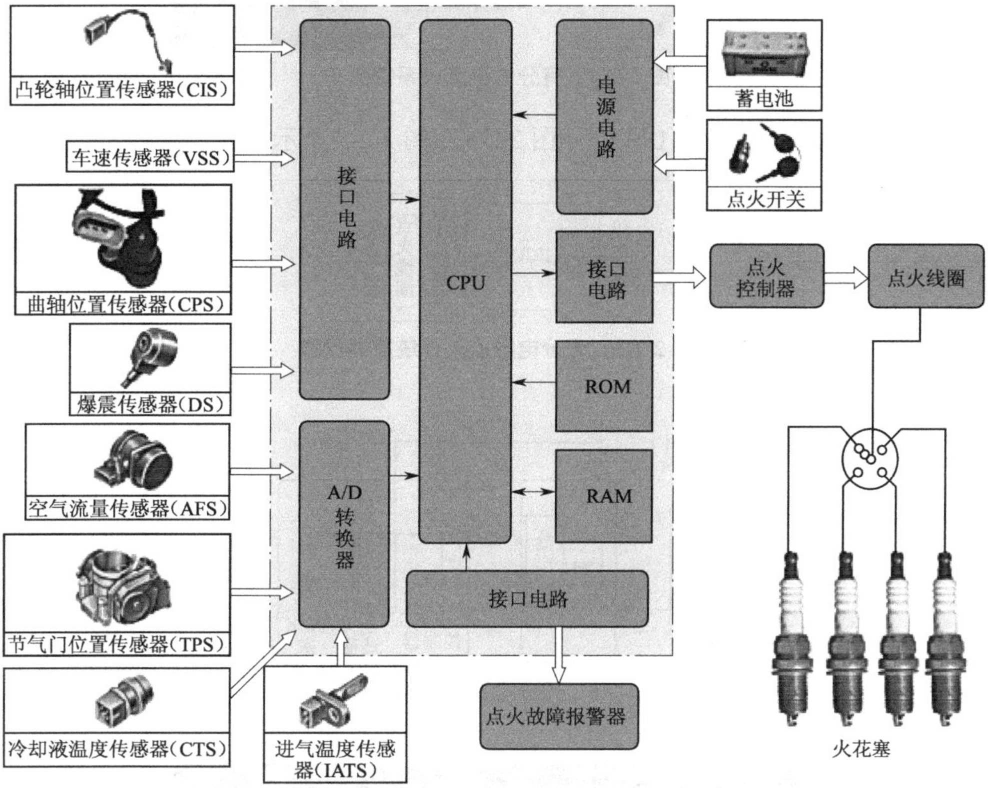

图 2-2-8　电控点火系统的组成

（1）低压电源点火系统的低压电源为蓄电池或交流发电机，标称电压一般为 12 V。低压电源的作用是为点火系统提供所需的电能。

（2）点火线圈构造与自耦变压器相似，主要由铁芯、初级绕组和次级绕组组成，其功用是将 12 V 的低压电转换成 15~20 kV 的高压电。

（3）点火控制器又称点火电子组件或电子点火器，由半导体器件组成电子开关电路，主要作用是根据点火信号发生器产生的点火脉冲信号，接通和切断点火线圈初级绕组电路。

（4）火花塞的作用是将点火线圈次级绕组产生的高压电引入汽缸燃烧室，产生电火花，从而点燃可燃混合气。

（5）点火开关的功用是控制点火系统的初级电路，点火开关一旦断开，发动机就会立即熄火。

（6）传感器是电控系统的基本组成部分，而在电控系统中，各传感器主要用来确定点火正时。

空气流量传感器（AFS）——确定基本点火提前角。

节气门位置传感器（TPS）——确定基本点火提前角。

曲轴位置传感器（CPS）——确定基本点火提前角。

凸轮轴位置传感器（CIS）——确定点火时机。

冷却液温度传感器（CTS）——修正点火提前角。

进气温度传感器（IATS）——修正点火提前角。

车速传感器（VSS）——修正点火提前角。

爆震传感器（DS）——修正点火提前角。

（二）发动机点火系统的工作原理

点火系统利用互感原理，发动机工作时，ECU 根据接收到的各传感器信号，按存储器中存储的有关程序和相关数据，确定该工况下最佳点火提前角控制参数（点火时间和通电时间），并向点火器发出指令。点火器则根据 ECU 的指令，控制点火线圈初级电路的导通和截止。当电路导通时，有电流从点火线圈中的初级电路通过，点火线圈将点火能量以磁场的形式储存起来。当初级电路中的电流被切断时，在次级线圈中将产生很高的感应电动势（15~20 kV）。而此时，随分电器轴一同旋转的分火头正好对准分电器盖上某缸的旁电极，高压电由分缸高压线送给火花塞，点火能量经火花塞瞬间释放，使火花塞跳火，产生的电火花点燃汽缸内的混合气，使发动机完成做功过程。

根据以上分析，点火系统的工作过程可分成三个阶段：初级电路导通，点火能量储存；初级电路截止，次级电路产生高压电；火花塞电极产生电火花，点燃混合气。

此外，在具有爆燃控制功能的电控点火系统中，ECU 还根据爆燃传感器的输入信号来判断发动机有无爆燃及爆燃的强度，并对点火提前角进行闭环控制。

【知识拓展】

不能点火的故障原因很多，首先要考虑的是油、液、气、电的供给情况，也就是说要检查启动系统、燃油供给系统，在确定它们没有故障的前提下，开始考虑点火系统是否出现问题。电路故障、元器件损坏等都会造成不能点火或者点火困难。下面以高压回路为例，进行点火系统的故障诊断，见表 2-2-1。

表 2-2-1　高压回路的检测

序号	图示	具体内容
1		检查火花塞外观： 1. 检查火花塞中心电极磨损情况； 2. 检查火花塞间隙； 3. 检查火花塞有无积炭； 4. 检查火花塞陶瓷有无裂纹
2	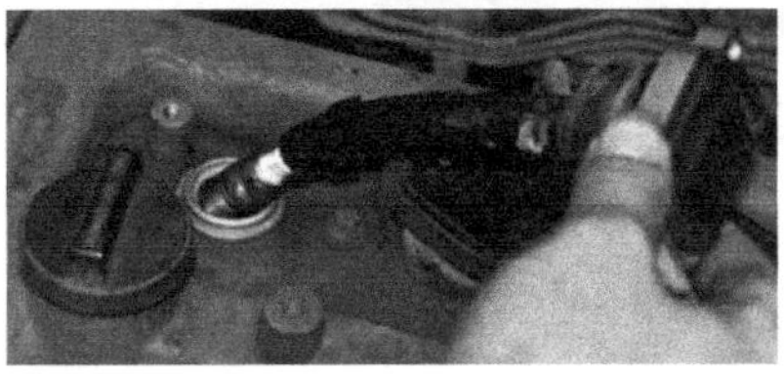 	检查高压导线： 1. 检查火花塞插头与高压导线是否连接正常； 2. 检查防干扰插头与高压导线是否连接正常； 3. 检查火花塞插头、高压导线、防干扰插头有无裂纹、腐蚀、老化等
3	 	检查点火模块： 1. 检查点火模块有无裂纹； 2. 检查点火模块有无变形； 3. 检查点火模块有无腐蚀
4	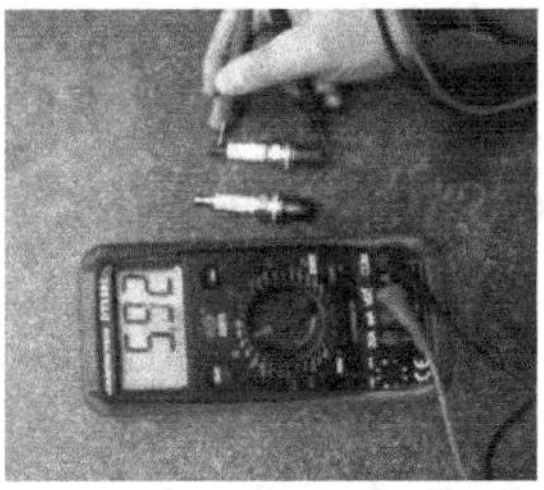	检查火花塞电极电阻： 正常值为 4~6 kΩ
5	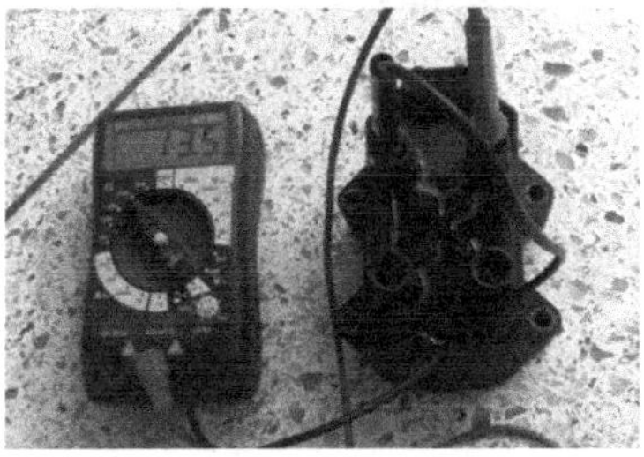	检查点火模块内阻： 点火模块电阻 4~8 kΩ

续表

序号	图示	具体内容
6		断开燃油泵保险
7	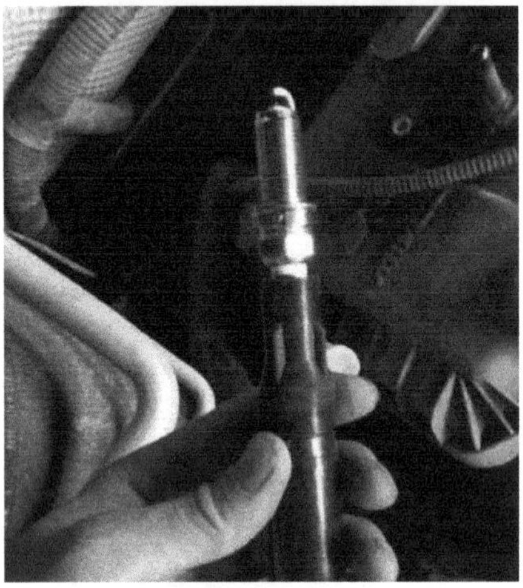	拔出高压导线，装上火花塞
8	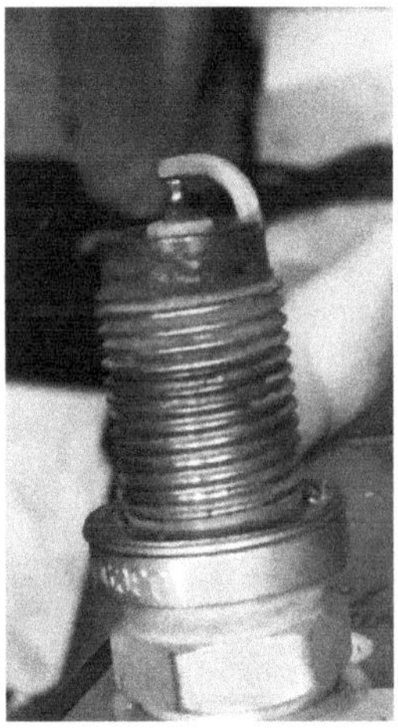	起动发动机，检查跳火情况

【思考与练习】

1. 简述电控点火系统的组成。

2. 简述电控点火的优点。

3. 简述有分电器点火系统和无分电器点火系统的相同点和不同点。

第 3 章

汽车底盘电控系统

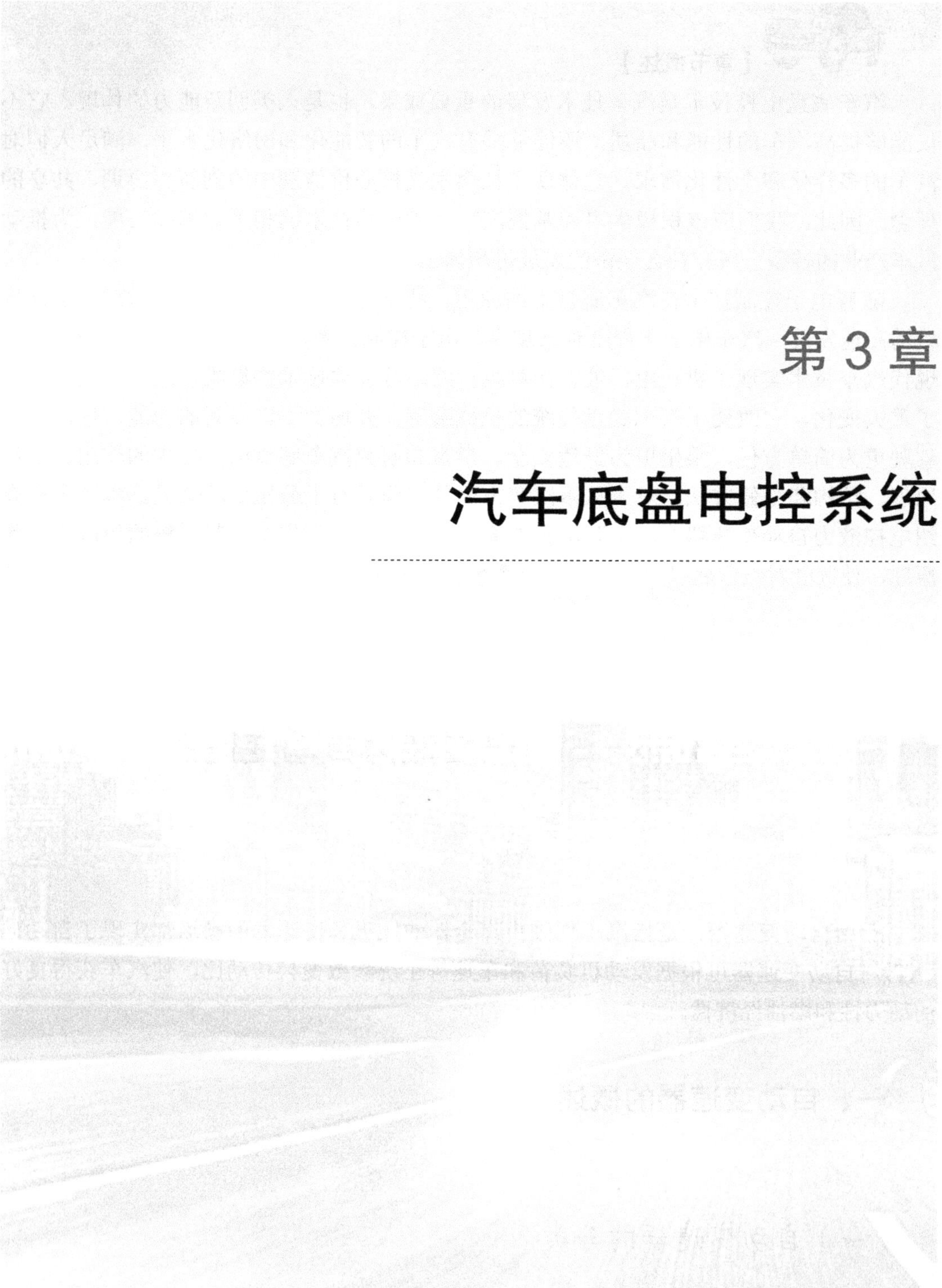

【章节概述】

汽车底盘电控技术是汽车技术发展的重要成果，也是人类创新能力的体现。它不仅能够提高汽车的性能和品质，还能够提升汽车的智能化和网络化水平，满足人们对汽车的多样化和个性化需求。它体现了社会主义核心价值观中的创新、协调、共享的理念。因此，我们应该积极学习和掌握汽车底盘电控技术的相关知识和技能，为推动汽车产业的转型升级和社会经济的发展进步做出贡献。

随着电子控制技术在汽车底盘上的应用，特别是大规模集成电路和微型电子计算机的高速发展，汽车电子化程度越来越高，电子控制技术在汽车上的应用越来越广泛。现代汽车技术实现了机、电、液、计算机、网络等多项技术的集成。汽车底盘也发生了重大变化，它改变了汽车底盘传统的机械装置，并增加了许多新的功能，使汽车的驾驶更为简单方便，乘坐更为舒适安全。学习和研究汽车底盘电控技术的作用、工作原理、结构和检修方法，对于从事汽车方面的工作具有十分重要的意义。本章主要介绍电控液力自动变速器、汽车防滑控制系统、汽车行驶与安全控制系统的组成及工作原理，使读者对汽车底盘电控系统有一个全面、系统的了解。

第 1 节　电控液力自动变速器

所谓自动变速器，是指汽车驾驶中离合器的操纵和变速器的操纵都实现了自动化（AT）。自动变速器可根据发动机负荷和车速等工况参数变换传动比，使汽车获得良好的动力性和燃油经济性。

一、自动变速器的概述

（一）自动变速器的分类

自动变速器可以按结构和控制方式、车辆驱动方式、挡位数的不同进行分类。

1. 按结构和控制方式

自动变速器按结构和控制方式的不同，可以分为液力式自动变速器、机械式自动

变速器、无级自动变速器和有级式双离合机械自动变速器。

（1）液力式自动变速器（HAT）（图3-1-1）是目前应用最广泛、技术最成熟的自动变速器。按照控制方式不同，液力式自动变速器可以分为液控流力自动变速器和电控液力自动变速器，目前轿车上都采用电控液力自动变速器；按照变速机构不同，液力式自动变速器可以分为行星齿轮自动变速器和非行星齿轮自动变速器，行星齿轮自动变速器又可分为辛普森式和拉维娜式。

图3-1-1　液力式自动变速器

（2）机械式自动变速器（AMT）（图3-1-2）是在原有普通有级式手动齿轮变速器的基础上增加了电子控制系统，以自动控制离合器的接合、分离和变速器挡位的变换。机械式自动变速器由于原有的机械传动结构基本不变，所以齿轮传动固有的传动效率高、结构紧凑、工作可靠等优点被很好地继承下来。

图3-1-2　机械式自动变速器

（3）无级自动变速器（CVT）（图3-1-3）采用传动带和工作直径可变的主、从动带轮相配合来传递动力，可以实现传动比的连续改变。这也是一种具有广阔发展前景的自动变速器，已在部分汽车上应用。

（4）有级式双离合机械自动变速器（DCT、DSG）（图3-1-4）有别于一般的自动变速器系统，基于手动变速器而又属于自动变速器，拥有手动变速器的灵活性及自动变速器的舒适性，因为拥有两套离合器，分别负责不同挡位时的动力传速，因此能提供无间断的动力输出。而传统的手动变速器使用一台离合器，当换挡时，驾驶员须踩下离合器踏板，使不同挡的齿轮做出啮合动作，而动力就在换挡期间出现间断，令输出

表现有所断续。

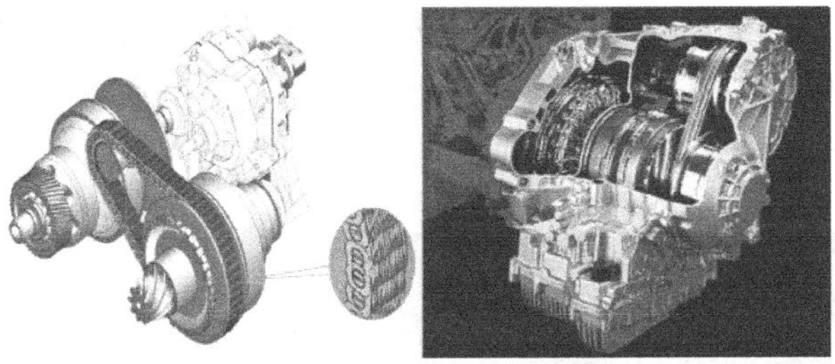

图 3-1-3　无级自动变速器

图 3-1-4　有级式双离合机械自动变速器

2. 按车辆驱动方式

自动变速器按车辆驱动方式的不同，可以分为后驱动自动变速器和前驱动自动变速器。后驱动自动变速器用于发动机前置后轮驱动的布置形式，变速器与主减速器、差速器分开;前驱动自动变速器用于发动机前置前轮驱动的布置方式，变速器与主减速器、差速器制成一个总成，如图 3-1-5 所示。

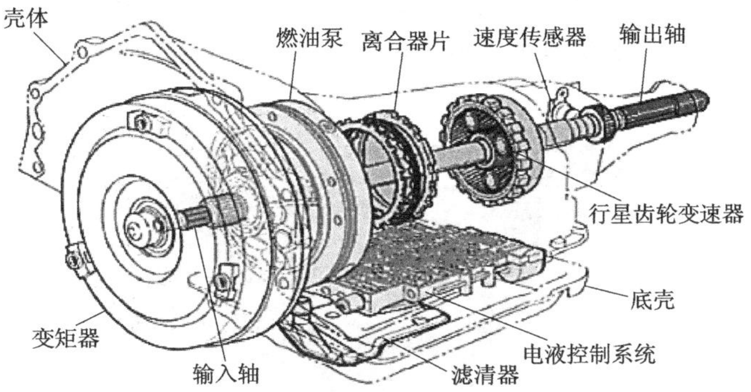

图 3-1-5　电控液力自动变速器的组成

3. 按自动变速器前进挡的挡位数

按照自动变速器换挡杆置于前进挡时的挡位数的不同，可以将其分为 4 挡、5 挡、6 挡等。

（二）电控液力自动变速器的基本组成

电控液力自动变速器主要由液力变矩器、行星齿轮变速机构、液压控制系统和电子控制系统四大部分组成。

1. 液力变矩器

液力变矩器是一个通过自动变速器油（ATF）传递动力的装置，它可以在一定范围内自动、连续地改变转矩比，以适应不同行驶阻力的要求。它还具有离合器的功用，在发动机不熄火、自动变速器位于动力挡的情况下，汽车可以处于停车状态，驾驶员可通过控制节气门开度控制液力变矩器的输出转矩，逐步加大输出转矩，实现动力的柔和传递。

2. 行星齿轮变速机构

与普通齿轮式手动变速器的作用相同，行星齿轮变速机构可形成不同的传动比，组合成电控变速器不同的挡位。它可以在液力变矩器的基础上将传动比的变化范围增大 2~4 倍，以提高汽车的行驶适应能力，还可以实现倒挡的传动。

3. 液压控制系统

1）换挡执行元件

电控液力自动变速器的换挡执行元件主要包括制动器、离合器和单向离合器。其作用与手动变速器的换挡拨叉、结合套等换挡元件类似，可以实现挡位和传动比的变换。

2）液压控制回路

电控液力自动变速器的液压控制回路主要控制换挡执行机构的工作，由液压泵及各种液压控制阀和液压管路等组成。

4. 电子控制系统

电子控制系统与液压控制系统配合使用，通常把它们合称为电液控制系统。电子控制系统主要包括电子控制单元、各类传感器及执行器等。电子控制系统中的传感器及各种控制开关将发动机工况、车速等信号传递给电子控制单元，电子控制单元发出指令给执行器，执行器和液压系统按一定的规律控制换挡执行机构工作，实现电控液力自动变速器自动换挡。

（三）电控液力自动变速器的控制原理

电控液力自动变速器是通过传感器和各种信号开关检测汽车和发动机的运行状态，接收驾驶员的指令，将发动机转速、节气门开度、车速、发动机冷却液温度、自动变速器液压油温等参数转变为电信号，并输入 ECU。ECU 根据这些信号，按照设定的换挡规律，向换挡电磁阀、油压电磁阀等发出电子控制信号。换挡电磁阀和油压电磁阀再将 ECU 发出的控制信号转变为液压控制信号，阀板中的各个控制阀根据这些液压控制信号，控制换挡执行机构的动作，从而实现自动换挡（图 3-1-6）。

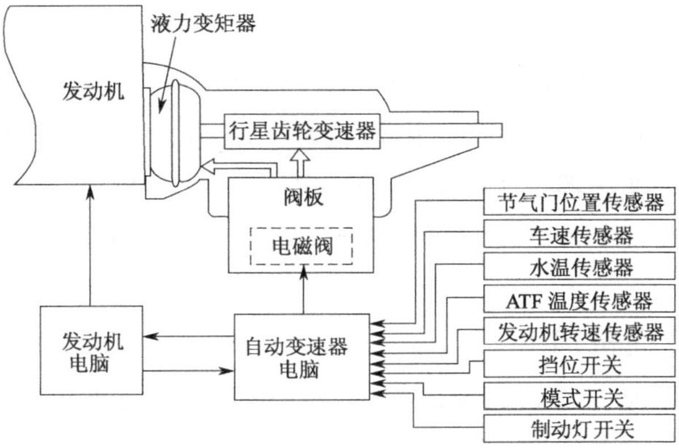

图 3-1-6　电控液力自动变速器的控制原理

长城 H6 采用 7 速湿式双离合变速箱，下面以双离合变速箱为例进行阐述说明。

二、电控双离合自动变速器检修

双离合自动变速器（DCT）有别于传统的液力自动变速器，是基于手动变速器发展而来的，应该是 AMT 机械式自动变速器中的一员。它除了拥有手动变速器的灵活和自动变速器的舒适以外，还能提供不间断的动力输出。装备双离合自动变速器的车辆相比装备手动变速器的车辆，在动力性和百公里加速上都具有明显的优势，而其城市工况和综合工况油耗，与装备手动变速器的车辆差不多，低于装备普通液力变矩器式 AT 的车辆。现在国内市场上，一汽大众、上汽大众等有些车型装备双离合自动变速器。

（一）双离合自动变速器的结构组成

双离合自动变速器的工作原理是将变速器挡位按奇偶数分开布置，分别与两个离合器连接，通过切换两个离合器的工作状况来完成换挡动作。

1. 整体结构组成

双离合自动变速器（图 3-1-7）主要由输入双离合器、电子液压控制系统和齿轮变速系统组成。

2. 齿轮变速系统

齿轮变速系统的结构（图 3-1-8）与手动变速器相似，是普通斜齿轮式的，有两根同心的输入轴和两根平行的输出轴，还有一根中间轴，也称为倒挡惰轮轴。

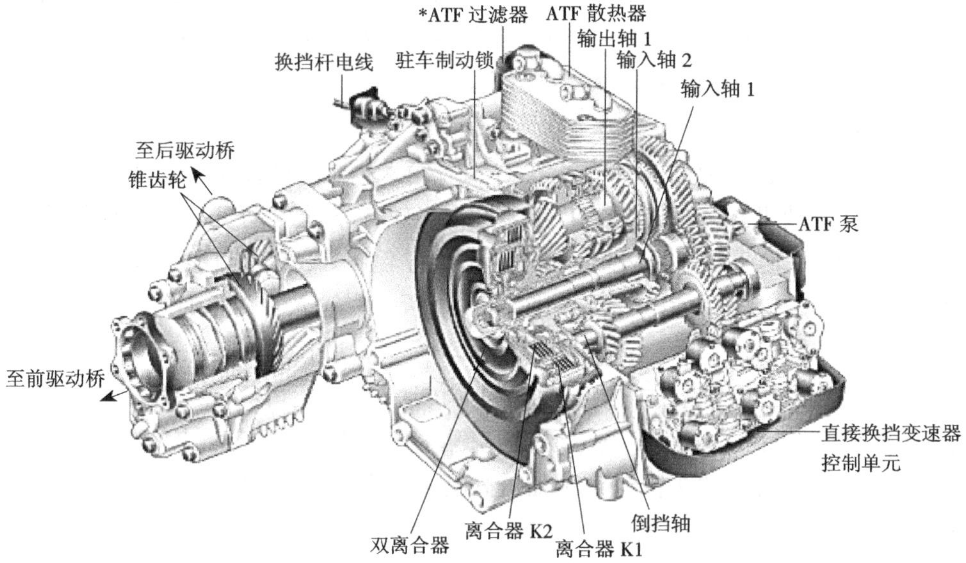

图 3-1-7 双离合自动变速器的组成

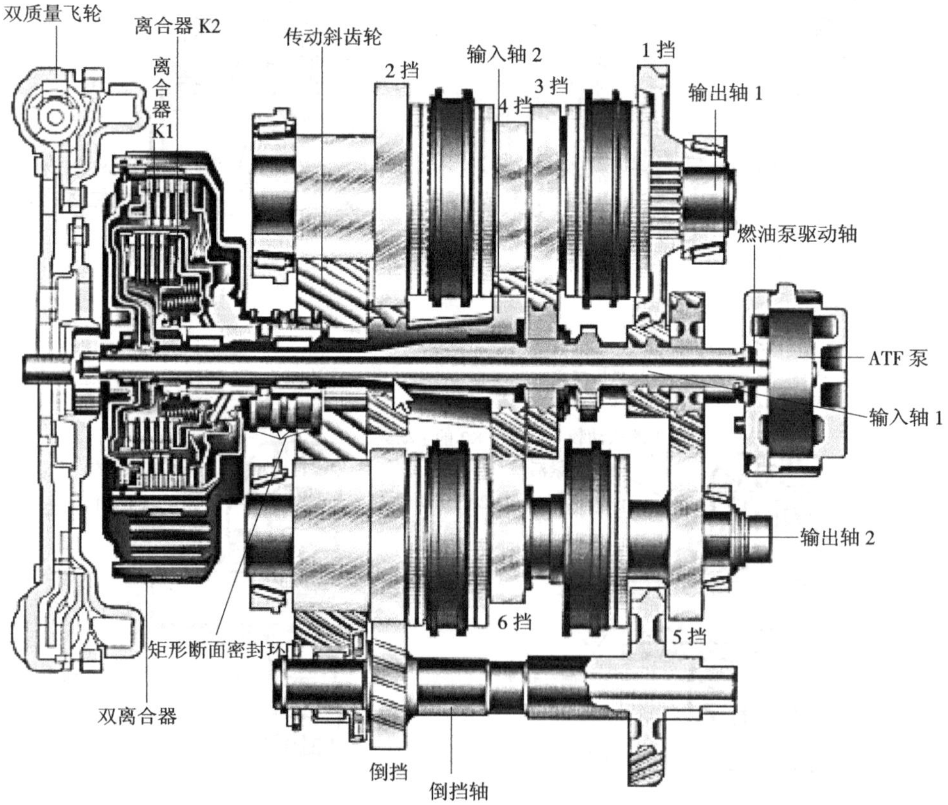

图 3-1-8 齿轮变速系统的结构

（1）变速器前端装有一个由两组离合器片集合而成的双离合器装置（K1 和 K2）

（图 3-1-9）。双离合器安装于一个充满液压油的封闭油腔里，离合器片之间也充满油液，其传动原理与普通 AT 里面的湿式多片离合器相同。这种湿式结构具有更好的调节能力和优异的热容性，因此能够传递比较大的扭矩。

（2）输入轴。

承接双离合器装置动力的是一个由实心轴（输入轴 1）及其外部套筒（输入轴 2）组合而成的双传动轴机构，离合器 K1 接合可将飞轮传来的发动机动力传递给实心轴 [图 3-1-10（a）]，即输入轴 1。输入轴 1 上有 1 挡 / 倒挡、3 挡和 5 挡主动齿轮，还有输入轴 1 转速传感器 G501 的信号轮，如图 3-1-11 所示。输入轴 1 可通过齿轮传动实现 1 挡、3 挡、5 挡和倒挡。

离合器 K2 接合可将飞轮传来的发动机动力传递给输入轴 2。输入轴 2 为套在输入轴 1 上的空心套筒 [图 3-1-10（b）]，通过花键与离合器 K2 相连，上有 2 挡、4 挡 /6 挡的主动齿轮，还有输入轴 2 转速传感器的信号轮，如图 3-1-12 所示。输入轴 2 可通过齿轮传动实现 2 挡、4 挡和 6 挡。

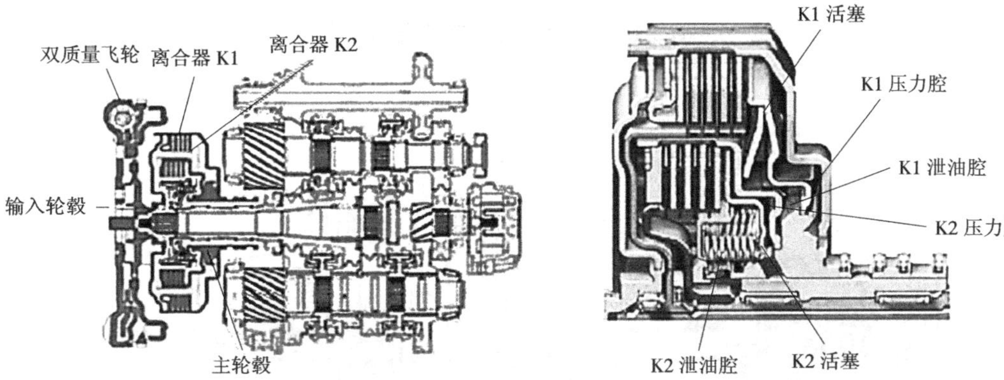

（a）　（b）

图 3-1-9　双离合器

（a）双离合器安装位置　（b）双离合器的结构

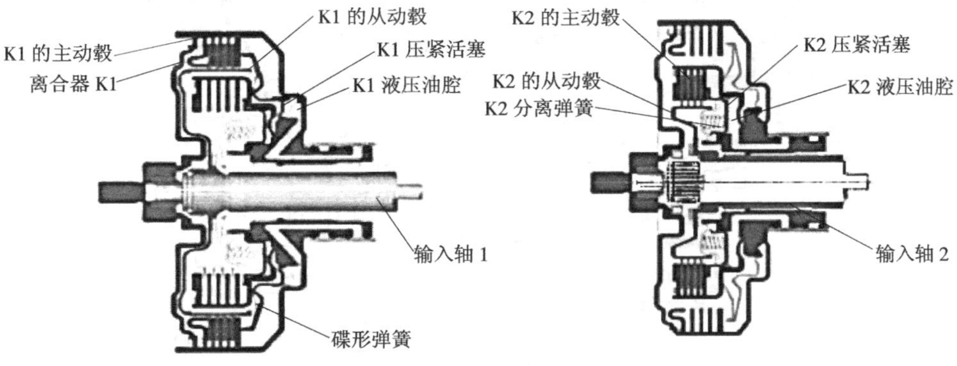

（a）　（b）

图 3-1-10　离合器 K1、K2 的结构

（a）离合器 K1　（b）离合器 K2

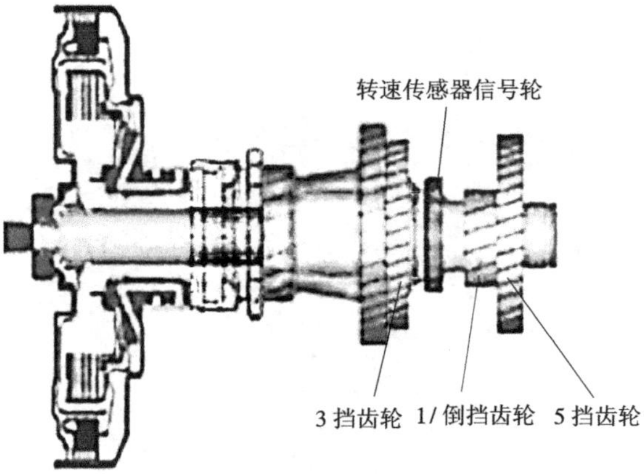

图 3-1-11　输入轴 1 的结构

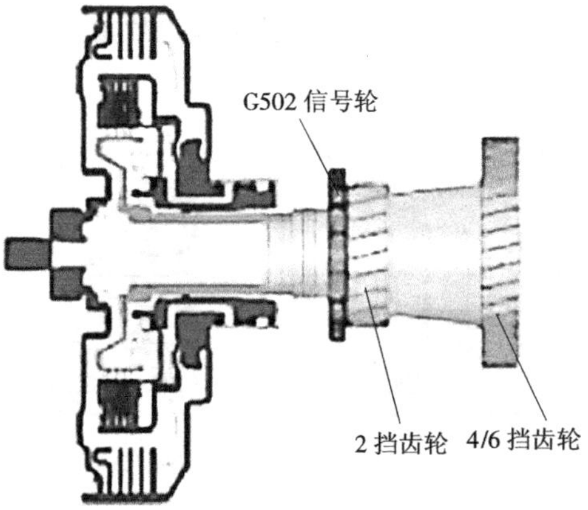

图 3-1-12　输入轴 2 的结构

（3）输出轴。

两根平行输出轴的输出齿轮都与主减速器的输入齿轮相啮合，其相对安装位置如图 3-1-13 所示。输出轴 1 的结构如图 3-1-14（a）所示，轴上有 1 挡、2 挡、3 挡、4 挡的从动齿轮，分别与输入轴上的 1 挡、2 挡、3 挡、4 挡主动齿轮啮合；还有 1 挡和 3 挡的换挡结合套及同步器、2 挡和 4 挡的换挡结合套及同步器，结合套及同步器的作用与手动变速器相同；另外输出轴 1 上面还有与差速器相连的输出齿轮。输出轴 2 的结构如图 3-1-14（b）所示，轴上有 5 挡、6 挡和倒挡的从动齿轮，与差速器相连的输出齿轮及相应的换挡装置。

（4）倒挡轴。

倒挡轴上有倒挡惰轮 1（大）和倒挡惰轮 2（小），分别与输入轴 1 上的倒挡主动齿轮和输出轴 2 上的倒挡从动齿轮相啮合，如图 3-1-15 所示。

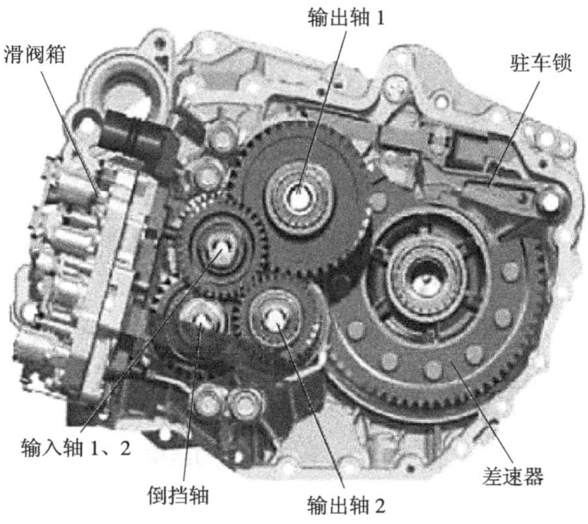

图 3-1-13　输出轴的安装位置

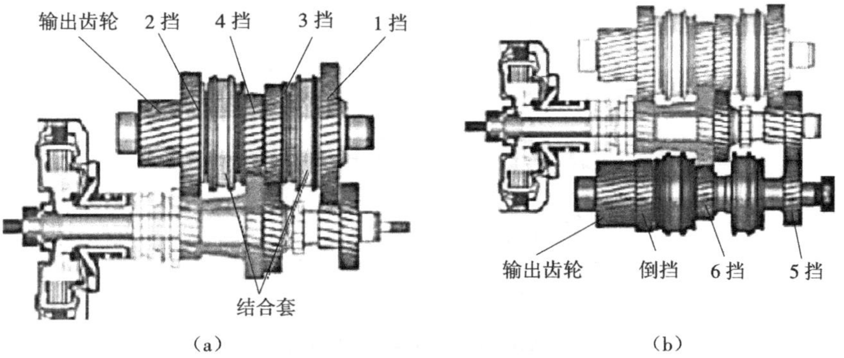

图 3-1-14　变速器的输出轴结构

（a）输出轴 1　（b）输出轴 2

（5）换挡机构。

换挡机构和手动变速器一样，由换挡拨叉推动结合套来完成，但是与手动变速器不同的是，双离合变速器不再需要手动推拨叉，而是由液压马达（或者称液压伺服机构）来推动拨叉完成换挡，如图 3-1-16 所示。每个换挡拨叉由两个被机电控制系统控制的液压马达来推动，而行程传感器是用来检测拨叉行程，确定挂挡是否到位的。

（6）其他辅助设备。

双离合变速器的 ATF 循环和供应如图 3-1-17 所示。双离合变速器因为采用湿式设计，使用单一的油液，ATF 油用量较大，所以设计了机油槽，并且拥有压力机油滤清器、机油冷却器以及靠曲轴动力驱动的机燃油泵等。

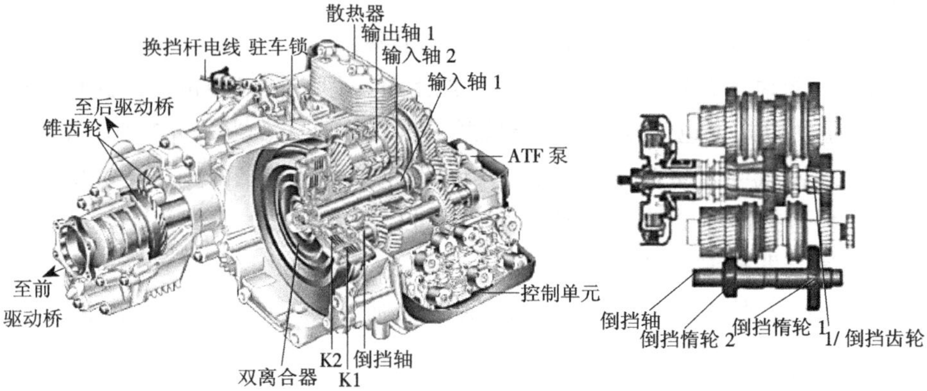

图 3-1-15　倒挡轴的结构和安装位置

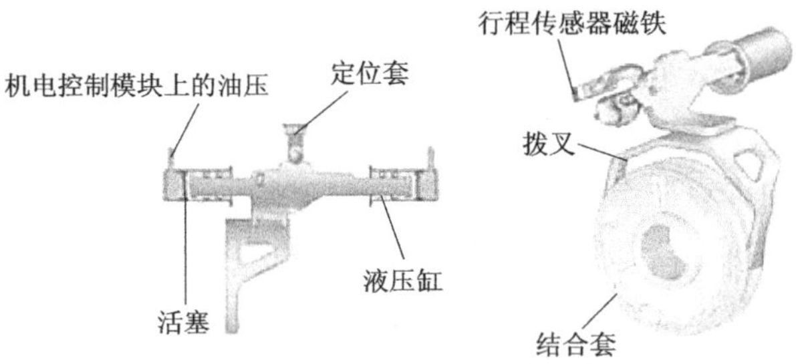

图 3-1-16　换挡控制

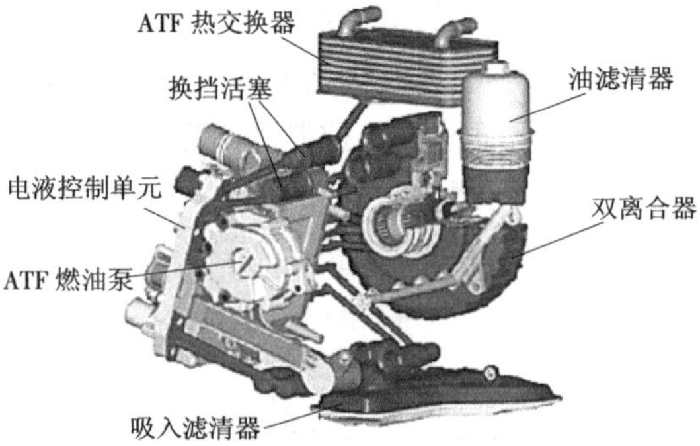

图 3-1-17　双离合变速器的 ATF 循环和供应

（二）双离合自动变速器的工作过程

双离合自动变速器在升挡或者降挡时，都是同时有 2 个挡位接合的。升挡时，比正在工作的挡位高一挡的挡位作为预选挡位而接合。如果 1 挡正在工作，则 2 挡位作为预选挡位而接合；降挡时，比正在工作的挡位低一挡的挡位作为预选挡位而接合。如果正在工作的是 6 挡，则 5 挡作为预选挡位而接合。双离合变速器的升挡或降挡是由

变速器控制器（TCU）判断的：踩油门踏板时，TCU 判定为升挡过程，做好升挡准备；踩制动踏板时，TCU 判定为降挡过程，做好降挡准备。

一般来讲，变速器升挡总是一挡一挡逐级上升，但降挡时经常会跳跃地下降。双离合变速器在手动模式下也可以进行跳跃降挡，例如，要从 6 挡降到 3 挡，连续按 3 下降挡按钮，变速器就会直接从 6 挡降到 3 挡，但是如果从 6 挡降到 2 挡，变速器就会先降到 5 挡，再直接降到 2 挡。也就是说，在进行跳跃降挡时，如果起始挡位和最终挡位由同一个离合器控制，则必须通过另一个离合器控制的挡位来转换一下，而如果起始挡位和最终挡位不是由同一个离合器控制的，则可以直接跳跃至所定挡位。

（三）电控模块

双离合器变速箱的机电控制模块 J743 是变速箱的核心控制单元。在该模块中，电子控制单元和电子液压控制单元整合成为一个部件。机电控制模块连接在变速箱上，并且是一个独立封闭的单元。它拥有独立的液压油回路，与变速箱机械部分的变速箱油回路完全隔离。

紧凑式封闭单元的优点在于：

（1）所有传感器和执行器都集成在机电控制模块内；

（2）机电模块中的液压油油量专门根据需要而定。

独立的供油系统防止变速箱机械部分的碎渣进入模块中。因为模块用油的黏度无须符合变速箱对用油的要求，所以机电控制模块的低温工作性能非常好。

机电控制模块的电子控制单元是变速箱的核心控制单元（图 3-1-18 和图 3-1-19）。所有传感器的信号和所有其他控制单元的信号都汇集于此，所有的行动从这里开始，并受它的监控。在电子控制单元中集成了 10 个传感器，仅变速箱输入转速传感器 G182 安装在控制单元外。电子控制单元通过液压控制和调节 8 个电磁阀，这些电磁阀用于换挡和控制离合器。电子控制单元匹配离合器的位置、匹配挂入挡位时换挡执行器的位置，并在今后的运行中注意这些部件的匹配。

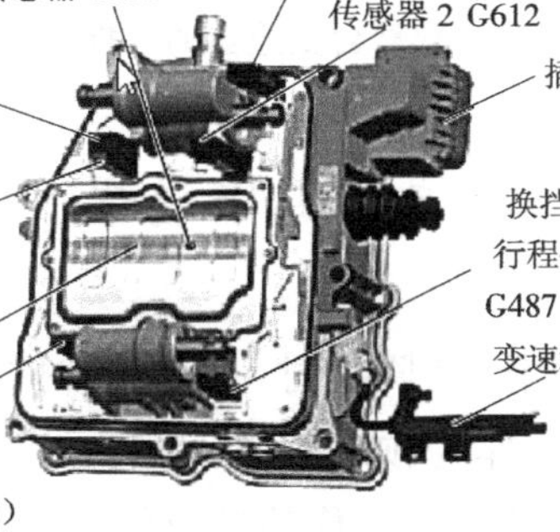

图 3-1-18　电控模块 1

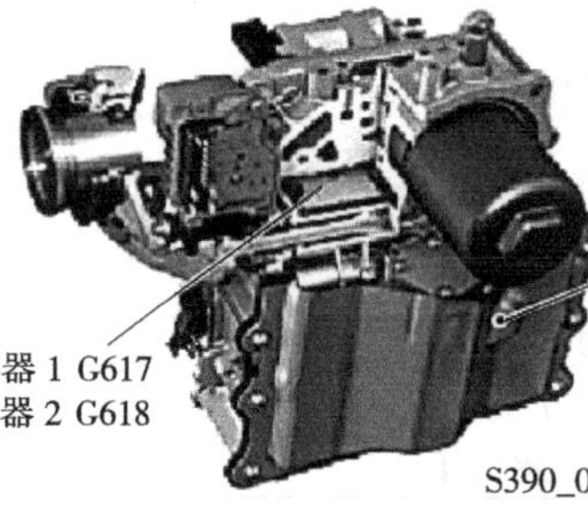

图 3-1-19 电控模块 2

电子液压控制单元集成在机电模块中（图 3-1-20），由它产生换挡所需的和控制离合器所需的液压。

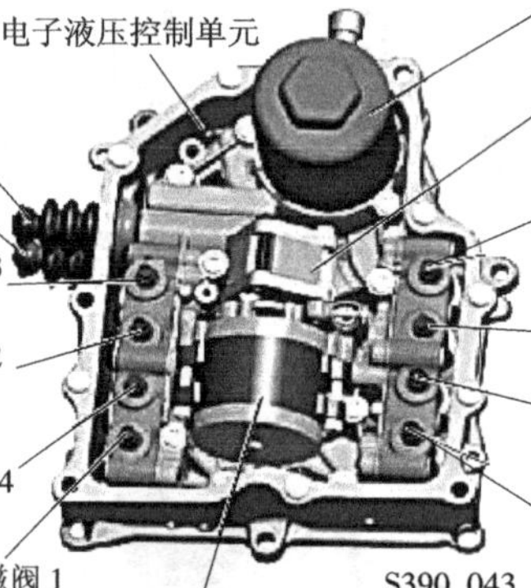

图 3-1-20 电子液压控制单元

其液压的产生和液压的基本控制由液压泵电机和与之相连的液压泵来实现。蓄压器保证电磁阀上一直有足够的液压可用。

双离合器变速箱内有两套相互独立的油液回路，各回路中使用的油液不同。

（1）变速箱机械部分的油液回路。

（2）机电控制模块的油液回路。

变速箱机械部分的供油原理与手动变速器类似，区别在于控制系统要相对复杂，液压控制模块与机械部分相互隔离，如图 3-1-21 所示。

液压泵总成（图 3-1-22）是控制系统的主要执行元件，安装在控制模块内，由液压泵及驱动电机组成。控制单元根据换挡需求，控制驱动电机工作状态，驱动电机与液压泵连接，从而实现管路中液压的控制。

液压泵由两个半径相等的齿轮相互啮合，在转动时，不停地将吸入侧的液压油输送到输出侧，在吸入侧形成负压，液压油根据转速的变化源源不断地进入泵体中，从而实现加压泵油的作用，输出侧的油压可以达到 80 bar 以上，如图 3-1-23 所示。

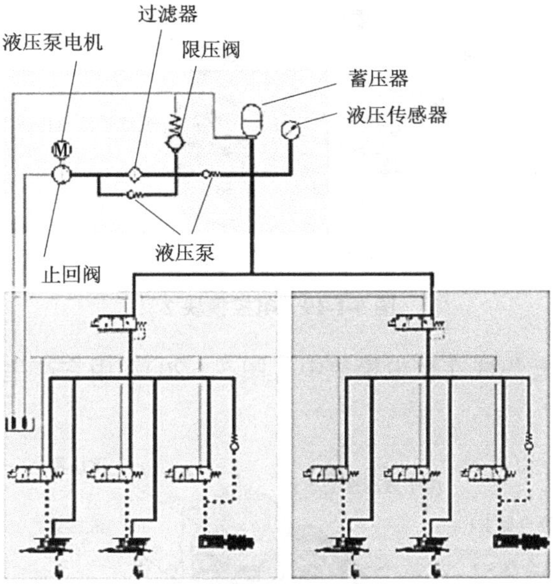

图 3-1-21　油液回路

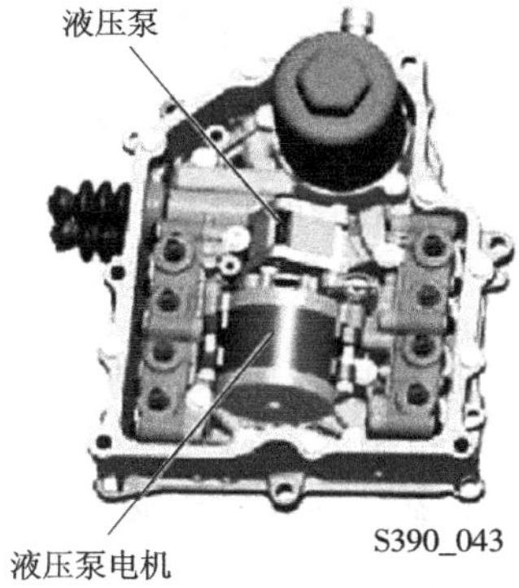

图 3-1-22　液压泵总成

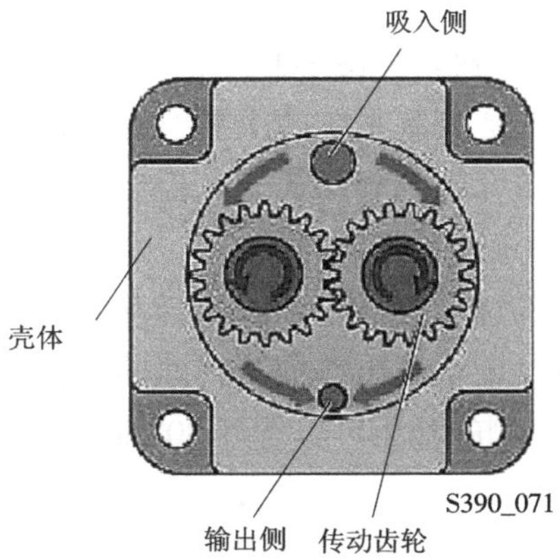

图 3-1-23　液压泵工作原理

液压泵电机为直流无刷电机，由定子和转子组成，其转子由6对永磁体组成，定子由6对电磁体组成，如图3-1-24所示。

无刷电机主要靠改变输入到无刷电机定子线圈上的电流波交变频率和波形，在绕组线圈周围形成一个绕电机几何轴心旋转的磁场，这个磁场驱动转子上的永磁磁钢转动，电机就转起来了，如图3-1-25所示。因为少了电刷的机械磨损，无刷电机的使用寿命更长，额定转速更高。

蓄压器（图3-1-26）以空气作为媒介为系统保压，当液压泵被关闭时，蓄压器为液压系统提供必要的压力。

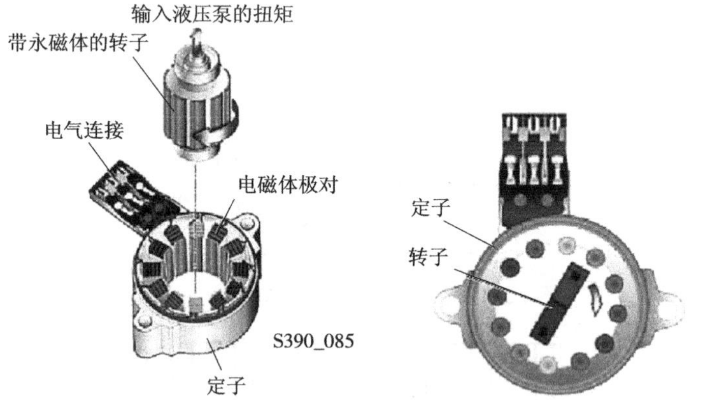

图3-1-24　液压泵电机构造

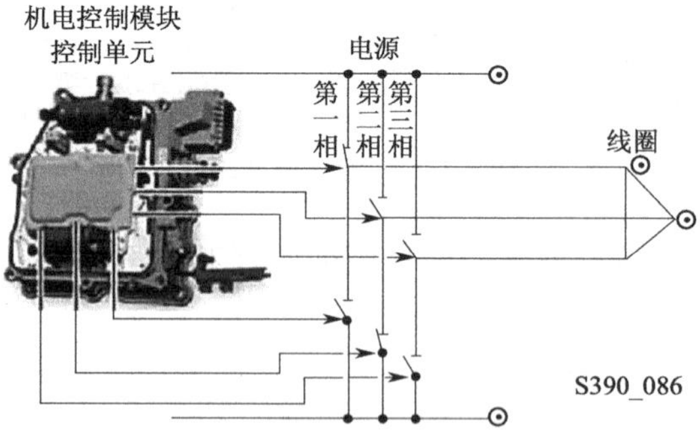

图3-1-25　电动控制图

第一相—接通正极；第二相—接通负极；第三相—断开

图 3-1-26　蓄压器

液压油回路如图 3-1-27 所示，主要包括压力调节电磁阀、换挡电磁阀以及离合器电磁阀等执行元件。

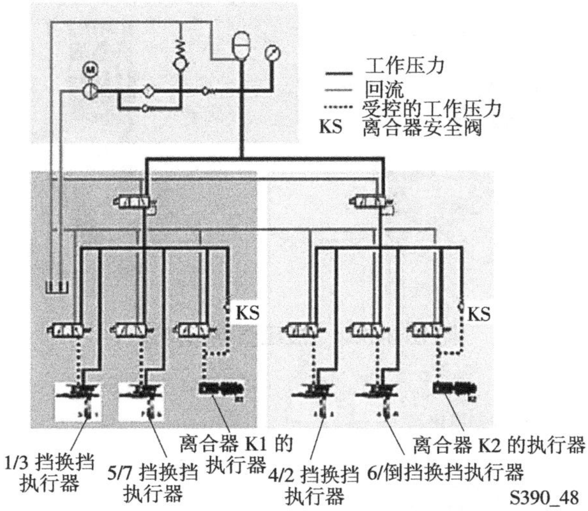

图 3-1-27　液压油回路

压力调节电磁阀主要进行分变速器内的油压调节，保证每个分变速器能够正常运行，如图 3-1-28 所示。

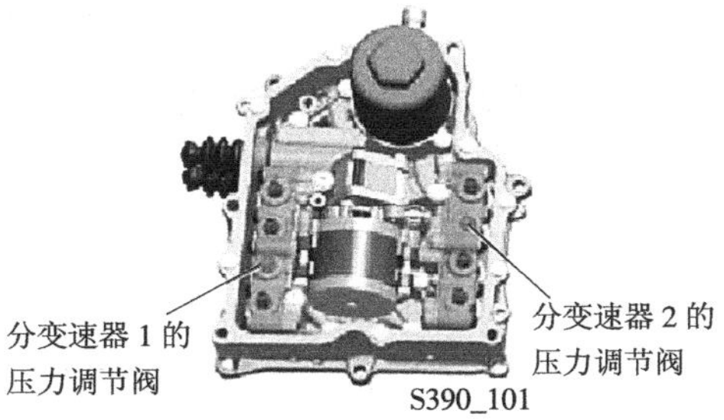

图 3-1-28　液压油回路电磁阀

换挡电磁阀（图 3-1-29）负责调节向换挡执行器输送的液压油油量。每一个换挡

执行器可以实现两个挡位。如果未挂入任何挡位，换挡执行器在油压的作用下停留在空挡。当换挡杆在P挡，且点火开关已关闭时，变速箱位于1挡。

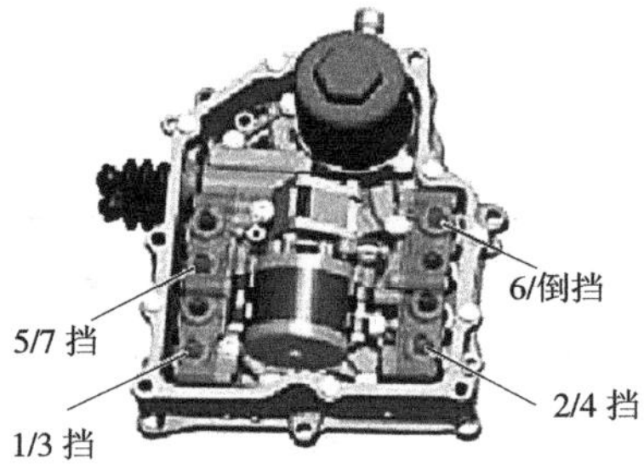

图 3-1-29　换挡电磁阀

离合器电磁阀（图 3-1-30）主要进行离合器执行器的液压油油量调节。通电时，离合器的接合和断开由离合器执行器进行控制。断电时，电磁阀和离合器处于分离状态。发生故障时，离合器安全阀可以排放液压油，从而使离合器分离。

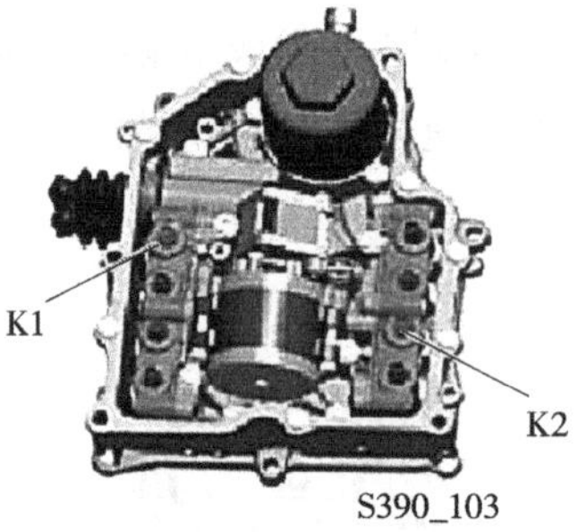

图 3-1-30　离合器电磁阀

双离合变速器的换挡由换挡拨叉拨动结合套，使不同挡位齿轮相互啮合，从而实现挡位的变化，每个换挡拨叉（图 3-1-31）负责 2 个挡位，位于变速箱壳体内两侧。

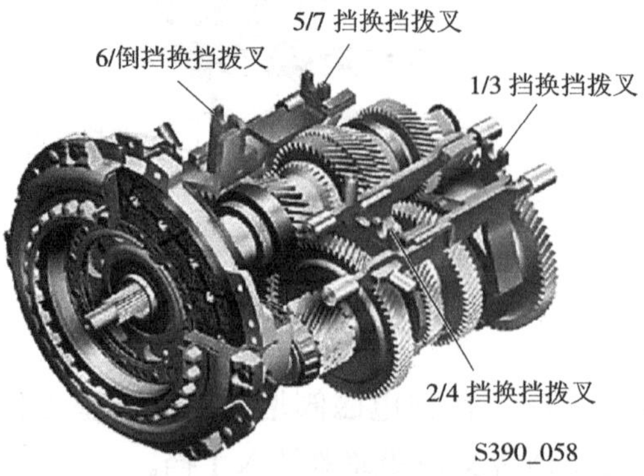

图 3-1-31　换挡拨叉

换挡时，机电控制模块控制液压泵向换挡执行器的活塞施加油压（图 3-1-32 和图 3-1-33），活塞推动拨叉移动，带动结合套和同步器将不同挡位齿轮啮合，传递动力，从而实现换挡。

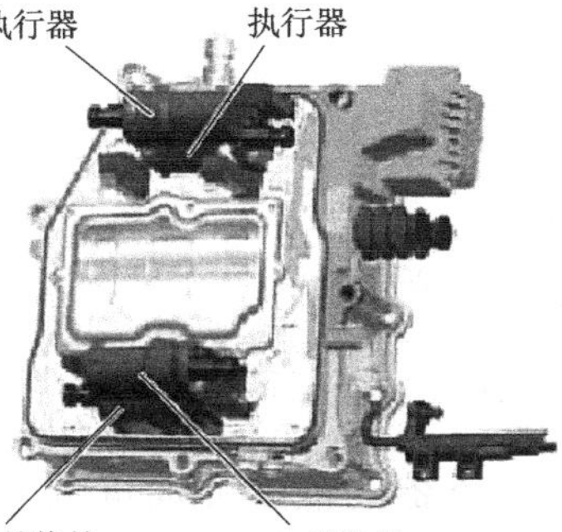

图 3-1-32　机电控制模块

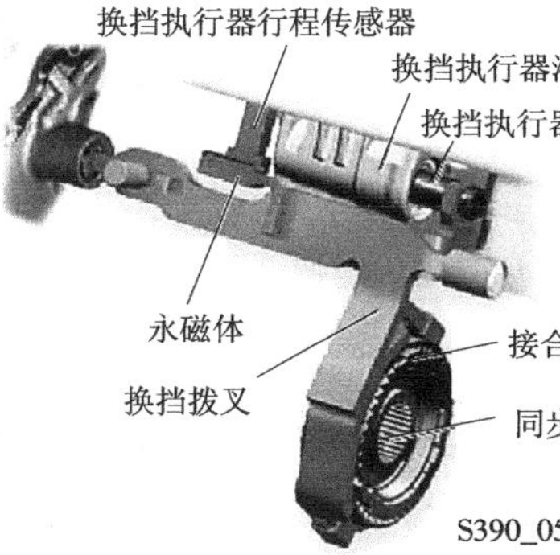

图 3-1-33　传感器位置

在起始位置（图 3-1-34）时，换挡电磁阀 N433 在油压作用下，换挡执行器活塞保持在 N 挡，挂入任何挡位，分变速器 1 中的 4 号电磁阀 N436 负责调节分变速器 1 中的油压。

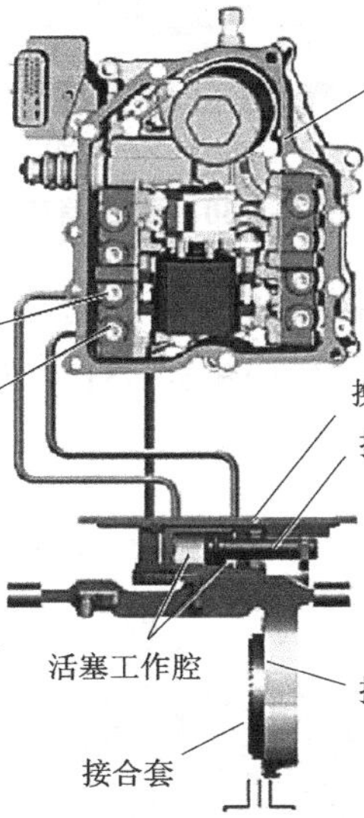

图 3-1-34　起始位置

挂入 1 挡（图 3-1-35）时，换挡电磁阀增大左侧活塞工作腔的油压，换挡执行器活塞向右移动，活塞连接换挡拨叉使变速器挂入 1 挡。

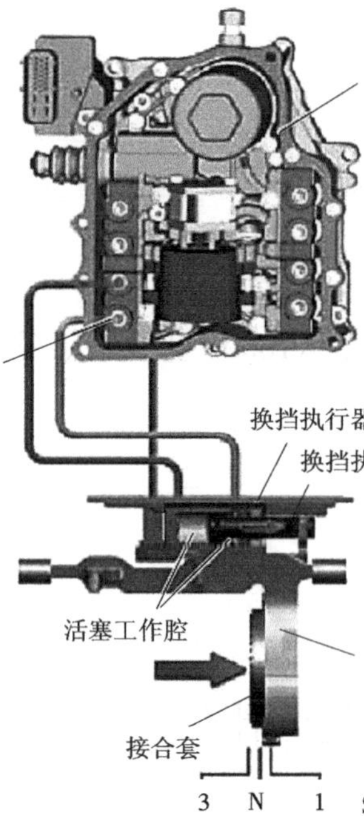

图 3-1-35　挂入 1 挡

离合器 K1 和 K2（图 3-1-36）由离合器执行器活塞控制离合器拨叉，实现离合器的结合与分离。特别说明的是在离合器执行器活塞上有一个永磁体，离合器行程传感器要通过永磁体来识别活塞位置。为了避免影响识别效果，离合器执行器液压缸和活塞不允许有磁性。

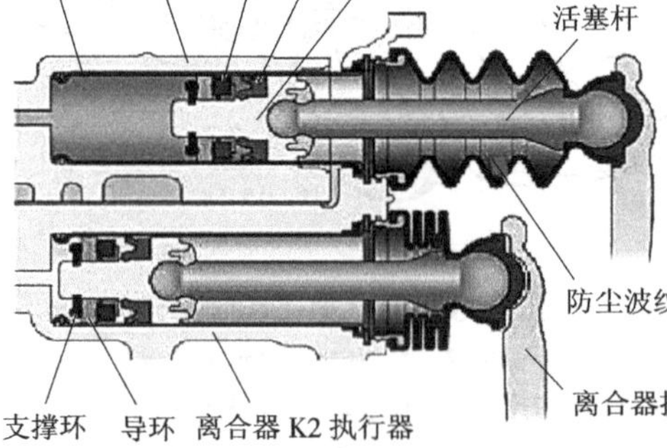

图 3-1-36　离合器执行器

【知识拓展】

一、准备工作

实训车辆（丰田卡罗拉轿车）；KT600、万用表、维修操作台等；维修手册、任务工单。

二、实施步骤

（一）找出电子控制系统元件位置

各元件位置如图 3-1-37 所示。

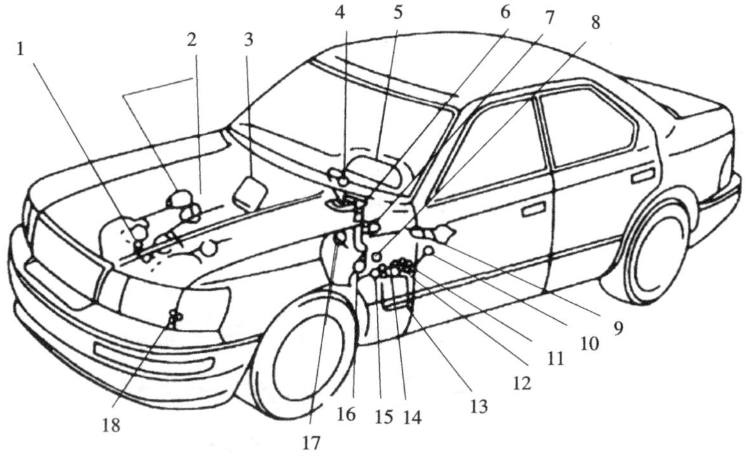

图 3-1-37　电子控制单元元件

1—发动机水温传感器；2—节气门位置传感；3—发动机与变速器 ECU；4—超速控制开关；5—0/D OFF 指示灯；6—行驶模式选择开关；7—制动灯开关；8—超速离合器转速传感器；9—1 号车速传感；10—2 号车速传感器；11—1 号电磁阀；12—2 号电磁阀；13—巡航控制 ECU；14—3 号电磁阀；15—4 号电磁阀；16—空挡起动开关；17—节气门全开强制降挡开关；18—发动机转速传感器

（二）认识 A341E 型自动变速器电控原理

A341E 型自动变速器电控原理如图 3-1-38 所示。

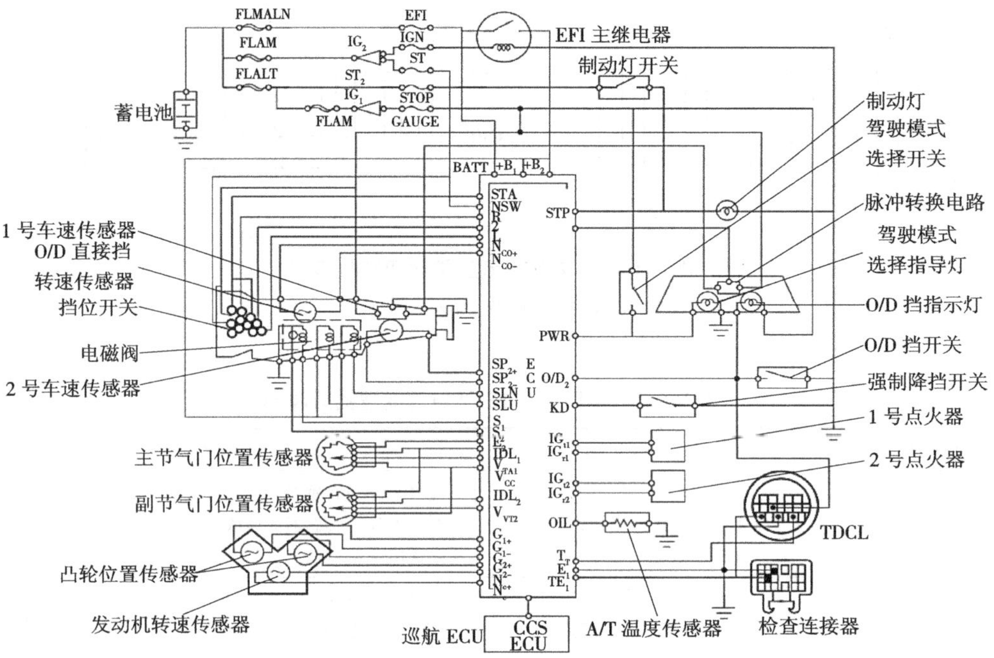

图 3-1-38　A341E 型自动变速器电控原理

(三)读取故障码

当计算机检测到电控系统存在故障时，就会在存储器中存储故障码。通常故障码既可以手工调出，也可以用诊断仪读出。

1. 用短接线读取故障码

(1)点火开关置 ON，O/D 开关置 ON。

(2)跨接 TDCL，或检查连接器的 TE 和 E1 端子(图 3-1-39)。

(3)由 O/D OFF 指示灯的闪烁(图 3-1-40)、读取故障码，含义见表 3-1-1。

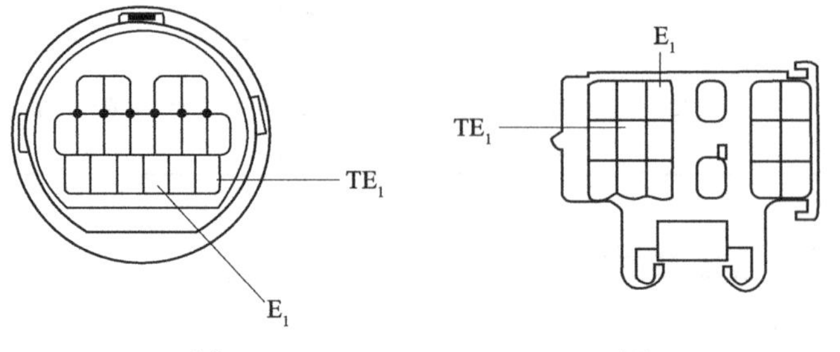

图 3-1-39　丰田 17PIN 半圆形故障诊断座

(a) TDCL　(b) 检查连接器

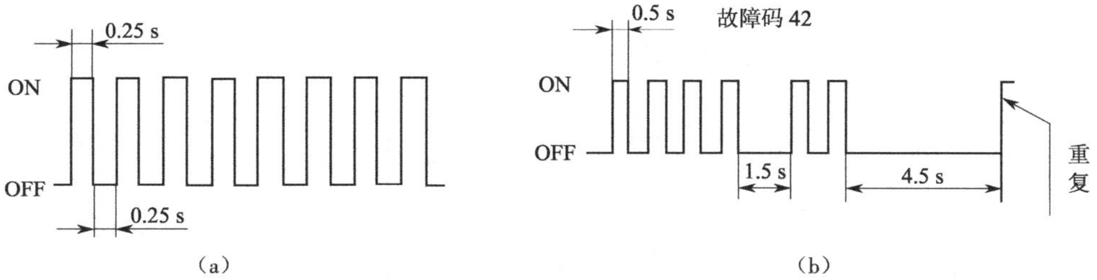

图 3-1-40　丰田车系正常代码和故障码

（a）正常代码　（b）故障码

表 3-1-1　丰田 A341E 型自动变速器故障码

故障码	含义	故障部位
42	1 号车速传感器故障	① 1 号车速传感器 ② 1 号车速传感器线速或连接器 ③ ECU
46	4 号电磁阀短路或断路	① 4 号电磁阀 ② 4 号电磁阀线速或连接器 ③ ECU
61	2 号车速传感器故障	① 2 号车速传感器 ② 2 号车速传感器线速或连接器 ③ ECU
62	1 号电磁阀短路或断路	① 1 号电磁阀 ② 1 号电磁阀线速或连接器 ③ ECU
63	2 号电磁阀短路或断路	① 2 号电磁阀 ② 2 号电磁阀线速或连接器 ③ ECU
64	3 号电磁阀短路或断路	① 3 号电磁阀 ② 3 号电磁阀线速或连接器 ③ ECU
67	O/D 挡转速传感器故障	① O/D 挡转速传感器 ② O/D 挡转速传感器线速或连接器 ③ ECU
68	KD 开关短路	① KD 开关短路 ② KD 开关短路线速或连接器 ③ ECU

2. 使用诊断仪读取故障码

（1）选择测试接头。

测试丰田 17PIN 半圆形诊断座车型选择“丰田-17”测试接头。测试丰田 17PIN 方形诊断座车型选择“丰田-17”测试接头。测试丰田 16PIN 方形诊断座车型选择 OBD-Ⅱ测试接头。

（2）找到诊断座位置。

17PIN 半圆形诊断座在仪表板左下侧。17PIN 长方形诊断座一般在引擎室内。16PIN 方形诊断座一般在驾驶室转向柱下方。

（3）认识诊断座形状。丰田车型的诊断座形状如图 3-1-41 所示。

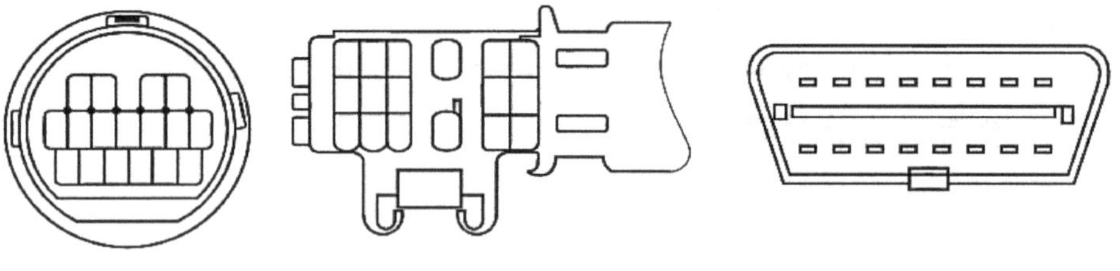

（a）　　（b）　　（c）

图 3-1-41　丰田车型的诊断座形状

（a）17PIN 半圆形　（b）17PIN 长方形　（c）16PIN 方形

（4）测试 OBD-Ⅱ 16PIN 方形诊断座，连接 KT600 诊断仪，如图 3-1-42 所示。

说明：丰田汽车 17PIN 半圆形诊断座不带电源可通过以下任一方式获取电源。①通过点烟器。取出点烟器，将点烟器电缆的一端插入汽车点烟器孔，另一端与 KT600 诊断仪测试主线的电源插头连接。②通过双钳电源线。将双钳电源线的电源钳夹在电瓶的正负极，另外一端插入 KT600 诊断仪测试主线的电源插头，如图 3-1-43 所示。

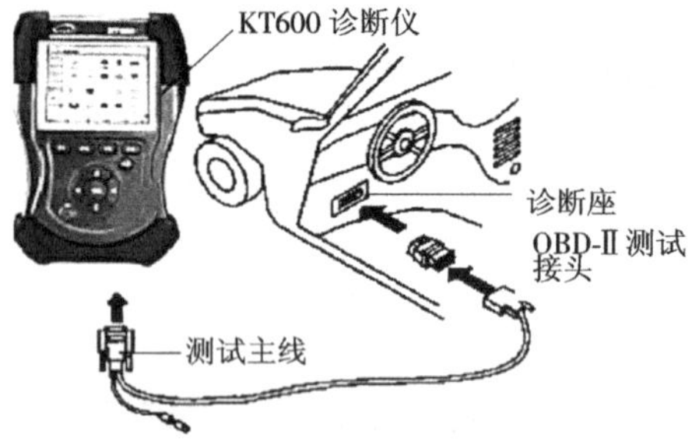

图 3-1-42　诊断仪的连接

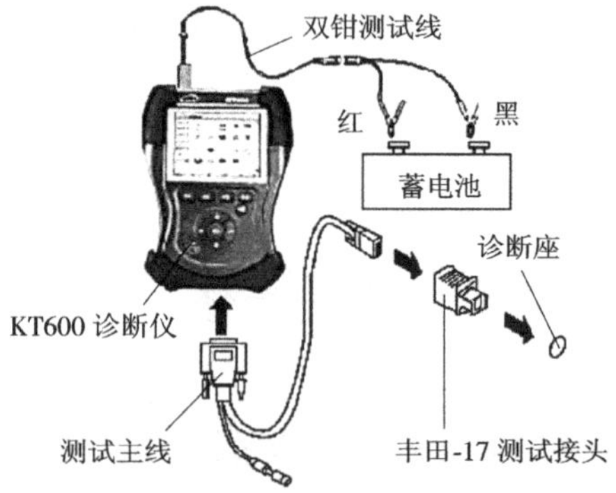

图 3-1-43　通过双钳电源线获取电源

（5）置点火开关于 ON 位置。

（6）按 POWER 键启动 KT600 诊断仪，启动完成后点击“开始”按钮并在其弹出菜单中选择“诊断程序”→“汽车解码程序”进入选择菜单。

（7）确认选择正确的测试接头并连接好仪器后点击“确定”按钮。

（8）点击“读取故障码”选项即可执行读取故障码功能。

如果读取故障码成功，屏幕将显示测试结果。如果系统有故障码，屏幕将显示故障码及其说明。

（四）故障码的清除

1. 手工清除故障码

（1）清除故障码的基本思路是将 ECT 的 ECU 断电，则存储在存储器中的故障码就被清除掉。

（2）点火开关置 OFF 取下 EFI 保险丝 10 s 以上，如图 3-1-44 所示。

2. 使用诊断仪清除故障码。

（1）连接诊断仪至 DLC3。

（2）置点火开关于 ON 位置。

（3）操作诊断仪清除故障码。

在功能菜单中点击“清除故障码”选项，再点击“是”按钮，执行清码操作；点击“否”按钮，退出并返回上一界面。

如果清除故障码成功屏幕显示：清除故障码成功。

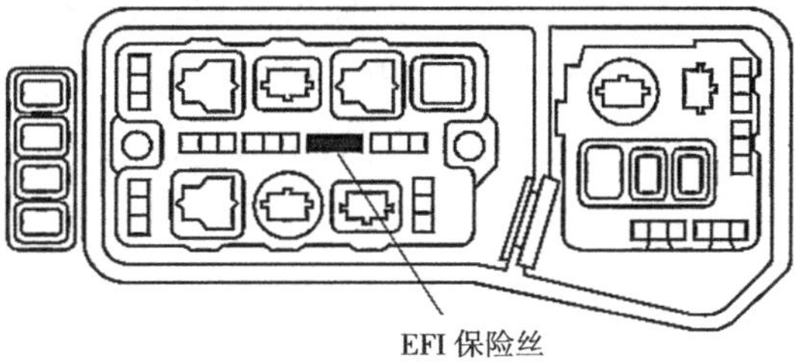

图 3-1-44　保险丝的位置

（五）电控系统检修

利用故障诊断仪读取故障码，可以找出控制单元大部分故障的大致范围，但要确定故障所在的具体部位，还必须使用万用表等简单工具，按照维修手册中提供的检测方法、检测步骤及标准数据，对各零部件进行检测。另外，一些执行器的机械故障（如卡滞、泄漏等）是无法被 ECU 故障自诊断电路检测出来的，只有通过实际检测才能发现。

（六）性能测试

电控自动变速器的性能检测是判断电控自动变速器故障的基础，电控自动变速器的故障往往可以通过相应的性能检测判断出故障类型和故障所在部位。

【思考与练习】

1. 简述电控液力变速器的基本组成。
2. 双离合变速器是如何工作的?
3. 如何排除变速器挂挡不走的故障?

第 2 节　汽车防滑控制系统

汽车防滑控制系统是汽车安全行驶的重要保障，是汽车安全技术的重要组成部分，也是人类科技进步的体现。它不仅能够提高汽车的安全性和可靠性，还能够增强汽车的操控性和舒适性，保障人们的出行安全和便利。它体现了以人民为中心、安全发展、共建共享的发展原则。因此，我们应该积极学习和掌握汽车防滑控制系统的相关知识和技能，为提高汽车行业的安全水平、维护社会交通安全秩序做出贡献。

汽车防滑控制系统主要包括防抱死制动系统（ABS）、驱动防滑控制系统（ASR）和电子稳定性控制系统（ESP）。ABS 系统的作用是通过对区域抱死车轮的制动压力进行自适应循环调节，来防止被控制车轮发生抱死。ASR 系统就是利用控制器控制车轮与路面的滑移率，防止汽车在加速过程中打滑，特别是防止汽车在非对称路面或转弯时驱动轮的空转，以保持汽车行驶方向的稳定性、操纵性和维持汽车的最佳驱动力以及提高汽车的平顺性。ESP 则整合了 ABS 和 ASR 的功能，通过有针对性的单独制动各个车轮，以在紧急躲避障碍物或转弯时出现转向不足或转向过度时，使车辆避免偏离理想轨迹，可降低汽车在各种场合下发生侧滑的风险。

一、防抱死制动系统的理论基础

（一）汽车的制动性

汽车在行驶过程中，强制地减速以至停车且维持行驶方向稳定性的能力称为汽车的制动性。

制动性能的主要评价指标如下。

（1）制动效能：汽车在行驶中，强制减速以至停车的能力称为制动效能，即汽车以一定的初速度制动到停车所产生的制动距离、制动时间、制动减速度。

（2）制动时的方向稳定性：汽车在制动时仍能按指定方向的轨迹行驶，即不发生跑偏、侧滑以及失去转向能力的性能称为制动时的方向稳定性。

（二）汽车制动时车轮受力分析

汽车制动时车轮受力分析如图 3-2-1 所示。

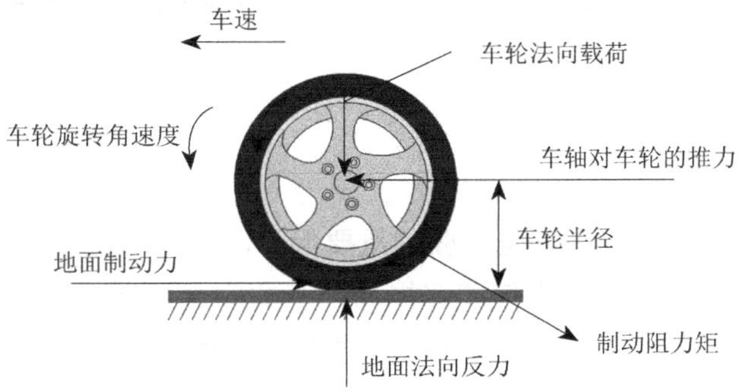

图 3-2-1　汽车制动时车轮受力分析

蹄与制动鼓（盘）压紧时形成的摩擦力矩通过车轮作用于地面的切向力称为制动器制动力 F_x。制动时地面对车轮的切向反作用力称为地面制动力 F_u。

地面对轮胎切向反作用力的极限值称为附着力，附着力取决于轮胎与路面之间的摩擦作用及路面的抗剪强度。

地面制动力、制动器制动力及附着力之间的关系如图 3-2-2 所示。

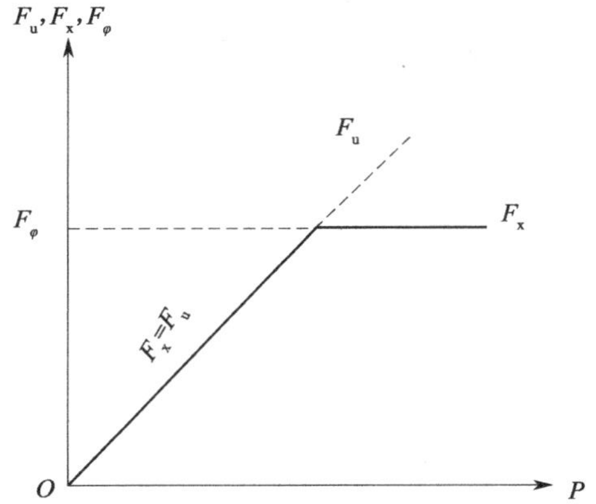

图 3-2-2　地面制动力、制动器制动力及附着力之间的关系

从图 3-2-2 可以看出，正常制动过程中，地面制动力 $F_u \leqslant$ 附着力 F_φ，此时车轮滚动；如果地面制动力 $F_u >$ 附着力 F_φ，则车轮抱死滑移。如图 3-2-3 所示，若需要增大

F_x，必须增大 F_φ。F_φ 取决于附着系数 φ，φ 又受滑移率 S 的影响。

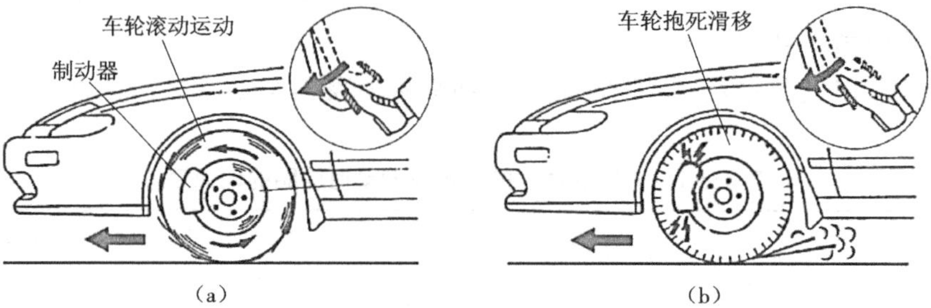

图 3-2-3　F_u 和 F_φ 的关系

（a）$F_u \leqslant F_\varphi$，车轮滚动　（b）$F_u > F_\varphi$，车轮抱死滑移

（三）附着系数 φ 与滑移率 S 的关系

制动时车轮在路面上的运动形式为滑移，表示车轮滑移的程度，用滑移率 S 来表示：

$$S=\frac{(v-\omega r)}{v}\times 100\%$$

式中　S ——车轮的滑移率；

v ——车轮中心的纵向速度（m/s）；

ω ——车轮的旋转角速度（rad/s）；

r ——车轮的自由滚动半径（m）。

附着系数 φ 与滑移率 S 的关系如图 3-2-4 所示。从图中可以看出，干的沥青路面和水泥路面的峰值附着系数最大，在冰面上较小。随着滑移率 S 的增大，横向附着系数 φ_S 一直下降，纵向附着系数 φ_B 先增加后降低，当滑移率 S 为 20% 左右时，φ_B 有最大值，φ_S 也较大，制动效果好，此时制动点称为最佳制动点，附着系数称为峰值附着系数。相同情况下峰值附着系数越大，制动效果越好。

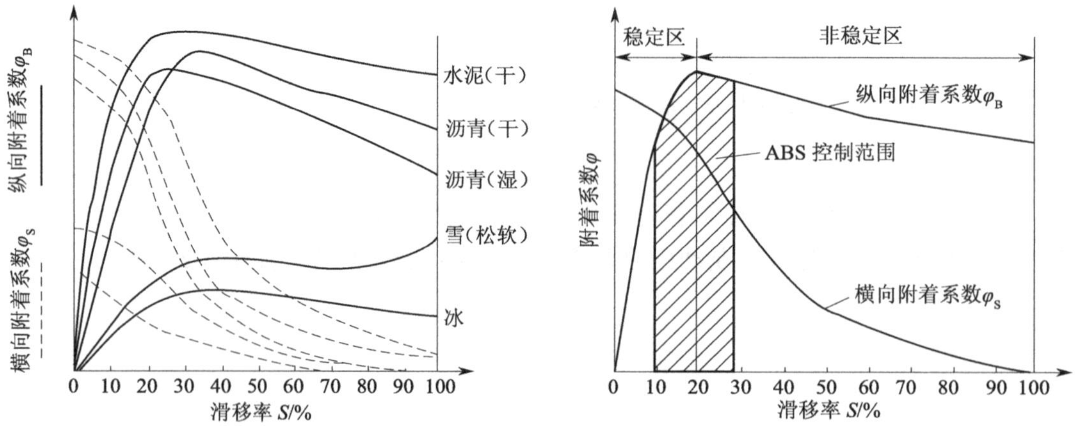

图 3-2-4　附着系数与滑移率的关系

通过分析可以得出结论：$S < 20\%$ 为制动稳定区；$S > 20\%$ 为制动非稳定区；将车轮滑移率 S 控制在 20% 左右，便可获取最大的纵向附着系数和较大的横向附着系数，是最理想的控制效果。

车轮制动时的关系及制动时轮胎的地面痕迹见表 3-2-1。

表 3-2-1　车轮制动时的关系及制动时轮胎的地面痕迹

车速与轮速的关系	车轮运动状态	滑移率	制动时轮胎的地面痕迹
$\omega r = v$（轮速 = 车速）	纯滚动	$S = 0$	路面痕迹与胎面花纹基本一致
$\omega r < v$（轮速 < 车速）	边滚边滑	$0 < S < 100\%$	边滚边滑，路面痕迹可以辨认出轮胎花纹，但花纹逐渐模糊
$\omega r = 0$（轮速 =0）	纯滑动（车轮完全抱死滑移）	$S = 100\%$	抱死拖滑，路面痕迹粗黑

（四）防抱死制动系统的作用

由于 ABS 能够使被控制的车轮获得较大的纵向和横向附着力，因此可以大大提高汽车的行驶性能，具体有以下几个方面的作用。

（1）缩短制动距离。ABS 能保证汽车在雨后、冰雪及泥泞路面上获得较高的制动效能，防止汽车侧滑甩尾（松散的沙土和积雪很深的路面除外）。

（2）保持汽车制动时的方向稳定性。

（3）保持汽车制动时的转向控制能力。

（4）减少汽车制动时轮胎的磨损。ABS 能防止轮胎在制动过程中产生拖痕，提高轮胎使用寿命。

（5）减少驾驶员的疲劳强度，特别是汽车制动时的紧张情绪。

二、防抱死制动系统的组成与工作原理

（一）防抱死制动系统的组成

一般来说，ABS 是在传统制动的基础上，增加了制动力调节系统，主要包括轮速传感器、ECU、执行器（即制动压力调节器）和 ABS 指示灯等，如图 3-2-5 所示。

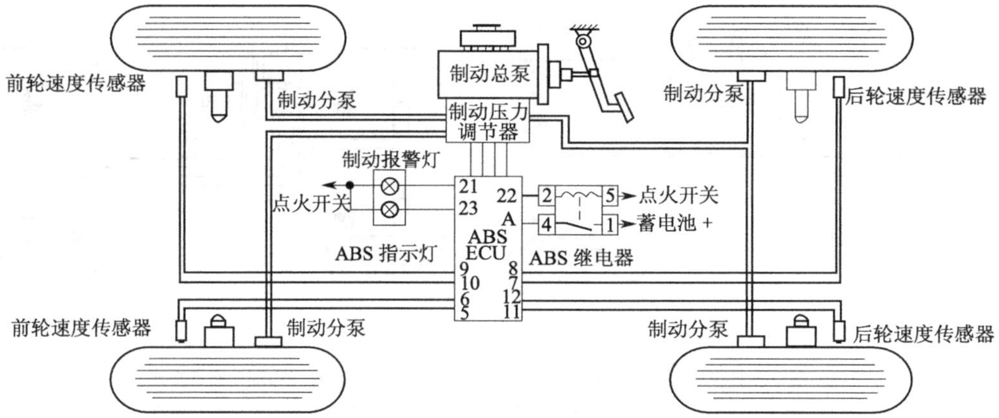

图 3-2-5 防抱死制动系统的组成

制动时 ECU 接收传感器的信号，车轮在将要被抱死的情况下，ECU 发出控制信号，通过执行机构控制制动器的制动力使车轮不被抱死。

（二）防抱死制动系统的分类

1. 按控制形式

ABS 工作时，能够独立进行制动压力调节的制动管路称为控制通道。如果每个车轮各占用一个控制通道，就称为独立控制式；如果两个车轮占用同一个控制通道，就称为同时控制。

当车轮采用同时控制时，如以保证附着系数较小的车轮不发生抱死滑移来调节制动压力，这两个车轮就是按低选原则进行控制的，简称低选控制（SL）；如以保证附着系数较大的车轮不发生抱死为原则来调节制动压力，则这两个车轮就是按高选原则来进行控制的，简称高选控制（SH）。

2. 按控制通道数目分

ABS 按照控制通道数目可以分为四通道 ABS、三通道 ABS、二通道 ABS 和单通道 ABS。四通道 ABS 的结构如图 3-2-6 所示。为了对四个车轮的制动压力进行独立控制，在每个车轮上各安装一个轮速传感器，并在通往各制动轮缸的制动管路中各设置一个制动压力调节分装置（通道）。由于四通道 ABS 可以最大限度地利用每个车轮的附着力进行制动，因此汽车的制动效能最好。但在附着系数分离（两侧车轮的附着系数不相等）的路面上制动时，由于同一轴上的制动力不相等，汽车产生较大的偏转力矩，从而产生制动跑偏。因此，ABS 通常不对四个车轮进行独立的制动压力调节，四通道 ABS 较少采用。

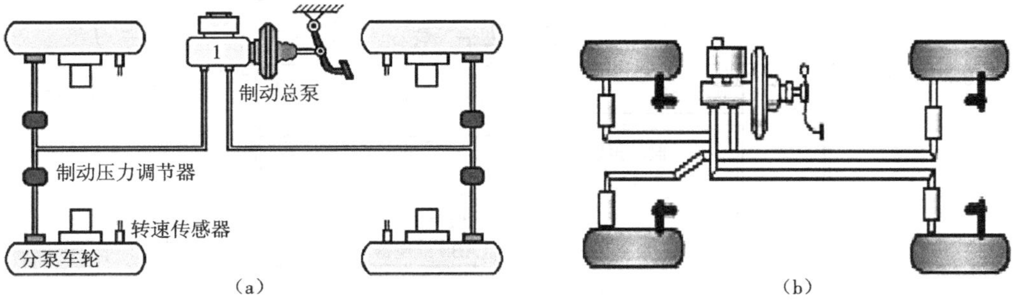

图 3-2-6 四通道 ABS 的结构

（a）四传感器四通道 / 四轮独立控制对应于双制动管路的 H 形（前后）布置形式

（b）四传感器四通道 / 前轮独立 - 后轮选择控制对应于双制动管路 X 形（对角）布置形式

四轮 ABS 大多为三通道 ABS，而三通道 ABS 都是对两前轮的制动压力进行单独控制的，对两后轮的制动压力按低选原则一同控制，如图 3-2-7 所示。这样对于后轮驱动的汽车可以只在变速器或主减速器中设置一个转速传感器来检测两后轮的平均转速。由于三通道 ABS 充分利用前轮附着力，因此制动距离短且方向稳定，被广泛采用。

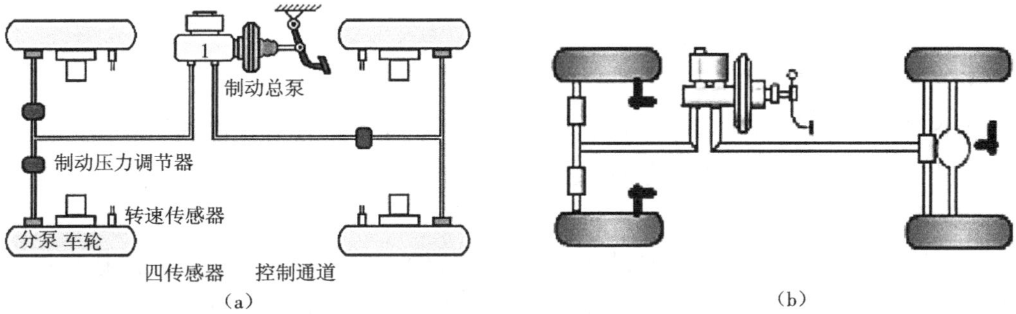

图 3-2-7 三通道 ABS

（a）四传感器三通道 / 前轮独立 - 后轮低选控制方式

（b）三传感器三通道 / 前轮独立 - 后轮低选控制方式

二通道 ABS 如图 3-2-8 所示。前后制动管路各设一个制动压力调节器，分别对两前轮和两后轮进行一同控制。两前轮可据附着条件进行高选和低选转换，两后轮则按低选原则一同控制。由于双通道 ABS 难以在方向稳定性、转向操纵能力和制动距离等方面得到兼顾，因此目前很少被采用。

单通道 ABS 如图 3-2-9 所示，所有单通道 ABS 都是在前后布置的双管路制动系统的后制动管路中设置一个制动压力调节装置，对于后轮驱动的汽车只需在传动系统中安装一个转速传感器。由于前制动轮缸的制动压力未被控制，前轮仍然可能发生制动抱死，所以汽车制动时的转向操作能力得不到保障。但由于单通道 ABS 能够显著提高汽车制动时的方向稳定性，又具有结构简单、成本低的优点，因此在轻型货车上得到广泛应用。

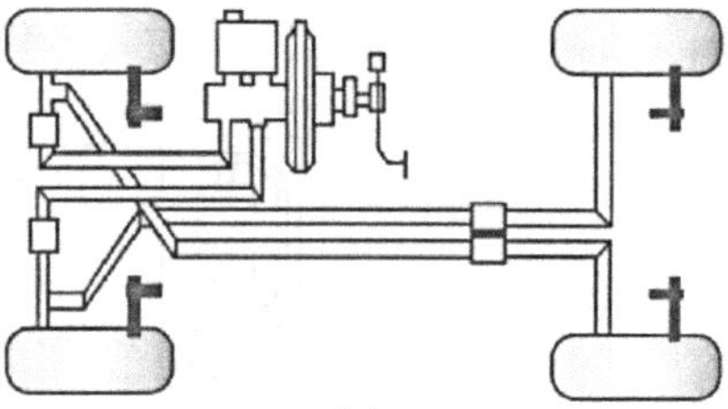

(a)

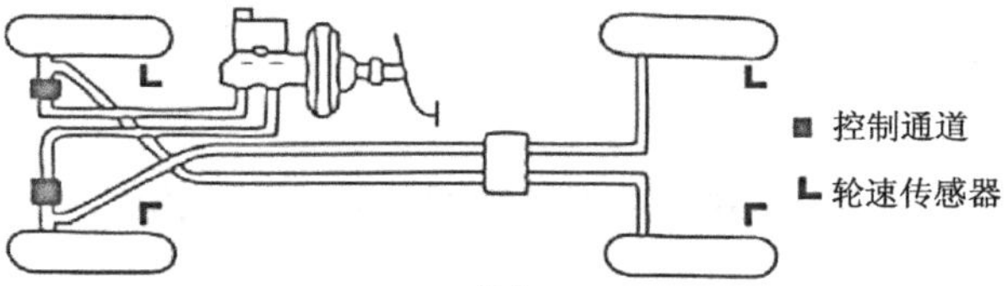

(b)

图 3-2-8 二通道 ABS

(a) 四传感器二通道 / 前轮独立控制方式

(b) 四传感器二通道 / 前轮独立 - 后轮低选控制方式

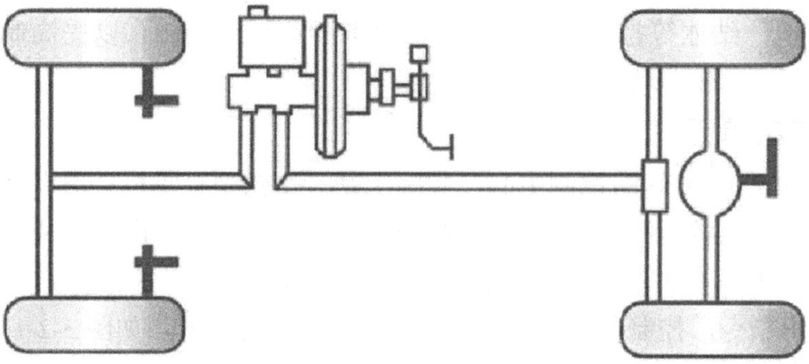

图 3-2-9 单通道 ABS

(三) ABS 主要零部件的结构与工作原理

1. 传感器

1) 轮速传感器

轮速传感器是在汽车行驶过程中将车轮轮速以电信号形式传给电子控制单元的传感器，经处理后判断车轮的运动状态而决定是否开始进行防抱死制动控制。一般安装在车轮处，但也有安装在主减速器或者变速器中的。轮速传感器的外形与基本结构如图 3-2-10 所示。

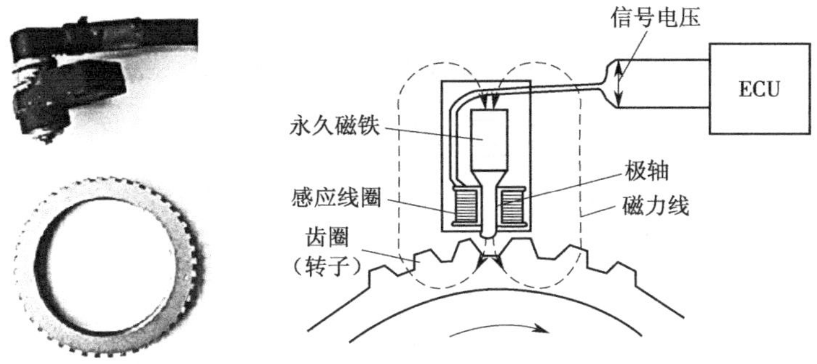

（a）　　　　　　　　　　　　（b）

图 3-2-10　轮速传感器的外形与基本结构

（a）外形　（b）基本结构

2）减速度传感器

减速度传感器的作用是在汽车制动时，获得汽车减速度信号。因为汽车在高附着系数路面上制动时，汽车减速度大；在低附着系数路面上制动时，汽车减速度小，因而该信号送入 ECU 后，可以对路面进行区别，判断路面附着系数的高低情况。当判定汽车行驶在雪地、结冰等打滑的路面上时，采取相应控制措施，以提高制动性能。减速度传感器多用于四轮驱动控制系统。

2. 电子控制单元

电子控制单元是 ABS 的控制中心，实际上是一个微型计算机，所以又常称为 ABS 电脑。ABS 的 ECU 由输入电路、数字控制器、输出电路和警告电路组成。其作用是接收轮速传感器以及其他开关的信号，进行放大、计算、比较，按照特定的控制逻辑分析、判断后输出指令，控制制动压力调节器进行制动压力调节，如图 3-2-11 所示。

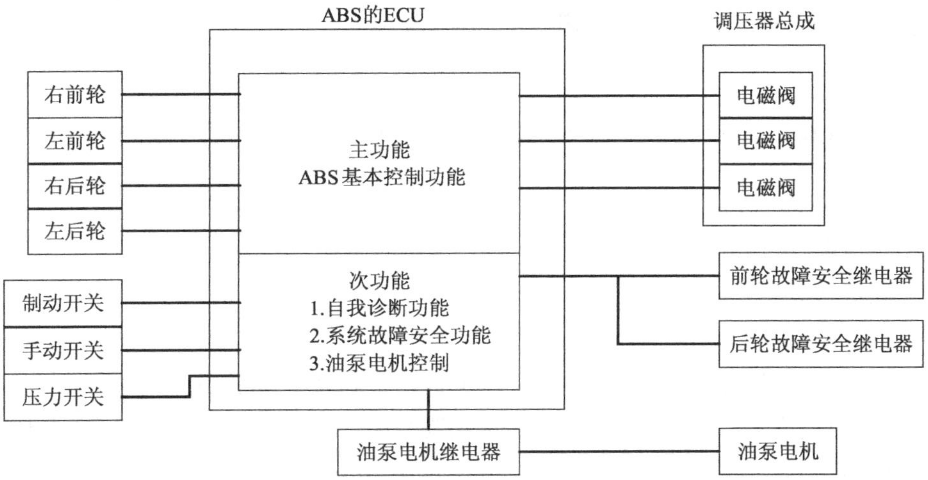

图 3-2-11　ABS 的 ECU 的组成

ECU 还有故障检测和失效保护功能。点火开关接通后，仪表板上的 ABS 警告灯闪烁几次后熄灭，表明 ABS 自诊断完毕，系统正常；如果不熄灭，则表明系统有故障。

在ABS失灵后，常规制动仍能够继续工作。

3. 制动压力调节器

制动压力调节器的作用是接收ECU的指令，通过电磁阀的动作来实现车轮制动器制动压力的自动调节。因车型不同，制动压力调节器的安装位置和制动管路的布置等均有所不同，但其本身的构造和工作则基本相同。制动压力调节器串联在主缸和轮缸之间，通过电磁阀直接或间接地控制轮缸的制动压力。通常，电磁阀直接控制轮缸制动压力的调节器称为循环式制动压力调节器，间接控制轮缸制动压力的调节器称为可变容积式制动压力调节器。

1）循环式制动压力调节器

循环式制动压力调节器（图3-2-12）是在制动总缸和制动轮缸之间串联一个电磁阀，直接控制轮缸的制动压力。其特点是常规制动油路和ABS控制压力油路相通，由电磁阀直接控制轮缸的制动压力，多采用三位三通电磁阀和二位二通电磁阀，三位三通电磁阀在ECU控制下使电磁阀处于增压、保压和减压三种位置。

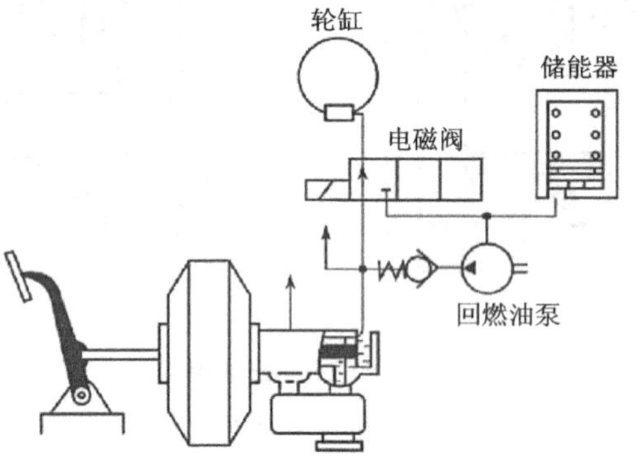

图3-2-12　循环式制动压力调节器

（1）三位三通电磁阀由进液阀、回液阀、主弹簧、副弹簧、电磁线圈及衔铁套筒等组成，如图3-2-13所示。

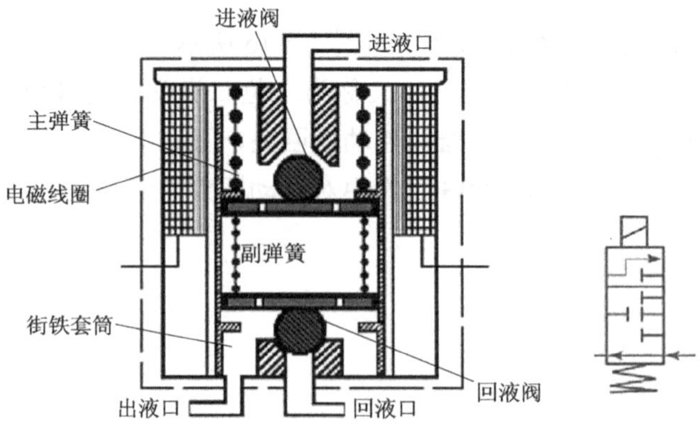

图3-2-13　三位三通电磁阀的结构及符号

（a）结构（b）符号

三位三通电磁阀工作过程如下。

增压：电磁线圈未通电时，在主弹簧张力作用下，进液阀打开，回液阀关闭，进液口与出液口保持畅通。

保压：电磁线圈通入较小电流（2 A），产生的电磁吸力小，吸动衔铁上移量小，但能适当压缩主弹簧，使进液阀关闭，放松副弹簧，回液阀并不打开，如图 3-2-14（a）所示。

减压：电磁线圈通入较大电流（5 A），产生的电磁吸力大，吸动衔铁上移量大，同时压缩主、副弹簧，使进液阀仍保持关闭，回液阀打开，如图 3-2-14（b）所示。

因为该电磁阀工作有三个状态（增压、保压、减压），即为“三位”，对外有三个接口（进液口、出液口、回液口），即为“三通”，所以该电磁阀称为三位三通电磁阀，常写成 3/3 电磁阀。

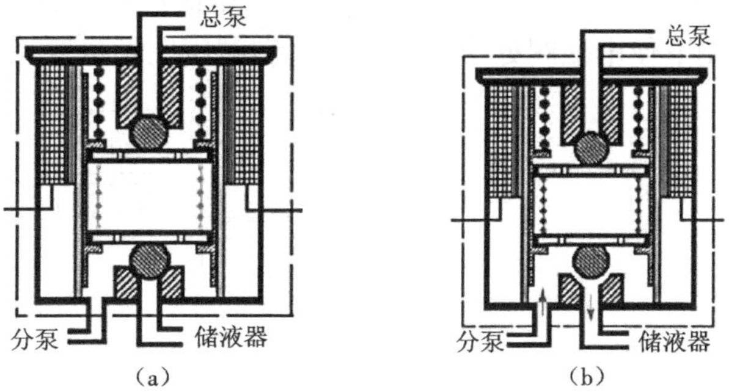

图 3-2-14　三位三通电磁阀

（a）保压　（b）减压

（2）二位二通电磁阀分为二位二通常开电磁阀和二位二通常闭电磁阀。两种电磁阀均由阀门、衔铁、电磁线圈、回位弹簧等组成。

常态下，二位二通常开电磁阀阀门在弹簧张力作用下打开，二位二通常闭电磁阀阀门在弹簧张力作用下闭合。

二位二通电磁阀的结构及表示符号如图 3-2-15 所示。二位二通常开电磁阀用于控制制动总泵到制动分泵的制动液通路，又称为二位二通常开进液电磁阀。二位二通常闭电磁阀用于控制制动分泵到储液器的制动液回路，又称为二位二通常闭出液电磁阀。两个电磁阀配套使用，共同完成 ABS 工作中对制动压力调节的任务。

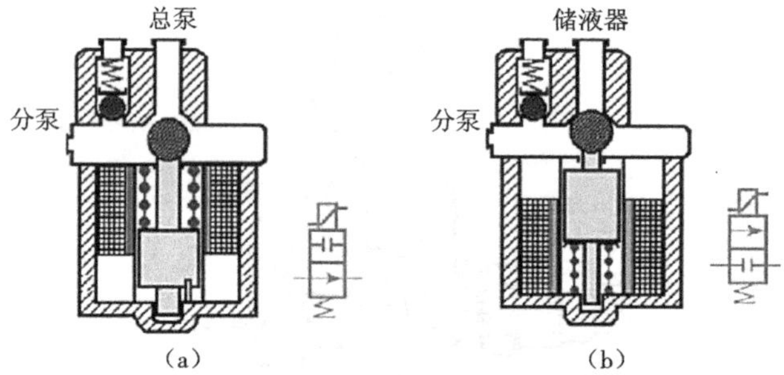

图 3-2-15 二位二通电磁阀的结构及表示符号

(a) 二位二通常开电磁阀 (b) 二位二通常闭电磁阀

(3) 回液泵与储能器。

电磁阀在减压过程中，从轮缸流出的制动液由储能器暂时储存，然后由回液泵泵回主缸，如图 3-2-16 所示。

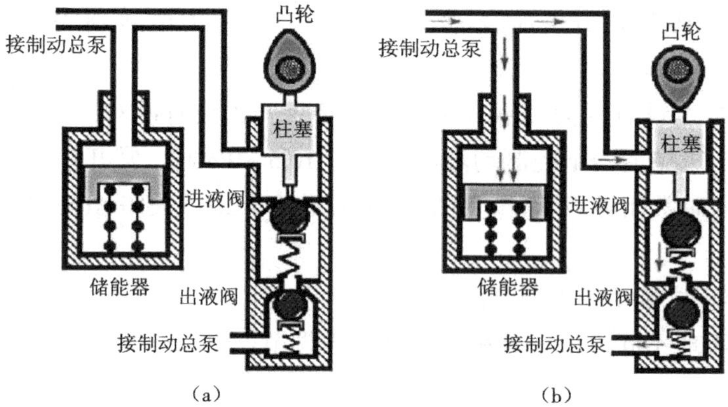

图 3-2-16 回液泵与储液器

(a) 回液泵不开启，不回油 (b) 回液泵开启，回油

储能器依据储存制动液压力的不同，分为低压储能器和高压储能器，分别配置在不同形式的制动压力调节系统中。

①低压储能器一般称为储液器，用来接纳 ABS 减压过程中，从制动分泵回流的制动液，同时还对回流制动液的压力波动具有一定的衰减作用。

储液器内有一活塞和弹簧。减压时，回流的制动液压缩活塞克服弹簧张力下移，使容积增大，暂时存储制动液。图 3-2-16 中的储能器即为储液器。

回液泵由直流电机和柱塞泵组成，柱塞泵由柱塞、进出液阀及弹簧组成。

②高压储能器与电动增压泵用于储存制动中或 ABS 工作时所需的高压制动液，如图 3-2-17 所示。高压储能器多采用黑色气囊状球体。黑色气囊状球体被一个膜片分隔成两个互不相通的腔室：上腔为气室，下腔为液室，与电动增压泵液道相通，盛装由电动增压泵泵入的制动液。

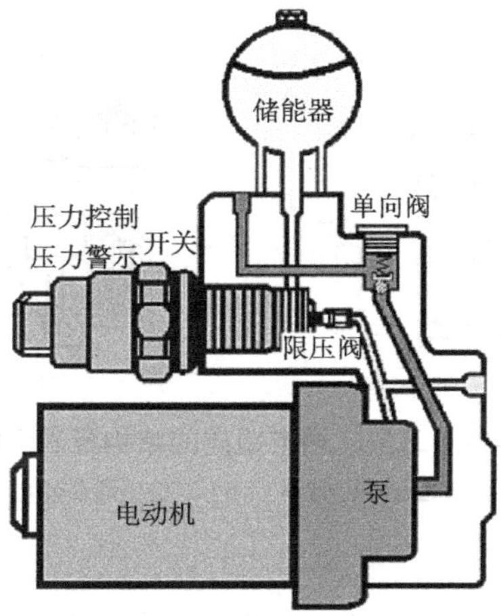

图 3-2-17　储能器与电动增压泵

高压储能器下端设有两个压力控制开关，用来检测高压储能器下腔制动液压力。当压力低于 15 MPa 时，开关闭合，增压泵工作；当压力达到 18 MPa 时，开关打开，增压泵停止工作。

电动增压泵上设有压力警示开关。压力警示开关设有两对开关触点，一对常开，一对常闭。当高压储能器下腔制动液压力低于 10.5 MPa 时，常开触点闭合，点亮红色制动警示灯；同时常闭触点断开，开将该信号送给 ECU，关闭 ABS 并点亮黄褐色 ABS 警示灯。

2）可变容积式制动压力调节器

根据控制原理不同，可变容积式制动压力调节器可以分为液压控制方式和直流电动机控制方式。

液压控制可变容积调压方式（图 3-2-18）在汽车原有制动系统管路中增加一套液压控制装置，用于改变制动管路容积，实现增压—保压—减压的循环调节。这种制动压力调节系统的控制液压油路和 ABS 控制的制动液油路是相互隔开的。

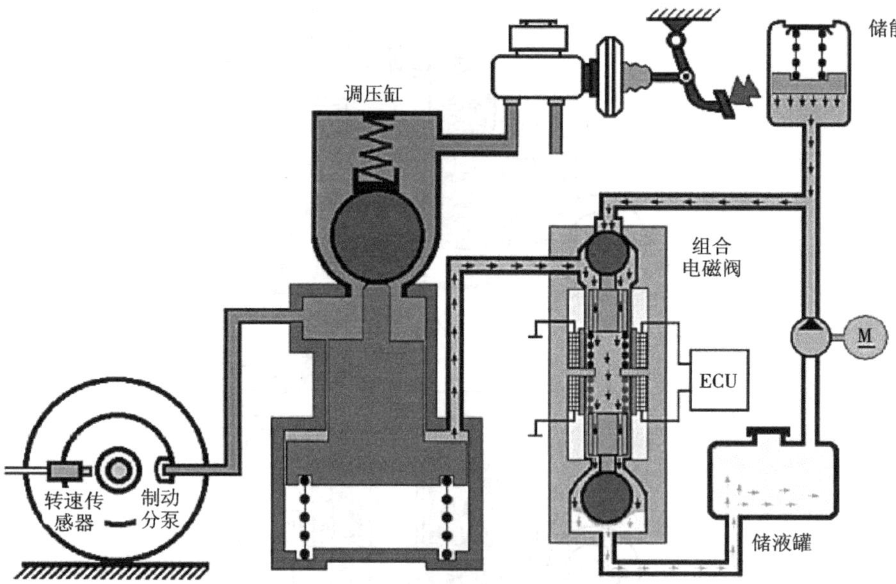

图 3-2-18　液压控制可变容积调压方式

液压控制可变容积调压方式工作过程如下。

常规制动：输入电磁阀断电关闭，输出电磁阀断电打开。调压缸活塞在弹簧作用下上移，将单向阀顶开。制动分泵压力将随制动踏板力的增大而增大，如图 3-2-19（a）所示。

减压：ECU 对两个电磁阀同时供电，输入电磁阀打开，输出电磁阀关闭，高压控制液经输入电磁阀流向调压活塞缸，活塞下移，容积增大，制动分泵制动压力减小，如图 3-2-19（b）所示。

保压：输入电磁阀断电关闭，输出电磁阀通电关闭。调压缸活塞位置保持不变，制动分泵制动液压力不变，如图 3-2-19（c）所示。

增压：输入电磁阀断电关闭，输出电磁阀断电打开泄压。调压缸活塞在弹簧作用下上移，容积减小，制动分泵制动液压力增大，如图 3-2-19（d）所示。

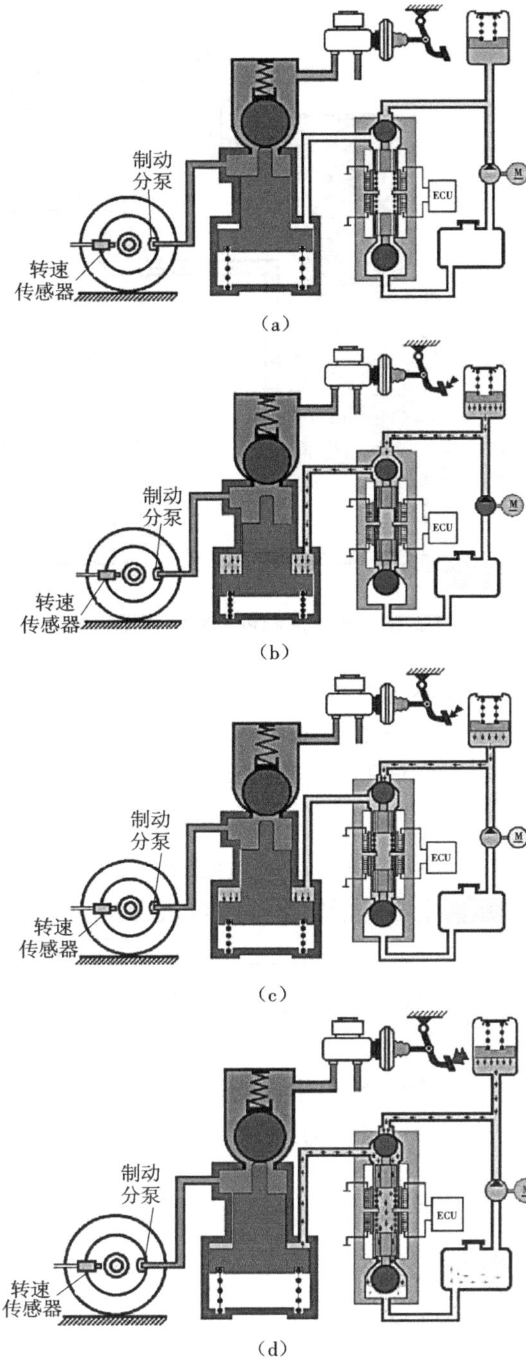

图 3-2-19 液压控制可变容积调压工作过程

(a) 常规制动 (b) 减压过程 (c) 保压过程 (d) 增压过程

三、ABS 的使用注意事项

（一）装备 ABS 的车辆容易出现的一些特殊现象

（1）发动机起动后，有时发动机舱内发出类似撞击的声音。

（2）某些装备 ABS 的汽车在发动机起动时，踩下制动踏板会弹起，而在发动机熄火时，制动踏板会下沉。

（3）制动时转动转向盘，会感到转向盘有轻微的振动。

（4）制动时，有时会感到制动踏板有轻微下沉或轻微振动，这是由于制动分泵高速收放时高压的制动液被频繁挤压造成的。

（5）高速行驶急转弯或在冰滑路面上行驶时，有时会出现制动警告灯亮起的现象。

（6）在积雪路面上制动时，有时制动距离较长。

（7）装备 ABS 的汽车在制动后期，车轮也会被抱死，在地面留下拖滑的痕迹，但与常规制动时的痕迹有所不同。

以上特殊现象属于 ABS 的正常反应。

另外，只有装有工作 ABS 的汽车的车速大于 5 km/h 时，才会对制动过程中趋于抱死的车轮进行防抱死制动的调节。低于该车速，制动时车轮仍可能抱死，这是因为在汽车速度很低时，制动抱死对汽车制动性能的影响已经很小，而且要使汽车尽快制动停车，必须使车轮制动抱死。

（二）使用装备 ABS 车辆的注意事项

（1）要保持足够的制动距离。

（2）切忌反复踩制动踏板。踩下制动踏板时，应使施加在制动踏板上的力持续且稳定。

（3）ABS 正常时，会产生液压工作噪声和制动踏板震颤，这属于正常现象。在紧急制动时，应直接将制动踏板踩到底，且不放松。

（4）不要忘记控制转向盘。

（5）在行车时应留意仪表板上的 ABS 警告灯情况，如发现闪烁或常亮，则说明其已不具备 ABS 功能，但常规制动系统仍起作用，应尽快到修理厂检修。

（6）要保持车轮传感器探头及齿圈的清洁。

（7）应严格按规定的轮胎气压标准加气，同时要保持同轴轮胎气压的均衡，严禁使用不同规格的轮胎。

（8）ABS 对制动液的要求非常高，用以保证 ABS 以 15~20 次 /s 的频率进行减压、

保压和增压的循环工作。

对制动液的要求：①沸点高，保证制动时不会产生“气阻”；②运动黏度要低，以保证制动时反应及时；③对金属橡胶无腐蚀性；④能长期保存，性能稳定；⑤吸湿沸点要高。

添加或更换制动液时应严格按照车辆使用说明书上的要求执行，禁止掺杂不同型号的制动液。

四、驱动防滑控制系统的理论基础

汽车驱动防滑控制（ASR）系统，主要应用在欧洲车型中。丰田等日本车型，应用 TRC 牵引力控制系统。而在现代、起亚等韩国车型则主要应用 TCS 牵引力控制系统（TCS）。

ASR 系统是继 ABS 后采用的一套防滑控制系统，是 ABS 功能的进一步发展和重要补充。ASR 系统和 ABS 密切相关，通常配合使用，构成汽车行驶的主动安全系统。因此 ASR 系统与 ABS 主要部件可以通用或共用。

（一）汽车车轮滑转时对汽车的危害

当汽车在低附着系数路面（如泥泞路面、冰雪路面）上行驶时，由于地面对车轮施加的反作用转矩很小，因此在起步、加速时驱动轮就会发生滑转，特别是在冰雪等光滑路面上还会出现方向失控的危险，如图 3-2-20 所示。

图 3-2-20　驱动轮打滑

当汽车在越野条件下行驶时，如果某个驱动轮处在附着系数低的路面上，汽车将无法前进，发动机输出的功率大部分消耗在车轮的滑转上，不仅浪费燃油，加速轮胎磨损，而且还会降低车辆的通过性能和机动性能。

（二）ASR 的功用

ASR 系统能在车轮开始滑转时，降低发动机的输出转矩，同时控制制动系统，以降低传递给驱动车轮的转矩，使之达到合适的驱动力，使汽车的起步和加速达到快速而稳定的效果，如图 3-2-21 所示。它的主要目的是防止汽车驱动轮在加速时出现打滑（特别是在下雨、下雪、下冰雹、路冻等摩擦力较小的特殊路面上）。当汽车加速时将滑动率控制在一定的范围内，从而防止驱动轮快速滑动。它的功能一是提高牵引力，二是保持汽车的行驶稳定。

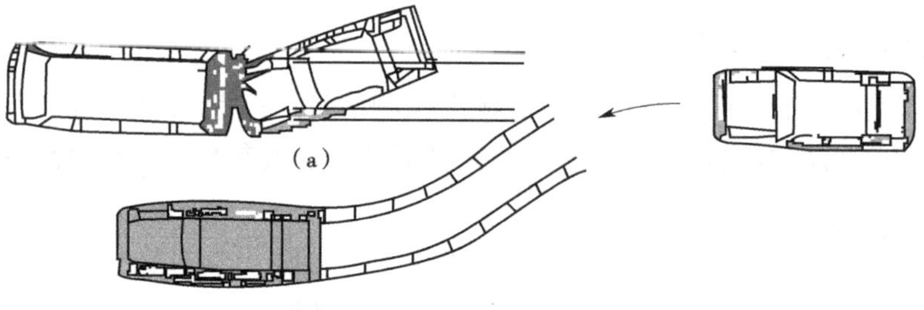

图 3-2-21　ASR 的功用

（a）车辆未装备 ASR 系统　（b）车辆装备 ASR 系统

通常用滑转率 S_d 表示驱动车轮的滑移程度。其公式如下：

$$S_d = \frac{v_c - v}{v_c} \times 100\%$$

式中　v_c——车轮圆周速度；

v——车身瞬时速度。

滑转率和附着系数的关系如图 3-2-22 所示。

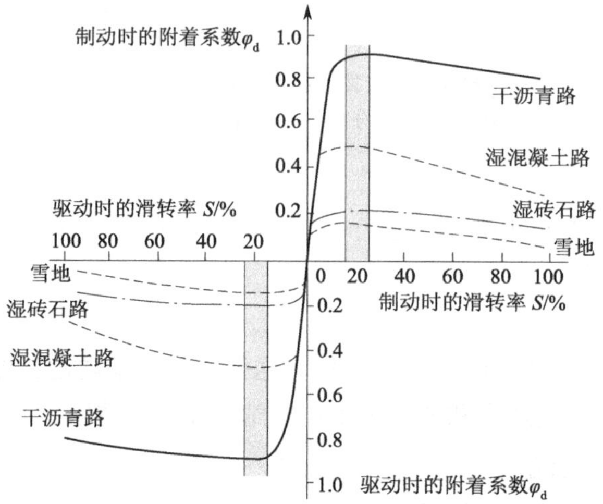

图 3-2-22　滑转率和附着系数的关系

（1）附着系数随路面的不同而呈大幅度变化。

（2）在各种路面上，S_d 为 20% 左右时，附着系数达到峰值。

（3）上述趋势无论制动还是驱动几乎一样。

实际进行驱动轮的控制过程中，由于各部分装置都有一定的延迟和滞后，因此不能精确地控制滑转率在最佳制动点（20% 左右）；同时，为防止车轮因滑转率过大而磨损过快，通常将车轮的滑转率控制在 5%~15%。

（三）ASR 的控制方法

1. 发动机输出功率控制

在汽车起步、加速时，ASR 控制器输出控制信号，控制发动机的输出功率，以抑制驱动轮滑转。常用方法有：辅助节气门开度调节、点火参数调节和燃油供给量调节。

1）辅助节气门开度调节

辅助节气门开度调节是指在原节气门管路上再串联一个副节气门，通过传动机构来控制其开度的大小，从而改变进气量，调节输出转矩，如图 3-2-23 所示。这种控制方式操纵稳定性较差，牵引性很差，但舒适性很好。

（a）　　　　（b）

图 3-2-23　发动机节气门开度调节

（a）辅助节气门部分开启　（b）辅助节气门全部开启

2）点火参数调节

点火参数调节是对点火提前角进行控制或对是否点火进行控制。减小点火提前角，可以适度减小输出转矩。

3）燃油供给量调节

减少供油和暂停供油，可以减小转矩，这是现代驱动防滑控制系统中比较容易的控制方式。这种控制方式通常和燃油电子控制结合在一起使用。

2. 驱动轮制动控制

直接对发生空转的驱动轮加以制动，反应时间最短。普遍采用 ASR 与 ABS 组合的液压控制系统，在 ABS 中增加电磁阀和调节器，从而增加驱动控制功能，如图 3-2-24 所示。

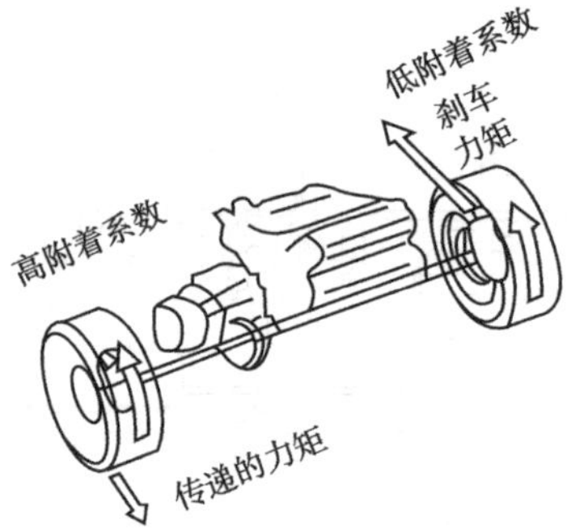

图 3-2-24　对驱动轮进行驱动控制

3. 同时控制发动机输出功率和驱动轮制动力

控制信号同时起动 ASR 制动压力调节器和辅助节气门调节器，在对驱动车轮施加制动力的同时减小发动机的输出功率，以达到理想的控制效果。

4. 防滑差速锁（LSD）控制

LSD 能对差速器锁止装置进行控制，使锁止范围为 0%~100%。当驱动轮单边滑转时，控制器输出控制信号，使差速锁和制动压力调节器动作，控制车轮的滑移率。这时非滑转车轮还有正常的驱动力，从而提高汽车在滑溜路面的起步、加速能力及行驶方向的稳定性。

5. 差速锁与发动机输出功率综合控制

差速锁制动控制与发动机输出功率控制相结合的控制系统可根据发动机的状况和车轮滑转的实际情况采取相应的控制，达到最理想的控制效果。

（四）ASR 系统的组成与工作原理

ASR 系统主要由传感器（车轮轮速传感器、节气门位置传感器），ESP 控制器总成 / 自动变速箱控制器，发动机 ECU 通信和执行器（制动压力调节器、节气门驱动装置）组成。

1. 传感器

（1）车轮轮速传感器：与 ABS 系统共享。

（2）节气门开度传感器：包括主、副节气门位置传感器，与发动机电控系统共享。

另外，可以人工控制 ASR 系统的开关。它有一个控制旋钮，如果想要人工控制，可以在适当的时机将系统关掉，此时 ASR 不起作用。

2. 控制单元（ECU）

ASR 的 ECU 也是以微处理器为核心，配以输入、输出电路及电源等组成的。由于 ASR 与 ABS 的一些信号输入和处理是相同的，因此，为减少电子器件的应用数量，ASR 控制器与 ABS 电控单元常组合在一起，如图 3-2-25 所示。

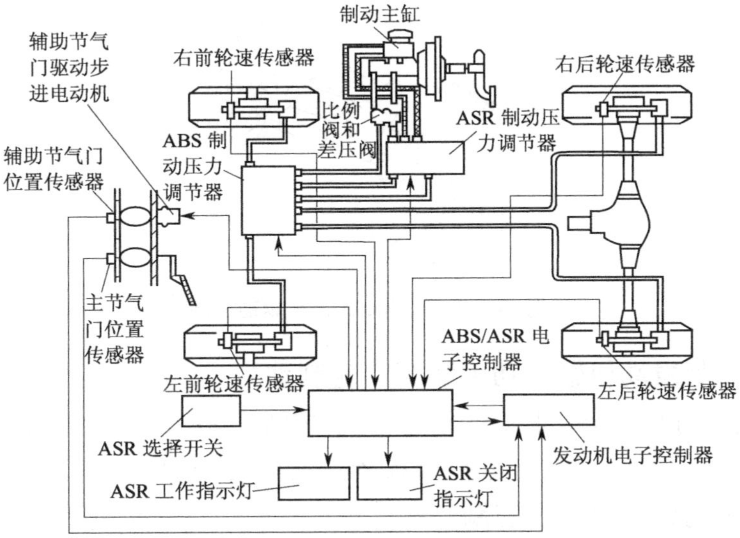

图 3-2-25　ASR 系统组成

ASR 依靠电子传感器探测到从动轮速度低于驱动轮时（这是打滑的特征），就会发出一个信号，调节点火时间、减小气门开度、减小油门、降挡或制动车轮，从而使车轮不再打滑。

ECU 的另一个功能是对故障进行报警或对故障码进行存储和显示。

3. 执行器

ASR 制动压力调节器有独立和组合两种结构形式。前者指 ASR 与 ABS 制动压力调节器彼此分立的结构形式，比较适合将 ASR 作为选装系统的车辆，布置较灵活，但结构不紧凑，连接点较多，易泄漏；后者是将两套压力调节装置合二为一的结构形式，特点与独立式结构相反。

1）独立调节方式

ASR 系统的工作过程与 ABS 相同，在制动过程中，也分为增压、保压和减压三个阶段。正常制动时 ASR 系统不起作用，电磁阀不通电，阀在左位，调压缸的活塞被复位弹簧推至右边极限位置。

起步或加速时若驱动轮出现滑转需要实施制动，ASR 系统使电磁阀通电，阀至右位，蓄压器中的制动液推活塞左移。

保压时，电磁阀半通电，阀在中位，调压缸与储液室和蓄压器都隔断，于是活塞保持原位不动，制动压力保持不变。

减压时，电磁阀断电，阀回左位，使调压腔右腔与蓄压器隔断而与储液室接通，于是调压缸右腔压力下降，制动压力下降。

2）组合调节方式

ASR 系统不起作用时，电磁阀 Ⅰ 不通电，ABS 起制动作用并通过电磁阀 Ⅱ 和电磁

阀Ⅲ来调节制动压力。驱动轮滑转时，ASR控制器使电磁阀Ⅰ通电，阀移至右位，电磁阀Ⅱ和电磁阀Ⅲ不通电，阀仍在左位。于是蓄压器的压力油通入驱动轮制动泵，制动压力增大。

保压时，ASR控制器使电磁阀Ⅰ半通电，阀至中位，隔断蓄压器及制动总泵的通路，驱动轮制动分泵压力保持不变。

减压时，ASR控制器使电磁阀Ⅰ和电磁阀Ⅱ通电，阀移至右位，接通驱动车轮制动分泵与储液室的通道，制动压力下降。

ASR系统通过改变发动机辅助节气门的开度来控制发动机的输出功率。节气门驱动装置由步进电动机和传动机构组成。步进电动机根据ASR控制器输出的控制脉冲转动规定的转角，通过传动机构带动辅助节气门转动。

控制过程如下：ASR系统不起作用时，辅助节气门处于全开位置。当需要减小发动机驱动力来控制车轮滑转时，ASR控制器输出信号使辅助节气门驱动机构工作，改变辅助节气门开度，如图3-2-26所示。

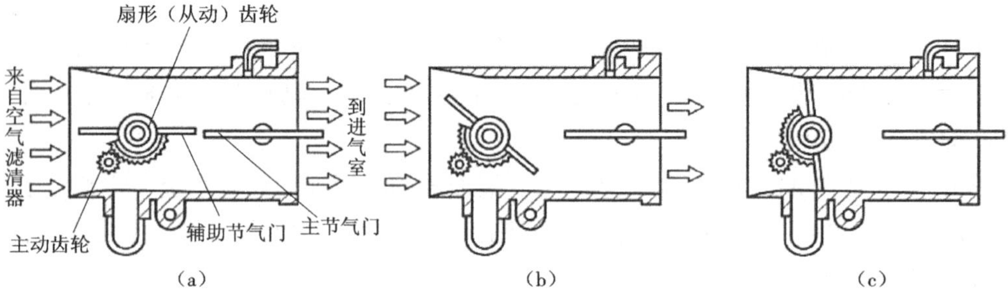

图3-2-26　辅助节气门的工作原理

(a) 全开位置　(b) 半开位置　(c) 全关位置

（五）ASR与ABS的区别

ASR和ABS都是控制车轮和路面的滑移率，以使车轮与地面的附着力不下降，因此二者采用的是相同的技术，它们密切相关，常结合在一起使用，通过共享许多电子组件和共同的系统部件来控制车轮的运动，构成行驶安全系统。ASR和ABS的不同点见表3-2-2。

表3-2-2　ASR与ABS的不同点

控制项目	控制系统	
	ABS	ASR
控制总目标	制动时控制车轮相对地面的滑动	驱动时控制车轮相对地面的滑动

续表

控制项目	控制系统	
	ABS	ASR
达到效果	提高制动效果确保制动安全	提高起步、加速及在光滑路面上的牵引力，确保行驶稳定性
控制对象	四轮	驱动轮
起作用时间	车速很低时不起作用	车速很高时不起作用

五、电子稳定程序系统（ESP）理论基础

（一）ESP 的作用

ESP 属于车辆的主动安全技术，在大众、奥迪、奔驰车型上均使用此简称。在其他车型上，相同或相近功用的系统采用不同的名字，如宝马称其为 DSC，丰田称其为 VSC，而本田称其为 VSA。

ESP 系统是在 ABS 和 ASR 的基础上发展而成的车辆辅助控制系统，它整合了 ABS 和 ASR 的基本功能，并大大拓宽了功能范围。其具体作用主要表现在以下三个方面。

1. 实时监控

ESP 系统是一个实时监控系统，每时每刻都在监控驾驶员的操控、路面反应、汽车运动状态，并不断向发动机和制动系统发出指令。

2. 主动干预

ESP 系统主动调控发动机的转速并可调整每个车轮的驱动力和制动力，以修正汽车的过度转向和转向不足。

3. 预警

ESP 系统还有一个实时警示功能，当驾驶员操作不当和路面异常时，会用警告灯警示驾驶员。

带有 ESP 系统和不带 ESP 系统的轿车在地面附着力相同的路面上行驶时会有很大差异，如图 3-2-27 所示。

图 3-2-27　有无 ESP 系统的行驶情况对比

（二）ESP 系统的组成

ESP 系统以 ABS 为基础，由各种传感器、电子控制单元和执行器三大部分组成，如图 3-2-28 所示。ESP 系统的大部分元件可以与 ABS 和 ASR 共用。在此基础上，增加了用于检测汽车状态的横摆率传感器、转向角传感器、侧向加速度传感器以及检测制动总泵压力的制动压力传感器。ESP 系统的电子控制单元一般与 ABS 和 ASR 的电子控制单元组合为一体，称为 ABS/ASR/ESP 电子控制单元。ESP 执行器在 ABS/ASR 执行器的基础上，改进了通往各车轮的液压通道，增加了 ESP 警告灯和 ESP 蜂鸣器等，如图 3-2-29 所示。

（三）ESP 系统的工作原理

在汽车行驶过程中，转角传感器感知驾驶者转弯方向和角度，车速传感器感知车速、油门开度和转速力矩，刹车传感器感知刹车力，而摆角传感器则感知车子的倾斜度和侧倾速度。ECU 了解这些信息之后，通过计算后判断汽车要正常安全行驶和驾驶者操纵汽车意图的差距，然后，由 ECU 发出指令，调整发动机的转速和车轮上的刹车力，从而修正汽车的过度转向或转向不足，以避免汽车打滑、转向过度、转向不足和抱死，从而保证汽车的行驶安全。从严格的角度来讲，ESP 系统实际上包括 ABS 和 TCS（牵引力控制系统）两大系统的功能，但又不是两者简单的叠加。它们之间的差别主要是 ABS 和 TCS 只能被动的作出反应，而 ESP 则能够探测和分析车况并纠正驾驶的错误，防患于未然。其工作原理如图 3-2-30 所示。

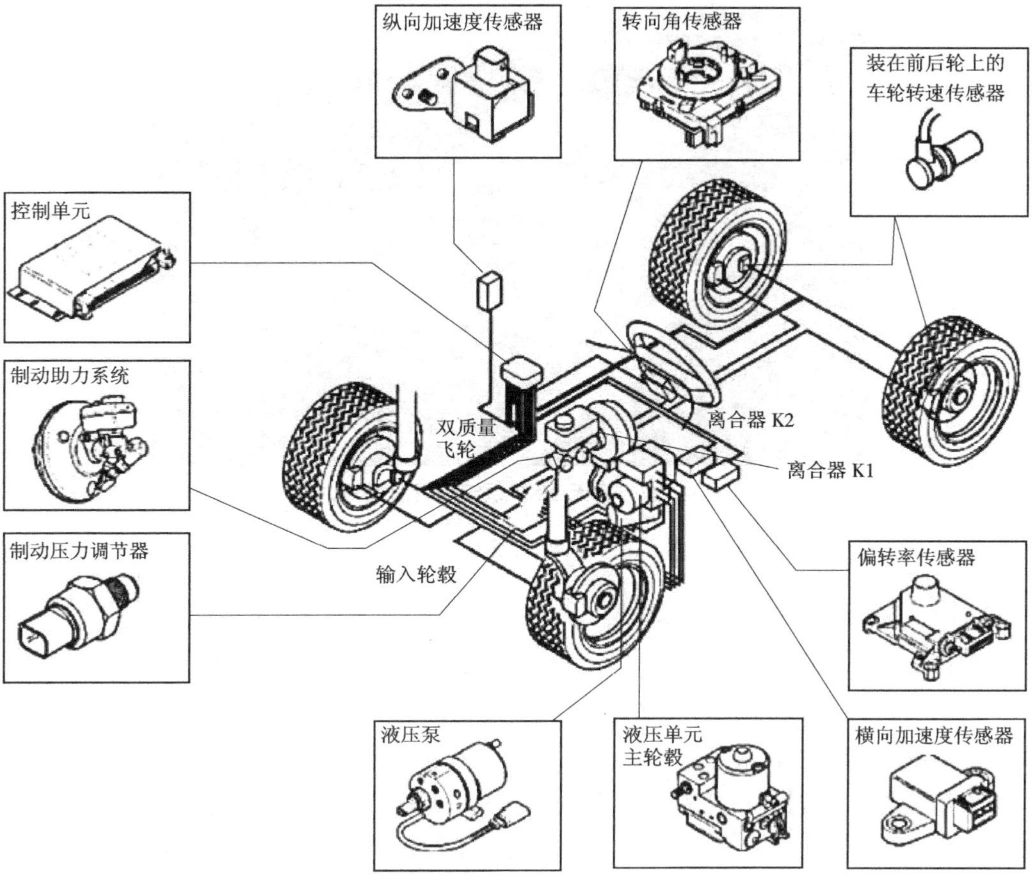

图 3-2-28　ESP 系统的组成

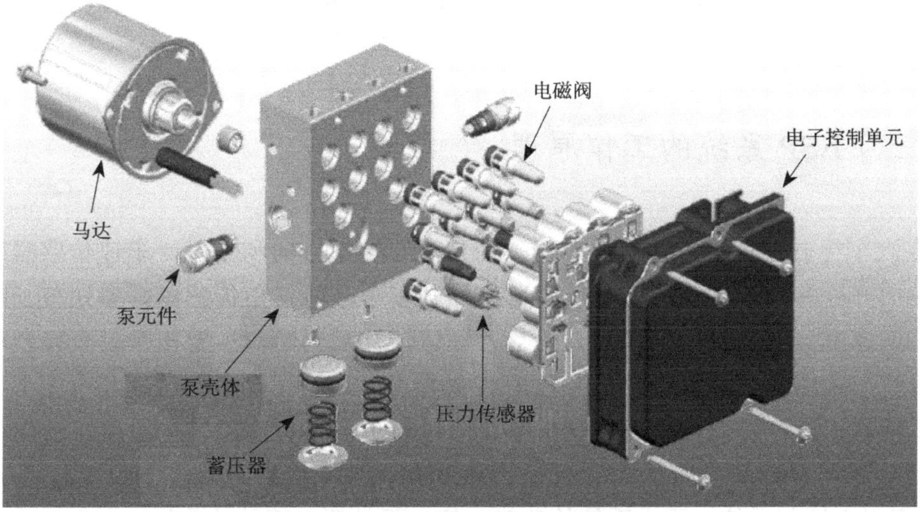

图 3-2-29　ESP 执行器总成实物拆解

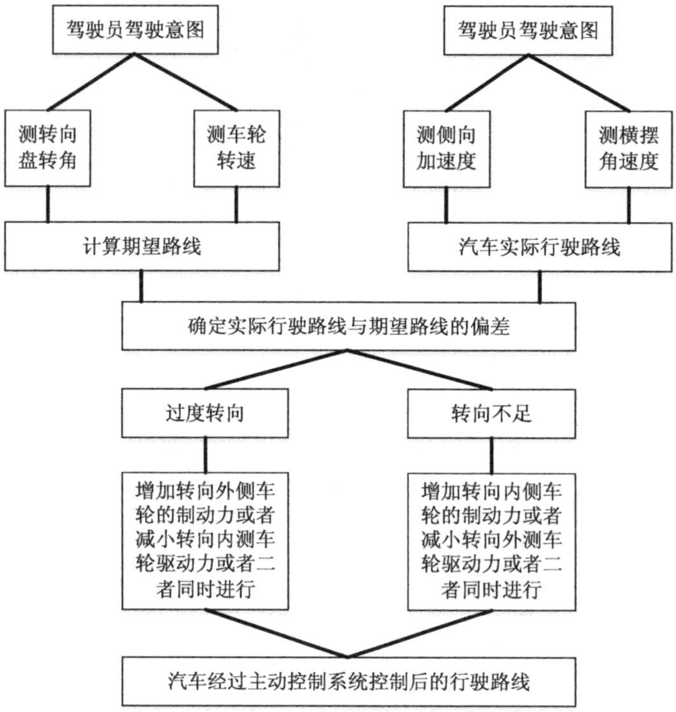

图 3-2-30　ESP 系统的工作原理

ESP 系统经由增压、保压、减压过程调节系统压力，以达到最佳制动压力状态，如图 3-2-31 所示，该系统采用 X 形布置，包含 1 个电机、2 个回流泵、2 个蓄能器与 12 个电磁阀，各部件名称缩写见表 3-2-3。ESP 与 ABS 控制器不同的是，ABS 控制器只有 8 个阀，而 ESP 控制器有 12 个阀。这是由于 ESP 系统在主动控制时需要形成一个封闭的液压回路，因此在 ABS 回路的基础上增加了 2 个阀（HSV），另外增加的两个阀（USV）则在 ESP 系统工作时打开，让马达泵从储液罐中泵油给制动轮缸，从而实现牵引力控制和稳定控制功能时动作。

哈佛 H6 制动系统模块出现故障时，ABS/ESP 报警灯在仪表板上显示，表 3-2-4 所示为系统出现不同故障时显示的标识，当刹车液位低于极限值时，仪表板点亮刹车液位低报警标识。

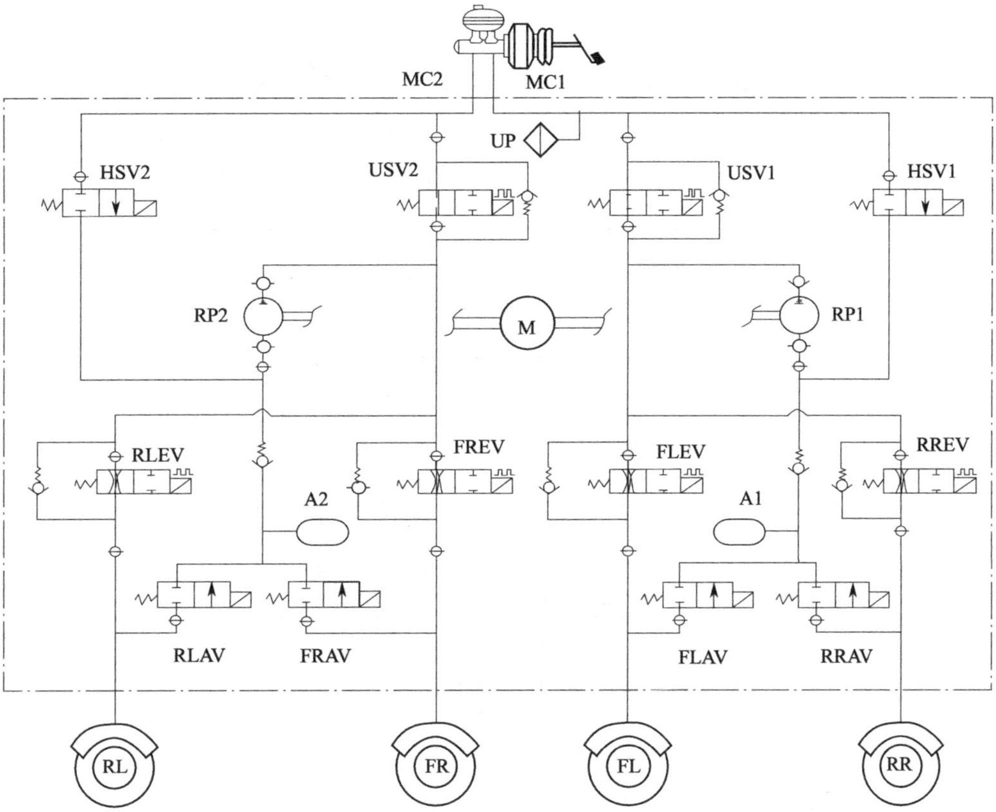

图 3-2-31　哈佛 H6 系统液压回路原理

表 3-2-3　哈佛 H6 系统液压回路各部件名称缩写

MC1	制动主缸第一回路	FLEV	左前轮进油阀
MC2	制动主缸第二回路	FLAV	左前轮出油阀
M	马达	FREV	右前轮进油阀
RP1	回流泵 1	FRAV	右前轮出油阀
RP2	回流泵 2	RLEV	左后轮进油阀
A1	蓄能器 1	RLAV	左后轮出油阀
A2	蓄能器 2	RREV	右后轮进油阀
FL	左前轮	RRAV	右后轮出油阀
FR	右前轮	HSV1	高压开关阀 1
RL	左后轮	HSV2	高压开关阀 2
RR	右后轮	USV1	回路控制阀 1
UP	压力传感器	USV2	回路控制阀 2

表 3-2-4　ABS/ESP 报警灯显示标识

报警灯名字	EBD	ABS	ESP
符号形状			
颜色	红	橘黄	橘黄
系统正常	不亮	不亮	不亮
行驶中 ASR 起作用	不亮	不亮	闪烁
行驶中 ESP 起作用	不亮	不亮	闪烁
点火开关 ON，仪表自检	常亮 2.5 s 后熄灭		
诊断模式（制动系统）	常亮	常亮	常亮
ABS 故障	不亮	常亮	常亮
EBD 故障	常亮	常亮	常亮
ASR 故障	不亮	不亮	常亮
ESP 故障	不亮	不亮	常亮
关闭 ESP 功能	不亮	不亮	常亮
没有收到 CAN 网络信号（制动系统）超过 500 ms	常亮	常亮	常亮

【知识拓展】

ESP 系统的检修

1. 问题

哈佛 H6 汽车打开点火开关，系统自检完毕，警告灯保持点亮。

2. 初步检查

在对 ESP 系统进行诊断前，应首先检查可能导致 ESP 系统故障并且容易接触的部件，目视检查和外观检查程序能快速确定故障，从而无须再做进一步的诊断。

（1）确保车辆上只安装推荐尺寸的轮胎和轮毂。同轴轮胎的花纹样式和深度必须一样。

（2）检查 ESP 液压调节器、制动管路及连接处是否有泄漏。

（3）检查 ESP 系统的保险丝，确保保险丝没有烧毁并且型号正确。38 pin ESP 系统有三个保险丝，分别是：泵电机保险丝（40 A），电磁阀保险丝（25 A），电子控制单元保险丝（5 A）。46 pin ESP 系统有三个保险丝，分别是：泵电机保险丝（40 A），电磁阀保险丝（40 A），电子控制单元保险丝（40 A）。

（4）检查蓄电池电压，检查蓄电池接线柱是否腐蚀或松动。ESP 系统的正常工作电压范围是 9~16 V。

（5）检查 ESP 系统接地线的搭铁点是否松动，搭铁位置是否被改变。

（6）对下列电气部件进行视检和外观检查：ESP 系统相关部件的线束和接插件是否连接正确、是否被夹伤或割伤；线束布线是否过于靠近高压或大电流装置，如高压电或部件、发电机和电机、售后加装的立体声放大器等，ESP 部件对电磁干扰（EMI）很敏感。如果怀疑有间歇性故障，检查售后加装的防盗装置、灯或移动电话是否安装正确。

3. ESP 系统检修流程

ESP 系统检修流程如图 3-2-32 所示。

4. 无故障码故障维修

如果制动系统存在故障，但 ESP 系统没有存储故障码，此类故障称为无故障码故障。无故障码故障一般由基础制动系统故障所致。

（1）制动液泄漏，可能引起制动偏软，制动踏板行程过长，严重的可能引起制动失效。

（2）使用劣质的制动液，会腐蚀制动管路和 ESP 液压调节模块内部元件，严重的还会导致制动失效。

（3）制动管路有空气，可能引起制动偏软，甚至制动失效。

（4）制动管路堵塞，可能引起制动偏硬，制动跑偏，甚至制动失效。

（5）制动盘过度磨损，可能引起制动偏软，制动踏板行程过长。

（6）助力器故障，可能引起制动偏硬或偏软，制动踏板行程过长，严重的还会导致制动失效。

（7）制动管路连接错误，可能引起 ESP 系统性能下降，出现摆尾，刹车距离长等现象。正确安装方法请参照 ESP 液压调节模块上油孔附近的标识：MC1 表示 1 号主缸油管；MC2 表示 2 号主缸油管；FL 代表左前轮缸油管；FR 代表右前轮缸油管；RL 代表左后轮缸油管；RR 代表右后轮缸油管。

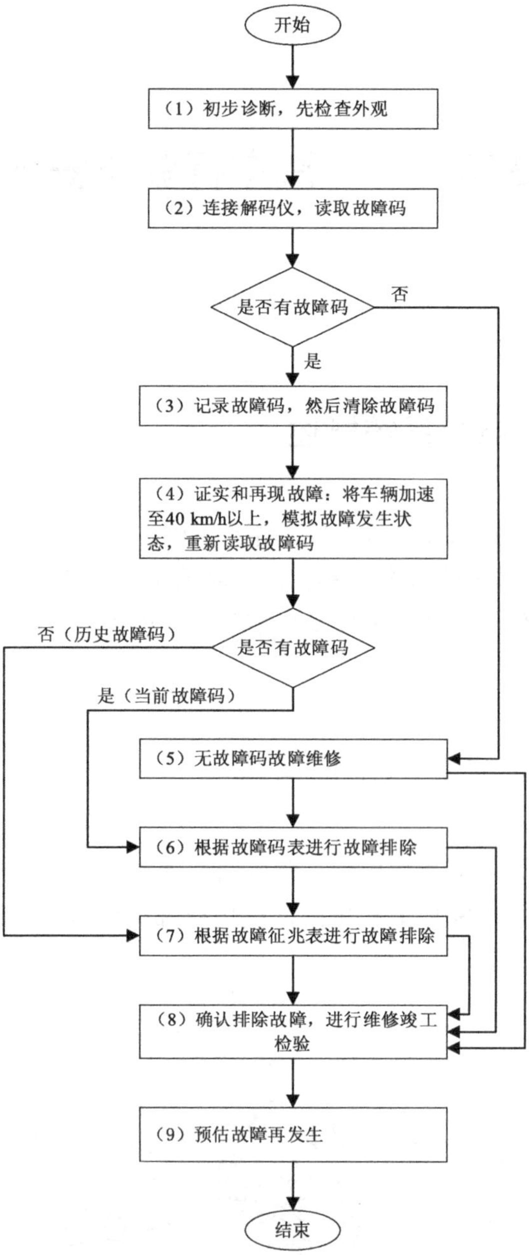

图 3-2-32　哈佛 H6 ESP 系统检修流程

【思考与练习】

1. 电控 ABS 由哪几部分组成？
2. 简述 ASR 和 ABS 的区别。
3. 简述 ABS 的功用及工作原理。
4. 简述 ESP 的常见问题及诊断流程。

第 3 节　汽车行驶与安全控制

一、汽车巡航电控系统概述

汽车巡航电控系统通常简称巡航控制系统（CCS）。汽车巡航是指汽车以一定的速度匀速行驶，故汽车巡航控制系统又称恒速控制系统。汽车巡航电控系统的功用是：根据汽车行驶阻力的变化，自动调节发动机节气门（或供油拉杆）的开度大小，使汽车保持恒定的速度行驶。

（一）汽车巡航电控系统的组成

巡航控制系统主要由车速传感器、节气门位置传感器或加速踏板位置传感器、巡航控制系统电控单元（CCS ECU）和执行机构等部件组成。如图 3-3-1 所示为某车型 CCS 控制部件的安装位置。

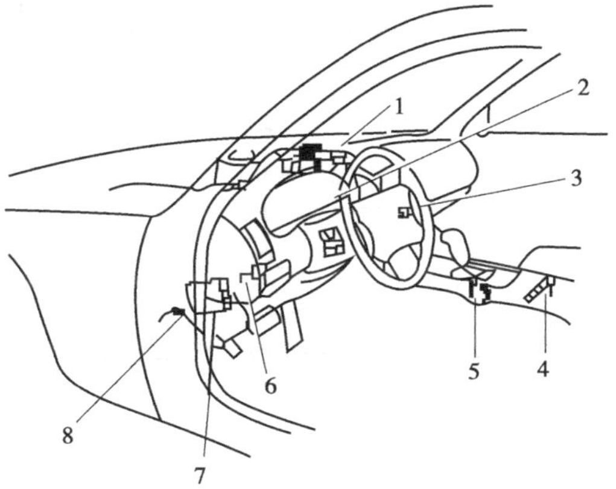

图 3-3-1　某车型 CCS 部件的安装位置

1—执行器；2—巡航指示灯；3—巡航开关；4—车速传感器；5—空挡启动开关；
6—制动灯开关；7—CCS ECU；8—驻车制动开关

巡航控制系统的车速传感器（VSS）、节气门位置传感器（TPS）或加速踏板位置传感器既可与发动机控制系统或电子控制自动变速系统公用，也可专门独立设置。

控制开关主要有巡航开关、制动灯开关、驻车制动开关、点火开关、离合器开关（仅对手动变速器汽车）或空挡启动开关（对自动变速器汽车）等。巡航开关的功用是将恒速、加速或减速、恢复原速以及取消巡航行驶等指令信号输入 CCS ECU，其他开关的功用是将各种状态信息输入 CCS ECU，以便 CCS ECU 确定是否进行恒速控制。

CCS ECU 是巡航控制系统的控制核心，具有数学计算、逻辑判断、记忆存储、故障自诊断等功能。

执行机构分为气动式和电动式两种。气动式主要由速度伺服装置和电磁阀等组成；电动式主要由电动机（永磁式或步进式电动机）、减速机构和电磁离合器等组成。执行机构的功用是根据 CCS ECU 指令，通过节气门拉索（钢索）或电子式节气门控制器调节发动机节气门的开度，使车速保持恒定。

（二）巡航控制系统的控制原理

巡航控制系统的控制原理如图 3-3-2 所示。输入 CCS ECU 的信号有两个：一个是驾驶员根据行驶条件，通过巡航开关设定的巡航车速指令信号；另一个是车速传感器输入的实际车速反馈信号。

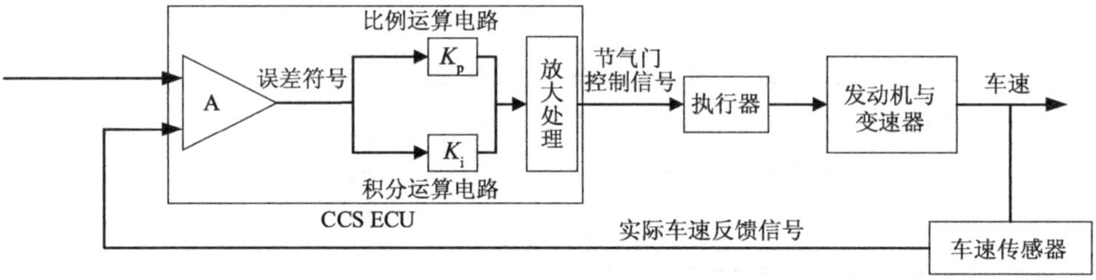

图 3-3-2　巡航控制系统的控制原理

当巡航车速指令信号和实际车速反馈信号输入 CCS ECU 后，CCS ECU 的比较器 A 经过比较运算便可得到两个信号之差，称之为误差信号。误差信号经过比例运算和积分运算后再经过放大处理就可得到控制节气门开度大小的控制信号，CCS ECU 将控制指令发送给执行机构，执行机构就可以驱动节气门拉索（或电子节气门控制器）调节节气门开度，将实际车速迅速调节到驾驶员设定的车速，从而实现巡航控制（即恒速控制）。在控制过程中，当实际车速低于驾驶员设定的巡航车速时，CCS ECU 将向执行机构发出增大节气门开度的指令，使实际车速升高到巡航车速。反之，当实际车速高于驾驶员设定的巡航车速时，CCS ECU 将向执行机构发出减小节气门开度的指令，使实际车速降低到巡航车速，以使实际车速基本保持在驾驶员设定的巡航车速不变。

（三）巡航车速的控制方式

当汽车在平坦路面上以设定的巡航车速 v_a 行驶时，设节气门开度为 θ_a。如果此时 CCS ECU 向执行机构发出指令使节气门开度保持不变，则汽车将以设定的巡航车速 v_a 行驶。但是，当车辆遇到坡道上坡行驶或遇到刮风逆风行驶时，由于坡道阻力或风阻增加将使车速降低到 v_b，而不能以设定的巡航车速 v_a 行驶。因此，CCS ECU 必须向执行机构发出指令使节气门开度增大（即节气门旋转角度增大$\Delta\theta°$），才能使车速接近设定的巡航车速 v_a（即实际车速比巡航车速 v_a 低Δv值）行驶。同理，当车辆下坡或顺风行驶时，节气门旋转角度将减小$\Delta\theta°$，实际车速将比巡航车速 v_a 高Δv值。

由此可见，为使汽车巡航车速 v_a 不受行驶阻力变化的影响，CCS ECU 内部积分运算放大电路 K_1 控制的控制线应尽可能使车速变化范围减小，因此，当汽车行驶在上坡、下坡道路以及风阻等因素导致行驶阻力变化时，控制系统只要将节气门开度调整的转角，就可将车速变化幅度限制在$\pm\Delta v$值的微小范围内。

（四）巡航控制系统的优点

巡航控制系统主要具有以下优点。

1. 减轻驾驶员的劳动强度，提高行驶安全性

在汽车行驶过程中，当车速达到一定值（超过 40 km/h）后，只要驾驶员操作巡航开关设定一个想要恒速行驶的车速，CCS ECU 就能自动控制发动机节气门开度使汽车保持在设定的速度恒速行驶，不需要驾驶员踩踏加速踏板。

2. 行驶速度稳定，提高乘坐舒适性

在巡航行驶过程中，无论汽车在上坡或下坡路面上行驶，还是在平坦路面或风向变化的情况下行驶，只要在发动机功率允许的范围之内，汽车行驶速度都将保持设定的巡航车速不变。

3. 节省燃料消耗，提高燃油经济性和排放性能

实践证明汽车在相同行驶条件下，利用巡航行驶可以节省 15% 左右的燃料。

二、汽车巡航电控系统的结构原理

（一）巡航控制开关

巡航控制开关主控开关一般为杆式开关，安装在转向柱上驾驶员容易接近的地方，

或将组合开关设计在方向盘上。大多数开关有三个挡位：设置 / 减速（SET/COAST）、取消（CANCEL）和恢复 / 加速（RES/ACC）挡。通常情况下，当车速超过 40 km/h 时，只要按下设定键，车辆就会记住当前的车速并保持定速行驶，当按下取消键时，恒速行驶立即停止。“恢复 / 加速”挡用于制动或换挡断开电路后，使车辆重新按设定速度行驶。汽车在自动巡航控制状态下，可以通过按加速键提高车速，或按减速键来降低车速，如图 3-3-3 所示。

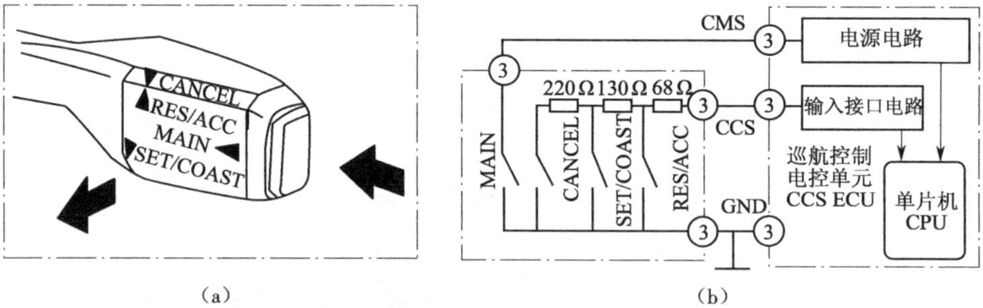

图 3-3-3　巡航开关操纵手柄的外形结构与内部电路

（a）操纵手柄外形结构　（b）巡航开关内部电路

（二）巡航控制系统电控单元

巡航控制系统电控单元（CCS ECU）又称为巡航电子控制器，巡航控制系统电控单元是巡航控制系统的中枢，其作用是接收车速传感器、巡航控制开关、制动灯开关等信号，经计算、记忆、放大及信号转换等处理后，输出控制信号，驱动执行器动作。电路框图如图 3-3-4 所示。

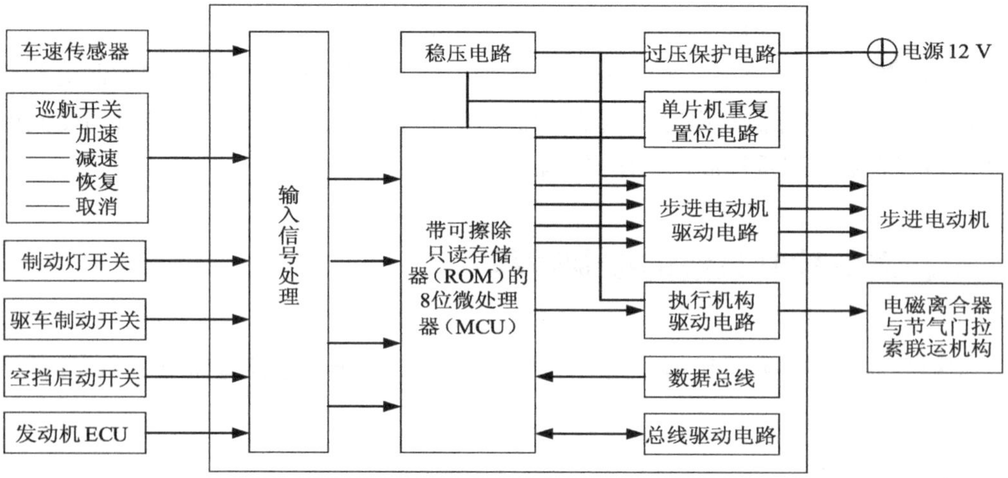

图 3-3-4　Motorola 数字式 CCS ECU 电路框图

（三）巡航执行机构

巡航控制系统的执行机构又称速度伺服装置，其功用是根据 CCS ECU 的控制指令，将电控单元输出的电流或电压信号转变为机械运动，进而控制节气门的开度，最终达到控制车速的目的。执行器有电动和气动操纵两种形式。巡航执行机构的结构组成如图 3-3-5 所示。

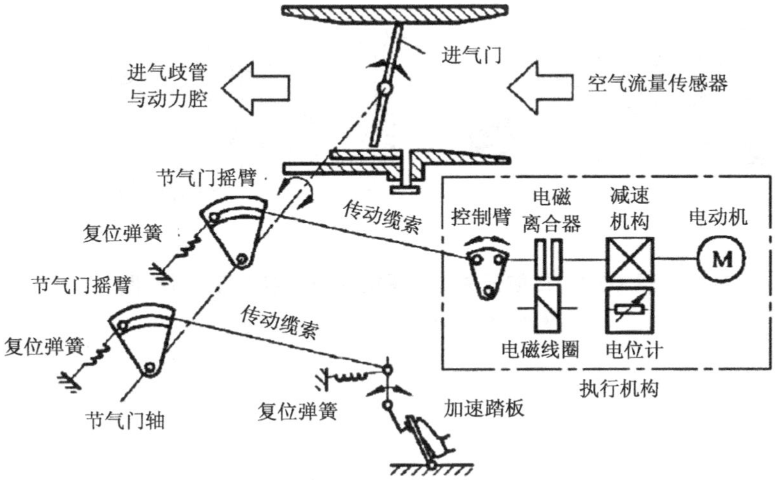

图 3-3-5　电动式巡航执行机构的结构组成

电动式巡航执行机构利用电动机的转动并带动控制摇臂摆动，可使节气门的开度变化，主要有电磁离合器、直流电动机或步进电机等。直流电动机是连续运转，它的运转速度与电控单元供给它的电压平均值有关；它的运转或停止，由电控单元输出的电压“有”或“无”来决定；它的运转方向，由电控单元输出的电压方向决定。步进电机的工作，是对其通电一次，电机轴就转过一定的角度。

电磁离合器的作用是，当电磁离合器通电时，电动机的轴与节气门控制摇臂结合在一起，当电磁离合器断电时，电动机轴与节气门控制摇臂分离，使节气门受到电动机和电磁离合器的双重控制，工作更可靠。

三、巡航控制系统的控制过程

巡航控制系统普遍采用闭环控制方式进行控制，巡航控制流程如图 3-3-6 所示。

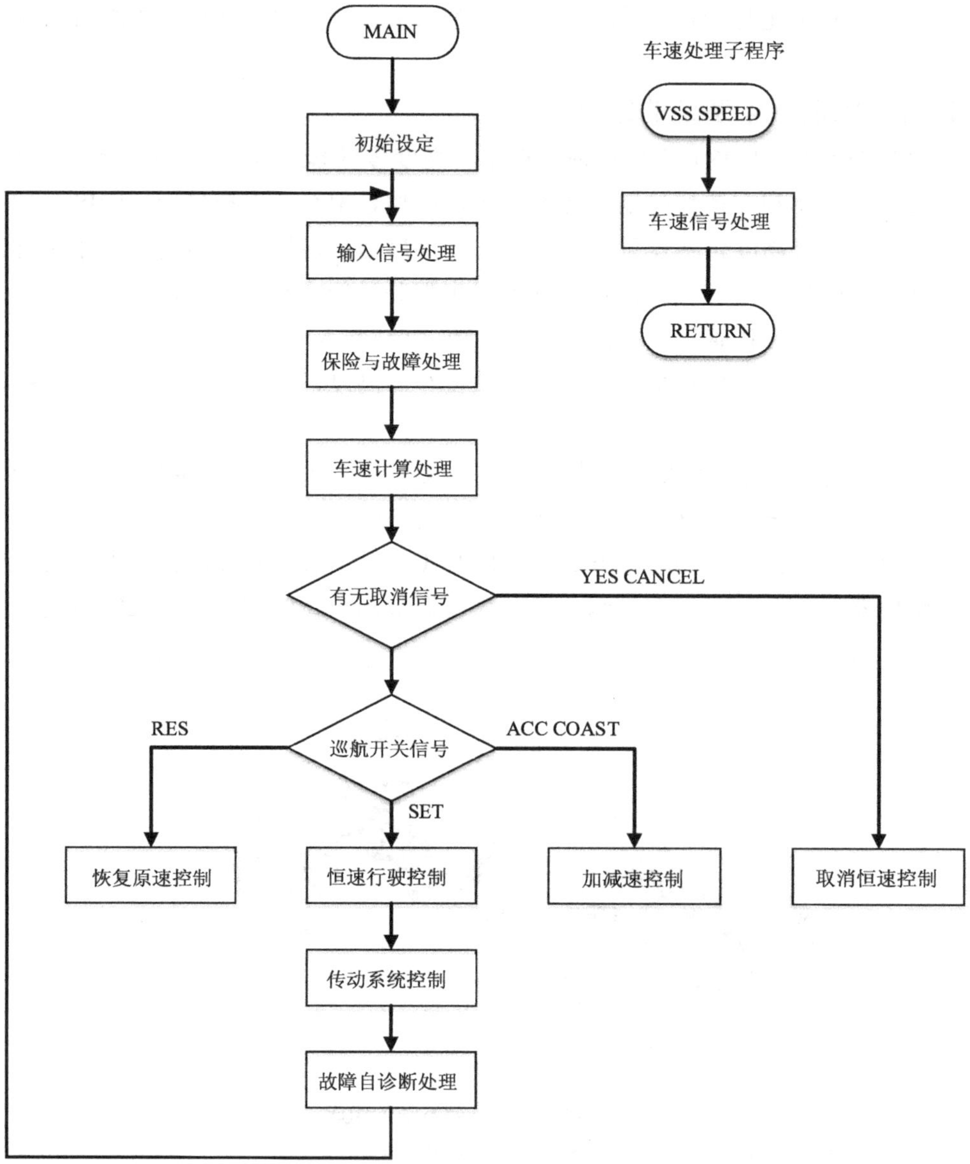

图 3-3-6　巡航控制流程

四、汽车电控悬架系统

（一）汽车电控悬架系统的组成

1. 汽车电控悬架系统的功用

汽车电控悬架系统的功用是：在汽车的行驶路面、行驶速度和载荷发生变化时，自动调节车身高度、悬架刚度和减振器阻尼的大小，从而改善汽车的行驶平顺性（即乘

坐舒适性）。其中阻尼指的是振动的物体或振荡电路的能量逐渐减少时，振幅相应减少的现象。

2. 汽车电控悬架系统的组成

电控悬架系统（EMS）主要由前、后车身高度传感器，转向盘转向与转角传感器，节气门位置传感器和车速传感器，控制开关，电控悬架系统电控单元（EMS ECU）和执行器组成。车身高度传感器采集前后车身的高度信号，转向盘转向与转角传感器采集汽车行驶方向信号，节气门位置传感器采集驾驶员加或减速信号，车速传感器采集汽车行驶速度信号。传感器和控制开关向 EMS ECU 输入车身以及汽车行驶状态信息，EMS 执行元件产生一定的机械动作，从而改变车身高度，空气弹簧的刚度或减振器的阻尼。

不同汽车电控悬架系统的功能与零部件组成各不相同。如图 3-3-7 所示，电控悬架系统主要由前、后车身高度传感器，转向盘转向与转角传感器，高度控制自动切断开关，驾驶模式选择开关，制动灯开关，EMS ECU，前、后悬架控制执行器，前、后高度控制继电器，前、后高度控制阀，储气筒与调节阀，高度控制空气压缩机，干燥器与排气阀总成等组成。

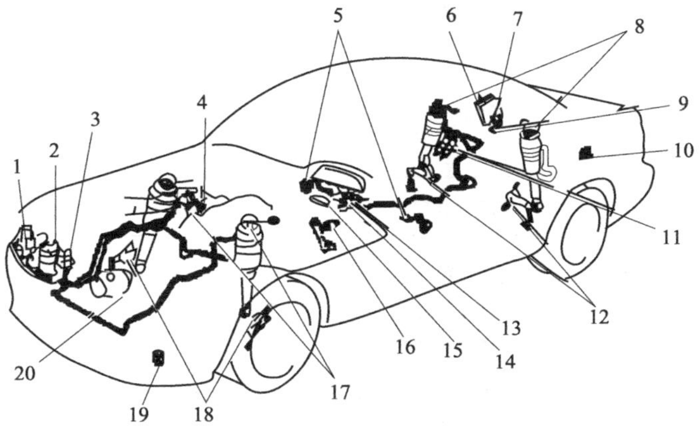

图 3-3-7 电控悬架系统的组成

1—干燥器与排气阀总成；2—高度控制空气压缩机；3—No.1 高度控制阀；4—主节气门位置传感器；5—门控开关；6—EMS ECU；7—No.2 高度控制继电器；8—后悬架控制执行器；9—高度控制连接器；10—高度控制自动切断开关；11—No.2 高度控制阀与溢流阀；12—后高度传感器；13—驾驶模式选择开关；14—高度控制开关；15—转向盘转向与转角传感器；16—制动灯开关；17—前悬架控制执行器；18—前高度传感器；19—No.1 高度控制继电器；20—储气筒与调节阀

高度控制开关设有“High（车身高）”和“Normal（车身高度正常）”两个挡位，操纵高度控制开关能使汽车车身的目标高度变为“Normal”状态或“High”状态。但是由于高速行驶时车身过高会降低车身的稳定性，因此，当高度控制开关处于“High”挡位且车速达到一定值时，高度控制系统能自动将车身高度降低到“Normal”状态，保证汽车的行驶稳定性和减小行驶阻力。当点火开关断开后，如果车身高度因乘员或载荷量变化而高于目标高度，那么高度控制系统能自动将车身高度降低到目标高度，从而改善汽车驻车时的姿态。

高度控制自动切断开关能使空气弹簧悬架系统关闭，防止车身过高或拖车时产生意外。驾驶模式选择开关用于选择减振器阻尼的工作模式，一般设有“自动”“坚硬”和“‘柔软”等工作模式。

当驾驶员踩下制动踏板时，制动灯开关信号将送到 EMS ECU，EMS ECU 将控制前部空气弹簧刚度和减振器阻尼变成“坚硬”状态，以便抑制汽车制动时的点头现象，使汽车姿态变化最小。

3. 电子控制悬架系统的分类

根据电子控制悬架系统的功能不同，目前采用的电子控制悬架系统主要有以下几种类型：

（1）车身高度电子控制系统（即电子控制变高度空气弹簧悬架系统）；

（2）电子控制变刚度空气弹簧悬架系统（即悬架刚度电子控制系统）；

（3）电子控制变阻尼减振器悬架系统（即悬架阻尼电子控制系统）；

（4）电子控制变高度与变刚度空气弹簧悬架系统（即悬架高度与刚度与电子控制系统）。

（5）电子控制变高度、变刚度空气弹簧与变阻尼减振器悬架系统（即悬架高度与刚度与阻尼电子控制系统）。

（二）电控悬架系统部分传感器

电控悬架系统主要传感器包括高度传感器、转向盘转角传感器、车速传感器、高度控制传感器、门控开关等。

1. 转向盘转角传感器

转向盘转角传感器用于检测转向盘中间位置、转动方向、转动角度和转动速度。电子单元根据车速传感器信号和转角传感器信号，判断汽车转向时侧向力的大小和方向，以控制车身的侧倾，图 3-3-8 所示为长城系列车型转向盘转角传感器。

图 3-3-8　长城 H6 转向盘转角传感器

在压入转向轴的遮光盘上有一定数量的窄槽，遮光盘的两端分别配有光电元件，一般是两个发光二极管和两个光敏三极管，组成两对光电耦合器（信号发生器）。当转动方向盘时，转向轴带动遮光盘旋转，当转到窄槽处时，光敏三极管感受到发光二极管发出的光，就会输出“ON”信号；当遮光盘转到除窄槽以外的其他位置时，光敏三极管感受不到发光二极管的光线，就会输出“OFF”信号这样随着转向盘的转动，两个光电耦合器的输出端就形成“ ON/OFF”的变换，如图 3-3-9 所示。

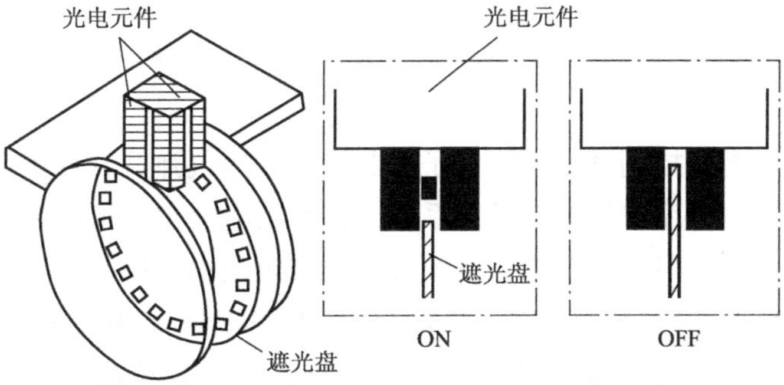

图 3-3-9　光电式转向盘转角传感器工作原理

2. 车速传感器

车速传感器通常与自动变速器系统共用。车速传感器的转子，由变速器输出轴通过齿轮驱动。转子轴每转一圈，传感器产生 20 个脉冲信号，输送至组合仪表，由组合仪表转换为转子轴每转一圈输出 4 个脉冲信号，该信号送至电子控制单元 ECU 中用来计算车速。长城 H6 车速传感器如图 3-3-10 所示。

图 3-3-10　长城 H6 车速传感器

3. 高度控制传感器

车身高度控制传感器检测行驶时车身高度的变化情况，常见的有光电式和可变电阻式，如图 3-3-11 所示。

图 3-3-11　光电式高度控制传感器

一般轿车安装4个车身控制传感器。光电式传感器有一根靠连杆带动转动的转轴，转轴上固定一个开有许多窄槽的圆盘，圆盘两边装有4组光电耦合器。当车身高度变化时，通过连杆可使转轴转动，因而4组光电耦合器可感应出4组脉冲信号，通过这4组脉冲信号的不同组合，可反映车高的高度范围，如图3-3-12所示。

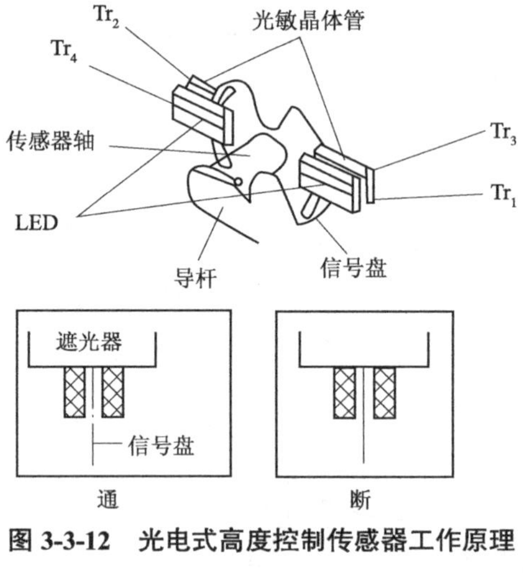

图 3-3-12　光电式高度控制传感器工作原理

4. 门控开关

门控开关负责检测车门是否打开。由于汽车停止后，悬架系统自动控制车身降低高度，若此时ECU检测到车门打开时，车高自动控制必须停止，以免造成危险，如图3-3-13所示。

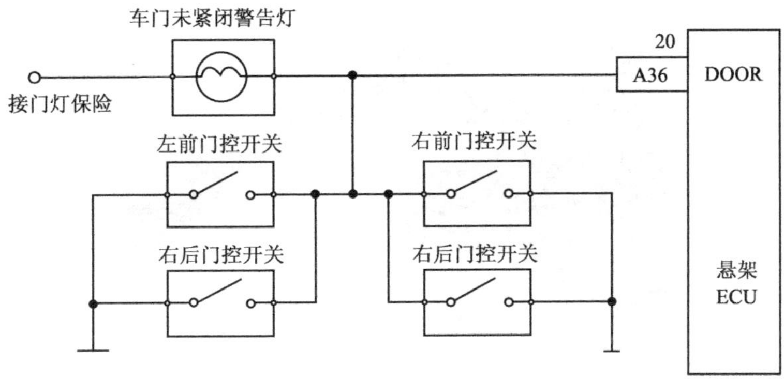

图 3-3-13　门控开关控制电路

（三）电控悬架系统控制单元

悬架控制系统的控制单元简称悬架 ECU 或 EMS ECU，主要由中央处理器 CPU、随机存储器（RAM）、只读存储器（ROM）、输入 / 输出接口（I/O）、模拟 / 数字（A/D）转换器等组成。各种传感器与执行元件是通过 I/O 接口电路来传递通信的，ROM 存储器储存着各种计算悬架控制的程序和运算所必需的数据，中央微处理器 CPU 负责按存储器的固有程序进行各种信息处理，将控制信号发送给执行器，控制执行器工作，如图 3-3-14 所示。

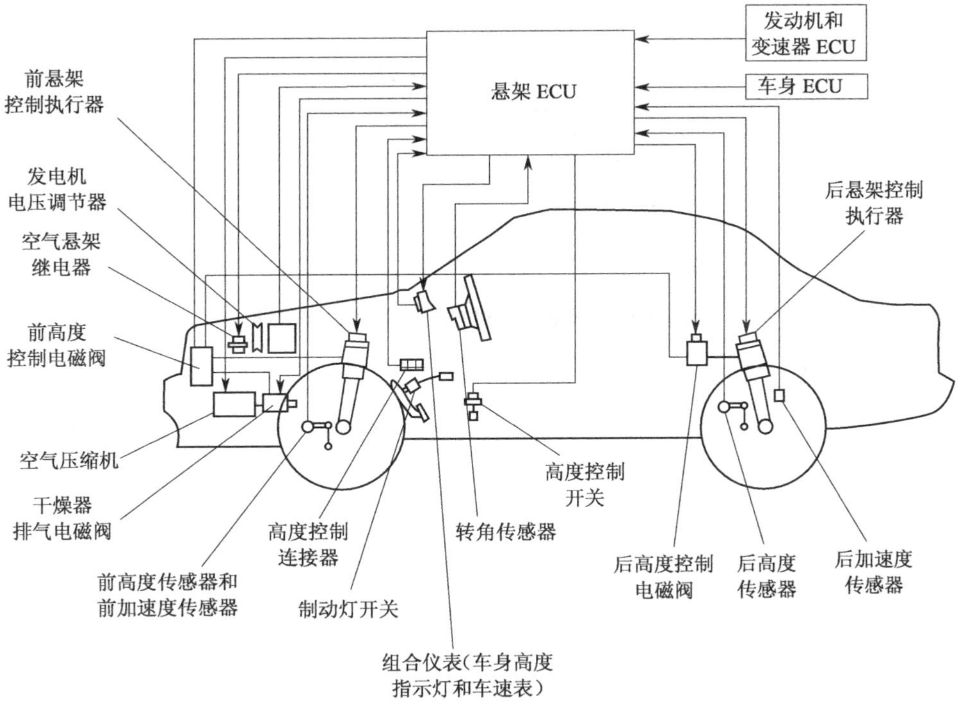

图 3-3-14　电控悬架系统的组成

（四）电控悬架执行机构

控制执行机构主要包括前悬架控制执行器、发电机电压调节器、悬架控制执行器、车身高度执行机构、空气压缩机等，主要影响电控悬架的高度、刚度等参数，如图 3-3-15 所示。

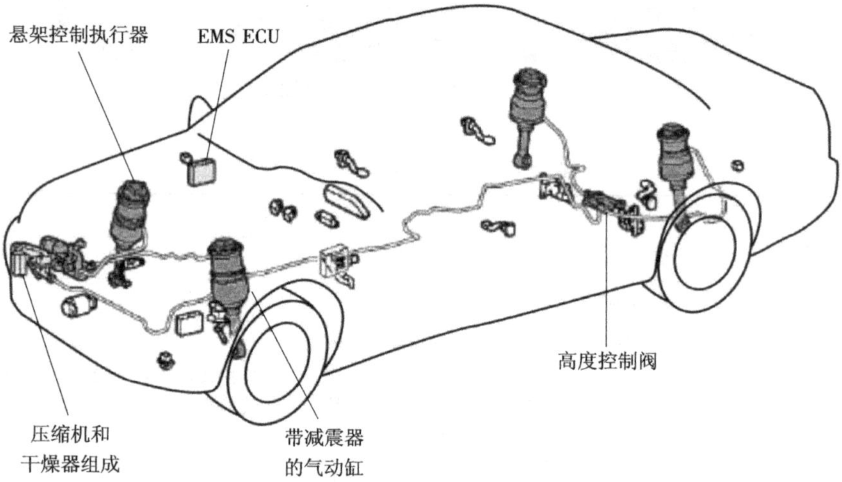

图 3-3-15　电控悬架系统执行机构

【知识拓展】

汽车自动驾驶系统简述

“长城汽车预计于 2025 年实现 Level5 级自动驾驶。”长城汽车总裁王凤英曾表示。科技迭代很快，如果需要将概念中 Level5 级别的自动驾驶形象化，那么汽车就是一台拥有人类感知、决策以及控制的代步机器。精细划分来看，实现一个自动驾驶系统，需要分为感知层、信息融合层、决策规划层以及控制层。

1. 感知层

汽车感知类比于人类用眼睛捕捉事物，自动驾驶汽车则需要用传感器感知事物，如图 3-3-16 所示。自动驾驶汽车想要安全行驶，首先需要了解周围行驶的环境，而传感器就是自动驾驶汽车了解环境的工具，目前自动驾驶汽车搭载的主要传感器包括摄像头、激光雷达、毫米波雷达以及超声波雷达等，见表 3-3-1。

图 3-3-16　自动驾驶感知层

表 3-3-1　四大传感器优缺点对比

性能	传感器			
	摄像头传感器	激光雷达传感器	毫米波雷达传感器	超声波雷达传感器
距离	6~50 m	100~200 m	>200 m	0.1~3 m
优势	成本低、全景泊车；可以识别障碍物形态（大小、距离及类别）	测距精度高，方向性明确，响应速度快，实时建立周围环境三维模型	探测距离远，不受天气影响	穿透力强、成本低、测试方便
劣势	对光线要求高，无法精确测距	成本高、易受天气影响	行人反射波弱，难以识别	测试角度小，需要安装多个

目前，摄像头普遍采用 CMOS 图像传感器，捕捉清晰图片帮助自动驾驶汽车输入数据参数。为了保证数据完整性，市面上的很多自动驾驶汽车都会采用 3~6 个摄像头。由于摄像头对于光线极为敏感，如果出现强、弱光的情况，普通摄像头捕捉的图像并不能直接被使用，或者会出现无法识别的现象，这对于自动驾驶汽车来说极为致命。所以，市面上的自动驾驶汽车一般都会采用动态范围 130 dB 以上的图像传感器。

雷达主要测量位置、速度以及方位角等三个参数。激光雷达算是汽车行业里的一个新贵，也被视为自动驾驶汽车未来最核心传感器之一。其主要通过发送直线激光束（非无线电波）的方式，根据激光遇到障碍物后的折返时间（TOF），计算目标与车的距离，如图 3-3-17 所示。激光雷达在精度、信息量以及安全性的方面，具有独到之处。但想要获得更高精度的测量数据，也意味着激光雷达线束需要增加，目前市面上比较常见的是 8、16 以及 32 线激光雷达产品，64 线比较少，这与成本也是成正相关的（激光线束越多，成本越高）。虽然，国内外如 Velodyne、Quangery 等科技公司一直在研发低成本、小体积的激光雷达，但由于单个成本居高不下，很难实现量产。

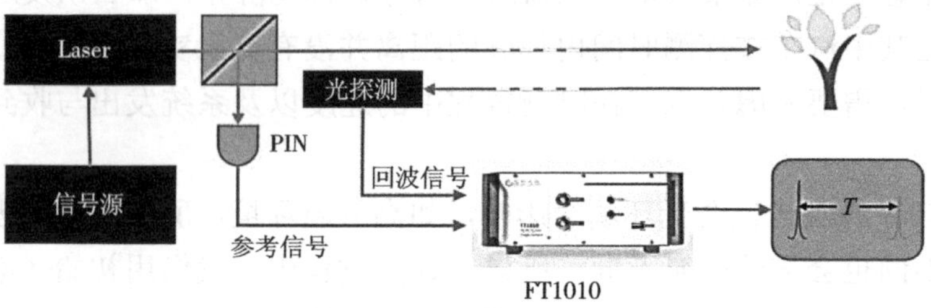

图 3-3-17 雷达工作原理

毫米波雷达，顾名思义是工作在毫米波波段（波长 1~10 mm，频率 30~300 GHz）的探测雷达。与激光雷达发送方式不同的是，毫米波雷达会发出锥状的电磁波。工作原理是根据回波时间差计算距离，其具有不受天气情况影响及超远测距的优势，雷达频段与测距成正相关，目前市面上主流有 24 GHz 和 77 GHz 两种，随着技术水平提升以及成本下降，此传感器逐渐被应用于 ADAS。

蝙蝠发出超声波探测物体的远近，自动驾驶汽车用超声波发现障碍物，两者原理一样。超声波属于机械波的一种，所以容易受传播介质的影响，如天气不同，传播速度不同。故为了充分利用超声波雷达穿透力强、测距方便以及成本低的优点，部分车企会在汽车车身四周置入大量的超声波雷达，如 L2-L3 级的特斯拉、奥迪等汽车中超声波雷达使用数量高达 12 个。

2. 信息融合层

信息融合层是比较关键的。自动驾驶汽车置入了如摄像头、激光雷达、毫米波雷达等多个传感器，我们需要用这些传感器感知、捕获数据。当汽车行驶至目标物一定距离内，摄像头和激光雷达同时检测出目标物时，为了让两个传感器检测出的目标物是同一个，需要对多传感器数据进行分析对比，如果相同，则进行信息融合，告诉汽车前面就是一个目标物，如图 3-3-18 所示。

图 3-3-18 自动驾驶信息融合层

信息融合是一个数据处理的过程，而且当数据量比较大的时候，信息融合时延会

加长。需要注意的是，如果汽车正在前进，前方目标物静止，那么从发送探测波到探测波返回，这其中汽车在探测时间内行驶的距离并没有算入实际距离中。所以，在计算时延的时候，需要考虑到汽车在时延过程中的速度以及系统发出与收到测试数据前后的时间差。

此外，频率的发送也会受环境的影响，如高低温环境，所面临的处理性能则可能不同。频率不同也会导致时延不同，所以在计算过程中，我们用初始（额定）频率去计算时延时，也会出现一定的误差。对于自动驾驶汽车而言，时间意味着安全，如果 1 s 计算错误，对于高速运行的汽车而言，都会产生致命的结果。

3. 决策规划层

决策规划层（图 3-3-19）即对融合的数据，根据驾驶需求进行任务规划以及决策。对于这点，业界看法比较多，目前只介绍两种比较宏观的看法。

（1）全局规划。这种方式需要借助地图信息，按照乘客的需求，选择最优的路径。

（2）局部规划。需要自动驾驶汽车根据全局规划，针对局部环境信息，规划最优的路线。

这个概念就相当于框架一样，需要自动驾驶汽车能够提前基于大数据对行程进行规划，这也是判断自动驾驶系统智能性的重要指标之一。

图 3-3-19　自动驾驶决策规划层

4. 控制层

自动驾驶汽车控制层（图 3-3-20）便是替代人为操作，根据获取的信息数据，将做出的决策规划落到实处，即实时操作。这需要车辆的控制系统与决策系统相配合，并且能够精确地按照需求，让汽车做出加速、减速、制动、转向、变道以及超车等操作。

图 3-3-20　自动驾驶控制层

可以看出，前面介绍的感知层、信息融合层以及决策规划层其实都是为控制层做铺垫，最终需要做出动作的还是控制层。

5. 总结

其实自动驾驶就是将人为开车的过程用硬件、软件技术体现出来，实现了某些过程替代人或者完全自动驾驶的目标。对于司机而言，开车过程中，身体与车的配合极为自然，自动驾驶其实也是一样，只不过它所有的信息获取以及判断不是通过眼睛和人脑，而是通过汽车自身的“眼睛”和“大脑”，解放了司机。

自动驾驶概念好理解，但实现的难度较大，正如汽车高德事业部总裁韦东所言，从普通的导航走向半自动辅助驾驶，更高自动化的辅助驾驶，再走向自动化，完全自动驾驶，一定是一步一步的。

【思考与练习】

1. 巡航控制系统主要由哪些部件组成？
2. 简述巡航控制系统各部件的功用。
3. 安全气囊系统的分类有哪些？
4. 汽车电子调节悬架系统主要由哪些部件组成？

第4章

车载网络技术

【章节概述】

随着现代汽车电子控制技术的要求日益增长，车辆内外的数据交互量越来越大，因此，车载网络系统在汽车数据通信中起到了至关重要的作用。车载网络系统是汽车电子技术的重要组成部分，也是人类信息化发展的体现。它不仅能够提高汽车的数据通信效率和质量，还能够简化汽车的线路结构和故障诊断，提升汽车的智能化和网络化水平，满足人们对汽车的高性能和高品质的需求。它体现了社会主义核心价值观中的创新、协调、开放的理念。因此，我们应该积极学习和掌握车载网络系统的相关知识和技能，为推动汽车产业的信息化和数字化转型做出贡献。随着汽车控制单元数量增加，在电子控制装置增加的同时，电器配线和信号配线也越来越多，许多汽车的线束质量和线束直径已分别达到甚至超过 40 kg 和 60 mm。由于导线太多，越来越难以将其安装到隐蔽的位置，而造成线路复杂、故障率增多、工作可靠性下降、维修困难，因此，在汽车上为了简化线路，提高各控制电脑之间的通信速度，降低故障率，车载网络系统应运而生，各大汽车生产厂家都先后应用了此技术。

第 1 节　车载局域网的分类及基本术语

一、汽车车载网络系统的分类

如今，已有多种网络标准，为方便研究和设计使用，美国汽车工程学会将汽车网络根据速率分为 A、B、C、D、E 五类。各类网络的特点见表 4-1-1。

表 4-1-1　车载网络的分类

类别	速率	应用范围	目前主要网络
A	1~10 kbit/s	面向传感器、执行器，主要应用于电动门窗、座椅调节、灯光照明等控制	TIP/A、I/LIN
B	10~100 kbit/s	面向独立模块间的数据共享，主要应用于车辆信息中心、故障诊断、仪表显示等系统	低速 CAN J1850

续表

类别	速率	应用范围	目前主要网络
C	125 kbit/s~1 Mbit/s	面向实时控制，主要用于与汽车安全相关，以及实时性要求比较高的地方，如动力系统	高速 CAN、TIP/C、FlexRay
D	250 kbit/s~400 Mbit/s	面向多媒体、导航系统等，主要用于娱乐和多媒体信息交换的车载网络	MOST
E	10 Mbit/s	面向乘员的安全系统，主要应用于车辆被动安全领域	Byteflight

目前多数乘用车的通信包括类 A，B，C，D 四类网络，构建起相对成熟得多网络车载通信系统，如图 4-1-1 所示 。

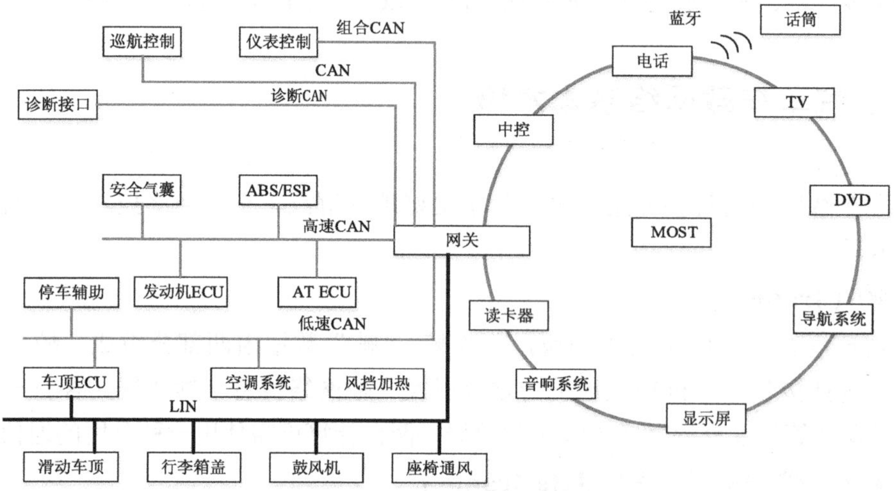

图 4-1-1　车载网络系统示意图

1. LIN

局域互联网络（Local Interconnect Network，LIN）是一种低成本的串行通信网络，用于实现汽车中的分布式电子系统控制。LIN 的目标是为现有汽车网络提供辅助功能，因此 LIN 总线是一种辅助的总线网络。在不需要 CAN 总线的带宽和多功能的场合，比如智能传感器和制动装置之间的通信使用 LIN 总线可大大节约成本。

LIN 通信是基于 SCI（UART）数据格式，采用单主控制器 / 多从设备的模式，仅使用一根 12 V 信号总线和一个无固定时间基准的节点同步时钟线。

这种低成本的串行通信模式旨在为汽车制造商以及供应商在研发应用操作系统降低成本。主要应用于对网络的带宽、性能或容错功能没有过高要求的信息传输。

2. CAN

CAN 是控制器局域网络（Controller Area Network，CAN）的简称，是由以研发和生产汽车电子产品著称的德国 BOSCH 公司开发的，并最终成为国际标准（ISO 11898)。

是国际上应用最广泛的现场总线之一。CAN 属于总线式串行通信网络。由于采用了许多新技术和独特的设计思想，与同类产品相比，CAN 总线在数据通信方面具有可靠、实时和灵活的优点。为使设计透明和执行灵活，CAN 遵循 ISO /OSI 标准模型。CAN 总线结构划分为两层：物理层和数据链路层（包括逻辑链路控制子层 LLC 和媒体访问控制子层 MAC）。

3. MOST

MOST 是一个面向媒体的信息传输系统，以光导纤维作为信息传导媒介，进行数字信号的传输。首先各控制元件将电磁脉冲信号转化为光脉冲信号，传送到光纤上，而后相应的接收电脑又将光脉冲信号转换回电磁脉冲信号，从而完成相应的控制功能。由于 MOST 系统的高传输速率，因此它可以做到只用两根光纤即可同时传递多路信号。由于智能化汽车的高速发展及以太网在大数据量高速传输中得到广泛应用，且其拥有无可比拟的多设备、多领域的互通兼容性，使得 MOST 已面临被淘汰的局面。

二、汽车车载网络基本术语

汽车车载网络有许多专用术语，为了更好地理解汽车车载网络技术，下面介绍一些常见术语。

1. 帧（frame）

将物理内存分为固定大小的块，称为帧。“帧”数据由两部分组成：帧头和帧数据。帧头包括接收方主机物理地址的定位以及其他网络信息。帧数据区含有一个数据体。为确保计算机能够解释数据帧中的数据，两台计算机需使用一种公用的通信协议。

2. CAN 数据帧（CAN data frame）

CAN 数据帧是数据链路层的协议数据单元。数据链路层的主要职责是控制相邻系统之间的物理链路，它在传送“比特”信息的基础上，在相邻节点间保证可靠的数据通信。为了保证数据的可靠传输，把用户数据封装成帧，组成传输数据的 CAN 协议帧所必需的有序位域，以帧起始（SOF）开始，以帧结束（EOF）结尾。

3. 标准帧（standard frame）

标准帧的仲裁域是连续的 11 位，可以出现 2^{11} 种报文，也就是帧 ID 的范围是 000~7FF。

4. 扩展帧（extended frame）

扩展帧的仲裁域有 29 位，可以出现 2^{29} 种报文，且在数据链路上是有间隙的（对操作者透明），帧 ID 的范围是 0000 0000~1FFF FFFF。

5. 数据包（packet）

单个消息被划分为多个数据块，这些数据块称为包，它包含发送者和接收者的地址信息。然后这些包沿着不同的路径在一个或多个网络中传输，并且在目的地重新组

合。一个单一的 CAN 数据帧就是一个包。当一条消息包含参数组的数据长度小于或等于 8 个字节时，这样的消息也称为包。

6. 地址（address）

地址是 8 位位域，用于决定消息源（或者目标）。

7. 消息（message）

消息指一个或多个具有相同参数组编号的 CAN 数据帧。

8. 位填充（bit stuffing）

位填充用于保证发送或接收的消息具有保持最小数量的显性位或隐性位跳变的处理程序，进而实现 CAN 数据帧中的位流正确同步。

9. 空闲状态

空闲状态指没有节点传输或试图传输数据时的 CAN 总线状态。

10. 首选地址（preferred address）

首选地址是在声明地址时，电控单元最先尝试使用的地址。

第 2 节　汽车多路传输系统机构与原理

汽车车载网络多路传输系统是实现在同一个信道上同时传输多路信号而互不干扰的一种技术电路或装置。多路传输是有线或无线同时传输许多信息，如数据信息等。多路传输技术使当今汽车网络控制成为可能，运用多路传输技术，可以使汽车省去许多电器设备、导线和连接器，可以减小质量、节省空间、改善可靠性。

一、多路传输系统（SWS）的技术特征

（1）模块已成为以中央处理器为核心的数字化设备，彼此通过传输媒体（双绞线、同轴电缆或光纤）以总线拓扑相连，多路传输系统总线控制器可对总线上的多个操作站、传感器及执行机构等进行数据存取。

（2）具有可靠性高、稳定性好、抗干扰能力强、通信速率快、系统安全、造价低廉、维护成本低等优点。

（3）数据总线的传输速率通常用比特率表示，比特率是每秒千位（kbit/s）或每秒兆位（Mbit/s）。数据传输速率受幅宽影响，32 位的数据传输量要比 8 位快 4 倍。

（4）互操作性。在遵守同一通信协议的前提下，可将不同厂家的现场设备产品统一组态，构成所需要的网络。

（5）开放式互联结构。既可与同层网络相连，也可通过网络互联设备与控制级网络或管理信息级网络相连。

二、多路传输系统的组成

多路传输系统主要由模块、数据总线、网络、架构、通信协议、网关等组成，如图 4-2-1 所示。

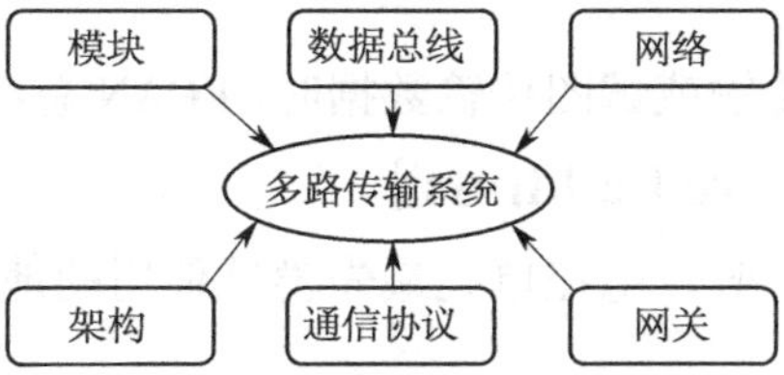

图 4-2-1　多路传输系统拓扑结构

1. 模块

模块是一种电子装置。简单一点的如温度和压力传感器，复杂的如计算机（中央处理器）。传感器是一个模块装置，根据温度和压力的不同产生不同的电压信号，这些电压信号在计算机（一种数字装置）的输入接口被转变成数字信号。在计算机多路传输系统中一些简单的模块也被称为节点，如图 4-2-2 和图 4-2-3 所示。

图 4-2-2　中央处理器

图 4-2-3　传感器

2. 数据总线

数据总线是连接智能现场设备和自动化系统的数字、双向传输、多分支结构的通信网络，是模块间运行数据的通道，它的关键标志是能支持双向多节点、总线式的全数字通信，如果模块可以发送和接收数据，则这样的数据总线就称为双向数据总线。数据总线如图 4-2-4 所示。

数据总线的结构形式很多，不同结构的价格不一样。在汽车车载网络中，数据总线必须避免无谓的高速和复杂。大多数的设计都有三种基本类型：低速型、中速型和高速型。表 4-2-1 列出了美国汽车工程师学会（SAE）推荐的汽车多路通信系统的等级分类。

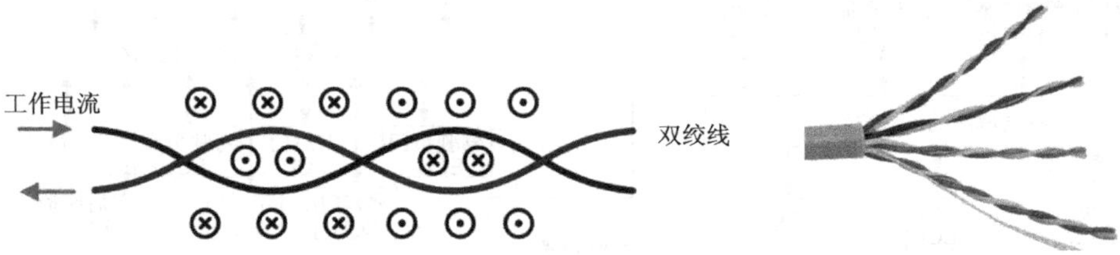

图 4-2-4　双绞线示意图

⊙—磁力线从纸面穿出；⊗—磁力线从纸面穿入

表 4-2-1　SAE 推荐的汽车多路通信系统分类

系统等级	信号种类	响应速度/ms
A	车身控制系统：灯具、继电器、电动门窗、电动座椅	20~50（低速）
B	动态信息系统：导航、电话、故障诊断	5~50（中速）
C	实时控制系统：发动机、传动系统、制动系统、悬架控制系统	1~5（高速）

3. 网络

网络是为了实现信息共享而把多条数据总线连在一起，或者把数据总线和模块当作一个系统。新型的 LS430 的几条数据总线间共有 29 块相互交换信息的模块，如图 4-2-5 所示，几条数据总线连接 29 个模块，总线又连接到局域网上，其中还有 3 个接线盒计算机（两个作为前端模块，一个作为后端模块），其作用是提供诊断支持（包括接插方便的接头及测试点）。从物理意义上讲，汽车上许多模块和数据总线距离很近，因此被称为局域网（LAN）。Motorola 公司设计的一种智能车身辅助装置网络，被称为局域互联网络（LIN）。

4. 架构

架构是信息高速公路的配置，其输入和输出端规定了什么信息能进和什么信息能出，如图 4-2-6 所示。架构通常包括一或两条线路，采用双线时数据的传输是基于两条线的电压差。当其中的一条线传输数据时，它对地有一个参考电压。架构要有特定的通信协议。

衡量数据总线及网络架构优劣的其他重要特征包括：

（1）能一起工作的模块数量；

（2）可扩展性；

（3）交互信息的种类；

（4）数据传输速度；

（5）可靠性或容错性，即抗故障性及数据交换的稳定与准确性；

（6）经济性。

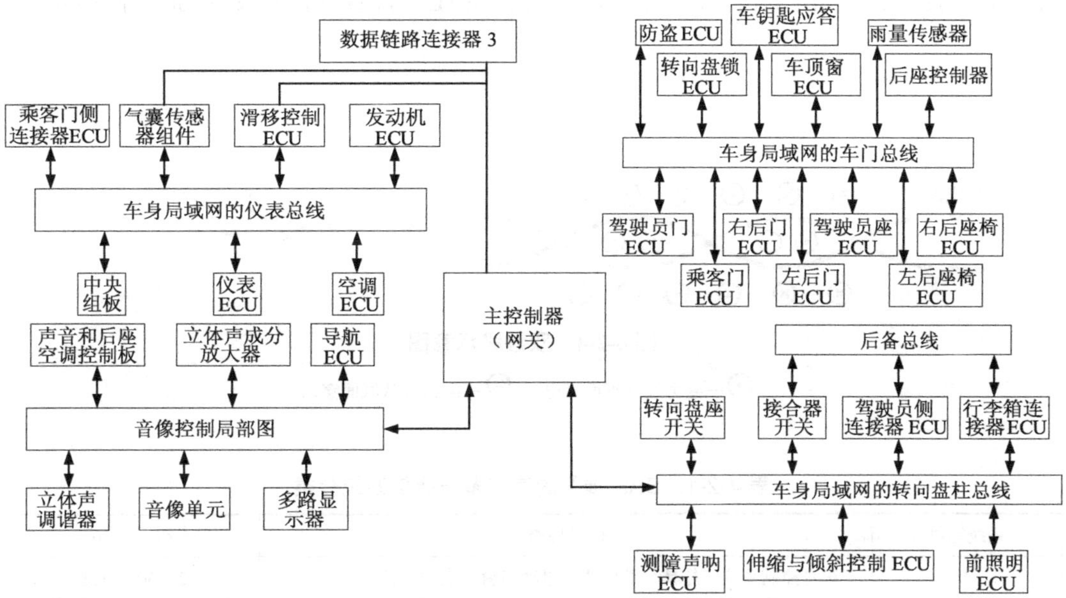

图 4-2-5　多路传输网络

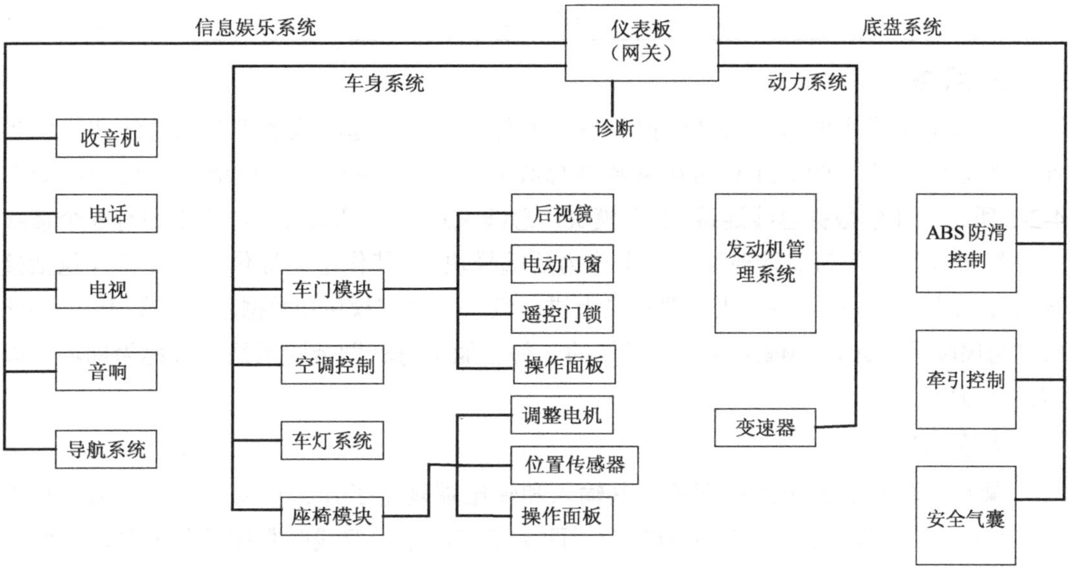

图 4-2-6　网络架构示意图

5. 通信协议

通信协议规定信号在数据总线上的通信规则。网络上的节点要成功实现通信，必须遵守相互识别、相互接受的约定和规则，建立通用的标准，用于各 ECU 之间进行通信。

通信协议的分类如下。

（1）直接型：点对点的链路直接通信，无须经过中间信息处理的通信协议。

（2）间接型：通过转接式通信网络或两个以上的网络进行信息交换的通信协议。

（3）结构优化型协议：按需要分成不同的层次，较低级别的功能在较低层次实现，同时它们又向较高层次的实体提供服务，是各层次协议的复合。

6. 网关

通常一辆车上配置了多种总线和网络，所以必须用一种方法来让它们达到共享和不产生协议间的冲突。例如，车门打开时发动机控制模块也需要被唤醒。为了使不同协议及速度的数据总线间实现无差错数据传输，必须使用一种特殊功能的计算机，这种计算机就叫作网关。

1）网关的作用

网关实际上就是一种模块，它自身的质量、功能和工作性能决定了不同的总线、模块和网络间通信的质量。对不兼容但却需要互相通信的总线和网络来说，网关起到了桥梁作用。如果信息不能传递，不一定是网关存在问题，也可能是通信链路、模块等设备存在故障。总而言之，新型汽车网络控制系统中“网关”的作用如下：

（1）它可以把局域网上的数据转变成可以识别的 OBDII 诊断数据语言，方便诊断；

（2）它可以实现低速网络和高速网络的信息共享；

（3）与计算机中的网关作用是一样的，负责接收和发送信息；

（4）激活和监控局域网络工作状态；

（5）实现车辆数据的同步性；

（6）对信息标识符作翻译。

2）网关的布置

如果两个 CAN 网络执行器是两片独立的芯片（图 4-2-7），中央控制器（单片微型计算机）为网关，那么 CAN 芯片就像灵巧的随机存储器被网关读写。一旦接收到信息，网关就会执行接收 CAN 芯片的外部读操作，接着执行转换信息的逻辑指令，然后执行外部写操作，对第二个网络的 CAN 芯片作传输编程。

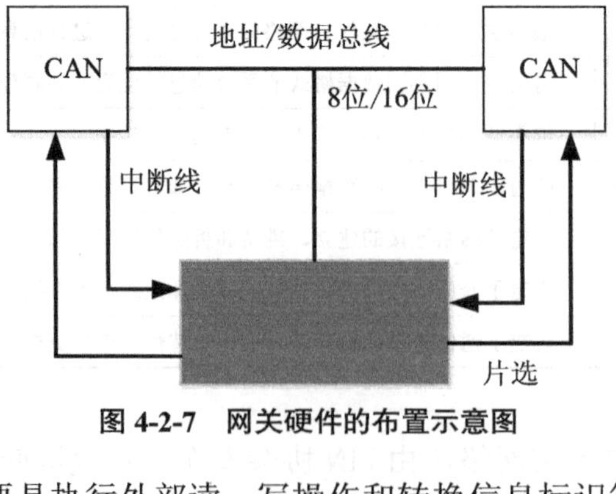

图 4-2-7　网关硬件的布置示意图

所以说，网关主要是执行外部读、写操作和转换信息标识符，而执行读、写操作的重要技术条件是时间，读、写所要求的时间又取决于网关和 CAN 芯片接口的定时

特性。

3）多路传输系统的通信协议标准

通信协议要解决系统优先权问题、灵活性问题、可扩展性问题、诊断接口问题、独立性问题、数据共享问题等，十几年来，已发展了几代通信协议，较早的有SAE推出的用于重型车的基于串行总线的标准，如SAE J1708、SAE J1587、SAE J1922，串行协议传输速率低、代码定义烦琐，除在诊断系统有一些应用外，基本已被取代。迄今为止，汽车应用的多种网络标准较典型的有LIN、CAN、J1850、MOST、TTCAN、TTP、FlexRay、J2284等。拓扑结构主要为总线式，如LINCAN、J1850、TTCAN。总线式网络为多个ECU共用一条传输线，信道利用率高，结构简单、布线容易、易于增加节点，每个系统对总线有相同权利，为多主方式工作，同一时刻只能有一个节点发送消息，网络延伸距离、网络容纳节点有限。ISO 7498把网络通信系统划分为七层结构，即开放式系统互联（OSI）的七层模型，包括物理层、数据链路层、网络层、传输层、会话层、表示层、应用层（图4-2-8），各层的作用见表4-2-2。汽车各网络协议一般只定义OSI结构中的底层协议，即物理层和数据链路层。

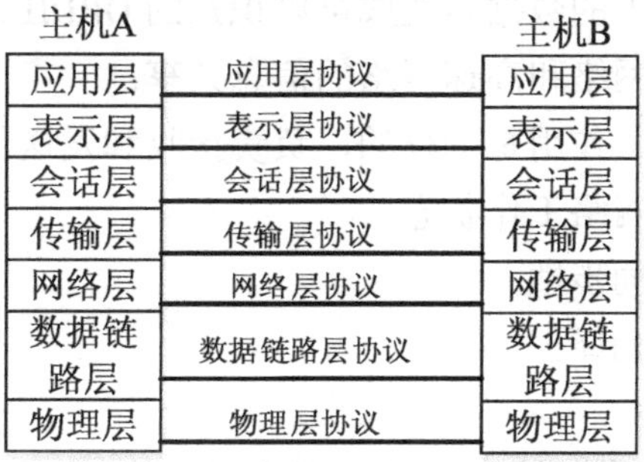

图4-2-8　ISO 7498规定的OSI的七层模型

表4-2-2　OSI开放系统互联模型各层作用

序号	层名称	作用
7	应用层	最高层，用户、软件、网络终端等之间用来进行信息交换，如DeviceNet
6	表示层	将两个应用不同数据格式的系统信息转化为能共同理解的格式
5	会话层	依靠低层的通信功能来进行数据的有效传递
4	传输层	两通信节点之间的数据传输控制，如数据重发和数据错误修复
3	网络层	规定了网络连接的建立、维持和拆除的协议，如路由和寻址
2	数据链路层	规定了介质上传输的数据位的排列和组织，如数据校验和帧结构
1	物理层	规定了通信介质的物理性，如电气特性和信号交换的解释

LIN总线是典型的A类网络，由LIN协会发布，是价格低廉的单总线低端网络，也称为经济型CAN网络。LIN是以广泛应用的通用非同步收发传输器（UART）为基础

定义的，物理层基于 ISO 9141，一般用于传输速度、实时性要求较低的车身系统，采用单主 / 多从机的通信模式，网络节点分为主节点和从节点。主节点执行主控发送任务，决定什么时候、哪一帧将在总线上传输，信息帧的长度是可变的，数据长度可为 2、4 或 8 个字节，目前我国自主开发的车身系统中 LIN 协议得到了一定的应用。

CAN 总线是在 20 世纪 80 年代中期，由德国 BOSCH 公司提出的，CAN 推出之后，很快世界上各大半导体生产厂商迅速推出各种集成有 CAN 协议的产品，如 Intel、Motorola、NEC、Philips 等公司都提供集成有 CAN 协议的芯片及 CAN 总线产品，此后越来越多的欧洲主要汽车制造商采用 CAN 总线构成其汽车网络，后来美国、日本的汽车公司也采用 CAN 构成其 B 级或 C 级网络。1994 年，SAE 所属的卡车和客车控制及通信附属委员会选择了 CAN 总线作为 J1939 标准（一个针对卡车和客车的高速网络标准的基础，添加了高层协议）。CAN 是目前唯一个取得国际标准的协议，包括高速的 ISO11898（C 类网）和低速的 ISO 11519（B 类网）。CAN 采用多主方式工作，网络上任一个节点均可在任意时刻主动向网络上的其他节点发送信息，而不分主从，网络上节点可根据不同的实时要求分成不同的优先级，当两个节点同时向网络上传递信息时，优先级低的节点主动停止数据发送，而优先级高的节点可不受影响地继续传送数据，具有点对点、一点对多点及全局广播的数据传送功能，通信速率可达 1 Mbit/s，每帧的数据字节数为 8 个，节点在错误的情况下，可自动切断它与总线的联系，以使总线上的其他通信不受影响。CAN 协议定义了两种通信格式，即标准信息帧和扩展信息帧，它们都具有 7 个位域，二者的差别在于仲裁域，标准帧有 11 位标识码，而扩展帧有 29 位。CAN 能够使用多种物理介质，如双绞线、光纤等。最常用的就是双绞线，信号使用差分电压传送，两条信号线被称为 CAN H 和 CAN L。随着 CAN 控制器成本的不断降低，且有大量产品支持基于 CAN 的系统，进一步降低了采用 CAN 控制系统的成本，因此 CAN 是目前应用最广泛的汽车网络。

在一辆车里通常有两条或三条独立的 CAN 总线。高速 CAN 用于发动机和底盘控制系统，低速 CAN 通常用于天窗、座椅、空调等舒适系统，高速 CAN 和低速 CAN 通过网关构成整个汽车网络，有些车辆的低速 CAN 被 LIN 网络取代，通过网关与 CAN 总线相连。SAE J1850 总线最初由美国三大汽车公司提出，主要是在通用公司的 Class 2 协议和福特公司的 SCP 协议基础上发展而来的，属于典型的 B 类网，这一标准已实施多年，得到广泛的接受与采用。美国很多车型采用 J1850，J1850 是比较成熟的协议，目前的 OBDI 诊断系统定义在 J1850，由于其通信速率低，只适合用于车身控制系统及诊断系统，目前在美国逐步被 CAN 所取代。

MOST 是采用光纤并用于智能交通及多媒体的网络协议，传输速率可达 22 Mbit/s。TTCAN 是基于时间触发的网络，是 CAN 总线与时间触发机制相结合产生的。其与基于事件触发的 CAN 协议的主要区别是：总线上不同的信息定义了不同的时间槽，避免了因总线仲裁使信息传输时间产生不确定性，改善了 CAN 总线的实时性能，可满足消息传输密度不断增长的需要。ISO 11898-4 定义了 TTCAN 协议。

FlexRay 是一种灵活的通信系统，能够满足未来先进汽车高速控制应用的需要，可补充 CAN、LIN 和 MOST 等主要网络标准。SAE2284 是基于时间触发的高速 CAN 网络，传输速率可达 500 kbit/s，主要用于轿车。汽车网络协议还有如 TTP/A、TTP/C、VAN 等。至今没有一个协议可以完全满足未来汽车成本和性能的要求，因此未来汽车网络仍将是多种协议共存，目前 CAN 或 LIN 是最好的选择。主要车载网络基本情况见表 4-2-3。

表 4-2-3　主要车载网络基本情况

车载网络的名称	概要	通信速度
CAN	车身 / 动力传统系统控制用 LAN 协议	1 Mbit/s
J1850	车身系统控制用 LAN 协议，以美国为中心	10.4 kbit/s
LIN	车身系统控制用 LAN 协议，液压组件专用	20 kbit/s
TTCAN	重视安全、按用途分类的控制用 LAN 协议，时间同步的 CAN	1 Mbit/s
Byteflight	重视安全、按用途分类的控制用 LAN 协议，通用时分多路复用	10 Mbit/s
FlexRay	重视安全、按用途分类的控制用 LAN 协议	5 Mbit/s
MOST	信息系统通信协议，以欧洲为中心	22.5 Mbit/s
IEEE 1394	信息系统通信协议	100 Mbit/s

【知识拓展】

哈佛 H6 防盗系统的检修

1. 哈佛 H6 防盗系统组成及电路图

哈佛 H6 防盗系统组成如图 4-2-9 所示。

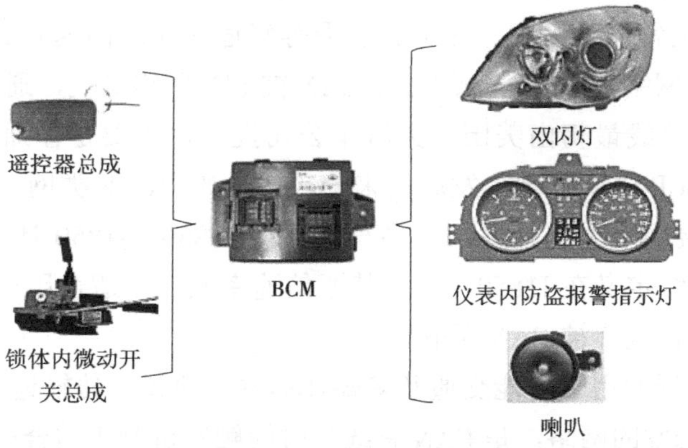

图 4-2-9　哈佛 H6 防盗系统组成

哈佛 H6 防盗系统电路图如图 4-2-10 所示。

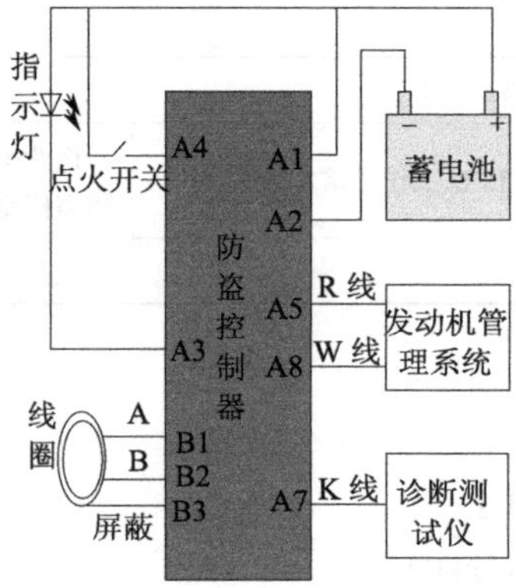

图 4-2-10　防盗系统外围电路图

2. 常见的故障现象及故障原因

常见的故障现象及故障原因见表 4-2-4。

表 4-2-4　常见的故障现象及故障原因

常见故障现象	可能故障原因	排除方法思路
无法检测到钥匙	1. 钥匙未匹配 2. 防盗线圈故障 3. 防盗控制器故障 4. 防盗转换器配件错误或损坏	1. 读取数据流，查看钥匙状态 2. 排除防盗线圈故障 3. 排除防盗器故障 4. 排除钥匙故障
防盗器无法和发动机 ECU 通信	1.W 线故障 2. 防盗控制器电源线和 IG 挡故障 3. 发动机 ECU 电源线和 IG 挡故障 4. 防盗控制器故障 5. 发动机 ECU 故障	1. 检查 W 线是否正常 2. 检查防盗器和发动机 ECU 的匹配状态 3. 检查防盗器和发动机 ECU 的电源是否正常 4. 重新匹配防盗器或发动机 ECU，无法排除则更换

3. 常见的故障代码含义

常见的故障代码含义见表 4-2-5。

表 4-2-5　常见的故障代码含义

故障代码	故障名称	可能的故障
B1000	防盗器内部故障	检查并考虑更换防盗器或防盗线圈及连接线束。此故障码一般不会单独存在，排除其他故障码即可
B3040	W 线上发生通信故障	检查与防盗器 W 线相连的线束，更换防盗控制器或发动机 ECU
B3042	W 线接地	检查防盗器 W 线是否有接地情况
B3043	W 线短接电源	检查防盗器 W 线和点火端、蓄电池正端管脚的连接线束

续表

故障代码	故障名称	可能的故障
B3045	LED 短接地或开路，LED 工作异常	检查 LED 与防盗器的连接线束，更换 LED 或防盗控制器
B3048	LED 与电源短路	检查 LED 与防盗器的连接线束，更换 LED

【思考与练习】

1. 多路传输系统由哪几部分组成?
2. 网络通信系统一般划分为几层结构？分别是什么?
3. CAN 数据总线传输系统的组成是什么?
4. 简述 CAN 总线的数据传输过程。